WRITINGS IN THE *SMART SET*

Collected Essays and Journalism of H. L. Mencken

H. L. MENCKEN

WRITINGS IN THE *SMART SET*

Volume 4: 1916–1917

Edited and Annotated by S. T. Joshi

Sarnath Press • Seattle

Contents

1916

1916

The Rescuers

A Study in the Art of Protecting Ladies

By Owen Hatteras

Her name was Camille Foe and that's what she was—decidedly *comme il faut*. You should have seen her skip across the Avenue de 'Opera and strike a pose-on the opposite curb! What an ensemble! What a blending and melting of lines and delicate tints!

> *"So fair*
> *She takes the breath of men away*
> *Who gaze upon her unaware."*

I know my dictionary of quotations!

The Bois de Boulogne, the Bois de Boulogne! 'Twas there that Georges Perrin, turning the bend of an unfrequented path, saw her struggling in the arms of a man. Georges was not uncompromisingly a man of action, but he realized the moral advantage he would acquire by saving her from her assailant. So he crept up behind them and planted the a healthy right under the ear, being careful to pick out the ear with the short hair above it. The owner of the ear sprawled upon the ground. In falling he upset Camille and she came to the earth in a crash of silks and laces; she lay still in decorous disarray.

Georges gave his fallen victim a kick.

"Go away," said Georges.

The fellow withdrew like a whipped boy. Georges turned to the girl. How beautiful she was as she lay there; how unspeakably lovely in her tumbled hand-embroidereds! He knew now that he loved her even more than he had before. But she must be revived. He knelt and raised her head. For a moment he gazed at her beautiful face; she opened her eyes.

"Eh?" she said.

"Are you all right?"

"*Mais oui*—what has happened?"

"Don't you remember? You were struggling in the arms of a brute. I arrived just in time and pulled him away. As I did so he struck at me but

Smart Set 48, No. 1 (January 1916): 205–6.

hit you and knocked you out. So I thrashed him and sent him away."

Camille rose and smoothed out her f rock.

"I'm sure I do not know how to thank you." He waved his hand grandly.

"'Twas nothing," he said.

"I must go home. Will you accompany me, Monsieur Perrin?"

"You might call me Georges now, Camille."

"Well, Georges, then."

She extended her hand with a cordial smile which went to his head. How wonderful she was! He didn't blame that ruffian; *eh, bien,* he wished he had his nerve! Her hand clasp was thrilling; her soft little palm pressed against his for an exquisite moment—how warm her lips must be! He seized her roughly.

"Stop! Stop!"

But he didn't stop, much to his own surprise. Her lips were warm, and soft and sweet to kiss! He held her tightly while she struggled to free herself.

"Here you!" A heavy hand seized him by the shoulder and drew him roughly away.

"*Eh? Est-ce possible! Georges Perrin!* Our own pretty little Georges!" cried his captor.

"Please take your hand from my shoulder," said Georges with the dignity that went so well with his little mustache. He knew that Gaston Morel had never liked him.

"Not yet," said. Gaston. "Did he hurt you, Camille?"

"Not—not very much. I am so glad you came, Gaston!"

He extended his free hand. She took it in both of hers.

"What shall I do with him? Make him beg your pardon?"

"No, let him go. His apology would be as worthless as he is."

Gaston gave Georges a shaking that sent his hat flying.

"*Allez! Vite! Depechez!*"

Like a whipped boy the other picked up his hat and slunk away.

"Contemptible little lap-dog," muttered Gaston. "Which way are you going?"

"*Chez moi.*"

"May I walk along?"

"I should be delighted."

They walked in silence for a while. Then Gaston smiled.

"Didn't he look funny when his hat flew off? Like a cartoon, *n'est ce pas?*"

Camille laughed, lightly at first, then heartily, then immoderately. *Dieu,* she was lovely when she laughed! The narrowed eyes, the gleaming teeth, the heightened color, the fluttering of her throat as the quick, spasmodic breaths forced their way through it! The melody of it! *Dieu!* And then, as she controlled herself, the laugh ended in a kind of snort, the very humanness of which was the finishing touch, like the signature on a masterpiece. Think of having a laugh like that on the other side of your coffee urn at *petit dejeuner!*

"Like a novel, is it not, Camille? Big, strong hero comes along in the nick of time, saves little heroine from villain and then goes through the rest of the book trying to do in his own way what the villain was trying to do in his. But I hate long stories, do not you, also?"

She was thinking of something else.

"Yes," she answered absently, after a while.

Dieu! There was no mistaking that!

She had paused a moment, thinking over his innuendo, and then had deliberately encouraged him.

"Camille! Sweetheart!"

"Do not! Oh, please do not! You :are hurting me!"

She struggled vainly in his arms. By this time she was quite adept at struggling. The big, strong Gaston thought it was merely womanly fervor. Suddenly there was a crash and for Gaston it was a dark night with lots of shooting stars.

Camille looked wildly from the fallen man to this latest rescuer.

"What have you done?" she cried; "you have killed him!"

The latest rescuer's reply is somewhat difficult to translate. But perhaps this will give an indication of his manner of speech:

"No, I ain't. Leave him lay. He'll come to after a while. Come on, sweetie, let's get out o' this."

Camille followed him at a trot. Presently they stopped and looked at each other. The man's hand went up to a swollen place under his ear.

"That fellow must have used brass knuckles on me."

"Are you all right now?"

"*Oui.* You are all right?"

"*Oui.*"

"Do you love me?"

He seized her in his arms.

"Do not! Please do not!" she cried.

"Why?"

"As I told you before, you will get my hair all mussed!"

She struggled vainly in his arms. But, fortunately, she had run out of rescuers.

Partly about Books

§1

The Dismal Art.—The massive example of George Henry Lewes (Mr. George Eliot) to the contrary notwithstanding, the average Anglo-Saxon critic, whether of the drama or of books, continues to dispatch his business with the heavy solemnity of a college professor, a newspaper editorial writer or an embalmer. Consider, for example, William Archer. What could be more depressing than his illuminating discussions of the Ibsen plays? He penetrates to the truth almost infallibly, but he does it as if he were cutting off a leg. Even George Bernard Shaw's essays on the theatre are seldom gay; the best that can be said of them is that they make use of a sour and cruel sort of humor as a moral weapon. In aim and essence they are as serious as the harangue of a Billy Sunday; Shaw is not only convinced that the stage-plays he discusses are frightfully important things, but also that anyone who disputes it (or even doubts it *in petto*) is a moral leper. Again, think of William Winter, with his childlike veneration for such empty mummers as Richard Mansfield and Henry Irving; and the late Clement Scott, with his Puritan determination to make of art a purely moral matter. . . . A salient exception is A. B. Walkley. The fact that this most un-British of all critics serves the super-British London *Times* is but one more proof that the universe is managed by a troupe of very talented comedians. . . . But isn't it significant that Walkley is quite unable to express his idea in the English language, that he is forever dropping into French, German, Latin and Greek, so that the average Englishman, who is belligerently unilingual, can't understand the half of him? The same peculiarity is to be noted in the only American dramatic critic comparable to him in nimbleness of wit, scope of professional knowledge and freedom from superstition. . . . Can it be that English lacks a critical vocabulary, that English critics have to step cautiously and heavily because they must pick out stepping-stones? Surely the Frenchman is at vastly greater ease in such adventuring, if only because his way is well-worn, and its very ruts are roomy and casual and comfortable.

Smart Set 48, No. 1 (January 1916): 304–10.

§2

Gliding Faded Lilies.—Some time ago, discoursing in this place upon music, I ventured the view that 'twould be a pretty thing for Richard Strauss to re-orchestrate the finale of Schumann's D minor
symphony. Let me now move with the sacrilege into beautiful letters.
Why not a new version of "Vanity Fair" by Arnold Bennett? Or a revi-
sion of Congreve and Wycherley by Shaw? (How I should like to see
"The Old Bachelor" revised and dephlogisticated by the Irish Puritan!)
Or an improved edition of Jane Austen by George Moore? Or of George
Eliot by Elinor Glyn? Or a complete recasting of Byron's poetry by Alfred Noyes . . . The plan, indeed, has endless possibilities. There is
scarcely a classic that is perfect as it stands; in every one of them, save
perhaps "Barry Lyndon," "Alice in Wonderland" and the prologue to
the Canterbury Tales, one can readily imagine improvements. How
greatly Stevenson, if he had had the courage, might have bettered most
of the Waverley Novels! What W. S. Gilbert might have done for
"Paradise Lost"! Or Eugene Field for "The Ring and the Book"!

§3

Conrad Again.—The best study of Joseph Conrad that has yet appeared is to be found in a little book by Wilson Follet, lately privately
printed by Doubleday, Page & Company. Why privately? God knows.
Perhaps because this same firm publishes Richard Curle's highly unsat-
isfactory tome on Conrad—ten per cent. sound criticism and the rest
wind and moonshine. Ask for a copy of the Follet book at once; it is
for free distribution so long as the supply lasts. It is full of sharp observation and intelligent discussion. I recall a haunting saying: "Under all
his stories there ebbs and flows a kind of tempered melancholy, a sense
of seeking and not finding . . ." Nothing could better describe the effect of such tales as "Almayer's Folly," "Nostromo" and "Lord Jim."
Even "Youth," though it interprets and celebrates the indomitable, yet
has defeat and tragedy in it; one sees the breakup of middle age beyond the Homeric endeavors of one-and-twenty. . . . Mr. Follet finds
the cause of Conrad's preference for *adagio* in the circumstances of his
own life—his double exile, first from Poland and then from the sea.
But this is surely stretching the facts until they squeak. Neither exile, in
truth, was enforced, nor is either irrevocable. Conrad has been back to
Poland, and he is free to 'round the Horn again whenever the spirit
moves him. Far better to look for the springs of his melancholy in that
deepest-lying race philosophy which seems to engulf all reflective men
soon or late. I mean resignationism.

All philosophies and all religions come to resignationism at the last. Once it takes shape as the concept of Nirvana, the desire for nothingness, the will to not-will. Again, it is fatalism in this form or that—Mohammedanism, Agnosticism, . . . Presbyterianism! Yet again, it is the "Out, out, brief candle!" of Shakespeare, the "Vanitas vanitatum; omnia vanitas!" of the Preacher. Or, to make an end, it is millenniumism, or the theory that the world is going to blow up to-morrow, or the day after, or two weeks hence, and that all sweating and striving are thus useless. Search where you will, near or far, in ancient or in modern times, and you will never find a race or an age that gave more than a passing bow to optimism. Even Christianity, starting out as "glad tidings," has had to take on protective coloration to survive, and to-day its chief professors moan and blubber like Iokanaan in Herod's rain-barrel. The sanctified are few and far between. The vast majority of us must suffer in hell, just as we suffer on earth. The divine grace, so omnipotent to save, is withheld from us. Why? There, alas, is your insoluble mystery, your riddle of the universe. . . .

This conviction that human life is a seeking without a finding, that its purpose is impenetrable, that joy and sorrow are alike meaningless, you will see written largely in the work of all great artists. It is obviously the final message, if any message is to be sought there at all, of the nine symphonies of Ludwig van Beethoven. It is the idea that broods over Wagner's Ring, as the divine wrath broods over the Old Testament. In Shakespeare, as Shaw has demonstrated, it amounts to a veritable obsession. What else is there in Turgenieff, Dostoievski, Andrieff? Or in the Zola of "L'Assommoir," "Germinal," "La Débâcle," the whole Rougon-Macquart series? (The Zola of "Les Quatres Evangiles," and particularly of "Fecondité," turned uplifter and optimist, and became ludicrous.) Or in Hauptmann, or Hardy, or Sudermann (I mean, of course, Sudermann the novelist; Sudermann the dramatist is a mere mechanician) . . . The younger men of today, in all countries, seem to cherish the philosophy of impotence and surrender. Consider the last words of "Riders to the Sea." Or Gorky's "Nachtasyl." Or Frank Norris' "McTeague." Or Dreiser's "Jennie Gerhardt." Or George Moore's "Sister Theresa." Or Conrad's "An Outcast of the Islands."

Conrad, more than any other of the men I have mentioned, grounds his whole work upon a sense of this "immense indifference of things." The exact point of the story of Kurtz, in "Heart of Darkness," is that it is pointless, that Kurtz's death is as meaningless as his life, that the moral of such a sordid tragedy is a wholesale negation of all morals. And this, no less, is the point of the story of "Falk," and of that of Almayer, and of that of Jim. Mr. Follet (he must be an American!) finds himself, in the end, unable to accept so profound a pessimism unadulterated, and so he injects a gratuitous and mythical optimism into it, and hymns Conrad "as a comrade, one of a company gathered under the ensign of hope for common war on despair." With the highest regard, Pish! Conrad makes war upon nothing; he is pre-eminently *not* a moralist. He swings, indeed, as far from moralizing as is possible, for he does not even criticise God. His undoubted comradeship, his plain kindliness toward the souls he vivisects, is not the child of hope but of pity. Like Mark Twain he might well say: "The more I see of men, the more I laugh at them—and the more I pity them." He is *simpatico* precisely because of his infinite commiseration. . . . I have said that he does not criticise God; one may imagine him even pitying God. . . .

As for Conrad the literary artist (opposing him here to Conrad the humanist), one cause of the startling vividness that he gets into his narrative is to be found in the dimness that he so deliberately leaves there. A paradox of course, but I do not devise it for its own sake, believe me. What I mean to say is that Conrad always shows us a picture that is full of the little obscurities, the uncertainties of outline, the mysterious shadings-off, that we see in the real world around us. He does not pretend to the traditional omniscience of the novelist. He is not forever translating the unknowable in motive and act into ready formulae; instead, he says frankly that he does not know, or, at best, "I believe," or "perhaps," or "Marlow thinks it possible." A trick? To be sure. But also much more than a trick, for its constant repetition not only constitutes a manner but also indicates a state of mind. Conrad knows his characters too well to explain them too glibly. They are too real to him (and to us) to be made quite understandable. They keep to the end all of that fine mysteriousness which forever hangs about those who are nearest and dearest to us. . . . A man may profess to understand the President of the United States, but he seldom alleges, even to himself, that he understands his wife.

§4

Cinderella the Nth.—There is nothing new in the story that Willa Sibert Cather tells in "THE SONG OF THE LARK" (*Houghton Mifflin*); it is, in fact, merely one more version, with few changes, of the ancient fable of Cinderella, probably the oldest of the world's love stories, and surely the most steadily popular. Thea Kronborg begins as a Methodist preacher's daughter in a little town in Colorado, and ends as Sieglinde at the Metropolitan Opera House, with a packed house "roaring" at her and bombarding her with "a greeting that was almost savage in its fierceness." As for Fairy Princes, there are no less than three of them, the first a Galahad in the sooty overalls of a freight conductor, the second a small town doctor with a disagreeable wife, and the third Mr. Fred Otterburg, the *Bierkronprinz.*

But if the tale is thus conventional in its outlines, it is full of novelty and ingenuity in its details, and so the reading of it passes very pleasantly. Miss Cather, indeed, here steps definitely

into the small class of American novelists who are seriously to be reckoned with. Her "Alexander's Bridge" was full of promise, and her "O Pioneers" showed the beginnings of fulfilment. In "The Song of the Lark" she is already happily at ease, a competent journeyman. I have read no late novel, in fact, with a greater sense of intellectual stimulation. Especially in the first half, it is alive with sharp bits of observation, sly touches of humor, gestures of that gentle pity which is the fruit of understanding. Miss Cather not only has a desire to write; she also has something to say. Ah, that the former masked less often as the latter! Our scriveners are forever mistaking the *cacoethes scribendi* for a theory of beauty and a rule of life. But not this one. From her book comes the notion that she has thought things out, that she is never at a loss, that her mind is plentifully stored. I commend her story to your affable attention—at least the first half of it.

§5

The Puritan.—One hears, in "The Song of the Lark," too little of old Kronborg, the father of Thea, a one-horse Methodist preacher in a one-horse town. To me, at all events, there is endless fascination in such a man. What American novelist will first depict and interpret the Puritan? (I do not mean the Puritan Father, for that has been attempted by Hawthorne and others, but the Puritan of today, the neighborhood uplifter, the advocate of harsh laws, the bitter critic and reformer of his brother over the fence). There is a brilliant flashlight picture in the second chapter of E. W. Howe's "The Story of a Country Town," but it is no more than a flash. Frank Norris was the man for a full-length portrait, but he was too much intrigued by the romance of commerce to give his attention to it. Perhaps Dreiser will some day undertake it. He has the capital advantage of being of un-Puritan blood, of having no race sympathy to overcome. But he lacks, alas, the bitter wit, the hand for satire. The Puritan is not to be dealt with calmly and scientifically, but savagely, joyfully, with gusto. What a job the Hilaire Belloc of "Emmanuel Burden" might have made of him! But that Hilaire Belloc, alackaday, is now no more! . . .

§6

The Shy, Shy Girls.—Before parting from Miss Cather, let us join in praising her for a rare sort of courage: she gives the exact date of her birth in "Who's Who in America." Do I spoof? Nay. Very few of our literary girls do it. Is Mrs. Atherton 27 or 72? You will never find out from that gaudy red volume, though the fact that she is a *g. g. niece* of Benjamin Franklin is duly set forth.

Another fair fictioner tells us that her father was the son of a sister of a president of the United States, but neglects to tell us how long she has been a student in the school of human experience. Yet another confesses that she has been "engaged in literary work since 1895," but doesn't say how old she was when she began. Yet another is careful to give the quite undistinguished occupation of her deceased husband, but goes no further with her confidences. Glancing through these humorless, telegraphic autobiographies, one happens upon various naïf and chatty things. One lady says that she has been to Europe five times; another that she writes about "women's capacity and potentiality;" another that she has "made a specialty of geography;" another that she has four children; another that she is a Colonial Dame; several boast bravely that they are unmarried; more than one admits having contributed to THE SMART SET, and even to *The Atlantic Monthly.* But none of these talkative girls tells us her age! . . . . Lest I be accused of foul injustice, or worthy ladies be wrongfully suspected, let me add that most of the gentle authors whose work is comparable to Miss Cather's are quite as honest as she is. For example, Miss Mary Johnston, Miss Ellen Glasgow, Mrs. Wharton, Mrs. Watts . . . four names are enough. In this field, indeed, reticence seems to be in indirect ratio to accomplishment.

§7

In Schwerer Zeit.—John Palmer begins his humorless, elephantine "epitaph" of George Bernard Shaw with the statement that "at midnight on August 4th, 1914, all that literature hitherto described as modern passed quietly away in its sleep." Almost a platitude!—at all events, in England. More than any other of the allied countries, England shows signs of surgical shock, of concussion of the heart and brain, of a spiritual collapse, and more than any other class of Englishmen, not even excepting the bishops and the politicians, the authors of the tight little isle are its victims. H. G. Wells, for example, has frankly gone to pot; the stuff he has done during the past year calls for charity rather than for criticism. And such fellows as Arnold Bennett, G. K. Chesterton and Rudyard Kipling have suffered even worse.

Kipling, indeed, has apparently passed into a state of mind which can only be described as pathological. The literary artist of yesteryear has departed, one fears forever; what remains is only a frightened house-holder in a flapping night-shirt, bawling for the police down a dark alley. . . . And what of Conrad? Has he been damaged as badly as the others? Despite the curious banality of his account of his Polish experiences, I presume to doubt it. While the others rant and blubber, he has next to nothing to say . . . . One detects in that silence something characteristically and magnificently ironical: the immigrant's but half concealed sneer at the native. For Conrad, after all, is not an Englishman, but a Pole. He comes of a race that is proud and undemocratic, a race that Nietzsche, with his fine sense of the heroic, regarded with almost superstitious veneration, a race that knows how to endure without complaint. One wonders just what, in his inmost heart, he thinks of the bellowing of Kipling, the feeble paralogy of Chesterton, the lower middle-class fustian of Wells and Bennett. What, indeed, must he think of (in Palmer's phrase) "insolence as a fine art"? Of the cad as artist?

§8

A Forgotten Holy Day.—Who knows that one single day of the year 1885, to wit, March 14th, saw the birth of two immortal works, "The Mikado" and "Huckleberry Finn"? Both light-hearted, both devoid of moral content—but both, I opine, destined to live. From end to end of the nineteenth century the English drama received no more novel, no more charming, and, for that matter, no more important accession than "The Mikado." It is worth today all the other stage plays and operettas written in England between the year 1800 and the first night of Pinero's "The Magistrate"—I mean all of them taken together—if only its own delightful predecessor, "Pinafore," be counted out. And it is a sounder, a more honest and a vastly more interesting piece of work than any single English play that has been written since. Moreover, its score contains some of the best music of the best British composer since Harry Purcell. For example, the chorus of schoolgirls, just before the "Three Little Maids" song. For example, "Tit Willow." For example, the finale of the second act. The man who wrote this music, true enough, was an Irishman, but the man who inspired it was an Englishman. England should be proud of Gilbert. He was the greatest librettist since King David. . . .

As for "Huckleberry Finn," its place among the truly great books of the world will not be understood for some time to come. But there is where it belongs, and there is where it will be found soon or late. It is easily the peer of "Don Quixote" and "Tristram Shandy"; nay, of

"Tom Jones." Curiously enough, its author had but a low opinion of it and wrote it rather grudgingly. You will find the whole story in Albert Bigelow Paine's "Mark Twain"—one of the most satisfying biographies, by the way, in many years. Mark labored over "Huck," off and on, for six or seven years, he was forever putting the manuscript aside and turning to more engaging tasks. In the end he probably fell into the stupendous error of ranking it below "Tom Sawyer"—an error into which he was helped by various college professor critics. It is as if Tolstoi's "What Is Art?" were put above "Anna Karenina." Or Leonardo's "Mona Lisa" before "The Last Supper." Almost as if Beethoven's Eroica Symphony were called greater than the Fifth, or the Pastoral set ahead of the Eighth . . . . Mark, in truth, was an incurable Philistine. "Lohengrin" always struck him as it might strike an average Congressman, theatre musician or Pullman porter—that is, as sheer noise and damnable to hear. This Philistinism colored his attitude toward his own works. The things he took most delight in were his clumsiest and most banal buffooneries and his heaviest attempts at sweet sentiment. To the day of his death it probably never occurred to him that "Huckleberry Finn" had made his fame secure.

§9

A Sound Workman.—"THE STAR ROVER," by Jack London (*Macmillan*), proves anew what I have often maintained in this place, to wit, that London is probably the most competent literary workman, the soundest and cleverest technician, now at work among us. His actual stories of late years have tended toward a feeble marvelousness and silliness (it is so of this one), but the manner in which they are written is always excellent and sometimes superb. Not only does he know how to devise and manage a fable; he also has a delicate taste in words, and seldom makes a tactical mistake in their use. Out of all this comes the charm, the plausibility, the address of the man, which is to say, his success. No current novelist writing in English, save perhaps H. G. Wells, comes closer to a mastery of the trade. . . . Style, of course, is the man. London writes pleasingly, not only because he is skilful, but also, and perhaps chiefly, because he must be a man of hearty and agreeable personality. One gets many amusing glimpses of him in "THE LOG OF THE SNARK," by his wife, Charmian Kittredge London (*Macmillan*), a chronicle of their journey to the South Seas in a 57-foot ketch.

§10

Department Store Literature.—The popular novels, so far as I can make out, do not get better as year follows year, but cheaper, emptier,

sillier. For example, consider "A MAN'S HEARTH," by Eleanor M. In-
gram (*Lippincott*). Here we are made privy to the regeneration of Tony
Adriance, son and heir to a notorious multi-millionaire. In order to escape from the clutches of Mrs. Lucille Masterson, who plans to divorce
her husband and marry him, Tony commits the crime hymeneal with a
beautiful nursemaid named Miss Elsie Murray and goes to work as a
chauffeur for his own father! In the end, of course, he becomes manager of the great Adriance paper-mill, working up to that post by his
own unaided efforts. . . . A stimulating dish of phosphates for the
brain-fagged! A soothing dose for lazy fat women while their husbands
sweat downtown! . . .

    "BELTANE THE SMITH," the last confection from the *fabrik* of Jef-
fery Farnol (*Little-Brown*), is a tale of amour in the Robin Hood manner, and starts off with such stylistic twitterings and grimaces as these:
"A mighty man was Beltane the Smith, despite his youth already great
of stature and comely of feature. Much knew he of woodcraft, of the
growth of herb and tree and flower, of beast and bird, and how to tell
each by its cry or song or flight; . . . versed was he, likewise, in the ancient wisdoms and philosophies, both Latin and Greek, having learned
all these things from him whom men called Ambrose the Hermit."
Under the cover of this quasi-archaic guff, Farnol slips over the
astounding news that Beltane (of course, after washing up) beguiles his
leisure by painting illuminations on vellum! Imagine it: the weary
blacksmith "teasing up" a Book of Hours! (What next? Jess Willard
studying Chopin? Hindenburg knitting socks for the Belgians?) . . .
But this marvel, fortunately enough, is not referred to often. Beltane,
after a while, has no time for the gentle monastic art; he is really, it
turns out, a duke, and he devotes himself to the ducal sports of
fighting and love-making. Incidentally, Mr. Farnol's delicate Old English breaks down toward the end. On page 569, for example, one encounters this: "And now Beltane's breath grew short and thick, his
strong hand trembled on the bridle, and he grew alternate hot and
cold." Almost American! Richard Harding Davis might have written
it. Or even Mr. Chambers. But immediately afterward Mr. Farnol
apologizes, as it were, with this: "So they rode into the echoing court-
yard, whither *hasted* old Godric to welcome them . . . Who so *mum-
chance* as Beltane, I say . . ." Or, for that matter, who so goustrous? Or
so noddypolled? Or so besniggled?

    The canned review of "HEART'S CONTENT," by Ralph Henry Bar-
bour (*Lippincott*), announces "nothing sordid, nothing that will offend
the most delicate taste, and yet much that will fascinate the most refined." But on page 108, there is a distinct and brazen mention of the
heroine's ankles, and not only of her ankles, but even of her actual feet;

and on page 204 she slides shamelessly into the arms of a man, and is roundly bussed in full view of the seven upstairs windows of a neighbor's house. Is this stuff for hiding under boarding-school pillows? . . . On page 8 of "THE WOOING OF ROSAMUND FAYRE," by Berta Ruck (*Dodd-Mead*) Miss Rosamund is writing love letters to Capt. Teddy Urquhart for and in the name of his cousin and fiancée, Miss Eleanor Urquhart, whom she serves as social secretary. I leave you to guess which of the two girls Teddy has in his arms on page 374. . . .

Such is the commercial novel, the best-seller. I have not described the worst, but almost the best.

§11

Blind Barabbases.—I am no believer, Got wot, in neglected geniuses; all the unpublished masterpieces that have come to me for reading have been atrociously bad. Nevertheless, the publishers of this fair republic often give color to the contrary superstition by a certain slowness of wit. It took two or three years for O. Henry to be discovered; the fact that he was destined to enchant the tired business man should have been obvious to the first publisher's reader who filched his postage stamps. Montague Glass had been bombarding the magazines for six or eight years before he was given his chance. Both men, true enough, were bound to be found out—but both had to wait. . . . How long will it take the most enterprising of American publishers (whoever he may be) to print the first book of John McClure, of Oklahoma? Here is a chance, not only to enlist a young poet who will probably be the rage in four or five years, but also to launch a literature. McClure is the first exponent of beautiful letters in Oklahoma, the Venerable Bede of that new empire, the *stammvater* of the Oklahoman hierarchy of bards. More, he is a maker and singer of very respectable parts, even when judged by the standards of our eastern Sodoms and Ninevehs. He has an extraordinarily delicate ear; his rhythms are full of Elizabethan surprises and syncopations; he uses words lovingly, reverently, beautifully. The influence of Ezra Pound is apparent in his work, but his is an altogether more graceful and delicate talent than Pound's. . . . Who will put him between covers?

Saved!

By William Drayham

It was the end.

For three long weeks they had struggled to make it go. They had cut, padded, changed the business, reduced the prices of the orchestra seats, raised them again, given souvenirs and hired three distinct sets of supers for the mob scene. The leading man had worked himself thin, the star had sacrificed scenes to which she felt she was entitled, the author, the stage manager, and the heavy had cursed in four different languages every day. They had rehearsed every morning. The dramatic critics had given the play splendid notices. One had compared it favorably with G. B. S.'s best work. Another had compared G. B. S.'s best work unfavorably with it. A third had extolled it as vivid and dramatic beyond any play of the season, and another had nothing but praise for the cast.

All of no avail. The public would not come.

On this Saturday night they felt it was the end. There had not been fifty dollars in the house. After the performance the manager sadly called the company onto the stage. His silence was ominous.

The leading man vented the feelings of all when he said, "Well, I suppose the jig's up?"

Too depressed to be grammatical, the manager could but respond with but a discouraged, "Yep, no use, folks. We close—"

He was interrupted by the entrance of the stage manager. Hair disheveled, collar torn, a wild light in his eyes, this worthy burst upon the stage like a cyclone. All present were petrified.

"What is it?" they exclaimed with one voice.

"Saved!" yelled the stage manager at the top of his voice. "Saved!"

"Whaddyemean saved?" said the manager excitedly.

The stage manager thrust a paper at him. The manager yelled and threw up his hat.

"What is it? What is it?" yelled the others, now as excited as he.

Smart Set 48, No. 2 (February 1916): 48.

"Look!" was the reply. "Look! George Jean Nathan says the show is absolutely rotten! Wow! Hooray! You're all raised fifty a week. Don't tell me there's no such thing as Providence."

Weeping for joy, the star clasped her little granddaughter to her bosom.

"It will be a white Christmas, darling," she laughed through her tears.

A Massacre in a Mausoleum

After all, what is reform but a laborious demonstration that 2 + 2 = 4? The true reformer, indeed, is no more than a donkeyish prattler of what should go without saying; the wildest heretic, at bottom, is merely a platitudinarian who has managed to make the obvious bear the agreeable aspect of the scandalous. So plain is this fact that we have put it into a saying: the heresy of to-day is the platitude of to-morrow. A platitude about a platitude! And, as usual with platitude, a sick and decrepit one. The truth is, of course, that there is actually an unmistakable difference in intrinsic veracity between the heresy of to-day and the platitude of to-morrow, for the latter is necessarily less true than the former, else the great majority of God-fearing men would not believe it. Thus it was quite true that Mother Church was a very dubious old baggage at the time the late Martin Luther stated it as a heresy, but it is no longer true to-day, with at least forty million patriotic Americans believing it. And by the same token it is true to-day that the two Houses of Congress are hypocritical, venal and dishonest but it will not be true after all the uplifters and bogus messiahs are orgiastically kicked out and the common people are thus made to believe it, nor was it true ten or twelve years ago, in the palmy days of the Interests, when no pop-eyed *villein* of the newspapers had the slightest doubt of it.

Here, discoursing upon platitudes, I platitudinize with the utmost ferocity—almost, indeed, like a Methodist bishop or a gentleman about to be hanged. Let my excuse be the fact that my intentions are humane—that what I chiefly seek to do is to obtain a merciful verdict upon Dr. Albert Mordell, the Philadelphia Georg Brandes, whose latest tome, "DANTE AND OTHER WANING CLASSICS," might otherwise excite the sensitive to lamentable cursing and swearing, or even to assault, mayhem and homicide. I grant you freely, gents, that it is hard to read this work and not go on the bust. When one encounters in it (page 12) an argument against Dante's "Divina Commedia" on the ground that some of the ladies and gentlemen pictured as in Hell therein "are punished in a measure out of proportion to their faults" and "should not have been put in Hell at all"; when one finds "Paradise Lost" denounced (page 64) because Eve's sudden acquirement of

Smart Set 48, No. 2 (February 1916): 151–57.

knowledge, on eating of the apple, is "not . . . a transformation that we have ever experienced," since "our knowledge is a matter of gradual growth and we have not been placed in a condition wherein from almost total insensibility we sprang instantly into the possession of great intellect"; when we are solemnly told (page 95) that the Confessions of St. Augustine are "distinctly old-fashioned Christian literature" and that "one thing that makes the Confessions tedious is that the book is addressed directly to God, and not to the reader"; when the author warns us (page 70) that Bunyan's "Pilgrim's Progress" is full of archaic theology and demonology, that "when we find Christian engaged in the struggle with Appolyon, who is covered with scales, wings and is belching fire and smoke, we say to ourselves: 'Now we have never fought this monster. He is the same old dragon who is a constant figure in medieval literature'"—when, as I say, we wade through page after page and chapter after chapter of such naif flapdoodle, of such high school platitudes, of such empty and obvious guff, the temptation is strong to run shrieking into the street and stuff the book down the gullet of the nearest sergeant of police. But second thoughts stay us. Second thoughts cure this damnable itch and pestilence of platitudes with still another platitude—to wit, with the platitude that, after all, such things must be said, somehow they must be put into words, someone must embalm them in a book. They may seem sour, stale, infinitely flat and brackish, but are college professors yet hep to them, are they known in Philadelphia, Raleigh, N. C., and Cambridge, Mass., have they reached (as sweet music) the ears of the poor schoolboys who are still doomed to sweat through "Paradise Lost" and the poems of Cowper, and to learn to "appreciate" (God help us!) such ghastly garbage as "Hudibras" and "An Essay on Man"?

I doubt it, and so doubting it, I offer a hospitable claw to this Quaker City Taine, this jitney Matthew Arnold of that singularly moral town. He has done a necessary job with commendable diligence and thoroughness, and if it be urged against him that he reveals a total lack of humor in the doing of it, the ready answer is that a total lack of humor was the chief thing that it demanded. A man of livelier and more facile wit could not have pushed it through. He would have paused too often, in his dehorning and disemboweling of such ancient frauds as Dante, Bunyan and Thomas à Kempis, to spoof them, to laugh at them, to tickle them in the ribs, or, even more probably, to snicker at himself for engaging in so grandiloquent and gratuitous a piece of hocus-pocus. Dr. Mordell never snickers once. Nay, he does not even smile. From beginning to end he proceeds solemnly, gruesomely, in such horrific style as this: "We cannot immediately (*sic*) resist thinking that a poet who teaches that the eating of an apple was the cause of the greatest misery that ever afflicted humanity has chosen a wretched and trite theme for a great poem." I can scarcely imagine a man more perfectly fitted for his work. He can give the simplest and most austere platitude—*e.g.,* "No character in Hell, human or diabolic, could think of amusement in playing a harp"—all the voluptuousness of a love-song by Ezra Pound and all the grim portentousness of a death sentence. Nature planned him for a Great Teacher, an American Thinker, an Uplifter. How his book will be hammered into all the prep school boys on that perhaps-not-distant day when the he-schoolmarms catch up to its heresies and so make articles of faith of them!

Let Dr. Mordell take the *Police Gazette* diamond belt. For lack of humor it would be extremely difficult to match him. But there is an ambitious young man in New York, Prof. B. Russell Herts by name, who may one day give him a very fair run for his money. Professor Herts' masterpiece, so far, is the discovery that Arnold Bennett "has not a great and mighty soul." You will find it embalmed on page 23 of his "DEPRECIATIONS" (*Boni*), a book of critical odds and ends, and of irritatingly uneven merit. On one page one finds such sweetmeats as this: "Abroad there is a variety of Social Classes. There are the dukes, marquises, barons, knights. Few of these labor and fewer possess capital. They are a true leisure class." And on another page, perhaps nearby, one finds certain observations of a considerable sagacity. Herts is at his best in the chapter entitled "Jottings in Europe." (The above quotation is not from it!) Here, for example, he states the whole case against Puritanism in a few words, and explains some of the late troubles of the English almost as accurately and as economically. He is at his worst when he discusses books and authors. He takes the cheap journalism of Bennett far too seriously; he hails Shaw meaninglessly as "the greatest progressive in history"; he makes the capital mistake of considering George Moore as a prophet, instead of as an artist.

This last error, of course, is no more than a proof of Herts' nativity; a man may revile the Republic all he pleases, but so long as he breathes its air and is nourished by its proteids there will be some flavor of the Puritan in him, and he will show it by an unescapable tendency to convert æsthetic issues into ethical issues, to discuss beauty in terms of morals. No American may ever hope to get rid of that habit entirely, at least so long as he remains on this side of the water. The miasma is as potent as mother's milk. Even an American who is professedly anti-Puritan and eager to prove it—for example, Theodore Dreiser—shows constant signs of what may be called morality-consciousness. That is to say, he is constantly forced to assume that this or that human act, intrinsically inert morally, has some sort of moral content, or at all events to waste a lot of time proving that it hasn't, and to a jury already committed to the other side. My learned brother, George Jean Nathan, is another immoralist who is a good American under his false whiskers. His recent volume, "Another Book on the Theatre," is full of naif moralizing; he is even indignant against chorus girls because many of them are, have been or hope to be kept ladies. I could cite from his work a score of specimens of moral sentiments that would be ratified without question by the Rev. Dr. Billy Sunday, Mr. Edward Bok or the Hon. Josephus Daniels. I myself have pious moments, and once denounced this same Dr. Sunday for sacrilege, a crime as purely mythical as seduction . . . Therefore, I plead for executive clemency for Herts. Let him be paroled. And let him make amends by writing an essay on George Moore the stylist. That stylist Moore is one of the most delicate craftsmen of our time; only Walter Pater and Oscar Wilde have made lovelier music of English prose. He stems, of course, not from Zola the moralist, as Herts, despite an attempt at differentiation, seems to suspect, but from Flaubert the artist. Moore is not "a gunshot at the conventions of this century"; if he were, Sudermann would be a salvo of Busy Berthas and Shaw would be a whole bombardment. He is not artillery at all: he is a lonely piper in a muggy London fog, playing a sweet, sad air from the childhood of the world.

II

Between the death of Tom Robertson, in 1871, and the first performance of Pinero's "The Profligate" in 1889—approximately a whole theatrical generation, for very few of us do much theater-going before seventeen, and no man of any intelligence ever frequents the playhouses, at least to see plays, after thirty-five—the current English drama consisted almost entirely of stealing from the French. Those were the palmy days of Sydney Grundy and his fellow adapters and chloride-of-limesters; nothing could exceed the ardor with which they pounced upon each new French play that saw the light in Paris, and prepared it for burial in the Puritan cerebrum. The process was beautifully simple. Wherever the French dramatist wrote adultery, the English aseptician scratched it out and put in flirtation, and where, at the end, the Frenchman made the outraged husband kick his guilty wife out of villa, village and vilayet and then hurl himself homerically into the arms of the nearest soubrette, the moral Briton brought the two down to the footlights for a handshake, a general amnesty and an amiable buss. In brief, the French originals were anatomized of everything that made them honest, naughty and charming, and so served up to the enchanted Londoners like chorus girls encased in flour barrels. During the whole of the eighteen years England did not produce n single play of the first rank, or even, indeed, of the tenth rank. Such a gaseous marshmallow as Henry Arthur Jones' "The Silver King" was actually the best that the country of Shakespeare and Sheridan, of Congreve and Wycherley, could produce of its own unaided effort. . . . And if the English drama of the time was thus a feeble imitation of the French, the American was a still feebler imitation of the English. Think, sweet one, of "Hazel Kirke"! Or of "The Young Mrs. Winthrop"!

Strangely enough, this so-copious borrowing from the French drama was accompanied by almost complete ignorance of it. That is to say, the London play-goers who, under the lash of Clement Scott, gave a lavish clapperclawing to the plays adapted—*i.e.,* stolen and mutilated—from Augier, Labiche, Meilhac, Halévy and the younger Dumas, knew no more about the original pieces of these gentlemen than an Eskimo knows of Michaelmas. Until Brander Matthews' "French Dramatists" was published, in 1881, there was actually no intelligible notice of them, nor of any one of them, in the English language, and even after this book was printed there was a wait of ten years before such fellows as Walkley, Shaw and Archer returned to the subject, and began to throw genuine light upon it. Then came the Ibsen bomb-explosion, with its ensuing spy hunt in England, and the French papas of the English drama were once more neglected. This neglect has run down to our own time. It is only during the past year or two, and through the efforts of one man, Dr. Barrett H. Clark, that any systematic effort has been made to translate the principal French plays of the nineteenth century into English. Clark entered the field by way of Brieux's and Hervieu's echoings of Ibsen, but he soon found, it would appear, that Ibsen, too, had forerunners, and now he plunges among those forerunners with a long series of excellent translations from Labiche, Feuillet, Meilhac, Halévy and Pailleron (*French*), and with a sightly volume entitled "FOUR PLAYS FROM THE FRENCH OF EMILE AUGIER" (*Knopf*).

The former already runs to twenty-five or thirty paper-bound volumes, and is to include specimens of the German, Russian, Spanish and Italian drama, and even a few plays from the Greek and Latin. Of the Russian drama we have had rather an overdose of late, and the more it is studied the more it is found to be soggy and witless, but there is plenty of room elsewhere for the enterprising pioneer, especially in France and Germany. Of the Sardou melodramas, for example, not three have been done into English; of the Labiche comedies not two; of the Dumas *fils* dramas of sex not one. Every American theater-goer has been thrilled at second-hand by Augier's "Le Mariage d'Olympe," for its grand scene (the belgianing of Olympe by the old marquis) was borrowed for Clyde Fitch's "The Marriage Game," but before Clark tackled it the actual text had never been done into English, nor was there any adequate critical discussion of its thesis and significance in the language, save in Dr. Matthews' forgotten book. Here is opportunity: here a useful job awaits the man. Two-thirds of what remains of Augier is almost as well worth translating, and two-thirds of Dumas *fils,* and probably a third of Sardou, and even some of Scribe, Feuillet, Meilhac, Dennery, Gondinet and Barrière. These birds taught our own theatrical canaries how to sing; they are the fathers of all our Thomases, Kleins, Walters, Sheldons, Armstrongs, Gillettes, Howards, Broadhursts and Megrues. More such sires are to be found across the Vosges; Clyde Fitch, for one, borrowed from the Germans even more than he borrowed from the French. It is to be hoped that Dr. Clark finds a German translator as discreet and efficient as he is himself. And think of Italy! How few of the new Italian plays have been Englished—the inane sardoodledoms of the mountebank, D'Annunzio; a single volume of Giacosa in the Modern Drama Series; and what else? And then there is Hungary. We know a play or two of Molnár's, and one of Menyhért Lengyel's, but what of Lászlo Beöthy, Lajos Biró, Sándor Bródy, Ferencz Herczeg, the Szász brothers, Rákosi-Malonyai, Viktor Tardos, Géza Gárdonyi, the enormously prolific Gergely Csiky? All of these are popular Hungarian dramatists, and most of them have been translated into German and the Slav languages. Again there are the Spaniards. We know only José Echegaray. Who will give us specimens of Jacinto Benvente, whose published plays run to eighteen volumes? Or of Fernando Periquet, the librettist of Enrique Granados, the Spanish composer? Or of Pérez Galdós, the Spanish Dumas? Or of such Portuguese dramatists as Fernando Caldeira, João de Camera, Camillo Castello Branco, the Marques de Costa, Francisco Serra, Gervasio Lobato, José de Souza Moneiro, Antoinio Joaquim de Carvalho and Francisco Gomes de Amorim? Here is a chance for Dr. Clark and his bilingual bravos to do a good service.

As for Augier, his fame must rest upon the fact that, even before Ibsen, he made a gallant effort to put the actual facts of life into the drama. "Le Mariage d'Olympe" was not the first of the so-called problem plays, but it was the first of them to steer wholly clear of mush and rumble-bumble. Compare it, for example, with Dumas' "La Dame aux Camélias." In the latter, the one object of the dramatist is to manufacture a false and mawkish sympathy for a hussy who is plainly seen to deserve the boot in her very first scene. Indeed, Marguerite Gautier is made out to be so innocent and pathetic that three generations of fat women have snuffled and slobbered over her, and cursed God for not making them red-haired, tubercular and immoral. Against this hollow sentimentality "Le Mariage d'Olympe" hurls a rock that finds its mark. The piece shows the prostitute as she really is: a grafter in skirts, with no more conscience than a police captain and no more real charm than a burlesque queen. . . . In closing, the *ordre pour la mérite* should be bestowed upon Mr. Knopf, who is a beginning publisher, for the attractive form that he has given to the Augier book. Inside and out it is a delight to the eye.

Of the other plays of the month, the only one worth noticing is George Middleton's "CRIMINALS" (*Huebsch*), a one-acter in which the dangers are seen of permitting a young girl to go to her marriage uninstructed in the appropriate facts of anatomy and physiology. Mr. Middleton is a competent workman and he has here made a plausible and actable little play, but his argument, after all, is chiefly of academic interest, for innocence is no longer a function of virginity. The sex hygienist have saved the flapper from her old ignorance, and she now goes to the altar with a learned and even cynical glitter in her eye. The veriest school-girl of to-day knows as much as the midwife of 1885. Worse, she spends a good deal more time discharging and disseminating her information. All this, of course, is highly embarrassing to the more romantic and ingenuous sort of men, of whom I have the honor to be one. We are constantly in the position of General Kitchener in Shaw's one-acter, "Press Cuttings," when he begs Mrs. Farrell, the talkative charwoman, to reserve her confidences for her medical adviser. One often wonders, indeed, what women now talk of to doctors. . . .

Please do not misunderstand me here. I do not object to this New Freedom on moral grounds, but on æsthetic grounds. In the relations between the sexes all beauty is founded upon romance, and all romance is founded upon ignorance, or, failing that, upon the deliberate denial of the known truth. To be in love is merely to be in a state of perceptual anesthesia—to mistake an ordinary young man for a Greek god or an ordinary young woman for a goddess. But how can this condition of mind survive the deadly matter-of-factness which sex hygiene and the new science (or is it sport?) of eugenics impose? How can a woman continue to love a man after she has learned, perhaps by affidavit, that his hæmoglobin count is 117%, that his blood pressure is 122/79 and that his Wassermann reaction is satisfactorily negative? . . . Moreover, all this new-fangled "frankness" dams up one of the principal wellsprings of art, to wit, impropriety. What is neither hidden nor forbidden is seldom very charming. If women, continuing their present tendency to its logical goal, end by going stark naked, there will be no more poets and painters, but only dermatologists and photographers.

As I have said, the other current printed plays are anything but inspiring. Percy MacKaye's "THE IMMIGRANTS" (*Huebsch*) marks the final eclipse of MacKaye the poet by MacKaye the brummagem soothsayer and uplifter. Between the two of them, Harvard University and the Drama League have darn nigh ruint Percy. . . . The English version of Franz Adam Beyerlein's "Zapfenstreich" by Charles Swickard, under the title of "TAPS" (*Luce*), is frankly put forward to cajole the more extreme Germanophobes and anti-militarists. The piece was first heard of so long ago as 1901, and four years later it was played with some success in London and Paris, though it was a complete failure in New York. The author is an Austrian Socialist, and the play embodies the damning accusation that a German officer is disinclined to marry a sergeant's daughter, even after she has succumbed to his blandishments. This accusation was heartily applauded by the French, German, Austrian and Belgian Socialists, who now follow their hated officers into battle with patriotic cries, and gloriously butcher one another. . . .

III

I wish I could give you a long list of lively and excellent novels, but the truth is that nearly all the new ones that have reached me have been intolerably stupid. For example, Arnold Bennett's "THE TWAIN" (*Doran*), the third (and, let us pray God, last) volume in the Clayhanger series. Most of us remember the joys of the first volume—and the keen disappointments of the second. Well, here is sorrow made doubly bitter. Bennett has simply filled 543 closely printed pages with empty and aimless details. One goes to sleep over it, dreams of dull sermons, awakens swearing, takes another hack at it, falls asleep again, awakens and tries it once more, and so on *ad infinitum*. It seems, in the end, no more than a vast effort to kill space, an enterprise infinitely huge and incredibly futile, a deafening howdy-do about nothing. Compared to it, Dreiser's "The 'Genius'" is a succinct and racy tale. . . . Turn now to Ian Hay's "SCALLY: THE STORY OF A PERFECT GENTLEMAN" (*Houghton*)—the usual sentimental story about a dog. Turn now to "SUNLIGHT PATCH," by Credo Harris (*Small-Maynard*)—the usual melodrama of the Kentucky uplands, with the usual uncut-diamond hero and the usual tedious dialect. And to "A DAUGHTER OF THE REVOLUTION," by Esther Singleton (*Moffat-Yard*), and to "THEN I'LL COME BACK TO YOU," by Larry Evans (*Ely*), and to "WINGS OF DANGER," by Arthur A. Nelson (*McBride*), and to "THE SON OF THE OTHER," by George van Schaick (*Small-Maynard*), and to "THE GLORY AND THE DREAM," by Anna Preston (*Huebsch*)—the usual sentimentality, the usual stale thrills, the usual hollow fustian, the usual stuff and nonsense of the 15-cent magazines. Nor can I find anything to excite and charm me in "THE FORTUNES OF GARIN," by Mary Johnston (*Houghton-Mifflin*), an historical novel printed twenty years after its time, nor in Maurice Hewlett's "THE LITTLE ILIAD" (*Lippincott*), nor in "MOYLE CHURCH-TOWN," by John Trevena (*Knopf*), nor in "THE ROSE OF YOUTH," by Elinor Mordaunt (*Lane*). All of these books show good workmanship; all of them avoid the cheapness just mentioned; but not one of them, I venture, will be alive two years hence; not one of them is of much more importance to beautiful letters than to-day's newspaper.

Eheu! what bad novels the publishers print! What a futile business to read them—with "Huckleberry Finn" on the shelf, and "Germinal," and "What Maisie Knew" and "Barry Lyndon"! Even when one is intrigued by a good beginning, it almost invariably leads to a banal and irritating ending. I dip, for example into "WESBLOCK," by Harry McDonald Walters (*Dent*), and am quickly interested by the autobiographical hero's account of his nonage. But on page 85 I am bludgeoned by such stuff as this:

> People are just like foods; if you have too much of them, they pall on you.
> There in only one way to love a woman, and that is to love her faults and all.

And on page 111 I am murdered in cold blood by this:

> I would rather have ten people remember me as "dear old Wesblock" than have a million remember me by the amount of money I left behind me.

So with Will Levington Comfort's "LOT & COMPANY" (*Doran*). The book starts out briskly, but soon shunts off into Comfort's characteristic mysticism. I confess frankly to a violent (and perhaps grossly unjust) prejudice against his whole menagerie of Messiahs, Voices, Unifiers, Gleams, Faraway Women and such-like fabulous fowl. He writes skilfully always, and sometimes beautifully, but I am quite unable to stomach his theology. . . .

IV

Let overpraise pursue him a year or two more, and Irvin S. Cobb will be so thrust through the vitals that he will never recover. His friends do him an ill service to compare him absurdly to Mark Twain and Poe; his publishers perform a thwack upon his caput when they tout his latest composition, "SPEAKING OF OPERATIONS" (*Doran*) as "the funniest book yet written by Irvin S. Cobb" and "the funniest book we know of." Snouting within, one finds half a dozen genuinely clever and amusing observations hitched to 60-odd pages of ancient vaudeville patter and funny-column wheezes—*e.g.,* the wheeze to the effect that in the days of the author's childhood "germs had not been invented yet" (page 17), the wheeze to the effect that doctors bury their mistakes (page 49), and the wheeze to the effect that the old-time doctor always prescribed medicines of abominably evil taste (page 66). Such humor, to be sure, has its place, but it is surely ridiculous to argue that it belongs to literature. What it actually does belong to is Dr. Ayers' Almanac.

V

Despite the war, with its blest reduction of all forms of the uplift to absurdity, the manufacture and marketing of "inspirational" books continues unabated in our fair confederation. Thus Prof. Seymour Deming, in "THE PILLAR OF SALT" (*Small-Maynard*), calls upon all college boys to join the revolution, whatever that may be, and Dr. Van Wyck Brooks, in "AMERICA'S COMING-OF-AGE" (*Huebsch*), instructs the rest of us in our opportunities in the manner of the *New Republic.* I see many more such hortatory and pontifical books: "NOTES ON RELIGION," by John Jay Chapman (*Gomme*); "THE SOCIAL PRINCIPLE," by Horace Holley (*Gomme*); "THE STORY OF CANADA BLACKIE," by Anne P. L. Field (*Dutton*); "THE NEARING CASE," by Dr. Lightner Witmer (*Huebsch*). . . . I turn from these pale blossoms of the uplift to the gorgeous rose-garden of Lord Dunsany—to the incomparable fantasies of his "BOOK OF WONDER" (*Luce*), and the exquisite miniatures of his "FIFTY-ONE TALES" (*Kennerley*). Dunsany doesn't give a hoot for the uplift; he is not a forward-looker. He is something infinitely better; he is something immeasurably more valuable than all the forward-lookers at present unhung: he is a fist-rate artist. . . .

The Great American Art

Let the bibliographical psychologists explain why it is that the first serious work upon bartending ever to reach the Library of Congress is the small volume by Dr. Alfred Jefferson entitled "THIRTY-FIVE YEARS OF PUBLIC LIFE" (*Huebsch*). One would think that a science so widely practised in Christendom and of such intimate and constant interest and value to so many men would have long ago brought forth a copious literature, but as a matter of fact the only books on bartending put into type before Dr. Jefferson's volume were absurd pamphlets of the "EVERY MAN HIS OWN BARTENDER" type. I myself, while still a high school student, compiled such a pamphlet, receiving for it the sum of $12.50 from a Boston publisher. Most of them (and at one time they were greatly in evidence on the bookstalls) were put together by hacks employed at weekly wages. My youthful introduction to the business brought me into contact with several such literati, and I found them to be, in the main, gentlemen whose literary daring was only equalled by their lack of information. One of them, still a vivid memory, told me that he had written no less than twelve books in one week, ranging in character from a hymnal for the use of colored Methodists in Virginia to a text book of legerdemain for county fair gamblers and Chautauqua magicians.

Dr. Jefferson's volume has nothing in common with the confections of such eighth-rate virtuosi. The learned doctor (whose title, though espoused only by custom and courtesy, is nevertheless as well deserved as that of any surgeon, evangelist or college professor in the land) is a man of long and profound experience, and of unquestionable professional dignity. He learned the principles of his invaluable art under the late Prof. Dr. Martin Dalrymple, for many years head bartender at the old Astor House. After seeing for five years under this incomparable mentor, young Jefferson spent a *wanderjahr* or two in the West, and among other adventures saw service at the Palmer House in Chicago and at the old Planters' Hotel in St. Louis. At the latter hostelry, then in the heyday of its eminence, he became intimately acquainted with Col. Lucius W. Beauregard, of Jackson, Miss., perhaps the greatest authority upon corn whiskey and its allied

Smart Set 48, No. 3 (March 1916): 304–10.

carbohydrates that the world has ever seen. Col. Beauregard took a warm interest in the young man, and one finds the marks of his influence, after all these years, in the latter's book.

After his service in the Middle West, Dr. Jefferson became head bartender at the old Shoreham Hotel in Washington, from which he was translated, in the middle eighties, to the post of head bartender and chief of the wine cellar at the Rennert Hotel in Baltimore, that last surviving bulwark of the palmy days of American epicureanism and conviviality. The so-called wine cellar at the Rennert, of course, was chiefly stocked, not with the juices of the grape, but with the rarer and more potent essences that come from the still. Here, when Dr. Jefferson took charge, were ten barrels of rye whiskey that had been released from bond in 1844. Here was a whole vat of Kentucky corn that registered no less than 166 degrees above proof. The greatest of America's connoisseurs visited the majestic vaults and dungeons of the old *gasthaus* as pilgrims might visit some holy shrine. Down in those aromatic depths Dr. Jefferson reigned a benevolent despot, and there he acquired his enormous knowledge of the history, etiology, chemical constitution, surface tension, specific gravity, flash point, muzzle velocity, trajectory and psychiatrical effects of each and every member of the standard repertoire of alcoholic drinks.

In one of his most interesting chapters he discusses the place that alcohol occupies in pharmacology, and shows clearly that the common notion that it is a stimulant is ill-founded. As a matter of fact it is not a stimulant at all, but a depressant. The civilized man does not drink alcoholic beverages to speed himself up but to let himself down. This explains the extremely agreeable sensation produced by a cocktail or two before dinner. One cocktail, if it be skillfully prepared, is sufficient to put a man into a mellow and comfortable frame of mind. It quiets his nerves by anæsthetizing the delicate nerve ends; it dulls his reactions to external stimuli by shrinking and blocking up the cutaneous follicles; it makes him less sensitive to all distracting ideas and impressions, whether of a financial, domestic or theological character; and so by the combination of all these processes it puts him into that placid and caressing mood which should always accompany the ingestion of food.

I speak here, of course, of its general effects—that is, of its effects upon the nervous and vascular systems, and through them, upon the mind. Its local effect upon the esophagus and the stomach walls is probably stimulating, at least momentarily. For one thing, it increases the secretion of most of the constituent elements of the gastric juices, particularly hydrofluoric acid and citrate of manganese, and thus must necessarily make digestion more facile. But even here it operates as a depressant eventually, for it is obvious to anyone familiar with elementary physiology that a rise in the activity of the stomach is invariably accompanied by a compensatory fall in the buzzing and bubbling of the cerebrum and cerebellum. Our mental reactions are always a bit dull after a hearty meal; hence the feeling of peace which overtakes us at that time. The same feeling is produced by a few ounces of diluted alcohol.

Of even more interest than his discussion of such scientific aspects of his art is Dr. Jefferson's account of what may be called its social or spectacular evolution. He has an interesting chapter, for example, upon the garb affected by bartenders in various ages of the Christian era. At one time, it appears, it was the custom for the bartenders in the chief American hotels to wear full dress when on duty, like head waiters, professional dancers and Pinero actors. (This same uniform, by the way, was worn by surgeons in England before the days of asepsis. It was considered a gross insult for a surgeon to operate on a pay patient in other habiliments. The sleeves of the dress-coat were provided with buttons like those on shirt sleeves, and the surgeon turned them back and fastened them with rubber bands before spitting on his hands and beginning his ministrations.) However, the claw-hammer disappeared from behind the bar during the Civil War and has not been seen since. Its departure was succeeded by an era of grave looseness in dress, and Dr. Jefferson says that there was a corresponding fall in the dignity of the bartender. In the shirt-sleeve days of the seventies, he was a nobody. It was a common custom, indeed, to address him indiscriminately as John, or even as Jack, much as one might address a waiter in a fourth-rate eating-house or a fellow convert at a revival. But once he got into his now familiar white coat, along about 1886, the gulf separating him from the public on one hand and from the caste of servants on the other began to widen rapidly, and in first-class barrooms he now occupies a position comparable to that of the druggist or the dentist, or even to that of the clergyman. He is no longer a mere pot-slinger, but a clean and self-respecting craftsman, whose pride in his subtle and indispensable art is signified by his professional accoutrements. This change in the public attitude toward him has naturally reacted upon the bartender himself. In the old days he took his swig from every jug and it was common for him to end his career in the gutter. But to-day he is a sober and a decent man and, unless fate has borne very harshly upon him, he has money in the bank against a rainy day, and dresses his wife and daughters as well as any other honest man.

Dr. Jefferson (whose æsthetic taste seems to be very advanced, for he quotes James Huneker's books and W. H. Wright's "Modern Painting," and is satirical at the expense of the impressionists) believes that the modern barroom is one of the most marked triumphs of American design. He says there are at least twenty barrooms in the United States that deserve to be ranked, in their separate way, with St. Thomas's Church in New York and the Boston Public Library. In his early days, he says, the present movement toward quiet refinement in barroom design was unheard of and the whole tendency of architects was toward an infantile gaudiness. The famous barroom of the Palmer House in Chicago—paved with silver dollars!—was its extremist manifestation. But for a half-dozen years past the architects have been putting away their old onyx pillars and rococo carvings and substituting plain hardwood and simple lines. The improvement is too obvious to need praise. The typical hotel barroom of to-day is not only a hospitable and a comfortable place, but also, and more especially, a noticeably beautiful place, and its effect upon those who visit it cannot fail to be inspiring. Even the ordinary saloon bar shows a certain forward movement. It is still, true enough, too flashily lighted, but its design is a good deal less delirious than it used to be. In particular, there is a benign passing away of its old intricate spirals and curlycues, and of its old harsh combination of mottled marble and red mahogany, and of its old display of mirrors, so reminiscent of the Paris bordello. One still fails, perhaps, to be soothed by it, but at all events one is no longer so grossly assaulted and tortured by it as one used to be.

Dr. Jefferson is an implacable antagonist of the American mixed drink, and all his references to it are unmistakably hostile, but nevertheless he is interested in it sufficiently to inquire into its history. Here, however, his diligence shows but meager reward. For example, he finds it quire impossible to determine the origin of the cocktail, or even the origin of its name. Its first mention in polite literature is in Nathaniel Hawthorne's "Blithedale Romance," published in 1852. But it seems to have been a familiar American drink a good while further back, for there is a legend in Boston that John Adams was very fond of it, and that he once caused a scandal by trying it upon the then rector of the Old South Church, the reverend gentleman quickly succumbing and taking the count. But this legend, of course, is merely a legend. All that one may safely say of the drink itself is that it was known in the first half of the Nineteenth Century, and all that one may safely say of its name is that it seems to be American. Even here, however, the pedant may be disposed to file a caveat, for the word "cock" passed out of usage in this country at a very early date, "rooster" taking its place, and so the primeval inventor of the drink, supposing him to have been American, would have been inclined to call it a roostertail rather than a cocktail. The explanation may be that the thing was invented on American soil, but by an Englishman.

A similar mystery surrounds the origin of "highball," despite the fact that the word goes back not more than twenty-five years. Why high? And why ball? In England, where the thing itself originated and where it has been familiar for many years, it is called a whiskey-and-soda. "Julep" presents equal difficulties. The etymologists say that it is an Americanized form of the Spanish word *julepe* (pro. hoo-*lay*-py), and derive the latter from the Persian *gul,* rose, and *ab,* water. But this derivation, as Dr. Jefferson justly points out, seems to be chiefly fanciful, and perhaps may be ascribed to some fantoddish journalist or college professor, either drunk or sober. It is highly improbable that the mint julep was known to the Spanish explorers of America, for they were not spirits drinkers but wine drinkers. Moreover, there is no mention of it in history until years after the last Spaniard had departed from these shores. Still more, it was first heard of, not in the Spanish parts of the country, but in the wholly English parts.

This scant and casual notice of Dr. Jefferson's book scarcely does justice to one of the most interesting of recent volumes. The common notion that a bartender is an ignorant man is here set at rest forever. The author reveals himself not only as a gentleman of sound information but also as one of cultured habits of reflection. His book is written in excellent English from cover to cover, and the arrangement of its materials certifies to his possession of a trained and orderly mind. It is sincerely to be hoped that he will not allow it to be his last essay in the philosophy of his ancient (and perhaps now dying) art. Bartending has suffered greatly from the ignorant and cynical attitude of mind of the general public. When the average man thinks of barrooms, his mind quickly turns to memories of some of his own worst stupidities and follies, and so he comes unconsciously to the notion that the man on the other side of the bar is an ass also. Nothing can be more grotesquely unjust and untrue. The typical American bartender in this year of grace 1916 is a man of education, intelligence and refinement. He must be able to meet all classes and conditions of men in a dignified and self-respecting manner; he must understand human vanity; he must keep himself steadfast in the midst of manifold temptations. Obviously, such a man can be no slouch. The boob, the osseocaput, the fat- or bonehead may get along very well in the pulpit, in business or at the bar, but it is quite impossible for him to survive *behind* the bar.

II

Various and numerous Old Subscribers write in to denounce me for 183 words of criticism printed in this place last month—criticism directed destructively at a little book called "SPEAKING OF OPERATIONS—" by Irvin S. Cobb (*Doran*). A good many of these protests, though mailed from cities as widely apart as New Orleans and Mil-

waukee, are in the handwriting of Robert H. Davis, more or less clumsily disguised, but the majority, I dare say, are quite genuine expres-
sions of public fever and discontent. In general, they are divided into
two sections, the first consisting of praise of Dr. Cobb, and the second
consisting of abuse of me. I am not unaccustomed to such epistles,
and, as a rule, they produce no more effect upon me than a discharge
of gravel might have upon the hide of an aurochs, but in this case they
came in so copiously and were so hot when they arrived that I confess
to having been considerably shaken by them. As a matter of fact, I was
so much shaken that I was eventually driven to a careful rereading of
Dr. Cobb's tome. This rereading I have since repeated three times. The
net effect of the process, I am glad to say, is that I am not only convinced that my former remarks in disparagement were well grounded,
but also that they were exceedingly inadequate.

But don't take my word for it. Instead, let us go through the book
page by page, noting simply and accurately what our revolving eyes
behold. What do we observe on page 1? On page 1, in the very first
paragraph, there is the old joke about the steepness of doctor's bills; in
the second paragraph, there is the somewhat newer but still fully adult
joke about the extreme willingness of persons who have been butchered by surgeons to talk about it afterward. These two jokes are all that
I can find on page 1. For the rest, it consists almost entirely of a reference to MM. Bryan and Roosevelt—a reference well known by all
newspaper paragraphists and vaudeville monologists to be as provocative of laughter as a mention of bunions, mothers-in-law or Pottstown,
Pa. On page 2 Bryan and Roosevelt are succeeded by certain heavy
stuff in the Bill Nye manner upon the condition of obstetrics, pediat-
rics and the allied sciences among whales. Page 3 starts off with the old
wheeze to the effect that people talk too much about the weather. It
progresses—or resolves, as the musicians say—into the wheeze to the
effect that people like to dispute over what is the best thing to eat for
breakfast. On page 4 we come to what musicians would call the formal
statement of the main theme—that is, of the how-I-like-to-talk-of-my-
operation motif. We have thus covered four pages.

Page 5 starts out with an enharmonic change: to wit, from the idea
that ex-patients like to talk of their operations to the idea that patients in
being like to swap symptoms. Following this there is a repetition of the
gold theme—that is, of the theme of the doctor's bill. On page 6 there
are two chuckles. One springs out of a reference to "light housekeep-
ing," a phrase which invariably strikes an American numskull as sala-
ciously whimsical. The other is grounded upon the well-known desire
of baseball fans to cut the umpire's throat. On page 6 there enters for
the first time what may be well called the second theme of the book.

This is the whiskers motif. The whole of this page, with the exception of a sentence embodying the old wheeze about the happy times before germs were invented, is given over to variations of the whiskers joke. Page 8 continues this development section. Whiskers of various fantastic varieties are mentioned—trellis whiskers, bosky whiskers, ambush whiskers, loose, luxuriant whiskers, landscaped whispers, whiskers that are winter quarters for germs. Let us here be just to Dr. Cobb. He has done some excellent work with the whiskers joke. But all the same, I cannot say with honesty that he has done better than other artists who have tackled it. An old contributor to THE SMART SET, Dr. William P. Ratcliffe, once filled two pages with far more amazing names for whiskers than any here set down—for example, chin lash and neck muff. But in this matter, perhaps, I am hypercritical, for, after all, Dr. Cobb's book is not about whiskers, but about his operation.

Returning to page 8, we find that it closes with a reference to the old joke about the cruel thumpings that medical gentlemen perform upon their patients' clavicles. On page 9 there is a third statement of the gold motif—"He then took my temperature and $15." Following it comes the dentist's office motif—that is, the motif of reluctance, of oozing courage, of flight. At the bottom of page 9 the gold motif is repeated in the key of E minor. Pages 10 and 11 are devoted to simple description, with very little effort at humour. On page 12 there is a second statement, for the full brass choir, of the dentist's office motif. On page 13 there are more echoes from Bill Nye, the subject this time being a man "who got his spleen back from the doctor's and now keeps it in a bottle of alcohol." On page 14 one finds the innocent bystander joke; on page 15 the joke about the terrifying effects of reading a patent medicine almanac. Also, at the bottom of the page, there is a third statement of the dentist's office joke. On page 16 it gives way to a restatement of the whiskers theme, in augmentation, which in turn yields to the third or fifth restatement of the gold theme.

Let us now jump a few pages. On page 19 we come to the old joke about the talkative barber; on page 22 to the joke about the book agent; on the same page to the joke about the fashionableness of appendicitis; on page 23 to the joke about the clumsy carver who projects the turkey's gizzard into the visiting pastor's eye; on page 28 to a restatement of the barber joke; on page 31 to another statement—is it the fifth or sixth?—of the dentist's office joke; on page 37 to the katzenjammer joke; on page 39 to the old joke about doctors burying their mistakes . . . And so on. And so on and so on. And so on and so on and so on. On pages 48 and 49 there is a perfect riot of old jokes, including the nth variation of the whiskers joke and a fearful and wonderful pun about Belgian hares and heirs. . . .

I proceed no further. My purpose is not to argue that the book is wholly bad, for, as a matter of fact, it contains here and there some excellent spoofing; but to show that it also contains a large quantity of the oldest and feeblest humor in the world—humor that was ancient and decrepit when Dr. Ayres compiled the first edition of his almanac. Such humor, I have no doubt, has its place in Christian intercourse, and I, for one, laugh at it without restraint when I am sufficiently in liquor. But it is surely open to attack when it appears in a book recommended by the publishers as "the funniest book written by Irvin S. Cobb" and "the funniest book we know of." This extravagant encomium appears upon the slip cover and is especially designed to catch the bookbuyer's eye. Do the publishers seriously believe what they say? If so, what is to be thought of their capacity for judging books? If not, what is to be thought of their attitude toward the reading public? In any event, it seems very clear to me that Dr. Cobb has been doubly injured—first, by his own act in signing his name to such laboured and empty snicker-squeezing, and, secondly, by his publishers' act in dabbing it with such excessive overpraise.

I thus, at the end, specifically refuse to withdraw the remarks printed in this place last month. I am still convinced that they were just. Needless to say, of course, this somewhat elaborate restatement of them is not the product of my animosity to Mr. Cobb. I have not, unfortunately, the honour of his acquaintance, but we have a great many friends in common and the latter all offer eloquent and constant testimony in his favour. Beside these friends in common, we also have many interests, aspirations and vices in common. Both of us are too fat; both of us are anti-Carranzistas; both of us prefer malt liquor to the juices of the grape; both of us are old newspaper men; both of us are unlucky at all games of chance; both of us have written very bad books; each of us is the Original Joseph Conrad Man. Nevertheless, despite these points of contact and amity, I cling tenaciously to the doctrine that "Speaking of Operations—" is a fifth-rate piece of writing, and go before the jury maintaining firmly that I myself have never written anything worse.

Incidentally, several of the kind friends who have come to Dr. Cobb's defence seek to stab and slaughter me with the old charge that I am a mere reviler of better men, and hence accursed. This allegation is one that every critic soon becomes painfully familiar with. It has been embodied in a thousand moral denunciations and epigrams, the burden of all of which is that a critic is a man who devotes himself to destroying that which he could not hope to create. As a matter of fact, this notion of critical destructiveness is anything but sound, for even the most bilious reviewer, whether of books, of plays, of music or of pictures, almost always praises many more works than he blames. Moreover, his praisings always get him into worse difficulties than his blamings, despite the common delusion that I have just mentioned. In my own case, for example, I have been far more vigorously attacked for arguing that Theodore Dreiser's "The Titan" is a great novel than I have ever been for arguing that this or that confection of the best-seller manufacturers was a bad one. Five or six years ago, when Joseph Conrad was still a mere name to the vast majority of American readers, I was denounced in a Boston newspaper for maintaining that he was a better novelist than Thomas Hardy and William Dean Howells. In exactly the same way I got a lot of pedantic, sophomoric abuse when I first voiced the theory that Mark Twain's "Huckleberry Finn" was the greatest of American novels, despite the fact that various older critics, including Sir Walter Besant, had subscribed to it before me. Finally, I am being hammered in the newspapers to-day for arguing that my learned colleague, Dr. Nathan, is a sounder critic of the drama than the senile infants who so vastly enchant the old maids and unsuccessful dramatists of the Drama League.

A critic, indeed, is forced in sheer self defense into a carping and hostile attitude toward the majority of books, for even setting aside the fact that they are undoubtedly bad, there remains the more important fact that readers and connoisseurs of criticism delight in brutality and esteem a critic in proportion as he is lethal. Here we alight upon the universal human appetite for roughhouse, for scandal, for the putting to death of the other fellow. Quite the easiest way to make a stir in the world is to engage in abuse in a wholesale and unconscionable manner. This and this alone is the secret of the popularity of such mountebanks as Dr. Bryan and Col. Roosevelt. It is equally the secret of the unpopularity of such suave, oleaginous fellows as Dr. Taft and Dr. Root. The first named gentleman, while President, committed the intolerable offense of refusing to give the mob a good show. True enough, the things that he and Dr. Root say are a million times more true and reasonable than the things said by Dr. Bryan and Col. Roosevelt. But the mere truth or reasonableness of an idea, of course, is nothing in its favour when one is addressing the mob. I speak here, not as a theorist, but out of a huge personal experience. I have been engaged in propagandist writing of one sort or another for seventeen years past, and have printed during that time enough argument, exposition and criticism to poison a whole herd of horned cattle. My writings have always failed of success when they were chiefly made up of praise, however well deserved; they have always been successful when they dealt principally in abuse, however ill deserved.

Moreover, they have always had a disconcertingly inverse effect upon the public repute and standing of the persons with whom they have dealt. That is to say, those persons that I have praised have shown, in the main, a certain damage, whereas those that I have denounced have shown an unmistakable benefit. Dr. Cobb offers a ready case in point. I have more than once called attention to his tendency to fall into feeble rubber-stamp humour, and what is more, I have supported my criticism of him with an overwhelming and staggering array of evidence. Nevertheless, his popularity continues to increase steadily, particularly, it would seem, among the very persons whom I have addressed so eloquently in his disinterest. The first time I wrote against him I got no more than four or five letters of protest. But the last time, even counting out the obvious sophistications of the spies and gunmen of Capt. Bob Davis, I got fully a hundred. Next time, I dare say, the very mails will be choked with them.

Such is the effect of criticism, however honest, however convincing, however sweet and mellow. The public views it as the ancient Romans viewed the art of the gladiator. Even though the gallery is always currently in favour of the fellow who is doing the walloping, the emotion it eventually carries away is sympathy for the fellow who has been walloped. The result is that the critic of the fine arts, if he is only belligerent enough, will always find it easy to drum up a crowd for his show, but by the same token he will always come to grief in the end, for just as, if he praises, he will be damned at once, so, if he blames, he will be damned after a little while. It is thus no wonder that the great majority of critics, whether of books, of music, of painting or of the drama, are hard drinkers, and that practically all of their classical forerunners came to evil ends.

Halls

by Owen Hatteras

It was a night of a thousand stars.

And in the palace of Haroun-al-Raschid was revelry and delight. In the great and golden hall of the palace, lit with torches and silver lamps, men drank and sang, women danced, and a hundred musicians made music with viols and tambourines, trumpets and tympanums. And Haroun the Caliph sat on his gilded throne in the white glare of it all, nodding like an owl.

One came to him, threading among the throng, and whispered into his ear.

"A holy man in the garden?" asked Haroun the Caliph. "Alone? And on this night of revelry? Order him to come in that he may partake of the feasting."

And by-and-by the servant returned, saying, "He will not come in."

"Strange," said the Caliph. "What manner of man might he be?"

"He is like the quiet and sombre men of the hill-country," said the servant, "and he will not come in."

Then an impulse seized Haroun-al-Raschid, who was ever a creature of whim. And he arose from his throne and stalked out of the great hall, brilliant with torches and silver lamps and the eyes of women, and penetrated the garden.

The holy man sat on his haunches near the base of an olive tree, peering at the sky,—a gaunt man with lean hand and a beard of the whiteness of milk which touched upon the ground.

"You are lonely here, old father," said Haroun-al-Raschid, "and there is revelry within. The great hall echoes with mirth, yet you are lonely here. Why will you not come in?"

The holy man smiled with a slight quivering of his long gray beard.

"And why should I desire to sit in the hall of Haroun-al-Raschid, in the golden hall of his palace that is lit with torches and silver lamps," he said, "I, who sit with God in the Hall of a Thousand Stars?"

Smart Set 48, No. 4 (April 1916): 65.

Notes from a Day-Book

By Owen Hatteras

1. Romeo in his cups in a public taproom, boasting of his conquest of Juliet. . . . .

2. Fame and shame: their difference: that between *ff.* and sh-h-h-h!

3. How much do you love me? I love you to the last full measure of devotion. And where is the proof of it? I am willing to marry you.

4. I believe that the first movement of Beethoven's Eighth Symphony is worth the souls of all the heathen in Africa. . . . .

5. What a difference between the advertisements and the goods! Consider, for example, Belgian hares. Or Belgian poets!

6. The aim of law is not to protect the strong in the enjoyment of their property, but to protect the weak in the enjoyment of theirs. This is why all weak and botched men—*i. e.,* all democrats—are such ardent believers in law.

7. A *salon* is impossible in America, not because we cannot produce a Mme. Récamier, but because our country is too prosperous. Here even a genius gets enough to eat, and so it is quite impossible to lure him into society with a glass of bad punch and a plate of ham sandwiches.

Smart Set 48, No. 4 (April 1916): 66.

The Publishers Begin Their Spring Drive

§1

On Journalism.—A lot of good-humored (though, at times, somewhat wistful) spoofing is to be found in "THE SERIO-COMIC PROFESSION," by L. J. de Bekker, of the New York *Evening Post,* but in its title, after all, is the best of its flings at the dolorous trade of writing for the press. That title describes journalism exactly. Your true journalist, at his noblest and most earnest, never quite rises to the dignity of a genuine professional man; he is always a bit of a comedian, a quack, a mountebank, and the fact that he commonly takes himself with deadly seriousness does not change the fact, nor even conceal it. The cause thereof, I daresay, is inherent in the very nature of his work; it demands that he deal readily and oracularly with a range of subjects quite beyond the capacity of any single human intellect. The result is an ardent cultivation of mere facility, at the expense (and even to the conscious disparagement) of all sound and well-ordered knowledge. The typical newspaper copy-reader (who is the archetype of the journalist) not only knows very little that is worth knowing; he actually regards it as somewhat affected and absurd to try to augment his stock. This explains, on the one hand, the amazing cocksureness of the newspapers, and on the other hand their abysmal ignorance. In the United States, at all events, they are content to shine forth with a speciousness and hollow smartness, and their point of view is frankly that of the mob orator. In Europe one finds a greater timorousness, a more willing dependence upon authority, a more unashamed respect for culture. But in the United States the stress is laid less upon what is acceptable to the mind than upon what will pop the eye. It is not a year ago that a dictated reference to the Beaux Arts went out upon the wires as Bozart, and so got into scores of American newspapers. It is not a month ago that a journal which boasts of being one of the oldest and most respectable in the United States transformed Richard Wagner into "Carl Maria von Wagner, the famous German poet." And how the gods are made gay daily by journalistic treatises upon taxation, military strategy, finance, police administration, penology and international law! . . .

Mr. de Bekker's book, however, is not so much a satire against

Smart Set 48, No. 4 (April 1916): 150–56.

journalism as a good-humored pasquinade upon journalists. He is one of them himself, and he understands accurately their glorious lack of logic, their boyish enthusiasm for the trivial, their heroic energy, their incurable romanticism. Journalism enlists thousands of men of vast force and genuine talents—enlists them, binds them upon its wheel, whirls the breath of life out of them, and then throws them upon its scrap-heap. To find a match for the crazy fidelity that it engenders one must go to religion or war. A true journalist is half a Jesuit and half a trooper in a Grande Armée that shoots its stragglers. He roars through the incomparable twenties, drags himself through the thirties, and is then left in a ditch at forty year. . . . De Bekker is old enough to begin to see the tragic farce of it, and to squeeze out a sentimental tear. He says on his title page that he has been in the game for twenty-five years, and probably stretches the facts very little. I worked with him seventeen years ago (we covered, in competition, a terrain which included a third of Baltimore, three rowdy suburban towns and the whole Chesapeake Bay littoral), and he was even then so far gone in the craft that he wore a Latin Quarter beard, rolled cigarettes with one hand, carried a walking stick two inches in diameter, and composed hymns to Pilsner, then still an exotic and actually known only to James Huneker and a few others. Even in those days of his nonage he stood a bit apart from the procession; he had a veneration, for example, for sound music, and scandalized police stations with garglings of the sword motive. That aloofness, no doubt, explains his capacity for seeing journalism somewhat objectively, and, per corollary, the charm of his little book. It is to be lamented that more such books do not come out of newspaper offices.

§2

The Red Cross.—In "MARXIAN SOCIALISM AND RELIGION" (*Huebsch*), John Spargo takes 187 pages to prove that Socialism is not antagonistic to religion, nor even (to make a distinction not intended to be invidious) to Christianity. A labor, surely, of supererogation, but one given some show of excuse by the Socialist war upon ecclesiasticism, and by the misconceptions arising therefrom, particularly among the ecclesiastics put to the torture. Nevertheless, a labor of supererogation still. Socialism and Christianity, in fact, are but facets of the same gem, and the doctrines actually preached by Christ were much nearer to the doctrines preached to-day by the more intelligent Socialists than to the doctrines revealed by the practice of any existing Christian church. At the bottom of Socialism and of pure Christianity there is exactly the same idea, to wit, that all men are equal before the Lord, and both address themselves to restoring the alienated rights of men of the more feeble and incompetent sorts, and to pulling them, by that process, on terms of equality with their betters. I cannot imagine a genuine Socialist dissenting from the Beatitudes. In their insistence that there is not only no discredit in weakness and unsuccess, but even a high and rare sort of virtue, they state his creed to the letter.

The only real difference between Socialism and this theology-purged Christianity is that the former demands the realization here and now of what the latter merely holds out as a promise of reward beyond the grave. In other words, the Socialist accepts the Christian theory of human values literally, and demands that it be put into effect at once. He thus rejects resignationism in this life, which, by reason of its superiority to Christian democracy in practical feasibility, has forced the latter aside, and appears to-day as almost the only philosophical content in Christianity. But in what they actually get, as opposed to what they demand, the Socialist and the neo-Christian are still brothers, for both, despite their theoretical right to an equal share in all the delights and usufructs of existence (and even to a lion's share as a makeweight for their past and present deprivation) are forced by a harsh fate to put up with a good deal less. Each philosophy embodies a scheme of rectification and a scheme of revenge. The Socialist is buoyed up, not only by the hope of getting what he thinks belongs to him, but also and more importantly by the hope of punishing the fellow who now has it, and who is trying hard to hold on to it. By the same token, the Christian is heartened and made happy, not only by the firm belief that his present going without will be stupendously compensated in a life beyond the grave, but also by the soothing confidence that those who are fat, prosperous, sinful and happy here will have to go to hell for it when they die. . . .

I speak here, of course, of Christianity in its pure form, and not of any definite Christian church. All the Christian churches that have attained to any actual position and influence in Christendom have had to yield something to the bitter facts of life. That is to say, they have had to wink at inequality, and some of them have even gone so far as to assume its inevitability and to woo its beneficiaries. This is only saying, of course, that pure Christianity is essentially impracticable—that, whatever its theoretical truth, it will not work. Socialism collides with the same difficulty. It is based in theory upon an idea of complete equality, a negation of caste, of authority and of vested right, but in practise it has to make various compromises. In the present book, for example, we see Dr. Spargo, a very intelligent Socialist, engaged in a deliberate effort to still the fears and cultivate the good will of the ecclesiastical hierarchy. I venture to believe that he will fail. In so far as he argues that religion and Socialism, as philosophical schemes, are not antagonistic, he merely says what is obvious, but when he tries to show that religion as organized politics and Socialism as organized politics can lie down together, or even exist together, he tackles a hopeless task, for the church *qua* church is always a snob and a tyrant, and this is true of the left wing as well as of the right. The Catholic Church, in its palmy days, was never more despotic than the Scotch kirk, nor, for that matter, than the Methodist Church in the least civilized parts of the United States to-day. It is, indeed, a sound instinct which ranges the vast majority of Socialists and trade-unionists against the Puritans who now seek to force their views upon the whole population under cover of the law, for prohibition and Sabbatarianism, in their essence, are quite as subversive of the lower man's rights and happiness as conscription, the Inquisition and the *droit de seigneur*. . . .

But, be this as it may, I think you will be interested by Mr. Spargo's book. I am no Socialist, God knoweth, but I always read him gladly and with profit. His Socialism lacks the crazy extravagance of the French brand; he mingles it with English caution and hardheadedness. It is such leaders that the Socialists must listen to if they are ever to get anywhere.

§3

A Novel of Distinction.—One finds in "THE MAN OF PROMISE," by Willard Huntington Wright (*Lane*), the precise group of qualities that distinguish the average American novel by their complete absence. That is to say, one finds a graceful style, a delicate and accurate sense of form, and an intelligible and interesting idea, competently worked out. Superficially, the thing suggests the method and point of view of John Galsworthy, say in "The Patrician" and "The Purple Flower," for there is on the one hand his scrupulous and a bit hard workmanship and on the other hand a contemptuous attitude toward the sentimentality of ordinary fiction, and no less of everyday life. But there is no sign of direct imitation, nor even of appreciable influence. Mr. Wright has plainly thought his thesis out for himself, and devised his own investiture for it. The result is a novel that, after the other novels of the day, with their maudlin idealism and emotion-monging, seems almost arctic in its restraint and remoteness, but that still leaves upon the civilized reader an effect of poignant drama, and even of tragedy. There is a touch of the Greek spirit in it. It makes its appeal, not to the tear ducts and the midriff, but to the centers of reflection, and even if it falls a bit short of its apparent aim, it is yet full of sense and dignity.

The idea underlying it is simple, and, at bottom, obvious enough, though Nietzsche's voicing of it brought down upon him the abuse of the pious. In plain words it may be conveniently stated thus: that the influence of women upon a man of any force and originality, far from being inspirational, is often intolerably hampering, and that in this business of holding him down what are called good women may be quite as inimical to him as what are called bad women. Stanford West, the hero of the fable, is a young American of inquiring habit and intellectual audacity, a fellow whose "obscure inner necessity" (as Conrad calls it) moves him to question some of the dearest *principia* of his day and race, and moreover, one with enough capacity for plausible utterance to do his questioning in a manner that arrests attention. But whenever he sets out for the field of battle he finds a woman hanging about his neck. First it is his mother; the rebellion that he raises at college (against academic numskullery and poltroonery) fills her with shame and grief, and he retreats to give her peace. Then it is his first mistress, the love of his youth; her demand for caresses stands between him and that indefatigable labor which alone can get him anywhere. Then it is another mistress, the ordinary type of preying woman: her crude harrowing of his emotions leaves him exhausted and almost hopeless. Then comes his wife; she, like his mother, shrinks from the social odium that goes with revolt, and he descends to facile novel-writing to gratify her vanity. A chance of release follows; he runs off with a woman who seems to be the rare miracle, the woman unlike all other women. But this delusion, of course, soon yields up its kernel of bitter truth: the miracle is hocus-pocus, the immemorial arms are around him still. In the end we see him make his final sacrifice to his daughter. In order that she may have her chance in the world, he surrenders his own, putting security above self-expression. As we part from him he flops into a chair in a fresh-water college, a safe man at last. His wife, triumphant, sees only contentment in his smile of tragic irony. . . .

Such is the story in its substance. It is worked out with quite unusual ingenuity and earnestness. There is, indeed, almost too fine a finish upon it; West's doom pursues him with an inevitableness which, in life, might be supposed to be tempered with more of the fortuitous and the incomprehensible. The drama is developed, in brief, in a manner that is just a shade too cold and scientific; it is, as a document in psychology, somewhat harshly well-made, as the plays of Scribe were well made, on the side of mere intrigue. But this, after all, is merit as well as defect, for the thing that the current American novel most sorely needs, even above that uncompromising honesty toward which Dreiser and his (very remote, alas!) followers show the way, is a more thoughtful artistic selection, better rhythm and organization, cleaner form. Our novels too often wobble and turn upon themselves; they show a woeful lack of plan; they are as full of chaos, discord and meaningless ornament as a block of dwelling houses in an American city. Wright, with his sounder æsthetic training, has laid out his book with more skill and sophistication. There is in it an agreeable air of the studied, of the imposing, almost of the symphonic. (First movement, West's mother and the two loves of his nonage; second movement, the melancholy *andante* of his marriage and of his days of surrender in London; third movement, the false *scherzo* of his flight with Evelyn Naesmith; *finale,* his disillusionment, his return to America, and his tragic collapse and defeat.) It is a novel that is straightforward, vigorous, earnest, young. The writer himself is still full of the divine sincerity of youth, and, reading him, one scarcely needs to be told the fact. At fifty, perhaps, he may feel moved to recast it in places, as George Moore recast "Evelyn Inness." He may ameliorate it, condition it, mellow it. But even as it stands, it hangs together admirably and deserves genuine respect. There is no hint of conventional charlatanism in it; it is enthusiastic, zealous, ardently thought out. Such novels are too rare among us to be lightly passed by. . . .

§4

More Fiction.—Of the other current novels, the most workmanlike and interesting is "THE STRANGERS' WEDDING," by W. L. George (*Little-Brown*). This George is the man who wrote "The Making of an Englishman" two years ago, by long odds the best novel that England has produced since H. G. Wells' "Tono-Bungay," and perhaps a shade the better of that. "The Strangers' Wedding," it may be said at once, is not its peer, but nevertheless the book reveals many excellences and amply confirms my view, hitherto expressed in this place, that George is the coming man in England, and will go beyond Wells, Bennett and the others of that group before he has lived ten years longer. At the moment, almost alone among the serious novelists of his country, he shows no sign of being demoralized by the current phobias and malaises. The easy opportunities of emotional journalism have not wooed him from his proper business; he is still writing novels, and not breathing red fire and chlorine in the penny press. Kipling is at the one end of the literary file, snuffling and sticking out his tongue like a small boy who has been birched. George is at the other end, an unruffled artist and a self-respecting man. . . . Is it merely a coincidence that he grew up in France, and is in truth, spiritually speaking, more than half a Frenchman?

"The Strangers' Wedding," in its essence, is an exhibition of the plain fact, so obnoxious to democratic sentimentalists, that the barriers of caste are very real things, and that the man who tries to knock them over can only come to grief. Roger Huncote, a young Englishman of good family and university education, goes into an East End social settlement to help uplift and unsettle the lower classes. There, taking his own sophomoric *flair* for the unwashed too seriously, he enters upon an idiotic marriage with Sue Groby, the daughter of a laundress. The thing, of course, is a failure from the start. It is quite as impossible for Sue to become a lady as it would be for a moving-picture actor to become a philosopher, and poor Roger, on his side, finds it utterly beyond him to get used to breakfasting daily with a woman who is not. In the end Sue solves the difficulty by eloping with one Bert Something-or-other, a fellow of her own tastes, traditions and station. As for Roger, he hunts up Theresa Underwood, who has employed a fork correctly and distinguished clearly between don't and doesn't since her sixth year . . . .

The story lacks something of the fine penetration and gusto of "The Making of an Englishman," perhaps because the transactions it sets forth are inherently less interesting than those of the other book. When George showed his young Frenchman's transmogrification into an Englishman, not only externally but in inmost thought and feeling, he showed something that was new to fiction and full of highly diverting odds and ends of reflection and revelation, but when he takes 412 pages to tell us that the Huncote-Groby marriage was a failure he merely tells us something that we understood the moment we heard of it. Even the details bear an air of the familiar, almost of the inevitable. One knows without being instructed just how such alliances go to pot. Moreover, the dénouement is stereotyped and hence banal, for the adulterous flight has been a commonplace of English fiction for years, and one finds it in at least eighty per cent. of second-rate English novels and third-rate English plays. . . . But for all this, "The Strangers' Wedding" is yet a book of genuine consideration. It is well designed; its people are not sticks; one can read it without any feeling of intellectual condescension. In it George marks time. I believe that he will take another step forward anon. . . .

Among the lesser novels are half a dozen or more that may be read without pain. Arnold Bennett's "THE GATES OF WRATH" (*Doran*), is a reprint of an extravaganza done in his first period. It is cleverly constructed, bouncingly written and immensely readable. (I read it on a train, and a hundred miles seemed as the leap of a frog, the gesture of a bartender.) Bennett's competence to tell a story, once he has a story to tell, is undeniable. He is dull only when he abandons the dynamic for the static. Another fair flower of fancy is Ellen Glasgow's "LIFE AND GABRIELLA" (*Doubleday-Page*), the story of a Southern girl's revolt against the superstition, incapacity and general dunderheadedness of the South, and of her struggle for existence in New York. Warring up-on Southern sentimentalism, Miss Glasgow here reveals it: the ultimate solution of Gabriella Carr's problem is love; the curtain comes down upon an amorous surrender, with the future serene. But the downright maudlin is very skillfully avoided, and if the book had no other virtue it would at least deserve praise for its pitiless picture of Gabriella's moth-er, a genuine Southern mush-worshipper. Miss Glasgow is much above the average woman novelist in America; she has sound and honest work to her credit; she belongs to that slender rank which includes Mrs. Watts and Miss Cather. . . . C. Allan Gilbert's frontispiece portrait of Gabriella, by the way, presents an extremely appetizing damsel, albe-it she hasn't brown hair like the authentic Gabriella (*vide* page 31), but black. One forgives the whole tribe of novel illustrators for one such sweetie. In my nonage I harbored the passion of a love for a girl who, if she had been more skillful at make-up, would have closely resembled this Gilbertian pseudo-Gabriella. . . .

In "HOMO SAPIENS," by Stanislaw Przybyszewski (*Knopf*), lately suppressed by the police in New York, I can find nothing of serious consequence, either morally or artistically. It is the story of a Polish Lothario, and it treats his commonplace amours and puerile philoso-phizings with heavy solemnity. A Frenchman would have made a com-ic novel of it, and not only improved its charm, but also evaded the constabulary wrath, for the Anglo-Saxon moralist is always disarmed by facetiousness. The same English play-censor who forbade the per-formance of Brieux's dramatized gospel hymns was himself the author of "Dear Old Charlie". . . . Two translations of far more bulk and beam are those of "JERUSALEM," by Selma Lagerlöf (*Doubleday-Page*), and of "TARAS BULBA," by Nicolai V. Gogol (*Knopf*), the former a study of Swedish peasants, particularly on the side of their religious mania, and the latter a classical picture of Russian Cossacks. Both are books of very high rank, and worthy of far more careful discussion than I could venture to give them here. The translators are Velma Swanston Howard and Isabel F. Hapgood respectively, two women whose services to the freedom of the sea in letters have been numerous and distinguished.

Various light and empty things: "THE ETERNAL MAGDALENE," by Robert H. McLaughlin (*Doran*), in which, despite a serious attempt to deal with a great human problem, the fable is spoiled by the conver-sion of a vice-crusader to toleration and understanding, a psychological impossibility; "A PAIR OF SILK STOCKINGS," by Cyril Harcourt (*Dodd-Mead*), a novelization of a popular farce; "HELD TO ANSWER," by Peter Clark Macfarlane (*Little-Brown*), a saccharine melodrama with a hero who takes to preaching; "A MAN'S REACH," by Sally Nelson Robins (*Lippincott*), in which Randolph Tuberville, a talented but thirsty young Virginia gentleman is saved from the Rum Demon by Miss Lettice Corbin, who tackles him with love, poetry, mental suggestion and the Jubilee Songs; "THE IRON STAIR," by "Rita" (*Putnam*), in which the hero is the Hon. Aubrey FitzJohn Derringham, son to Lord Dulcimer, and there is an air of high life; and "PERSUASIVE PEGGY," by Maravane Thompson (*Stokes*), a bubbly confection of the "Bambi" school. I find such volumes very heavy going. And almost as heavy are "MILDEW MANSE," by Belle K. Maniates (*Little-Brown*), "FELICITY CROFTON," by Marguerite Bryant (Duffield), and "THE IMMORTAL GYMNASTS," by Marie Cher (*Doran*). Let me make up for them by commending to you five novels that, whatever their defects, are at least capably written and inoffensive to the higher cerebral centers, to wit, "DAVIS PENSTEPHEN," by Richard Pryce (*Houghton*), "THE REAL ADVENTURE," by Henry Kitchell Webster (*Bobbs-Merrill*); "DUKE JONES," by Ethel Sidgwick (*Small-Maynard*); "ROSE COTTINGHAM," by Netta Syrett (*Putnam*), and "THE OAKLEYITES," by E. F. Benson (*Doran*). Four of these are English and one is American. Not one of them is first-rate, even as novels go to-day, but in all of them you will find civilized entertainment.

§5

A Conrad Book.—Between novels Joseph Conrad publishes a collection of short stories, by name "WITHIN THE TIDES" (*Doubleday-Page*). One of them, "The Planter of Malata," is a novelette as long as "The Point of Honor." It is a tale of the Eastern islands, and full of Conrad's brooding and melancholy irony. Its machinery is characteristic; it proceeds by indirection; the true Conradean vagueness of outline is there. Of the other three stories, one is a melodrama of the English coast, the second is a tale of the Peninsular War, and the third goes back to the East. Ranged beside such masterpieces as "Youth," "Falk," "Typhoon" and "Heart of Darkness" these pieces reveal a common weakness: what they lack is the allurement of fantastic and powerful character. No figure in them, indeed, is even remotely comparable to Falk, to Captain MacWhirr, to Kurtz or to Captain Whalley. Nor, for that matter, do they show the dramatic force and poignancy of the stories just named. But though they thus fall a good deal below Conrad's best, they are still tales of unmistakable merit, and any lesser romancer might well point to them with great satisfaction. . . . Which suggests the happy thought that Spring is here again, and that the time has thus come again to reread "Youth." I shall not miss it, believe me! I would as lief miss rereading "Huckleberry Finn," the central business and delight of my Springs since the year 1888. Has anyone ever noticed that the two stories are as alike as two peas, that the fundamental idea of the one is the fundamental idea of the other, that their very management is identical? . . . Two immortal and profoundly moving evocations of the True Romance, and in neither is there a hint of sex, a word of love! . . .

Two other volumes of unusual short stories are "WITH A DIPLOMA," by V. I. Nemirovitch-Dantchenko (*Luce*) and "THE BET AND OTHER TALES," by Anton Tchekhov (*Luce*). Tchekhov's work is already well known in this country and here he is represented by some of his best. It would be difficult, indeed, to exceed the sardonic humor of "A Tedious Story" (the longest of the thirteen), or, for that matter, of "'The Bet." The ghastly humor of the Russian, with its undertones of the macabre, is in both stories. The writings of Dantchenko are less familiar; the present volume, I believe, is the first translation to be published in America. It contains two longish tales. The first, "A Diploma," deals with village life in Little Russia; the second, "The Whirlwind," is a story of St. Petersburg society in the days before the Russo-Japanese war. In each there is enough of novelty and enough of literary distinction to suggest the hope that more of this author's work will be done into English. He belongs to the generation between that of Tolstoi and that of Gorki and Andrieff. His life has been that of a man of the world, and so his pictures of his countrymen should be penetrating and entertaining.

The Bleeding Heart

By Owen Hatteras

By all means," she faltered, "you must go. He may come at any moment."

Burton's lips twitched. His face was painful to see. He fumbled nervously with a button of his coat. And as he gazed into the frightened blue eyes of the little woman at his side, he felt a vague, dumb sensation as if his heart were broken.

"The telegram was plainly delayed in transmission," he said. "You are right. I must go. So this is the end."

In silence they watched the sheets of grey rain that surged past the window in the street outside. Burton wondered at the little fountains of water that leaped up by the thousands where the raindrops struck the pavement. There was such an air of finality about all this. It dazed him.

"Dearest," he said. "I will leave town on the first train, and, God willing, I will never see you again. How I shall live from now on, I don't know. I don't know what I shall be able to do. The days will be so vacant, so empty, dear."

The blue-eyed woman began crying softly.

"With you out of my life, I will be purposeless and hopeless. The. days will be empty—empty. Three hundred and sixty-five in every year. And what can I do to pass them away? What can I do?"

"I—I don't know," sobbed the woman. "I don't know, George. But think of *me!*"

"My life is empty," he said. His throat choked as he tried to continue. It was all so final. "I don't know whatever I shall be able to do, sweetheart," he said. . . .

As the train whistled and slowly drew away from the station, Burton sank as comfortably as might be into a chair in the smoker. His heart was broken. He knew in very truth that it *ought* to be broken. Hang it, it *was* broken. He lit a cigar and puffed softly.

The sun was out, shining like summer, although it was but the first week in March. A stream of comforting heat rose from the recently

Smart Set 49, No. 1 (May 1916): 262.

drenched fields at the roadside. It was a magnificent day. Burton peered out the window, looking quietly. The houses, the clumps of trees, the fields, swept past monotonously, crowding one upon the other. The fat man in the next seat was asleep and snoring. . . .

By-and-by Burton realized with a laugh that for an hour and a half he had, with keen pleasure, been counting the telegraph poles.

The Deathbed

By William Drayham

As he mounted the steps Randall looked at his watch. He was on time. From inside the house he could hear the sobbing of children and a murmur of low voices. He knocked softly.

The white-haired doctor opened the door and, nodding, motioned him in. The red-eyed woman with a soiled handkerchief in her hand sobbed a greeting. Randall clasped her hand in silence, pressing it hard. He could have wept for the pity of it.

"If you feel you can stand it," said the doctor, "we will leave it with you till daylight. Mrs. Crabbe needs sleep terribly and I'm worn out myself. If anything extraordinary develops, you will find me here on the couch."

Randall nodded and quietly entered the sick-room. The light was turned very low and he could see only with difficulty the emaciated figure on the bed. The room was deathly still. With a shrug of his shoulders Randall sat down in the chair at the bedside to watch the hours out. He felt quite at his ease with the ticking of his watch for company. But the tragedy of it weighed heavily on him.

The lean drawn face of his old friend resembled but little the smiling countenance of a month before. The arms that had once been strong with muscles like whip-cord now lay limp on the sheet, mere skin and bone. He had to watch carefully to detect the slightest sign of breathing. And with a feeling of deep sadness he realized that the friend of old days had but a few hours to live. The pity of it!

Randall gazed queerly at the pale face on the pillow. He thought of the plans that this dying man had made—his hopes—his dreams. How his face had beamed when he had spoken of them! Many a talk the two had had together, Randall and he. He was such a dreamer, with so many hopes, and all so golden. It was terribly sad. And terribly unjust, Randall thought.

For here were he and a million others as happy as ever. Their busy lives would go on with all the pleasures of the world next week, next month, next year. And here this man, with the most golden dreams of

Smart Set 49, No. 1 (May 1916): 276.

them all was to die—with his work unfinished, his dreams unfulfilled, his hopes defeated. Perhaps before dawn he would be dead. It was terribly unjust.

"And in the morning," Randall philosophized, "the wagons will bustle up and down the streets, people will chatter on the corners, cars will run and bells will ring, whistles will blow—the life of the city will be the same, busy and happy as ever. And he will never know. All that will be nothing to him."

It was unjust—utterly unjust. For his friend's sake, a wave of indignation swept over Randall, indignation against life, against God. The pity of it! Randall sighed and hung his head. The small lamp in the far corner of the room flickered queerly.

At daybreak when the white-haired doctor softly opened the door he, gave an exclamation of surprise. The man on the sick-bed was breathing peacefully. At his side sat Randall, the watcher for the night, with his head hanging limp on his breast. Hastily the doctor examined him. He was dead.

"Hm!" muttered the doctor. "Heart failure."

Tra-la! Tra-la-la! Tra-la-la-la!

The dog-star rages! nay, 'tis past a doubt,
All Bedlam, or Parnassus, is let out!
        —*Alexander Pope.*

Again that dulcet chirping, that whistling and bird-calling, that trilling and roulading, that gargling and grace-noting, that gentle puffing and snorting, that tuning of harps and sackbuts, that shoving and pushing, that shuffling of feet and beating on the door! Again it is Spring, and the poets rave and accumulate in my ante-chamber, each with his tome of strophes, his pamphlet of twitters, his sheet of gurgles! A heavy clay for my sergeant-at-arms, Unteroffizier Rufus Johnson, a blackamoor of courtesy all compact, himself a passable performer upon the banjo, violoncello and pianoforte da gamba. It is his duty, in all diligence and mercy, to save the poets from one another, to keep that herculean Oklahoma trioletist from stamping out the life of Harvard's favorite Homer, to rescue the fat and helpless Gilbert K. Chesterton from the devil's hooves of Louis Untermeyer, to remove the gnarled fists of Joyce Kilmer from the tender eyes of Don Marquis, to patch up a *trouga Dei* between the Prussian firebrand, Joseph Bernard Rethy, and the Anglo-Saxon pacifist, Morris Rosenfeld. No easy job, I assure you. Poets are tough, and not oppressed by conscience. More than once, at our annual soirées, I have had to call out the gendarme to prevent murder, or even worse. The pounding on the door is deafening, titanic, horrible. The very wall is bulged and crinkled by the impatience of the vernal choir. . . .

But fear not! Johnson is an old artillerist, a veteran of endless famous victories. He fought at Antietam, Gettysburg, Seven Oaks, Chancellorsville, Port Arthur, San Juan Hill, Omdurman, Modder River, Tannenburg, Neuve Chapelle, Jena, the Dardenelles, Agincourt, Przemysl, Bull Run, Ladysmith, Bannockburn, Yorktown, Bunker Hill, Waterloo. He will hold the portal, you may be sure. More, he will reduce that wild mob to order, peace, discipline. He will range the poets whose names begin with A first, and then the poets whose names begin with B, and then the poets whose names begin with C, and so on. And he will let them in that way and no other way, one quietly following another. . . . As behold: the first being Prof. George B. Adams. . . .

Let us now glance at the compositions of these bards as they come in, keeping a wary eye for what is sweet.

II

> Poets lose half the praise they should have got,
> Could it be known what they discreetly blot.
> —*Edmund Waller.*

ADAMS, George B.: "Outward Bound" (*Privately Printed*)— Exultations of a somewhat dampened, cerebral species. The lines of a poet who loves beauty, but is not easily fooled by it. Exhibit:

> The sky is calm,
>   The air is still,
>   The stars in quiet sleep;
> And yet we struggle
>   Up life's hill—
>   Mud ninety inches deep.

Not a superfluous word here; the thought slips out through an almost arctic reticence. Perhaps the "ninety inches" may be criticised as exaggeration, excess, exuberance. If so, change it to "nineteen". . . . Another world tragedy is squeezed into even tighter stays:

> There was a young man,
> And his cheek was very wan,
> 'Cause he loves a young girl named Ella;
> And the trouble seemed to be
> (Just 'twixt you and me)
> That she was rather fond of another fellah.

One gathers, from his title-page, that Dr. Adams is no more. Alas, that this should be so!

AIKEN, Conrad: "Earth Triumphant" (*Macmillan*)—This poet comes with encomiums in his hands, and his publishers send word that his book is "a credit to American literature." I find in it a number of fluent and graceful pieces of verse, but surely nothing to stagger humanity. The thoughts expressed in these poems are familiar and obvious, and they are clothed in phrases that seldom show the slightest feeling for the music and magic of words. All the old-timers are here: "a trembling kiss," "silver laughter," "a flash of feet," "mysterious dawn," "silent spaces," "brazen laughs," "endless pain," "gentle rhymes," "eager glance," "weight of grief," "scarlet maple," "myriad rain-drops," "bacchic mirth," "bitter north wind," "whirling whiteness," etc. It is not often that Mr. Aiken attempts anything original in image or epithet, and when he does the result is usually far from felicitous—as, for example, when he tries to represent the awakening of Spring aurally, and falls into far-fetched gabble about "an under-earth trombone." Moreover, his verse is frequently made lame by elisions, particularly of the articles. . . . What remains is simply a respectable facility, a neat hand for putting lines together. And in content, he usually mistakes the merely incongruous for the striking and moving. Why, save for the empty scandal of it, make the philosopher in "Earth Triumphant" fall in love with a Broadway chorus-girl—or, as the poet himself once calls her, a chorine? What could be more gratuitous, or cheaper? . . . Mr. Aiken formally confesses, in a preface, that he has read and admired Masefield, but assures the reader that his own poems are original. Let him be easy in mind. No one who knows Masefield will fail to mark a difference.

ANONYMOUS, John W.: "The House of My Dreams" (*Sherman-French*)— Harmless jingles, often of a pious caste. In one of them "hate" is rhymed with "snake." In another the negro form of "me" is spelled "mah," but rhymed with "tree."

ANONYMOUS, William P.: "The Major of the Kettle-Drum" (*Wells*)—Doggerel on political themes.

APPLETON, Everard Jack: "The Quiet Courage" (*Stewart-Kidd*)— The second edition of a book first printed in 1912. Sentimental, "inspirational" rumble-bumble, with no more poetry in it than a college yell. The Herbert Kaufman school.

BANGS, John Kendrick: "A Quest for Song" (*Little-Brown*)—The unsuccessful comedian, turned uplifter, at last achieves his first aim.

BARNES, Djuna: "The Book of Repulsive Women" (*Bruno*)— Moral philippics against sinful ladies, couched in high, astounding terms. The breasts of one are grandly denounced as udders. Another is depicted as with her legs "half-strangled," whatever that may be. I can find nothing here but a sophomoric effort to horrify the advanced thinkers of Washington Square.

BINYON, Laurence: "The Winnowing Fan" (*Houghton-Mifflin*)— War poems of a childish fustian. Pothouse braggadocia set to bad rhymes. In five years, Mr. Binyon will be blushing whenever he thinks of them.

BOURINOT, Arthur S.: "Laurentian Lyrics" (*Copp-Clark*)—No great poetry here, nor even poetry at all, but often a pleasant fancy, a pretty conceit. For example:

I cannot bring thee worldly things,
  Love with thy laughing lips,
Only a little song that sings,
  Blithe and free as it trips.
I merely bring thee simple things,
  Love with thy smiling eyes,
Dreams o' the blue of a blue-bird's wings,
  Only a rose that dies.

BRALEY, Berton: "Songs of the Workaday World" (Doran)—A book of newspaper verse, inspired as to both matter and manner by a diligent study of Kipling. Some of the things in it, indeed, are no more than variations of ballads that Kipling himself has actually written. There is even an imitative use of characteristic Kipling words and phrases—*e. g.,* "bloomin'"—in pieces dealing with American workingmen. A considerable metrical facility is visible, but the sense is often tortured to fit the rhyme.

BROOKE, Rupert: "Collected Poems" (*Lane*)—The circumstances of this poet's untimely death in Greece (he was on his way to the shambles of the Dardanelles) have surrounded him with a sentimental interest which greatly conditions judgment of his poetic achievement. As Dr. Gilbert Murray has said, he is already "almost a mythical figure." The result is a vast emission of overpraise, with the lady critics of the newspapers, male and female, leading in the benign business. Such sweet bosh is cruel to the fame of Brooke, for it sets up an expectation which his work, as published, can only disappoint, The truth about him is that he was a young man of the highest promise, a natural poet of undoubtedly excellent gifts, but that he died before he had quite found himself. Some of the poems printed in the present volume—for example, "A Channel Passage," in which the poet describes how his "retchings" made him forget the "sobs and slobber" of his love—are little more than the easy impudences that all of us write when we are young. Even in a few of his later pieces—for example, the song beginning "All suddenly the wind comes soft," and "Beauty and Beauty"—one finds little save the obvious, either in content or in form. But before he died Brooke rose to at least two eloquent and unforgettable bursts of song, first in "The Great Lover" and secondly in his five sonnets on the war. The former is a magnificent hymning of life as a great adventure, an endless pursuit of joy by curiosity, and there is something almost orgiastic in its ecstasy. The latter are, by long odds, the best poetry yet produced in England by the war, particularly the third and the fifth of them. Here, indeed, Brooke stands in no need of the snuffling encomiums of the literary ladies. As for his other things, most of them will be mercifully forgotten in a few years.

BROWN, Robert Carlton: "My Marjonary" (*Luce*) and "Tahiti" (*Bruno*)—This Brown joins the immortals as the discoverer of the essential humor of imagism, of the charming adaptability of *vers libre* to the uses of buffoonery. Don't mistake me: he is not a mere parodist. His innovation is more profound than parody: he does for the new verse forms (or non-forms) what Beethoven did for the bull-fiddle in the *scherzo* of the C minor symphony. For example:

> I like long prayers,
> The kind that stretch
> Like elastic hands.
> I always sit around,
> Holding my breath,
> Hoping they'll snap back
> And hit the preacher
> On the nose.

Again, this one:

> I'm tired of hearing praises sung
> In pale-checked
> Sad-eyed
> Virgins
> Who keep the vestal lights aglow.
> I sing to the red-checked,
> Healthy
> Modern maids
> Who keep the cheery
> Red light burning!

I quote only short ones. They show the manner of the poet, but they fail, of course, to show his more elaborate effects—effects which, in such pieces as "Aladdin," "Circus Follower" and "Who Shall Throw the First Shoe?" are extraordinarily vivid and amusing.

BURNET, Dana: "Poems" (*Harper*)—Sheer competence here makes an extremely interesting book of verse. Mr. Burnet has nothing very novel to say, nor does he say it with any great show of emotion (at all events his emotion is not contagious), but on the side of mere grace and dexterity his accomplishment is undeniable. It is not often, indeed, that one encounters more workmanlike verse. From end to end of his volume, 268 pages, I can't find a single forced rhyme, or a single stumbling line, or a single descent to the ridiculous. Even his war poems, though the ideas in them must have occurred simultaneously to at least ten thousand other bards, still have a certain bounce and freshness, and so leave at first glance an impression beyond their intrinsic deserts . . . . In brief, sound stuff. Magazine poetry at its best.

CARPENTER, Fred Warner: "Verses From Many Seas" (*Elder*)—Let us hear this Mr. Carpenter on the subject of war:

> Should I, a ruler—should any man be free
> Such great, inhuman, awful things to do,
> And claim the country's good demands it, of a few,
> To save one people from a Christian brother's knife?
> Ah, no! Twenty centuries of Christian life
> Should end such legalized and barbarous strife.
> The day has passed when other thoughts were rife.

All praise to Mr. Carpenter: he might have made it longer!

CHESTERTON, Gilbert K.: "Poems" (*Lane*)—Nothing of any pretensions here, but chiefly verses of occasion, some of them ten years old. Now and then a slashing, sonorous line; sometimes a whole stanza. The recreations of one who takes poetry lightly.

CLARK, Charles Badger, Jr.: "Sun and Saddle Leather" (*Badger*)—Rhymes of the cow country.

CONKLIN, Grace Hazard: "Afternoons of April" (*Houghton-Mifflin*)—A book of modest but often very charming verse. For example, this little song:

> As I went down the cedar stair,
> I saw the river pacing fair
> Between its tender tilted lawns,
> And past a thousand sailing swans.
> And I forgot strange talk of wars,
> To see its ripples swarm with stars;
> And all the thoughts that I could think
> Were swans along the river-brink.

Many of the poems in the volume deal with music—an art in which very few American poets seem to be interested—and one of them is a program for a proposed symphony, "In a Mexican Garden." The thing has plenty of color in it: where is the American composer to set it?

COX, Eleanor Rogers: "Songs of Eireann" (*Lane*)—Metrical versions of Irish legends, with a few songs added. Well-contrived, but I find nothing in them to loose an adjectival flow.

CROMWELL, Gladys: "Singing Fires of Erin" (*Sherman-French*)—Stereotyped, empty verses.

DE LA MARE, Walter: "The Listeners" (*Holt*)—Partly character sketches not unlike those in the Spoon River Anthology, though in more conventional forms; partly songs of a mystical flavor. One and all, they leave me cold.

DRAPER, John W., Jr.: "Exotics" (*Bruno*)—Very, very, very bad verse.

FICKE, Arthur Davison: "The Man on the Hilltop" (*Kennerley*)—Suave stuff. Occasionally, as in "The Three Sisters," a praiseworthy lyric. Less often, as in "To a Child—Twenty Years Hence," a genuinely excellent poem. For the rest, suave stuff.

FITZ SIMMONS, Theodore Lynch: "To One From Arcady" (*Sherman-French*)—Laborious, artificial pieces, wholly devoid of poetry.

FLETCHER, John Gould: "Irradiations: Sand and Spray" (*Houghton-Mifflin*)—A book of imagist verse, brilliant in color and (despite its superficial looseness) very careful in form. In the preface the imagist theory is stated briefly, sensibly and persuasively.

FOSTER, Jeanne Robert: "Wild Apples" (*Sherman-French*)—Workmanlike verse in many forms, always escaping poetry.

FRANK, Florence Kiper: "The Jew to Jesus" (*Kennerley*)—In the main, third-rate writing, but now and then, when the author's feelings are genuinely aroused (as, for example, in "The Jewish Conscript"), a piece of sound and moving verse.

FRANK, Henry: "The Clash of Thrones" (*Badger*)—Banal sonnets upon the war, containing all the ideas that would naturally occur to a talented high-school poetess.

HARTMANN, Sadakichi: "Tanka and Haikai" (*Bruno*)—Experiments in two Japanese verse-forms, the *tanka* of five lines and the *haikai* of three. An example of the latter:

> Butterflies a-wing—
> Are you flowers returning
> To your branch in Spring?

JOHNSON, William Samuel: "Prayer for Peace" (*Kennerley*)—Dithyrambs, chiefly very bad, by a minnesinger praised by Col. Roosevelt, who used his title poem as the preface of a campaign book. It is a pity that the vastly superior suitability of "The Egoist" (page 69) escaped the colonel's notice.

KEELER, Charles: "Songs of the Cosmos" (*Bruno*)—A performance of the Ninth Symphony upon a tin whistle.

KETCHUM, Arthur: "Profiles" (Badger)—Second-rate magazine verse.

KILMER, Joyce: "Trees and Other Poems" (Doran)—A somewhat toilsome effort to extract poetry from the commonplace. For example, a long poem in praise of delicatessen dealers. A gallant enterprise—but the poet is much more interesting when he backslides to stars and trees.

KREYMBORG, Alfred: "To My Mother" and "Mushrooms" (*Bruno*)—Dull prose sawed into irregular lengths.

LONGLEY, Snow: "Sonnets of Spinsterhood" (*Elder*)—A tedious sequence of stupid sonnets.

MACKAY, Helen: "London, One November" (*Duffield*)—A book of *vers libre* on the war, impassioned and yet empty.

MCLEOD, Irene Rutherford: "Songs to Save a Soul" (*Huebsch*)—Poems in obvious imitation of Francis Thompson, greatly over-praised by several critics. One called "Ships" offers a fair example of their commonplace style and puerile content:

> The rivers splendidly flow
>> Out to sea,
> And noble ships come and go
>> Statelily
> Whither and whence I do not know.

> I think the ships are like men
>> Setting forth for the wide
> With their cargoes of thoughts, and then,
>> With a change of tide
> And a newer load, coming back again.

MARQUIS, Don: "Dreams and Dust" (*Harper*)—A book of newspaper verse, graceful and workmanlike.

MILLER, Alice Duer: "Are Women People?" (*Doran*)—A new horror: a suffragette rabble-rouser taking to the pipes. Worse, rather clever tooting.

NOYES, Alfred: "The Lord of Misrule" (*Stokes*)—The sonorous nothings of a versifier who has mastered the forms of his craft without penetrating to its mystery. A No. 1 hack poetry.

O'HARA, John Myers: "Manhattan" (*Smith-Sale*)—A superbly printed volume, but in content no more than a respectable saying of what has been said before.

PHILLIPS, Stephen: "Panama and Other Poems" (*Lane*)—The poems of Phillips' last and saddest stage. The author of "Ulysses" and "Herod" reduced to silly jingles.

RAND, Kenneth: "The Dreamer" (*Sherman-French*)—Pedantic strophes.

REDPATH, Beatrice: "Drawn Shutters" (*Lane*)—Not so much poems as rough notes for poems—and not much in the notes to make one impatient for the poems.

RETHY, Joseph Bernard: "The Song of the Scarlet Host" (*Smith-Sale*)—Earnest, and often indignant, pieces. Two of them are addressed to Col. Roosevelt, and their collocation has a curious tang, for one of them hails him as a Moses and the other denounces him as a mountebank and a low-life. Mr. Rethy knows how to write a purple, resonant line, but he seems to be deficient in Hebrew, for on page 10 he employs the plural noun, *cherubim,* in the singular.

REYNOLDS, Elizabeth: "On the Lake" (*Badger*)—A book of songs for music, most of them bad. Not a few, indeed, suggest the translations from Heine and Goethe that one encounters in concert programs.

RICH, H. Thompson: "Lumps of Clay" and "The Red Shame" (*Bruno*)—An apparent effort to put all of the worst poems of this poet into two thin volumes. A success.

ROBBINS, Tod: "The Scales of Justice" (*Ogilvie*)—Ponderous doggerel.

SARGENT, Daniel: "Our Gleaming Days" (*Badger*)—More.

SCOLLARD, Clinton: "Italy in Arms" (*Gomme*)—Extremely bad stuff by a poet who, in his day, has done creditable work. Such poems as "Out of Rome" and "At the Vatican" are really quite pathetic.

SPENCER, Carl: "Poems" (*Badger*)—A posthumous collection, uncritically put together. Here and there, in the midst of much feebleness, a pretty song.

STORCK, Charles Wharton: "Sea and Bay" (*Lane*)—A prose tale in labored blank verse, with occasional songs. The chorus from one of the latter:

> We was joggin' along, joggin' along,
>   Joggin' along by the moon's pale light;
> Joggin' along, singin' a song,
>   Comin' home from the huskin' bee.

TEASDALE, Sara: "Rivers to the Sea" (Macmillan)—Saving only Lizette Woodworth Reese, Miss Teasdale (by book and bell, Mrs. Filsinger) is easily the first of living American lyric poets. Between the two, indeed, there are many resemblances. Each works in fragile and delicate forms; each returns always, after whatever excursion, to the *chant triste;* each shows a curious liking for the bald monosyllable, and particularly for the Anglo-Saxon monosyllable. Here, for example, is a little song that either might have written:

> The roofs are shining from the rain,
>   The sparrows twitter as they fly,
> And with a windy April grace
>   The little clouds go by.
>
> Yet the back-yards are bare and brown
>   With only one unchanging tree—
> I could not be so sure of Spring
>   Save that it sings in me.

The author here, it so happens, is Miss Teasdale, but if it had come to me unsigned I should have guessed Miss Reese. I do not hint, I need not add, at imitation. Miss Teasdale is too genuine a poet to need to borrow from anyone. But the concept of beauty cherished by the one woman is obviously nearly identical with the concept cherished by the other, and both give voice to it with the same apparent artlessness that conceals profound and dignified art. Miss Reese, it seems to me, is the better poet; at all events, Miss Teasdale has yet to write anything of the noble rank of the sonnet, "Tears." But with the simple lyric, often of but eight lines, the latter has achieved effects that no poet writing in English to-day has surpassed. In these songs one finds the very acme of simple melodiousness; they sing exquisitely, and they fix a mood with sure enchantment. Nothing, indeed, could excel the beauty of such things as "Morning," "The Sea-Wind," "Gifts" and "The Kiss," in the present volume. In more ambitious forms Miss Teasdale is less successful. But what of it? She has written at least twenty perfect songs, and that is more than most poets do in all their lives. . . .

THOMAS, Edith M.: "The White Messenger" (*Badger*)—The war is playing havoc with the poets. Here is one who, in the past, has done very good verses, and yet, on the war, the best she offers is stilted and bombastic, and the worst is downright ludicrous.

THOMPSON, Vance: "Verse" (*Kennerley*)—An undoubted eloquence is in some of these stanzas, despite a frequent preciosity, a visible striving for effect. They are by no means first-rate poems, but one somehow feels that a very fair poet was spoiled when Mr. Thompson took to journalism.

THOMSON, O. R. Howard: "Resurgam" (*Bains*)—Pretty things.

TOWNE, Charles Hanson: "Today and Tomorrow" (*Doran*)— Another victim of the war. Once he forgets it, Mr. Towne resumes the writing of poetry. For example, the ballad, "Assunta." For example, "The Quiet Years."

TROMBLY, Albert Edmund: "Love's Creed" (*Sherman-French*)— Sonnets, rondeaux, Pindaric odes and other things, chiefly bad.

UNDERWOOD, Edna W.: "The Book of the White Peacocks" (*Bruno*)—Words, words, words!

UNTERMEYER, Louis: "—And Other Poets" (*Holt*)—A book of parodies by the cleverest all-'round versifier in America today. This Untermeyer, indeed, seems to be a virtuoso in every branch of the grand old art of rhyme, for on the one hand he can fashion a pretty love song with the best of them, and on the other hand he can make blank verse that is genuinely imposing, and on the third hand, as it were, he is perhaps the deftest jingler in the whole camorra. His parodies in the present volume are often amazingly apt and deadly; he has caught the exact spirit, for example, of Miss Teasdale's plaintive lyrics, and then burlesqued it with diabolical accuracy of aim. All of the current metricians take their turns upon his operating table: Edgar Lee Masters, Ezra Pound, Amy Lowell, John Masefield, Rudyard Kipling, Alfred Noyes, William Watson and Vachel Lindsay among them. More, he attempts, and with success, the amalgamation of two styles in one poem—for example, those of Ben Jonson and Harry B. Smith. Altogether, a very cunning piece of fooling, and the fruit, I dessay, of many a tortured hour at the desk. Let him have a glass of beer for his pains.

WIDDEMER, Margaret: "The Factories" (*Winston*)—The poem which gives this volume its title attracted much attention when it was first printed, and is no doubt familiar. The other things are of uneven merit. The best are the love songs; the worst, it almost goes without saying, are the poems on the war.

WIGHTMAN, Richard: "Ashes and Sparks" (*Century*)— Workmanlike but uninspired stanzas.

WILLIAMS, Mark Wayne: "Babble o' Green Fields" (*Sherman-French*)—Rhymed platitudes.

WOOD, Charles Erskine Scott: "The Poet in the Desert" (*Privately printed*)—A long philosophical poem in the form of a dialogue between Truth and the Poet.

III

One who shall fervent grasp the sword of song
As a stern swordsman grasps his keenest blade—
————*Alexander Smith.*

In all, sixty-three books of poetry—and not four good ones. Among all the rhymers, whether American or English, Miss Teasdale stands easily in first place, with Mrs. Conkling second. The poets hailed with the most deafening plaudits—*e. g.*, Mr. Aiken, Miss McLeod and the late Mr. Brooke—offer almost unmixed disappointment. Among them all, only Mr. Brooke seems to me to have been a genuine poet, and his remains, removing what is merely facile and clever, consist of a sonnet sequence, two or three songs, and no more. . . . Are we to assume, then, that poetry is dead among us? Not at all. In the department of the lyric, at least, the United States is producing a large quantity of sound and beautiful verse to-day. The trouble is that it takes the publisher too long to discover it. A book of John McClure's songs, though it would be small, would stand above any book noticed above save Miss Teasdale's and Mr. Brooke's. A book of Muna Lee's would rank nearly as high. So would a book of Odell Sheperd's or Orrick Johns'. . . . And why are there no new volumes by Miss Reese, Bliss Carman, George Sterling, Marjorie L. C. Pickthall?

IV

> There is a pleasure in poetic pains
> Which only poets know.
> —*William Cowper.*

At the end a few volumes of translations, and a couple of anthologies. Miss Rittenhouse's two collections, "The Little Book of Modern Verse" and "The Little Book of American Poets" (*Houghton-Mifflin*) are both intelligently selected and attractively printed. It is inevitable, in such cases, that one should be dismayed by omissions, for every one of us has favorites that make little appeal to others. As for me, I wonder why Miss Rittenhouse put third-rate newspaper verse into the first of her two books and then forgot the lovely songs of Robert Loveman and Folger McKinsey, but nevertheless she has got together many beautiful things, and it will be a joy to go through them on dull days.

The Braithwaite "Anthology of Magazine Verse" (*Gomme-Marshall*) is too well known to need description. Here again one is occasionally brought up by what seems an unaccountable perversity of judgment, but in the main the collection is sound and interesting, and the editor's introduction and appendices are full of careful criticism and useful information. The 1915 volume bulges to 296 large pages—a sufficient proof that poetry is prospering in our fair republic. THE SMART SET poets are represented by no less than 29 poems "of distinction" . . . Two other collections of unusual interest are "Some Imagist Poets" (*Houghton-Mifflin*) and "Others," edited by Alfred Kreymborg (*Knopf*). The former I noticed last year, on its publication in England. There have been some changes in its contents, not always for the bet-

ter, but it still shows three or four things of excellent quality. . . . In
"Others" a youthful audacity often makes up for the lack of ideas.
There is an erotic flavor to the book, and much talk in it of forbidden
things. Searching it diligently, I can find nothing properly describable
as poetry, but all the same it is diverting stuff, and the pother over it
will to some good. I like to see the boys and girls of Parnassus leaping,
whooping and kicking up their legs. Now and then, perchance, they
will strike a nose, and let out a therapeutic stream of blood. And even
if they do not, they at least give an amusing show . . .

The translations of the year include "Russian Lyrics," by Martha
Gilbert Dickinson Biachi (*Duffield*); "Japanese Lyrics," by Lafcadio
Hearn (*Houghton-Mifflin*); "The Ebon Muse" (poems by Leon
Lavieux), by John Myers O'Hara (*Smith-Sale*); "Poems and Transla-
tions" (from the German) by J. H. Hyslop (*Small-Maynard*); "Selec-
tions from Catullus," by Mary Stewart (*Badger*); Morris Rosenfeld's
"Songs of Labor," by Rose Pastor Stokes and Helena Frank (*Badger*);
Theodore Botrel's "Songs of Brittany," by Elizabeth S. Dickerman
(*Badger*); and the "Poems of Emile Verhaeren," by Alma Strettell
(*Lane*). Poems from the Russian, Japanese, French, Latin, German and
Yiddish. The translators of Botrel and Rosenfeld tackled the hardest
tasks: it is easy enough to turn sonorous lines in one language into the
poetical jargon of another, but when one comes to transmuting simplicity the touching is very apt to slip over into the banal. Miss Dickerman fails almost utterly; Mrs. Stokes and Miss Frank less often. Of
the other translators the most skillful is Miss Stewart: she has really
done well with Catullus. But the books of most interest are Hearn's
volume of literal translations from the Japanese, and O'Hara's collection of songs by Lavieux, the only modern poet, so far as I know, who
has ever attempted to hymn the beauty of the darker races. . . .

Contribution toward a List of Euphemisms for "Drunk"

By James P. Ratcliffe, A. M., Ph. D. (Harvard), LL.D. (Oxon.)

A

Aslant   Awash
Atrophied   Awry-eyed

B

Banjoed   Blazing
Barrelled   Boiled
Bashed   Boozed
Bazooed   Broiled
Bished   Buttered

C

Calcified   Coppered
Carburetted   Corked
Chloroformed   Corkscrewed
Confubsticated   Corned

D

Dipped   Doused
Drenched   Dripping

E

Edged   Embalmed
Electrified   Enameled
Electrocuted

F

Fiddled   Frazzled
Fixed   Fricasseed
Flooded   Fuddled
Floored   Full

Smart Set 49, No. 2 (June 1916): 99–100.

Flummoxed   Fumed
Flustered

G

Galvanized   Greased
Gassed   Grogged

H

Half-shot   Hooked
Ham-strung   Horned
Het

I

Illuminated   Inflated

J

Jagged   Joyful
Jingled   Jugged

K

Keel-hauled   Knee-haltered
Kegged

L

Larded   Liquored
Left-hooked   Lit up
Loaded   Lushed
Lubricated

M

Malted   Muddled
Mellow   Mushed

O

Oiled   Ossified
Oozed   Oxidized

P

Paralyzed   Pifflicated
Petrified   Piped
Phosphorescent   Plastered
Pickled   Polluted
Pie-eyed   Primed
Piffed   Pruned
Piffled

Q

Quagmired   Queered

R

Rattled   Rouged
Refrigerated

S

Schoonered   Snagged
Scorched   Snooted
Screwed   Soaked
Sewed up   Soused
Shelled   Spangled
Shot   Splashed
Siphoned   Squiffed
Slanted   Star-lit
Slobbered   Stewed
Slopped   Straffed
Sloshed   Submerged
Sloughed   Swilled

T

Tambourined   Tight
Tangled   Tingled
Tangle-footed   Tipsy
Tanked   Tooted
Tattooed   Torpedoed

U

Unmanned   Upholstered

V

Varnished   Verdigrised

W

Wet-nosed   Whooped
Wobbly

Y

Yeasty   Yoked

Z

Zig-zagged   Zipped

A Soul's Adventures

§1

The New Fiction.—A fellow of naif and believing habit, despite the uric acid diathesis, I was bemused into looking for a grand crop of masterpieces of fiction by the Spring announcements of the publishers. Not a few of them, indeed, ascended to specific promises: they had new novels on the press that reduced "Barry Lyndon" to feebleness and "Jennie Gerhardt" to downright imbecility. The ensuing reviews in the newspapers bore out this extremely favorable prognosis; for a month or two, at the height of the merchanting (and advertising), another heaven-kissing genius was hymned every day. But an inspection of the actual books, alas, blew up my sweet anticipations. What I found in nine-tenths of these *chefs-d'oeuvres,* painfully wading through them, was not originality, not a sense of beauty, not the profound study of man, but merely the old superficiality and sentimentality, the old salvo of rubber-stamps, the old guff. The Spring novels, in brief, turned out to be Spring novels and no more, and I contemplate the stack of them to-day with sincere apologies to my eyes.

Consider, for example, "Just David," by Eleanor H. Porter (*Houghton-Mifflin*), author of "Pollyanna," that favorite sugar-teat of yesteryear. Here we have a frank return to the style of the Sunday-school books of fifty years ago—the style so ferociously burlesqued by Mark Twain in "The Story of a Good Little Boy." The thing, in truth, is almost unbelievably silly; it is quite impossible to imagine sane adults snuffling over such ludicrous rubbish. The hero, *aet.* ten, is on the one hand so innocent that he can't differentiate between sleep and death and is quite unconscious of evil, and on the other hand so gifted that he speaks French and German fluently and improvises on the violin with the facility of a Joachim. The orthodox "Oh, sirs" and "Oh, thank you, sirs" are forever in his mouth; he has a talent for mellifluousness and addresses the women who pet him in such terms as "O Lady of the Roses"; he reunites separated lovers and amazes the yokels of his habitat with flights of transcendental poetry; the bad boys of the vicinage try to assassinate him—unluckily, in vain!—he is a saccharine, sticky amalgam of the Good Angel, Cinderella, Herbert Kaufman, the

Smart Set 49, No. 2 (June 1916): 150–56.

infant Mozart (of the celebrated picture), Henry Van Dyke and Florence Nightingale. That so obvious and silly a piece of tear-squeezing should be taken seriously, even by sedentary and love-crossed fat women, is, as I have said, almost unimaginable. And yet, as everyone knows, books of this same garrulous mushiness are printed in the United States by the score, and publishers of decent position put their imprints on them and advertise them as Great Fiction, and they are praised lavishly in the newspapers as full of Optimism, Gladness and Human Nature, and the women's clubs sob and slobber over them, and pale divines preach on them, and they arise from the book-counters in huge stacks. What is to be thought of a literature which produces such scented piffle? What is to be thought of a nation which swallows it with sober gusto?

Put beside so empty a mess of bosh, such a bouncing boob-tickler as E. Phillips Oppenheim's "An Amiable Charlatan" (*Little-Brown*) takes on a considerable probability, and even a touch of literary consideration. This Oppenheim, in fact, is a good deal better than he is commonly painted; at his worst, he always manages to draw a satisfying scoundrel or two, and his writing is often very fair. Much the same half-skill is visible in "The Curved Blades," by Carolyn Wells (*Lippincott*), a detective story with the usual murder mystery; and in "The S. S. Glory," by Frederick Niven (*Doran*), the tale of a thrilling trip across the Atlantic in a cattle-boat; and in "Behind the Bolted Door," by Arthur E. McFarlane (*Dodd-Mead*), another detective story; and in "The Least Resistance," by Kate L. McLaurin (*Doran*), a chronicle of stage life with a tragic ending; and in "Exile," by Dolf Wyllarde (*Lane*), a melodrama with its scenes laid in a far-flung outpost of the British Empire. So, too, one finds a certain readableness, though precious little else, in three current romances of the Far West, to wit, in "The Phantom Herd," by B. M. Bower (*Little-Brown*), "The Shadow Riders," by Isabel Paterson (*Lane*), and "The Heart of Thunder Mountain," by Edfrid A. Bingham (*Little-Brown*). All of these confections, with the possible exception of Miss McLaurin's, will be dead and forgotten long before we go back to medicated flannels, but they at least reveal an occasional mark of respect for the reader's intelligence.

It is possible to say the same for Mrs. Atherton's latest offering, "Mrs. Belfame" (*Stokes*), but no more. In plan it is a very conventional mystery story, with the blame laid upon a woman who is innocent in fact, though guilty in intent. The actual culprit, in the end, turns out to be a suffragette. Not the slightest ingenuity is shown in the working out of this banal plot; its machinery is absolutely true to type, and its people include the inevitable stupid policemen, impertinent newspaper reporters and gloating neighbors. There is even a standard-model deathbed confession in the last chapter. Nevertheless, the publishers announce the book with a deafening blast of trombones, and argue gravely that it is "the only modern story in which crime and mystery are combined with a high order of literary merit." More, they break out with the modest doctrine that Mrs. Atherton is "the ablest American novelist," and quote such authorities as Sir W. Robertson Nicoll and the Hon. William H. Taft in support of it. The *Review of Reviews* is also put upon the witness stand; it compares the fair author to George Eliot, George Sand and Mme. de Staël. Here we have a match for the theory, so lately promulgated by another firm of zealous Barabbases, Irvin S. Cobb's "Speaking of Operations—" is "the funniest book we know of." Surely the news that Mrs. Atherton leads all the rest will be surprising to the admirers of the ancient but still sportive William Dean Howells, and to those of Mrs. Wharton, not to mention those of Dreiser and the late Frank Norris. Moreover, when this astounding award of bays was made, Henry James was still alive. . . . Read publishers' announcements if you would enjoy a refined dissipation! They are vastly more imaginative and amusing than the works of their authors! . . .

More harmless but hollow stuff. "Babette," by F. Berkeley Smith (*Doubleday-Page*), is a stupid and cheaply sentimental romance, the scenes laid in France, with an astoundingly hideous chromo by Oliver Herford as its frontispiece. I have found it quite impossible to get to the end by the lawful route, but by skipping two hundred pages I discover, not much to my surprise, that the rascally M. Pierre Raveau has given over his evil courses and married Mlle. Babette Pivot, and that they have a little Babette aged five, and that they are happy. In "The Fifth Wheel," by Olive Higgins Prouty (*Stokes*), we encounter a social butterfly who takes to the suffrage; in "Adam's Garden," by Nina Wilcox Putnam (*Lippincott*), we have another (this time male) who takes to adventure and amour. Two very dull novels. "The Blind Men's Eyes," by William McHarg and Edwin Balmar (*Little-Brown*), is merely one more mystery story. "Beggars on Horseback," by F. Tennyson Jesse (*Doran*), is a collection of mediocre short stories. "Instead of the Thorn," by Clara Louise Burnham (*Houghton-Mifflin*), is another piece of solferino taffy. "Behold the Woman!" by T. Everett Harré (*Lippincott*), is a sweet mixture of voluptuousness and piety—the very stuff to shock and enchant the lady Brandeses and Brunetières. "The Light That Lies," by George Barr McCutcheon (*Dodd-Mead*), is a tale in which love invades the jury box, and is written with skill and vivacity, as Mr. McCutcheon's endless best-sellers always are. "The Sentimental Dragon," by Nina Larrey Duryea (*Doran*), and "Mr. and Mrs. Pierce," by Cameron Mackenzie (*Dodd-Mead*), are two stories of social striving, neither getting very far, but both readable. "The Bars of Iron," by Ethel M. Dell (*Putnam*), is the history of a gentleman who falls in love with the widow of the gentleman he has killed. "A Hero of Our Time," by M. Y. Lermontov (*Knopf*), is a Russian novel of very old-fashioned cut, with a Byronic superman for its hero. . . . I draw the veil. A full catalogue of the Spring trade goods would only bore you.

§2

Better Fables.—Various novels of a greater pretension follow, but even here I find little that is inspiring. One of the best of them is "The Buffoon," by Louis U. Wilkinson (*Knopf*), a story that is somewhat talky at the start, but that soon settles down to a sharp and excellent character study. Its pictures of intellectual society in London are full of a devastating humor; Wilkinson does on a large scale what Willard Huntington Wright barely blocked out in "The Man of Promise." But his chief virtue, like Wright's, lies in his point of view rather than in his actual assembling of materials. He sees life ironically; he is a wit and a satirist; later on, I make no doubt, he will be a novelist to take into very serious account. Another sound piece of writing is to be found in "Green Mansions," by W. H. Hudson (*Knopf*), a romance of the Demarara *hinterland*. It is introduced by a foreword by John Galsworthy, in which Hudson is hailed as "a very great writer . . . the most valuable our age possesses." Not many readers, I fear, will be disposed to go with Galsworthy so far. Without question, Hudson is a stylist of considerable talents, and without question some of his pictures of the tropical forest are extraordinarily rich in beauty, but to me, at least, his story is only faintly interesting, and ranged beside even the second-best of Joseph Conrad it at once shows its limitations.

Other workmanlike books which still fall far short of the first contemporary merit are "The Rudder," by Mary S. Watts (*Macmillan*); "Children of Hope," by Stephen Whitman (*Century*), "John Bogardus," by George Agnew Chamberlain (*Century*); "The Little Lady of the Big House," by Jack London (*Macmillan*); "The Amateur," by Charles G. Norris (*Doran*), and "Her Husband's Purse," by Helen R. Martin (*Doubleday-Page*). Mrs. Watts' story, like "Van Cleve" and "The Rise of Jennie Cushing," deals with life in Cincinnati and is done with all her customary vivacity, but I find it much less interesting than the others despite a couple of very brilliant character sketches. The Whitman story, though extremely well written, is also disappointing, for it represents Whitman's abandonment of realism for what seems to be an imitation of the sentimental humor of W. J. Locke. So with London's "The Little Lady of the Big House." London, as I have often remarked, is a fictioneer who pursues his craft with almost Prussian thoroughness; there is nothing about the manufacture of popular novels that he doesn't know. But here he tries to entertain us with a superman who, in the last analysis, fails to convince, and so the product of all his skill is only tediousness. So again with "John Bogardus" and "The Amateur," the first the chronicle of a college professor who, after many psychical storms and alarms, settles down to Service, and the second the tale of a young artist's adventures, professional and amorous, in New York. These are well-meaning stories; they are written seriously and with due respect for the reader; but they miss force and gusto; they leave an impression of flatness. "The Conquest," by Sidney L. Nyburg (*Lippincott*), is even worse. This Nyburg, a year or two ago, published a book of very respectable short stories, but in this, his first novel, he runs aground on the Uplift, and his lawyer-hero, at the end, seems a vacant and silly fellow.

Here, perhaps, I yield to prejudice. The uplifter, whether in or out of fiction, is a fowl whose plumage sets me to swearing. I know too much about his ways and means to have any belief in him, or any love for him, or any respect for him. He is, when honest, little more than an ignorant and cocksure dunderhead, and when cured of honesty, the most insidious and dangerous rogue that this fair republic of rogues has yet produced. . . . Call it prejudice, if you will. Criticism itself, at bottom, is no more than prejudice made plausible. The judicial temperament, like moral beauty, is merely a phrase that men use to fool themselves. When I put on my hangman's gown of criticism and buckle on my celluloid sword, I make a mental oath that I will be as fair, as honest and as charitable as any judge on the bench. I succeed, like the judge, in being as fair, as honest and as charitable as any lawyer at the Bar.

§3

Good Short Stories.—The best of the Spring fiction, when all is said and done, is to be found in two books of short stories—"The River of Life," by Alexander Kuprin (*Luce*), and "Stamboul Nights," by H. G. Dwight (*Doubleday-Page*). Both are exotics, for Kuprin is a Russian and Dwight deals entirely with life in Turkey, in which country he has spent many years. It is a long while since these eyes have encountered better short stories than Kuprin's "Captain Ribnikov," the tale of a Japanese spy, or Dwight's "The House of the Giraffe." The former lifts itself enormously above the common run of spy stories, now so popular among lovers of tin-pot melodrama. It concerns itself, not with the objective work of the spy, but with the subtle effects of that work upon his innermost soul. It has sharp glances in it, and intimate revelations; the man, at the end, is astonishingly real. The other tales in Kuprin's volume fall a good deal below this one, but taken together they still show plainly that he is a man of genuine talents, and thus greatly above the jitney Russian geniuses who are being forever introduced with such gaudy encomiums. The fashion for Cossackian pathology will presently die out, but I believe that some of the work of Kuprin, along with the best of Andrieff and Gorky, will survive it.

"The House of the Giraffe" is a somewhat elaborate character study of a Turkish functionary of the old régime—a milk-brother of Sultan Abdul Hamid, and hence a personage of high privileges in Constantinople. Among those privileges is a sort of *droit de seigneur*, whereby this gallant Nousret Pasha honors the wives of his acquaintances with his favor. The story deals with his pursuit of such a pleasant affair, and of the catastrophe which overtakes it and him when dear old Brother Abdul Hamid is suddenly deposed. The color is brilliantly laid on; the Turkey of yesterday becomes not only gorgeous, but even understandable. Excellent writing is also to be found in "The Glass House," in "In the Pasha's Garden," and, above all, in "The *Leopard of the Sea*," the last an account of the comic opera voyage of a Turkish cruiser. To me, at least, the Turks are a people of much charm; they stand clearly above Christian sentimentality, and have courage, masculinity and a sense of beauty. Not since Demetra Vaka's "Haremlik" have I read a book which dealt with them more sympathetically, or made their point of view more comprehensible.

§4

Printed Plays.—Of the current play books, the only one that interests me is "Plays of the Natural and the Supernatural," by Theodore Dreiser (*Lane*), a volume containing seven pieces, four of which have been printed in THE SMART SET. Of the seven, that which shows the best promise of popular success is "The Girl in the Coffin," a somewhat obvious piece of realism but with saving overtones. The four plays of the supernatural are: "The Blue Sphere," "Laughing Gas," "In the Dark," and "The Spring Recital." In each of them Dreiser tries to depict dramatically the blind, unintelligent, unintelligible forces which lie behind all human motives and acts. Superficially, they may seem to reveal an abandonment of his "chemic" theory for mysticism, but that seeming is only seeming. The two are really no more than diverse aspects of a single philosophy. That philosophy, like Joseph Conrad's, has for its central idea the fortuitousness and inexplicability of human life, and you will find it running unbrokenly through all of Dreiser's books, from "Sister Carrie" down to this last one. The criticism which deals only with externals often praises him for making Carrie Meeber so clear, for understanding her so well, but the truth is that his achievement in his study of her consists rather in making visible the impenetrable mystery of her, and of the vast complex of muddled striving and aspiration of which she is so helplessly a part. It is in this sense and not in the current critical sense that "Sister Carrie" is a profound work. It is not a book of glib explanations, of quasi-scientific cocksureness; it is, beyond all else, a book of wonder.

Dreiser's characteristic lack of technical cunning is plainly seen in some of these plays. "The Girl in the Coffin," for example, is too long. Its content and doctrine would be better discerned if it were not so heavily blanketed with words. Again, "The Spring Recital" seems but half worked out, and "The Light in the Window," in more than one place, comes perilously close to banality. But these defects are more than made up for by the photographic observation shown in "Old Rag Picker" and by the disarming plausibility and impressiveness of "The Blue Sphere" and "In the Dark." If these pieces had been done by Maeterlinck or by some fantastic Russian, the noise of their celebrity would be filling the ears, but with Dreiser's name upon them, I doubt that they will arouse much enthusiasm among the lady critics, male and female, of our fair republic. These pious numskulls, in truth, seldom consider him as an artist; they almost always content themselves with belaboring him as an immoralist. The reviews of "The 'Genius'" themselves reviewed, would make a curious contribution to Puritan psychology, and if my health holds out, I may attempt its confection later on. The book was read with a salacious eye, as Sunday School boys read the Old Testament, and then denounced pontifically as naughty. I wonder what the smut hounds will find to shock them in his plays!

The remaining dramatic books need not detain us. "The Unchastened Woman," by Louis Kaufman Anspacher (*Stokes*) and "Quinneys," by Horace Annesley Vachell (*Doran*), are popular pieces that the estimable Nathan has already noticed. "The Nameless One," by Anne Cleveland Cheney (*Stokes*), is a heavy attempt at a poetical drama. "The Technique of Play Writing," by Charlton Andrews (*Home*), is a labored effort to reduce one of the fine arts to the level of a somewhat feeble legerdemain. Such works, I daresay, find a ready market among the hordes of bank clerks, bartenders, sempstresses, locomotive engineers and vaudeville actors who bombard the poor managers with impossible scripts, and dream of rivalling Sardou, Theodore Kremer, George Broadhurst and the late Charles Klein. Such naif aspirants have great faith in what they call "technique"; they believe that it may be acquired by reading a book by a man who lacks it himself. The same sort of public leaps to such absurd compositions as "The Universal Plot Catalogue," by Henry Albert Phillips (*Stanhope-Dodge*), a professor

whose curious contributions to the literary art I have hitherto smothered with praise. As Phillips depicts it, writing a short story is as easy
as slicing a *blutwurst*. So it is—if you want to write that sort of short
story. Look through the 15-cent magazines, and you will find hundreds of them.

§5

Three Americans.—Three typical Americans, though at first blush
each seems to stand miles apart from the other two, tell their stories in
"An Autobiography," by Edward Livingston Trudeau (*Doubleday-
Page*), "Notes of a Busy Life," by Joseph Benson Foraker (*Stewart-
Kidd*), and "The Story of an American Singer," by Geraldine Farrar
(*Houghton-Mifflin*). In all three of these self-chroniclings the quality
dominatingly revealed is audacity. Each is a tale not of genius, but of
mere unflagging hope and brilliance. Trudeau, broken in health and of
almost incredibly meagre equipment otherwise, revolutionized the
treatment of tuberculosis in America, saved thousands of useful lives,
and made himself a world figure; Foraker, by sheer industry and alertness, forced himself to the very door of the White House; and the fair
Geraldine, with a pretty face and an endless belief in herself, attained to
such a celebrity at twenty-five that the opera-houses of Christendom
were flooded with the tears of envious rivals, most of them vastly better singers. You will not find any false modesty in these books. Foraker
and the Farrar boast unblushingly, and even Trudeau does not belittle
his own achievements. But in each of them the story told is of interest
enough to apologize for its lack of reticence, and the character revealed
is thoroughly American from head to heels.

Trudeau, I daresay, will be held in memory long after the other
two are forgotten. Already, indeed, he begins to take on the proportions of a legendary and half-fabulous figure. And no wonder! With
the body of a sick child, he spent thirty years fighting and conquering
two great dragons—one the dragon of his own crushing illness, and
the other and even greater, the dragon of suspicion and ignorance. All
revolutionaries, medical or otherwise, have hard battles, but his was
much harder than most, for the cure that he advocated involved patient
submission to exposure and suffering for months and even years, and it
was difficult to get recruits for the experiment, and twice as difficult to
get medical approval of it. Nevertheless, Trudeau persisted, and bit by
bit he won his way. It is curious to note how much even he himself
took on trust. The open-air treatment for tuberculosis originated with
two Germans, Brehmer and Dettweiler, and Trudeau appears to have
adopted it on the strength of a brief notice or two in an English medi-

cal journal. Knowing no German, he was unable to consult the original reports, nor could he, later on, read the epoch-making announcement by Dr. Robert Koch of his discovery of the *tubercle bacillus*. He studied Koch's historic monograph in a rough English translation, made in a common copy-book and at the expense of a lay friend! The American medical journals of that time wholly neglected the subject. They printed nothing whatever about Brehmer's and Dettweiler's work, and so little about the new science of bacteriology that Trudeau had to seek the assistance of a German-trained colleague when he essayed to duplicate Koch's experiments. His story of his adventures in his improvised laboratory at Saranac makes one of the most interesting chapters of his book. . . . He lived to see his ideas accepted everywhere, and sanitariums springing up on all sides. Those ideas, at bottom, were borrowed; the true pioneering was done across the water; but surely it was Trudeau who gave them their present wide validity and significance, and so turned them to the uses of humanity. He was, beneath his puny form, a first-rate man.

The Foraker book would have been better stuff had Foraker gone to less pains to depict himself as a democratic saint. His long career in politics, as the record shows, was anything but discreditable. A man of firmness and intelligence and an orator of ingratiating sweetness, he devoted himself, first and last, to combating the worst vagaries of a mobocracy on the loose, and particularly to war upon the quacks who sought to inflame and beguile it. This was a useful and honorable enterprise. His days in public office were the days of the dawn of the uplift; men with courage enough to speak out against it were rare; he was one of the few who remained steadfast to the end and accepted the extreme penalty. But now, instead of discussing frankly the plain evils of mob-rule, he seems eager to have himself thought of as a pious believer in it, and so his story acquires pecksniffian touches and is disappointing where it should be instructive. It is the story, in brief, not of a man who boldly offers a reasonable philosophy to account for his acts, regardless of its popularity, but of a man eager to make a good impression upon his inferiors. Here we come to the central defect of American politics, and the cause of our utter dearth of statesmen. Our politicians, even at their best, always keep their eyes on the newspapers and the mob; we have yet to produce one willing to disregard superficialities and tackle mob-rule head-on. They all disguise themselves as true believers, even when their acts show that they are not. . . . The Farrar's saucy chronicle I leave to your own enchanted inspection. It does full justice to her talents.

§6

Much in Little.—Have I ever advised you to lay in a set of "The Everyman Encyclopedia" (*Dutton*)? If not, I do so now, and with full confidence that you will be delighted with the twelve little volumes that a few dollars will get for you. The trouble with all the larger encyclopedias, as practicable reference books, is that they are far too bulky and prolix. Going to them to ascertain some single name or fact or date, one is staggered by treatises that take hours, and sometimes even days, to read. The Everyman avoids that capital defect; its twelve volumes are of the size of the other books in the Everyman's Library, and their contents are admirably well-ordered, succinct and satisfying. I have used, in my time, all of the other encyclopedias in English, including the last edition of the Britannica, but I have now discarded them all in favor of the Everyman's. It answers a larger proportion of the questions that I ask of it, and more quickly and briefly, than any other. For detailed and technical information, of course, one must go elsewhere, but for the simple facts about what the preface calls "the affairs of everyday life" one need not proceed further. . . . Here and there, to be sure, errors and omissions are encountered, particularly in the articles on American topics. For example, Richard Croker is called "an American statesman," and there is no mention whatever of his leadership of Tammany Hall. Again the New York *Tribune* is described as a five-cent paper, and then, quite as absurdly, as "the pioneer of the halfpenny paper, of which the *Daily Mail* is the English equivalent." Yet again, there are irritating slips of the pen, as when the Canal du Drac in France, which is 446 miles long, is said to "affect an area of 18,600 acres." Finally, there are certain serious weaknesses on the biographical side, and one gasps to find such a stupendous figure as Johann Muller, the founder of cellular pathology, given less space than any other Muller. . . . But those defects, after all, are not very numerous, and every other encyclopedia also shows them.

The Puritan

By Owen Hatteras

§1.

The main service of the Puritan to practical religion is to be found in the fact that he saved the sport of heretic-hunting at a time when the rising tide of enlightenment threatened it. That rescue was effected by the simple device of changing the old crime against revealed doctrine into a crime against revealed ethics. Awakened by the Reformation and the Renaissance, the men of Northern Europe were beginning to take all pretensions to doctrinal infallibility very lightly, and so they revolted against the Inquisition. But they were still ready to grant that, in matters of conduct, there were absolute and immovable standards, and the Puritan very deftly turned this willingness to his uses. Instead of ferreting out and burning heretics for questioning the pope or the Trinity, he ferreted them out and did execution upon them for living in adultery, or for wearing gay clothes, or for affronting the Lord God with fiddle music, or for breaking the Sabbath. This innovation showed that he had a profound understanding of the popular mind, for it was based upon two sound assumptions as to the workings of that mind, the first being that the great masses of men are always convinced that right and wrong are absolute values, even after they have been induced to change those values by appeals to their emotion, and the second being that the great masses of men delight in barbarous punishments, and are always eager to join in the pursuit and destruction of offenders.

§2.

Puritanism and democracy are thus brothers, for both capitalize the mob-man's hatred of the individualist, and particularly of the individualist who is obviously having a better time in the world—*e.g.*, the millionaire, the wine-bibber, the king, the adulterer. This explains why it is that Puritanism has been most prosperous in democratic countries. In these countries the whole political theory of the people is based on the axiom that whatever the masses of undifferentiated and unsuccessful men think,

Smart Set 49, No. 3 (July 1916): 219–22.

desire and have to put up with is more creditable to the men themselves and more pleasing to a just God than what the minority of distinguished and successful men think, desire and are able to get. The ethical ideas at the bottom of Puritanism, like the ideas at the bottom of the Beatitudes, represent no more and no less than an effort to make a virtue of necessity. True enough, the mob-man, by his own enterprise, is quite incapable of erecting this assumption of superiority to his betters into a coherent ethical system, and doubly incapable of forcing it upon them. But there are always. resourceful and competent men who, in return for public honor and profit, are willing to turn against their class to serve him and lead him. Of such are all the great company of mob-masters, clerical and lay. These mob-masters exploit the envy of the mob in their own interest. They become eminent lawmakers, heretic- hunters, evangelists, scandal-mongers, reformers, heads of the state. They descend into democratic history as saviors of the common people and enemies of sin in high places. They constitute, while alive, the Puritan hierarchy.

§3.

The true Puritan always tries to make the world believe (and not infrequently he undoubtedly believes it himself) that his rigorous rules for the conduct of the non-Puritan are altruistic—that he seeks the other fellow's advantage against the latter's will. This is the excuse commonly offered for prohibition, vice-crusading, the laws against horse-racing, and so on. The pretension, of course, is false, even when made honestly. The Puritan would not actually like it if the other fellow were saved, either here or in some theoretical hereafter. His joy in his own peculiar virtue, indeed, lies precisely in the feeling that it gives him an advantage—that he himself, in return for his sacrifices of joy in this life, will be rewarded with illimitable joy in some future existence, whereas the other fellow will have to go to hell. Take away hell for the other fellow, and Puritanism would straightway lose most of its meaning, and what is more, most of its charm.

§4.

Moreover, the Puritan knows by experience that the sacrifices his ethical theory imposes upon him are hard to make, and so his successful achievement of them reinforces his feeling of superiority. The average man, he thinks, is not equal to them; they are the exclusive possession of a special class. Hence the Puritan venerates himself as an artist of unusual talents, a virtuoso of virtue. . . . His error consists in mistaking for a merit what is intrinsically rather a weakness. That is to say, his capacity for doing without is usually not so much a sign of strength as a sign of lack of originality, courage and enterprise. The truly strong man does not hesitate and refrain; he takes what he wants, and cheerfully pays the price. What keeps the Puritan faithful to his principles, nine times out of ten, is no more than a double-headed fear: first, of the consequences provided by his own system of morality, and secondly, of the probability that he would be unable to drag himself back, once he had stepped aside. The warmest advocate of prohibition that I know once confessed to me that he had a pathological thirst for whiskey, and that one drink would start him upon a debauch. One need be no very profound psychologist to see much the same fear in the Puritan howlers against what is called the double standard of morality. The trouble with these impassioned reformers is obviously temperamental. They are cursed with an extraordinary susceptibility to sex ideas and suggestions, and so they greatly exaggerate the susceptibility of others, and overestimate the importance of combating it. The Puritans who try to set up an extravagant censorship of art and literature suffer from the same disease. Here the inquiries of Dr. Sigmund Freud offer overwhelming support for what is a matter of common observation.

§5.

The truth about the Puritan is that, despite his superficial success at controlling his desires, he really has a good deal less power of inhibition than the average non-Puritan. The choice before him is not between abstinence and moderation, but between abstinence and excess. Recognizing his weakness, and greatly in fear of it, he attempts to conquer it by *force majeure*. He is in the condition of one who, fearing injury in a fight, incontinently assassinates his antagonist. Proceeding from the theory to the facts, we find that the Puritan, as encountered in the world, is almost always a poor stick of a man. His ethical theory is based frankly upon the needs and desires of eighth-rate men, and only eighth-rate men can get any genuine satisfaction out of it. No man of the first rank ever was a Puritan. No Puritan ever wrote a poem worth reading, or a symphony worth hearing, or painted a picture worth looking at. The Puritan doctrine peoples hell with the greatest men of all time, from Shakespeare to Beethoven, and from Sophocles to Frederick the Great. Even in the department that the Puritan has sought to claim for his own—that of lawmaking—he has done only second and third-rate work, The only really valuable contributions to law that have been made in two thousand years—*e.g.,* Magna Charta, the American Constitution, the Code Napoleon, and Bismarck's so-called social legislation—have been the work of non-Puritans. In the United States, with Puritans in complete control of most of the lawmaking bodies, the legislation of the past half century has been marked by a progressive decay in intelligence and effectiveness.

§6.

In judging the inherent virtue of the Puritan it is important to remember that, even when he seems to shine with rectitude, that shining may be no more than an appearance produced by his possession of the prerogative of defining the thing itself. In the Anglo-Saxon countries, at least, he has been in control of the law-making machinery for nearly three hundred years past, and during that time he has contrived to make crimes of most of the acts agreeable to the other fellow, while carefully allowing full legality to many of the acts most agreeable to himself. These valuations, I need not add, are disputed by non-Puritans. Not many of the latter, even when they obey the law, believe that it is intrinsically immoral to go fishing on the Sabbath, or, *per contra,* that it is intrinsically moral to play the spy and informer upon one's neighbors in the familiar Puritan manner. In themselves, indeed, many characteristic Puritan acts of faith and grace would seem to be far more dangerous to civilized order and decency than the characteristic acts of such favorite butts of Puritan attack as gamblers, saloonkeepers and even prostitutes. If the Puritan laws prevailing in England and the United States were suddenly repealed and the code of any Continental country—*e.g.,* France, Germany, or even Russia—were enacted in their place, fully a half of the persons under indictment for misdemeanor would be liberated forthwith, and a good many popular reformers and examples-to-the-young, it is likely, would go to jail instead. In France, for example, it would be quite impossible for a group of pornographic old men to form a private organization for unearthing and pursuing prostitutes. The police would quickly suppress the club as subversive of public order.

§7.

The Puritan's obsession by concepts of legality and illegality is proof enough, of course, that he lacks æsthetic sense, for morality and beauty, despite much thoughtless gabble about moral beauty and the laws of art, are inherently antagonistic things. The phrase "moral beauty," indeed, is comprehensible only in a somewhat far-fetched figurative sense; read literally, it is meaningless. A thing cannot be both moral and beautiful, for the essence of beauty is enjoyment and the essence of morality is renunciation. As well speak of "self-sacrificing self-indulgence." There is, of course, such a thing as moral voluptuousness, and one observes it plainly in most Puritans, but no long exposition is needed to show that it is related to true beauty only as a song in ragtime is related to a symphony by Brahms. The Puritan reveals his moral voluptuousness, not in the rules of conduct he imposes upon himself, but in the rules of conduct he imposes upon the other fellow. In this business, it may be said with some plausibility, he plays, momentarily, the part of an artist, for the satisfaction he seeks is not so much that of having refrained from something pleasant (an act of morality) as that of having achieved something pleasant, *i.e.,* the military conquest of the other fellow. But in general he seldom allows himself an indulgence in æsthetic feeling. Even in the case we have been considering his feeble æstheticism shows itself in the primitive form of cruelty, an element not lacking, true enough, in the higher manifestations of the æsthetic spirit, for they all involve the satisfaction of the will to power by forcing recalcitrant agencies to submit to design, but still an element that is usually well concealed by other and more rarefied factors. The Puritan can never imagine beauty as a thing in itself, an end in itself. It must be, at the best, no more than a bedizenment of morality. Even music, the purest form of beauty, he apprehends only as a sort of uproarious reinforcement of moral precepts—a rhythmic hammering, as it were, upon the consciousness.

§9.

Wherever the hand of Puritanism has fallen, there ugliness has spread like some foul pestilence. The original Puritans in England stripped the churches of all beautiful things, and the Puritan of to-day carries on the tradition. The altar that he rears to his harsh and glowering god is bare and unlovely; he houses it in a misshapen and hideous church; the ceremonial with which he serves it is austere and without imagination; the very garb of his priests and bishops suggests the Sunday gauds of so many plumbers and farmhands. The ancient office of the mass, so profound in its mysticism and so pervasive in beauty, he has degraded to the level of an ill-natured harangue, with music almost identical, in its violent rhythms and cheap sentimentality, to the tunes of a brothel. There is in his act of worship no effort to evoke the infinite mystery and majesty of the Most High, but only an effort to reduce the inscrutable decrees and desires of the Most High to the facile logic of a pothouse. He is, in brief, a spiritual vandal as he is an æsthetic vandal, and his antagonism to that ineffable beauty which lies within the dreams and aspirations of man is scarcely less bitter than his antagonism to that outer beauty which lies before man's eye. He translates kismet into the terms of a police court. He turns the prophets of God into pettifogging lawyers. He reduces the unknowable to the not worth knowing.

§9.

Puritanism and democracy: twin facets of the same gem! Both set the opinion of the incompetent above the opinion of the competent; both war upon beauty as the chief of all the handmaidens of joy; both are attempts to cast a mystical glamour, an air of transcendental impeccability and grandeur, about the mob-man's envy and distrust of his betters: both afford appeasement to his will to power. When they come to die, they will die together, as they have lived and flourished together. When democracy, proceeding from excess to excess, reaches at last that king excess which will destroy it, Puritanism will be destroyed with it. Aristocracy, order and discipline, a sound vision of progress, the concept of life as a beautiful adventure and civilization as a work of art—these things are as incompatible with Puritanism as they are with democracy. The two must perish in their day as all other great delusions have perished. And once they have passed even the report of them will cease to have any gripping substance. The Puritan Sunday, in the time to come, will take on the unreality of the Roman saturnalia; the whole Puritan scheme of ethics will grow as archaic and incredible as the laws of the Salic Franks; such great Puritan prophets as Calvin, Wesley and Billy Sunday will become as fabulous as Torquemada. . . . But it will take waiting, Messieurs: it will take waiting!

Savonarolas A-sweat

I

One William T. Ellis, an author, lately filled the *Bulletin* of the Authors' League with moving bellows against a publisher, alleging atrocities of the classical sort, but worse. The name of this Ellis arrests me; I seem to remember him as one who loves his fellow men to distraction, and gallops to save them from hell for modest honoraria. Isn't he the same, in fact, who is staff expert in piety to the Philadelphia *North American,* that loveliest flower of consecrated journalism? Isn't he Ellis the jitney Savonarola, the emblem wholesaler in Sunday-school lessons, the endless perspirer for the Uplift, the author of "Men and Missions" and other great doxological works? Isn't he the ecstatic one who hymned the late vice crusade in lascivious Atlanta—now, alas, almost forgotten!—as "more fun than a fleet of air-ships," and urged the moral sportsmen of other towns to go to it? I suspect that he is, and if so I have venerated him for years. Let a tear fall for him. If he does not gild his tale of woe, his hornswoggling was cruel, indeed. . . .

But enough of this grand young man. He appears in the chronicle only incidently, and as complaining of his royalties on his *magnum opus,* "Billy Sunday: the Man and His Message." This great critical biography, he says, has sold 300,000 copies within a year!—and is still going like Coca-Cola in "dry" Georgia! . . . Har, har, me luds! Where are your best-sellers now? What becomes of McCutcheon, MacGrath, Chambers, the Glyn? Who will now whisper the figures for "Pollyanna," "Trilby," "Eben Holden," "Dora Thorne"? More, this Ellis tome is but one of several on the same subject. I have another before me; it is "The Real Billy Sunday," by the Rev. Dr. Ram's Horn Brown (*Revell*), and if the signs and portents go for anything, it has sold even better than the Ellis book. The plates, indeed, show signs of usage; it has been rolled off by the hundred thousand. And in the city where I bought it, just outside the gates of Dr. Sunday's vast arena of God, the official bookseller told me that it was the best-seller of them all, and worth ten times the dollar that he asked for it.

Nevertheless, the fellow had a heart and so offered me *lagniappe.* He was sworn on the Four Gospels, he said, to sell the book for no less

Smart Set 49, No. 3 (July 1916): 292–98.

than a dollar, but if I would take it without parley, passing over the Ellis book, he would give me something instructive as makeweight. This
something as makeweight turned out to be a gaudy pamphlet entitled
"Fighting the Traffic in Young Girls, or, War on the White Slave
Trade," by Ernest A. Bell, "secretary of the Illinois Vigilance Association, superintendent of Midnight Missions, etc." Another great tussler
for rectitude. The Ellis, no doubt, of Cook county. The beyond-
Parkhurst. But himself, it would appear, rather daring, and to the evil-
minded, perhaps even somewhat racy. Several of the full-page half-
tones give us flaming views of brothel parlors, with the resident staff at
persiflage with the visiting fireman; another shows the exterior of "a
gilded palace of sin," with a stained glass *porte-cochère;* yet another (a
photograph) shows a plump *geisha,* in skirts almost as short as a débu-
tante's, in the lewd act of plaiting her hair. In a fourth appears "the
white slave clearing-house," with a gospel meeting going on across the
street. In a fifth we are introduced to a lady uplifter "pleading with a
lost one to give up her sinful life," the "lost one" being by far the better looking. In a sixth we see a white slave trader plying his abominable
arts upon a simple country girl in an ice-cream parlor. In a seventh—

But I spare you any further carnalities in effigy. The text of the
work is horrifying enough. Not only Dr. Bell himself, but various other virtuosi, each of learning and cunning, encourage the popping eye-
ball. One of them is the Hon. Edwin W. Sims, district attorney in
Chicago during the palmy days of the white slave uproar, and secretary
to the immortal Chicago Vice Commission, whose report was barred
from the mails by super-uplifters at Washington. The unctuous Sims
protests that he has "strong personal feelings against appearing in print
in connection with a subject so abhorrent," but swallows them in order
to warn all country girls that "the ordinary ice-cream parlor is very likely to be a spider's web." Another "expert" is Principal D. F. Sutherland, "of Red Water, Texas," who tells the sad story of the kidnapping
of Estelle Ramon of Kentucky and of her rescue by the valiant William
Scott, an old beau. Many more are mentioned on the title-page, but I
fail to find their contributions inside. The explanation appears in an
advertisement on the back cover. This advertisement shows that the
present volume is no more than a sort of bait or pilot for a larger work
of the same title, the which sells to connoisseurs at a dollar and a half.
("Fastest selling book of the age! Agents wanted! Write for terms and
outfit!") A chance for the young gentlemen of the Y. M. C. A. to dedi-
cate themselves to Service. Pornography for the plain people. . . . Too
late, alas, too late! The copyright of the oleaginous Bell is dated 1910.
That was the golden age of vice crusading, the year of unparalleled

harvests for the snouting fraternity. To-day only the old-fashioned believe in white slavery; there are other bugaboos for the progressive.

No wonder Dr. Sunday's bookseller was so free with his *lagniappe!*
. . .

As for the actual Sunday book, dated 1914, it already tells an old story, for the sweating doctor has since done such press-agenting as not even a whole library of books could do, and his public eminence in these States is scarcely less exalted than that of Col. Roosevelt, Jess Willard, Henry Ford and the Kaiser. Dr. Horn-Brown reviews his career in phrases of laudation—a career of double distinction, for he was a celebrated baseball-player before he became the American St. Paul. (Joseph Smith, William Miller, Mary Baker G. Eddy, John Alexander Dowie, Sam Jones, William A. Sunday: we have produced some noble theologians!). His paternal grandfather was a Pennsylvania Dutchman named Sontag, but on the distaff side he stems from Lord William Corey, "who married the only daughter of Sir Francis Drake." The family of Corey de Pittsburgh de Reno is apparently the *jüngerer Linie*. Bill, our present hero, was converted in Chicago at the Pacific Garden Mission, in 1886 or thereabout, and after getting clear of his baseball contracts became assistant secretary of the Chicago Y. M. C. A. Then he got a job as advance man for J. Wilbur Chapman, an itinerant evangelist. When Chapman retired, in 1896, Sunday took over his trade, and has since gone steadily ahead. For fifteen years he worked the water-tanks, snaring the sinful tobacco chewers for the heavenly choir. Then he struck out for bigger game, and today he performs only in the main centers of population. He has saved Philadelphia, Baltimore, Kansas City and Pittsburgh; he is headed for Boston, Chicago and New York. He has been lavishly praised by the President of the United States, is a Freemason and a Doctor of Divinity, and has enjoyed the honor of shaking me by the hand.

So much for the facts of his career, and the book of Dr. Horn-Brown. In laborious preparation for the review of that book I went to hear the whooping doctor himself. I found him vastly more interesting than any tome that these old eyes have rested upon in many a day. He was engaged, as I entered his vast bull-ring for the first time, in trying to scare a delegation of Civil War veterans into some realization, however faint, of the perils of hell, and when I took my seat in the pen reserved for the *literati,* directly under the eaves of his pulpit, I was sprinkled copiously with the dew of his frenzy. On it came, dribble, dribble, splash, splash, every time he executed one of his terrifying revolutions. It was like holding the bottle for a Russian dancer with a wet sponge strapped to his head. Of a sudden he would rush to the edge of the platform—his pulpit is as long as a barroom, but is without rails—, scream hysterically, and then bring himself up with a jolt and spin 'round like a top, his arms flung out and saline globules leaping from his brow in a pelting shower. He shed, I daresay, at least eight ounces of sweat between 7.45 and 9.00 P. M., and though he mopped his brow constantly and tried to be polite, a good deal of it escaped into the air, and so begemmed my critical gown. . . . Revolting details, but the love of all truth is above all prudery!

Of the *sforzando* doctor's actual discourse, that night or on the other nights I heard him, I have only a faint memory. Some sweet mush about the joys of heaven, with dogs and children playing on the grass; a long review of the life and times of King Solomon, with incidental railings against money; the orthodox arguments against ethyl alcohol, of no effect upon my thirst; high words against deacons who roll their eyes on Sunday and rob the widow on Monday; the joys of hell in detail, with not a singe omitted—all the orthodox camp-meeting stuff, howled from a million stumps by Methodist dervishes since the days of Wesley, and before them by Puritans of one sort or another since the croaking of the captive in Herod's rain-barrel. Out of all this I could get nothing; it was as empty of ideas as an editorial in the Boston *Transcript*. But away with ideas, and their pursuit. It was not by ideas that the downpouring doctor bemused those sinful veterans, and white-faced shop girls, and quaking Sunday School teachers, and staggered fat women; it was by his sheer roar and outcry. He survives in the cortex, not intellectually or visually, but purely aurally—as an astounding and benumbing noise, a riot of unearthly sound, an ear-torturing cacophony. Time and again he would have to pause for breath. Time and again he would make a megaphone of his hands to give the yell more pedal. Time and again you could see the elect in the front rows shrink and quiver beneath the gargantuan wallop of his shouts. I have fought through four wars; I have been a boilermaker; I have heard "Feuersnot." But never have I eared such a flabbergasting caterwauling; never have I suffered such a racking of the fenestra rotunda. It penetrates the capital ivory like a bullet, and sets up a raging pyemia. Sunday tells the simplest anecdote with the triumphant yelp of Satan sighting another archbishop in the chute. He utters such bald words as "Yes" and "No" with all the withering passion that the Old Guard put into its naughty reply at Waterloo. In the midst of a quite banal sentence his voice flies off into a shrill falsetto, and he clubs the side of his desk as if it were the very door of hell.

No wonder the candidates down in the arena are raised to incandescence, and begin screaming to be saved! Imagine the balcony scene in "Romeo and Juliet" with Juliet bellowing like Klytämnestra in the last round of "Electra," and Romeo howling up at her like an auctioneer, and both Swinging Indian clubs, and revolving like pinwheels, and sweating like the colored waiters in a Pullman diner! Imagine "Nearer, My God, To Thee" accompanied by anvils, tom-toms, ophicleides, bass-drums and artillery, and a committee sticking pins into the tenors to make them squeal! No wonder the frontal celluloid is pierced and set afire! No wonder the devil flees in alarm, and takes refuge in some quiet Unitarian church! . . . Losing, alackaday, not much! Robbed of very little appetizing stock! The converts, indeed, are but feeble specimens of God's handiwork. Those I saw seemed anthropoid, but no more. In all my life I have never looked into more stupid and miserable facts. At least half of the aspirants for harps were adolescent and chlorotic girls; most of the males were of the sort one finds in water-front missions and at Salvation Army Christmas dinners. Even an osteopath, glancing at the former, would have noted a deficiency in haemoglobin, a disturbance below the diaphragm and above the neck, a profound veneration for moving picture actors. Some of them seemed to be flirting with tuberculosis; many of them had heads of curious shape and eyes that did not match; nearly all looked pitifully poor and wretched and godforsaken. Of such, perhaps, are the kingdom of heaven. They, too, have immortal souls, as much so as Claude Debussy, General Carranza or the Hon. Josephus Daniels. Let us hope, at all events, that somewhere or other they will get square meals, and less work, and a chance to be care-free, and sinful, and happy.

Such is my memory of four nights of the Rev. Dr. Billy Sunday, now the emperor and pope of all our uplifters, the beyond-Gerald Stanley Lee, the super-Herbert Kaufman, the Augustine of American theology, the heir of Bryan, Dowie and Barnum. Let it stand as a review of Dr. Horn-Brown's instructive book, the which I commend to your study. Buy a couple of copies. Give one to your pastor, that honest man. But if it sets him to whooping like Sunday, then I advise you, in all charity, to have your gunmen do execution of the *lex non scripta* upon him. You will never stand such *fortissimos*—as a steady diet. Now and then, like laparotomy or mania-à-potu, a benign stimulant, but not for every Sunday! . . . I depart from the Doctor Seraphicus et Ecstaticus with a specimen of his official hymnology. The copyright is owned by his *kappelmeister*, the Rev. Dr. Homer A. Rodeheaver (plain "Rody" to the purged), but I take a chance. So:

> Do not wait until some deed of greatness you may do,
> > Do not wait to shed your light afar:
> To the many duties ever near you now be true,

*   *   *

Brighten the corner where you are!
Brighten the corner where you are!
Some one far from harbor you may guide across the bar,
Brighten the corner where you are!

The words, it appears, are by Miss Ina Dudley Ogdon. Ina has the gift. Let her plod at her art; she will go far.

II

Mush by the Pound.—After all, Inspiration is the safest and fattest business in the United States today. Give them the soapy platitude, the boshful burble, the rolling eye, and they will fall for it even more ecstatically than for smut. The true best-sellers are not the lingerie confections of Chambers and the Glyn, but the uplifting tomes of such astounding Poloniuses as Orison Swett Marden, Herbert Kaufman and Gerald Stanley Lee. Kaufman is the reigning king of them all in the newspapers; there is scarcely an American town of 10,000 inhabitants that doesn't devour his mellow nonsense every Sunday. But Lee seems to be the champion between covers. His books sell enormously; they are bought wholesale by "inspired millionaires" and retailed to the gaping groundlings; *Life* has solemnly pronounced his "Crowds" "the most religious book published in this country since 'Uncle Tom's Cabin'"; Prof. Richard Burton, in the *Bellman,* hails it as "greatness," and bids us take our hats off. Go read it for yourself. I hesitate to offend your piety, maybe you will like it. . . .

Lee's latest is called "We" (*Doubleday-Page*), and runs to 728 pages. It is printed with limp covers, and on thin, hard paper not unlike that found in Oxford Bibles. A holy book for the plain people; a testament of sentimentality to be carried about in the hip-pocket, and milked of its sweets in the pauses of the day's traffic. One finds in it, at a casual glance, portentous and penetrating thoughts: that the war was caused by the German's ill-treatment of their women; that "Say! Look! Listen!" are "beautiful, wistful, plaintive words"; that "all there is to self-defense is being known and being ready to be known"; that Dr. Wilson "on ordinary days" is like Abraham Lincoln on "days of stupendous wars and of tragic crises." On such rare delicacies the forward-looking feed. Such is the current philosophy of our great moral commonwealth. You will find it imitated and poll-parroted on all sides; it gets into the newspapers mixed with ditch water. . . . I leave it to the cultural pathologists of the days to come.

III

The Tone Art.—Snowbirds in hell, Presbyterians in Paris, blondes along the Niger, musical critics in the United States! All of them who actually know what a sonata is could be numbered on the fingers of the two hands, and of these all save a few confine themselves to transient and trivial reviewing in the newspapers. As for bound books on music, we do not average one good one a year. James Huneker, in fact, has produced nearly a half of all we have printed since 1890: he is the only American musical critic who has any existence across the ocean. Henry Edward Krehbiel, the dean of the New York critics, will leave little behind him save some dreary records of performances, and a few elemental volumes for the newly cultured. His most respectable book, that on negro folksong, impresses one principally by its incompleteness; it is a creditable rough sketch, but surely no full-length work. The trouble with Krehbiel is that he mistakes mere diligence for criticism. He is an adept at accumulating facts, but he doesn't know how to write, and so his compositions are chaotic and tedious. W. J. Henderson, of the *Sun,* carries no such handicap. He is as full of learning as Krehbiel, as his small book on early Italian opera shows, but he also wields a slippery and intriguing pen, and could be vastly entertaining if he would. Instead, he has devoted himself chiefly to manufacturing petty school-books, and one finds little of the charm of his *Sun* articles between his covers. Lawrence Gilman? The perfect type of the *dilettante* turned professor; he says much, but has little to say. Philip H. Goepp? His three volumes on the classical symphonies are pedantic and irritating. Philip Hale? His gigantic annotations and footnotes scarcely belong to criticism at all; they are musical talmudism. Beside, they are buried in the programme books of the Boston Symphony Orchestra, and might as well be inscribed on the walls of Baalbec. As for Upton and other such fellows, they are merely musical chautauquans, and belong to *Ladies' Home Journal* Kultur. One of them, a Harvard *maestro* named Daniel Gregory Mason, has published a book on the orchestra in which, on separate pages, the reader is solemnly presented with pictures of first and second violins!

In view of all this paucity, such a volume as "Music After the Great War," by Carl Van Vechten (*Scribner*), takes on a considerable importance, despite its modest size and range. This Mr. Van Vechten, I believe, hires his ears and soul to the New York *Times,* and is a prophet of the extremest heterodoxy in music. His revolt, indeed, goes so far in mad, mad daring that one hears in it the gurgle of the *vin rouge* of Greenwich Village, and abroad it would probably attract the attention of the *polizei.* For example, he lifts a scornful eyebrow to Brahms, sniffs

at string quartets, and argues that the C minor symphony should be embalmed in some museum. Even Debussy begins to bore him; he has
heard nothing interesting from that quarter for a long while. As for present-day Germany, he finds it a musical desert, with Arnold Schoenberg
behind the bar of its only inviting *gasthaus.* Richard Strauss? Pooh!
Strauss is an exploded torpedo, a Zeppelin brought to earth, "he has
nothing more to say." (Even the opening of the Alpine symphony, it
would appear, is mere stick-candy.) England? Go to! Italy? Back to the
barrel-organ! Spain, Holland, Scandinavia, the United States? It is to
laugh, perchance to die! . . . Where, then, is the *post bellum* tone poetry
to come from? According to Mr. Van Vechten, from Russia. It is the
steppes of that prodigal and prodigious empire which will produce it,
or, more specifically, certain of the fauna thereof, especially Prof. Igor
Strawinsky, author of "The Nightingale" and of various revolutionary
ballets. In the scores of Strawinsky, says Van Vechten, music takes a
large leap forward. Here, at last, we are definitely set free from melody
and harmony; the tonal fabric becomes an ineffable complex of time
signatures; "all rhythms are beaten into the ears."

But is such purged thumping actually of the future? Is it really
new? I have not yet heard these powerful shiverings and tremblings of
M. Strawinsky, but all the same I presume to doubt it. "The ancient
Greeks," says Van Vechten, "accorded rhythm a higher place than either melody or harmony." Perhaps they did, but what of it? So did the
ancient Goths and Huns, the more ancient Assyrians and Dravidians.
So do the modern niggers and New Yorkers. But do these admitted
facts dispose of the *Wohltemperirtes Clavier?* Surely not. The simple
truth is that the accentuation of mere rhythm is a proof, not of progress in music, but of a reversion to barbarism. The African savage,
beating his tom-tom, is content to go no further; the American composer of popular dance music gives him eager support. But music had
scarcely any existence as a civilized art until melody came to rhythm's
aid, and its fruits were little save a childish prettiness until harmony
began to support melody. To argue that naked rhythm, unaided by anything save a barbaric tone-color, may now supplant them and oblite-
rate them is to argue something so absurd that its simple statement is a
sufficient answer to it.

The rise of harmony, true enough, laid open a dangerous field. Its
exploration attracted meticulous and rabbinical minds; it was rigidly
mapped out, in hard, geometrical lines, by dry-as-dust professors
(think of Jadassohn, Prout!); in each succeeding age it tended to become unnavigable to the man of living ideas. But there were always
plenty of champions ready to put the pedagogues to flight—Haydn,
Mozart, Beethoven, Wagner—and surely there is no lack of them to-

day. No melodramatic rejection of melody and harmony is necessary to work such reforms as remain to be achieved. The dullest conservatory pupil has learned how to pull the nose of Goetschius; no one cares a hoot any more about the ancient laws of preparation and resolution; the rules grow so loose, indeed, that I myself begin to write tone-poems. But out of this seeming chaos new laws will inevitably arise, and though they will be much less stiff than the old ones, they will still be coherent and logical and intelligible. One needs but glance through such a book as René Lenormand's "Etude sur l'Harmonie Moderne," indeed, to see that a certain order is already showing itself, that even Debussy and Ravel and Florent Schmitt know precisely what they are about. And when the present boiling in the pot dies down, the truly great musicians will be found to be, not those who have been most extravagant, but those who have been most discreet and intelligent—those who have most skillfully engrafted what is good in the new upon what was sound in the old. Such a discreet one, I believe, is Richard Strauss—not a hollow iconoclast, as Strawinsky seems to be, but an alert and skillful musician. His music is modern enough, God knows, but he stops before it ceases to be music. One turns from a hearing of it to a reading of it with a sense of surprise at its essential simplicity and soundness. The performance reveals so many purple moments, so staggering an array of lusciousness, so gorgeous a musical Bull Moosery, that the ear is deceived into hearing scales and chords that never were on land or sea. What the exploratory eye subsequently discovers in the score, perhaps, is no more than our stout and comfortable old friend, the highly well-born *hausfrau,* Mme. C. Dur—with a hooch of successive ninths in her afternoon *schokolade,* and a vine-leaf or two of C sharp minor or B flat major in her hair.

I thus repudiate the heresies of Prof. Van Vechten, but praise him for a brisk and stimulating little book., At all events, he has got away from the *kindergarten.* He rises above the parlor vocalist and the automatic piano-player. Let him print more.

IV

In the remaining books of the month I can find little of interest. "Nights," by Elizabeth Robins Pennell (*Lippincott*), introduces us pleasantly to intellectual society in Rome, Venice, London and Paris twenty years ago, but tells us little that is new about its lions. The book's merit is its graceful style; Mrs. Pennell writes very well. "The Challenge of the Future," by Roland G. Usher (*Houghton-Mifflin*), presents a college professor's speculations in the international politics of the future. It is suave and cocksure, but not always convincing.

"Souls on Fifth," by Granville Barker (*Little-Brown*), is a sweet piece of tear-squeezing. "John Bannister Tabb," by Sister Mary Paulina (Miss M. S. Pine) (*Printed for the Georgetown Convent*) is the first accurate biography of the priest-poet and contains much new matter about him, but is marred by a too pious and gushing style. "The Best Short Stories of 1915," edited by Edward J. O'Brien (*Small-Maynard*), presents the selections of a critic who awards first honors to the story that has brought him "the most definite message of idealism."

The novels, in the main, seem to be rubbish. "The Daredevil," by Maria Thompson Daviess (*Reilly-Britton*), is the usual sentimental mush, with the war to help it out. "Hearts and Faces," by John Murray Gibbon (*Lane*), is a tale of artists and their models. "Viviette," by William J. Locke (*Lane*), is a melodrama with a sugary ending, and fortunately shorter than most of Locke's recent books. "Those Gillespies," by William J. Hopkins (*Houghton-Mifflin*), is a story of Boston, and has an air of smartness without actually saying anything or getting anywhere. "The Road to Mecca," by Florence Irwin (*Putnam*), is a chronicle of social climbing. "Susan Clegg," by Anne Warner (*Little-Brown*), is a warming over of old wheezes. . . . I put aside "The Red Stain," by Achmed Abdullah (*Fly*), and "Love in Youth," by Frank Harris (*Doran*), for notice next month. Also, four or five story-books by Rupert Hughes, a very clever fellow. . . .

Now for a ham sandwich and a bottle of synthetic beer.

A Footnote on the Duel of Sex

If I were a woman I should want to be a blonde, with golden, silky hair, pink cheeks and sky-blue eyes. It would not bother me to think that this color scheme was a flaunting badge of stupidity; I would have a better arm in my arsenal than mere intelligence; I would get a husband by easy surrender while the brunettes attempted it vainly by frontal assault.

Men are not easily taken by frontal assault; it is only strategem that can quickly knock them down. To be a blonde, pink, soft and delicate, is to be a strategem. It is to be a ruse, a feint, an ambush. It is to fight under the Red Cross flag. A man sees nothing alert and designing in those pale, crystalline eyes; he sees only something helpless, childish, weak; something that calls to his compassion; something that appeals powerfully to his conceit in his own strength. And so he is taken before he knows that there is a war. He lifts his portcullis in Christian charity—and the enemy is in his citadel.

The brunette can make no such stealthy and sure attack. No matter how subtle her art, she can never hope to quite conceal her intent. Her eyes give her away. They flash and glitter. They have depths. They draw the male gaze into mysterious and sinister recesses. And so the male behind the gaze flies to arms. He may be taken in the end—indeed, he usually is—but he is not taken by surprise; he is not taken without a fight. A brunette has to battle for every inch of her advance. She is confronted by an endless succession of Dead Man's Hills, each equipped with telescopes, semaphores, alarm gongs, wireless. The male sees her clearly through her densest smoke-clouds . . . But the blonde captures him under a flag of truce. He regards tenderly, kindly, almost pityingly, until the moment the gyves are upon his wrists.

It is all an optical illusion, a question of color. The pastel shades deceive him; the louder hues send him to his artillery. God help, I say, the red-haired girl! She goes into action with warning pennants flying. The dullest, blindest man can see her a mile away; he can catch the alarming flash of her hair long before he can see the whites, or even the terrible red-browns, of her eyes. She has a long field to cross, heavily under defensive fire, before she can get into rifle range. Her quarry has

Smart Set 49, No. 4 (August 1916): 1–2.

a chance to throw up redoubts, to dig himself in, to call for reinforcements, to elude her by ignominious flight. She must win, if she is to win at all, by an unparalleled combination of craft and resolution. She must be swift, daring, merciless. Even the brunette of black and penetrating eye has great advantages over her. No wonder she never lets go, once her arms are around her antagonist's neck! No wonder she is, of all women, the hardest to shake off!

All nature works in circles. Causes become effects; effects develop into causes. The red-haired girl's dire need of courage and cunning has augmented her store of those qualities by the law of natural selection. She is, by long odds, the most intelligent and bemusing of women. She shows cunning, foresight, technique, variety. She always fails a dozen times before she succeeds; but she brings to the final business the abominable expertness of a Hindenburg, a Joffre; she has learnt painfully by the process of trial and error. Red-haired girls are intellectual stimulants. They know all the tricks. They are so clever that they have even cast a false glamour of beauty about their worst defect— their harsh and gaudy hair. They give it euphemistic and deceitful names—auburn, bronze, Titian. They overcome by their hellish arts that deep-seated dread of red which is inborn in all of God's creatures. They charm men with what would even alarm bulls.

And the blondes, by following the law of least resistance, have gone in the other direction. The great majority of them—I speak, of course, of natural blondes; not of the immoral wenches who work their atrocities under cover of a synthetic blondeness—are quite as shallow and stupid as they look. No one ever heard a blonde say anything worth hearing; the most they ever achieve is a specious, baby-like prattling, an infantile artlessness. But let us not blame them for nature's work. Why, after all, be intelligent? It is, at best, no more than a capacity for unhappiness. The blonde not only doesn't miss it; she is even better off without it. What imaginable intelligence could compensate her for the flat blueness of her eyes, the xanthous pallor of her hair, the doll-like pink of her cheeks? What conceivable cunning could do such execution as her stupendous appeal to masculine vanity, sentimentality, egoism?

If I were a woman I should want to be a blonde. My blondeness might be hideous, but it would get me a husband, and it would make him cherish me and love me.

A Panorama of Babies

By W. L. D. Bell

Babies smelling of camomile tea, cologne water, wet laundry and dog soap. Red, rough-looking babies with heads resembling rubber bath sponges. Babies who appear old, disillusioned and tired of life at six months. Babies who cry "Papa!" to blushing youths of nineteen or twenty at church picnics. Fat babies whose ear-lobes turn out at an angle of forty-five degrees. Soft, pulpy babies asleep in perambulators, the sun shining straight into their faces. Babies gnawing the tails of synthetic dogs. Babies without necks. Pale, scorbutic babies of the third and fourth generation, damned because their grandfathers and great-grandfathers read Tom Paine. Babies of a bluish tinge, or with vermilion eyes. Babies full of soporifics. Thin, cartilaginous babies that stretch when they are lifted. Warm, damp, miasmatic babies. Affectionate, ingratiating, gurgling babies: the *larvæ* of life-insurance solicitors, fashionable doctors, Episcopal rectors, dealers in Mexican mine stock, handshakers, Sunday-school superintendents. Babies with heads of thick, coarse, black hair, seeming to be in toupées. Unbaptized babies, dedicated to the devil. Eugenic babies. Babies that crawl out from under tables, and are stepped on. Babies with lentils, grains of corn or shoe-buttons up their noses, purple in the face and waiting for the doctor—or the embalmer. A few pink, blue-eyed, tight-skinned, clean-looking babies, smiling upon the world. . . .

Smart Set 49, No. 4 (August 1916): 54.

Degenerate Days

By William Drayham

I feel sad this morning because of the things and customs that have fallen on degenerate days and given themselves over to base and trivial uses. I am sick of the vapid, formal, unmeaning handshakes I exchange with those to whom I am introduced . . . I remember how it used to be that men held each other's right hands strongly when they talked together, lest one should draw his sword in sudden wrath and slay the other.

I am disgusted with canes, those dainty survivals of virile weapons that men carried for offense and defense.

Little by little empty symbols are taking the place of reality.

The other night I went to a banquet where men came in with shiny top-hats. I thought how once the latter served as glorious helmets, the real mark of an aristocracy of courage. But now they are put on merely when one wants to go on an afternoon or Sunday walk, to march in some civic parade, to go to a place where one hears overmuch talk about things which do not matter . . . *they,* that are survivals of courageous steel casques worn by knights and earls, princes and kings who rode forth to fight for nothing less than the restoration to Christendom of the very burial place of the God of all creation.

And, now that I come to think of it, not only do the old things fall into desuetude. How rapidly the present becomes merely a shadow of past glory. How swiftly new things join in the degeneracy of the old.

Yesterday I walked with a shudder under those three golden balls that once shone regally in the Da Medici coat of arms . . .

And there I pawned, for the price of a square meal, the watch that had once so passionately kept me informed concerning the approach of the exquisite hours I spent with the woman I loved!

Smart Set 49, No. 4 (August 1916): 112.

A Litany for Hangmen

By Owen Hatteras

From clients who delay the exercises by pausing to make long and irrelevant speeches from the scaffold, or to sing depressing hymns; and from medical examiners who forget their stethoscopes and clamor for waits while messenger boys are sent for them; and from official witnesses who faint at the last minute, and have to be hauled out by deputy sheriffs; and from undertakers who keep looking at their watches, and hinting obscenely that they have other engagements at 10.15; and from spiritual advisers who crowd up at the last minute, and so fall through the trap with the condemned, good Lord, deliver me!

Smart Set 49, No. 4 (August 1916): 112.

The Ulster Polonius

I.

The general formula of George Bernard Shaw, to wit, the announcement of the obvious in terms of the scandalous, is made so palpable in his new book, "ANDROCLES AND THE LION" (*Constable*), that even such besotted Shawolators as George Jean Nathan will at last perceive and acknowledge it. Here, indeed, the Irish Herbert Kaufman indulges himself in a veritable debauch of platitudes, and the sickly music of them fills the air. In the long and indignant preface to "AN-DROCLES" (it runs to 114 pages) all he manages to say about Christianity is what every man of the slightest intelligence has been thinking for years; and yet he gets into his statement of all this trite stuff so violent an appearance of radicalism that it will undoubtedly heat up the women's clubs and the newspaper reviewers, and inspire them to hail him once more as a Great Thinker. It is amusing to rehearse in cold blood some of his principal contentions: (*a*) that the social and economical doctrines preached by Christ were indistinguishable from what is now called Socialism, (*b*) that the Pauline transcendentalism visible in the Acts and the Epistles differs enormously from the simple ideas set forth in the Four Gospels, (*c*) that the Christianity on tap to-day would be almost as abhorrent to Christ, supposing Him returned to earth, as the theories of Nietzsche, George Moore or Emma Goldman, (*d*) that the rejection of the Biblical miracles, and even of the historical credibility of the Gospels, by no means disposes of Christ Himself, and (*e*) that the early Christians were persecuted, not because their theology was unsound, but because their public conduct constituted a nuisance. Could one imagine a more abject surrender to the undeniable? And yet, as I say, these empty platitudes will probably be debated furiously as revolutionary iconoclasms, and perhaps even as blasphemies, and the reputation of Shaw as an original and powerful metaphysician will get a great boost.

In this new book his method of making a scandal with embalmed ideas is exactly the same that he used in all his previous prefaces, pontifications and pronunciamentos. That is to say, he takes a proposition which all reflective men know and admit to be true, and points out ef-

Smart Set 49, No. 4 (August 1916): 138–44.

fects and implications of it which very few men, reflective or not, have the courage to face honestly. Turn to "Man and Superman" and you will see the whole process. There he starts out with the self-evident fact, disputed by no one, that a woman has vastly more to gain by marriage, under Christian monogamy, than a man, and then proceeds to manufacture a sensation by exhibiting the corollary fact that all women know it, and that they are thus more eager to marry than men are, and always prove it by taking the lead in the business. The second fact, to any man who has passed through the terrible decade between twenty-five and thirty-five, is as plain as the first, but its statement runs counter to many much-esteemed conventions and delusions of civilization, and so it cannot be stated without kicking up a row. That row stems from horror, and that horror has its roots in one of the commonest of all human weaknesses, viz.: intellectual cowardice, the craven yearning for mental ease and safety, the fear of thinking things out. Shaw is simply one who, for purposes of sensation, resolutely and mercilessly thinks things out—sometimes with much ingenuity and humor, but often, it must be said, in the same muddled way that the average "right-thinker" would do it if he ever got up the courage. Remember this formula, and all of the fellow's alleged originality becomes no more than a sort of bad-boy audacity. He drags skeletons from their closets, and makes them dance obscenely—but everyone, of course, knew that they were there all the time. He would produce an excitement of exactly the same kind (though perhaps superior in intensity) if he should walk down the Strand naked to the waist, and so remind the horrified Londoners of the unquestioned fact (though conventionally concealed and forgotten) that he is a mammal, and hence outfitted with an umbilicus.

This is all I can get out of the long and highly diverting preface to "ANDROCLES": a statement of the indubitable in terms of the not-to-be-thought-of-for-an-instant. His discussion of the inconsistencies between the Four Gospels is no more than a réchauffé of what everyone knows who knows anything about the Four Gospels at all. You will find all of its points set forth at great length in any elemental treatise upon New Testament criticism—even in so childish a tract as Ramsden Balmforth's. He actually dishes up, with a grave air of sapience, the news that there is a glaring inconsistency between the genealogy of Jesus in Matthew, I, 1–17, and the direct claim of Divine Paternity in Matthew, I, 18. More, he breaks out with the astounding discovery that Jesus was a good Jew, and that Paul's repudiation of circumcision (now a cardinal article of Christian faith) would have surprised Him, and perhaps even shocked Him. Yet more, he takes thirty or forty pages to prove that the essential ideas of Jesus, stripped of the interpolations of Paul and all the later volunteers, were the ideas of a militant communist, and hence of a Socialist—a notion so obvious that it occurred to me (a man but little concerned with either Socialism or Christianity) fully a dozen years ago, and so much a part of my common stock of platitudes that I embalmed it in print last April in a tedious, rubber-stamp review of John Spargo's "Marxian Socialism and Religion." Of such startlingly "original" propositions the preface to "ANDROCLES" is all compact. Searching it from end to end with eagle eye, I have failed to find a single fact or argument that has given me any sense of novelty—despite the circumstance, as I say, that I pay little attention to exegesis, and so might be expected to be surprised by its veriest commonplaces.

Nevertheless, this preface makes bouncing reading—and for the plain reason that Shaw is a clever workman in letters, and knows how to wrap up old goods in charming wrappers. When, in disposing of the common delusion that Jesus was a long-faced tear-squeezer like John the Baptist or the average Methodist evangelist, he arrives at the conclusion that He was "what we should call an artist and a Bohemian in His manner of life," the result, no doubt, is a shock and a clandestine thrill to those who have been confusing the sour donkey they hear every Sunday with the genial, good-humored and likable Man they affect to worship. And when, dealing with the Atonement, he argues against it that it puts a premium upon weakness, and that the man who doesn't accept it is apt to be a more careful and unflinching fellow than the man who does, he gets the easy dramatic effect of a raid upon the very sanctuary, and so achieves a pleasant devilishness. But, as I have said, these ideas are not, in themselves, new ideas, nor are they really very naughty. I have heard the first of the two maintained by a bishop, and as for the second, I myself urged it against a chance Christian encountered in a Pullman smoking-room three or four months ago, and snickered comfortably while he proceeded from an indignant repudiation of it to a reluctant confession of its practical truth. I remember well how staggered the poor old boy was when I complained that my inability to accept the orthodox doctrine put a heavy burden of moral responsibility upon me, and forced me to be more watchful of my conduct than the elect, and so robbed me of many good chances to make money. I was very considerate in dealing with this pious gentleman. So far as I remember, I avoided tackling him with any idea that was not wholly obvious. And yet, in half an hour, he was full of the same protesting (and subtly yielding) horror that afflicts the simple folk who support the fame of Shaw.

A double joke reposes in the Shaw legend. The first half of it I have expounded; the second half is to be found in the fact that Shaw is not at all the heretic his fascinated victims see him, but an orthodox Scotch Presbyterian of the most cock-sure and bilious sort. In the theory that he is Irish I take little stock. His very name is as Scotch as haggis, and the part of Ireland from which he comes is peopled almost entirely by Scots. The true Irishman is a romantic; he senses religion as a mystery, a thing of wonder, an experience of ineffable beauty; his interest centers, not in the commandments, but in the sacraments. The Scot, on the contrary, is almost devoid of that sort of religious feeling; he hasn't imagination enough for it; all he can see in the Word of God is a sort of police regulation; his concern is not with beauty, but with morals. Here Shaw runs true to type. Read his critical writings from end to end, and you will not find the slightest hint that objects of art were passing before him as he wrote. He founded, in England, the superstition that Ibsen was no more than a tinpot evangelist—a sort of brother to General Booth, Mrs. Pankhurst, Mother Eddy and Billy Sunday. He turned Shakespeare into a prophet of evil, croaking dismally in a rain-barrel. He even injected a moral content (by dint of abominable straining) into the music dramas of Richard Wagner, surely the most colossal slaughters of all moral ideas on the altar of beauty ever seen by man. Always this ethical obsession, the hall-mark of the Scotch Puritan, is visible in him. He is forever discovering an atrocity in what has hitherto passed as no more than a human weakness; he is forever inventing new sins, and demanding their punishment; he always sees his opponent, not only as wrong, but also as a scoundrel. I have called him a good Presbyterian. Need I add that, in "ANDRO-CLES," he flirts with predestination under the scientific euphemism of determinism—that he seems to be convinced that while men may not be responsible for their virtues, they are undoubtedly responsible for their sins, and deserve to be clubbed therefor? . . . And this is Shaw the revolutionist, the heretic, the iconoclast! Next, perhaps, we shall be hearing of Woodrow the immoralist, of Pius the atheist, of Nicholas the Hindenburgista!

II.

Barabbas the Inexplicable.—Myself concerned all my adult years with the merchanting of printed matter, and in endless confabulation with publishers of all sorts, I nevertheless find myself, at the threshold of senility, in complete ignorance of the principles upon which the rev. Barabbases do business. Surely no trade in all the world is more mysterious, more gaudy with anomalies, more replete with a gay damphoolishness. Why is this book published, and the other one passed over? On what theory do reputable houses affix their imprints to three-

fourths of the novels that reach me? On the theory that they are literature? Pish! Even a publisher is at least as intelligent as a bull-frog. On
the theory that they will sell? Pish again! It would take a public of maniacs to buy most of them; the majority are so atrociously tedious that
they are scarcely praised by the New York *Times*. How many, indeed,
actually sell 1,500 copies? Not one in eight. And yet, as I say, they
pour from the presses in chromatic streams, and what is more, the
whole cost of printing and marketing them is borne by the publishers
themselves, for though it is almost the rule to make a poet pay for his
book, the novelists, however bad, are seldom squeezed. I know practically all the American poets, male and female, who have ever actually
sold poetry to the magazines, and a canvass of them shows that 88.7
per cent. have been shaken down, at one time or another, by "co-
operative" publishers. I know perhaps twice as many bad novelists, and
yet not one of them, so far as I can determine, has ever had to fork up
a cent. The Barabbases take all the risks and all the losses—and keep on
doing it over and over again, spitting experience in the eye each time.

The history of American literature (and of English literature no
less) is one long chronicle of publishers' imbecilities. The early books
of Edgar Allan Poe, now run up in the auction rooms to hundreds and
even thousands of dollars, were brought out, not by the leading publisher of Poe's time, nor, indeed, by any recognized publisher at all, but
by what were really no more than neighborhood job printers. So with
the books of Whitman; even to this day he is printed, not by the solemn booksellers who gabble about their high services to literature, but
by smaller and more obscure fellows. Try to pick up the early books of
Ambrose Bierce; you will find imprints you never heard of before. As
for Mark Twain, he had to start a publishing house of his own to get a
free hand. True enough, when this venture failed (through the fault of
his partners) he went back to a regular publisher—but with what result? With the result that it is quite impossible to buy a satisfactory edition of his collected works to-day. The only edition on the market
contains many volumes that lack all or a major part of the original illustrations. Imagine "Huckleberry Finn" without Kemble's pictures—
the best illustrations, it seems to me, that any book in English has ever
had! Moreover, six years after his death his posthumous works remain
unpublished, and among them, according to his biographer, are at least
two books in his very best manner.

A glance at the first editions of Joseph Conrad (now selling for as
much as $30 apiece, though the earliest goes back no further than
1895) shows what a hard time he had finding an appreciative publisher. The first eleven bear six different London imprints. His American
editions tell an even stranger story: the first six of them were brought

out by six different publishers. When, a few years ago, the firm of Doubleday, Page & Co. conceived the plan of reprinting his books in a uniform edition, it was found impossible to bring together the widely dispersed rights to all of them, and the uniform edition is still full of gaps, and such important works as "Nostromo" and "An Outcast of the Islands" are not in it. I salute this firm for its enterprise—but do not forget that its chief claim to fame is that it suppressed Dreiser's "Sister Carrie." To-day it makes amends by publishing Gerald Stanley Lee and Gene Stratton Porter—surely sweet companions for Conrad, who is bedizened for the department-store trade, by the way, in navy-blue limp leather and all the other gaudy trappings of Corn Belt *Kultur*. The Harpers, after an obscure publisher had shown the way, took over "Sister Carrie"—and then make their own bid for immortality by jumping from under "The Titan." The present publisher of the leading American novelist is the *English* firm of John Lane. . . . Somewhere on the tablet let us scratch the name of the Houghton-Mifflin Company. Observe its imprint on Eleanor H. Porter's "Just David"—and let your tears flood Boston Common!

It would be easy to string out the tale to endless lengths. Two or three more examples and I pass on. The late John Millington Synge managed to find an English publisher for "Riders to the Sea," but after that masterpiece had come out the bookselling gentlemen washed their hands of him, and all his later books were printed by a small publisher in Dublin. The manuscript of "The Aran Islands" knocked about the London publishers' offices so long that it wore out, and had to be re-typed. Lord Dunsany, undoubtedly the greatest of the neo-Celts after Synge, had to publish his earlier books (that is, in England) at his own expense. Finally, there is the case of the English translation of Nietzsche. An eminent Anglo-American firm brought out four or five volumes, and then lost stomach for the enterprise, and no other publisher would touch it. After long delays, a private admirer of Nietzsche, Dr. Oscar Levy, undertook it at his own expense, and pushed it to rapid completion. The inevitable followed. The books that all the wiseacres of Grub Street had been afraid of made a big success, and Dr. Levy soon had to reprint many of the volumes. When the war came, and all England began reading Nietzsche in search of deviltries, the doctor began rolling up a handsome profit. The firm which had abandoned Nietzsche before Levy entered the lists took over the American rights to the Levy edition later on—and promoted it in a characteristically Barabbasian manner by publishing some of the eighteen volumes in one binding and the rest in another and very different one.

Such is the art and craft of the publisher. Books of intolerably bad poetry reach me almost every day, and once a year I call a holiday and divert the vulgar by exposing their imbecile contents. But no publisher, as yet, has bethought him to publish the *good* poetry of John McClure, though I have made outcry of its existence more than once; nor the poetry of Muna Lee, nor that of Odell Shepard, nor that of Ruth Comfort Mitchell—all of them vastly better poets than two-thirds of the burbling college professors hymned by the *Dial*. Down in Louisville there is David Morton, with the best volume of sonnets I have seen for a long while. Morton is not unknown; his work has appeared in the magazines; there are plenty of folks who like it. But he will probably cut many a bale of blue grass before he finds a publisher willing to print him between covers. In the end, perhaps, his experience will be that of my old *corpsbruder* at Oxford, Folger McKinsey. McKinsey, in the intervals of heavy newspaper work, has written many very lovely lyrics; I wish I could get a steady supply of them for THE SMART SET. But when he put together his first book, the impossibility of finding a publisher for it quickly became manifest, and so he had it put into type by a bankrupt who kept a bookstore in a provincial city. The joke was then on the publishers, for it sold 3,000 copies within a year—almost a record for poetry in the United States. I offer a keg of Coca-Cola to any publisher who will say that the average for the poetry books that *are* published is more than 300.

Another mystery of publishing is to be found in the incomprehensible system by which review copies are distributed. I have been reviewing books for fifteen years past, and have had that system under my eye all the while, and yet I do no more understand it to-day than I understand liturgical Russian. Whenever I find an author who pleases me and take to praising him lavishly in these pages and calling upon all Christian men to buy him and read him, his publisher is sure to stop sending me his books. And if, on the contrary, I try some poor devil of a scribbler by the *lex talionis* and do execution upon him with Prussian frightfulness, his publisher invariably sends me all of his ensuing works, and favors me with idiotic circular letters testifying to their unquestioned merit. I get, almost every week, books that, under no imaginable circumstances, could be reviewed to any purpose in THE SMART SET—for example, books for little girls, books upon economics and trade, and even scientific books. At least twice during the past year I have been at pains to explain that I do not review war books—that it is the policy of this magazine (copiously supported by the gratitude of its readers) to avoid any discussion of the war, even in fiction or poetry. Nevertheless, I continue to receive nearly all the war books that are published, including the current treatises unpreparedness by college boys, old maids, newspaper reporters and job-seekers. More, this present note will not shut off the stream. During the month following its publication I shall receive at least thirty such tomes, despite three fair warnings that all of them will go into my hell-box unread. The Barabbasian skull seems to be of four-ply celluloid; it takes a fearful battering to penetrate it. Or can it be that publishers never read reviews? I begin to harbor a suspicion that way. It is supported by the obvious fact that they never read the books they publish.

III.

The Labial Infamy.—Despite a great laboriousness in the collection of materials, I can find nothing that is novel and little that is sound in "A Bundle of Kisses," by Dr. R. McCormick Sturgeon (*York Comp. Co.*), a York, Pa., savant. Dr. Sturgeon, indeed, takes a thoroughly sentimental view of the thing he presumes to vivisect, and so his book is no more than a compendium of mush. Even when, putting on a scientific black cap, he essays to describe the act of osculation in cold terms, he gets no further than a sonorous gabble about heaving bosoms, red lips, electric sparks and such-like imaginings. The truth is that the physiology of the kiss, like its psychology, has been unaccountably neglected. What reason have we for believing, as Dr. Sturgeon does, that the lungs are "strongly expanded" during the act? My own casual observation inclines me to hold that the opposite is true: that the lungs are actually collapsed in a pseudo-asthmatic spasm. Again, what is the ground for arguing that the lips are "full, ripe and red"? The real effect of the emotions that accompany kissing is to empty the superficial capillaries and so produce a leaden pallor. As for such salient symptoms as the temperature, the pulse and the rate of respiration, the learned pundit passes them over without a word. Mrs. Elsie Clews Parsons would be a good one to write a sober and accurate treatise upon kissing. Her books upon "The Family" and "Fear and Conventionality" indicate her possession of the right sort of scientific learning and accuracy. Even better would be a tome by Havelock Ellis, say, in three or four volumes. Ellis has devoted his whole life to illuminating the mysteries of sex, and his collection of materials is unsurpassed in the world. Surely there must be an enormous mass of instructive stuff about kissing in his card indexes, letter files, book presses and archives.

Just why the kiss as we know it should have attained to its present popularity in Christendom—or, as Dr. Sturgeon puts it, its universal veneration—is one of the things past finding out. The Japanese, a very affectionate and sentimental people, do not practise kissing in any form; they regard the act, in fact, with an aversion matching our own aversion to the rubbing of noses. Nor is it in vogue among the Moslems, or among the Chinese, who countenance it only as between

mother and child. Even in parts of Christendom it is girt about by rigid taboos, so that its practise tends to be restricted to a few occasions.
Two Frenchmen or Italians, when they meet, kiss each other on both
cheeks. One sees, indeed, many pictures of General Joffre thus bussing
the heroes of Verdun; there has even appeared in print a story to the
effect that one of them objected to the scratching of his moustache.
But imagine two Englishmen kissing! Or two Germans! As well imagine the two former kissing the two latter! Such a display of affection is
simply impossible to men of Northern blood; they would die with
shame if caught at it. The Englishman, like the American, never kisses
if he can help it. He even regards it as bad form to kiss his wife in a
railway station, or, in fact, anywhere in sight of a third party. The Latin has no such compunctions. He leaps to the business regardless of
place or time; his sole concern is with the lady. Once, in driving from
Nice to Monte Carlo along the lower Corniche road, I passed a hundred or so open taxicabs containing man and woman, and fully 75 per
cent. of the men had their arms around their companions, and were
kissing them. These were not peasants, remember, but well-to-do persons. In England such a scene would have caused a great scandal; in
most American States the police would have charged the offenders
with drawn revolvers.

The charm of kissing is one of the things I have always wondered
at. I do not pretend, of course, that I have never done it; mere politeness forces one to it; there are women who sulk and grow bellicose unless one at least makes the motions of kissing them. But what I mean is
that I have never found the act a tenth part as agreeable as poets, the
authors of musical comedy librettos, and (on the contrary side) chap-
erons and the *gendarmerie* make it out. The physical sensation, far from
being pleasant, is intensely uncomfortable—the suspension of respiration, indeed, quickly resolves itself into a feeling of suffocation—and
the posture necessitated by the approximation of lips and lips is unfail-
ingly a constrained and ungraceful one. Theoretically, a man kisses a
woman perpendicularly, with their eyes, those "windows of the soul,"
synchronizing exactly. But actually, on account of the incompressibility
of the nasal cartilages, he has to incline either his or her head to an angle of at least 60 degrees, and the result is that his right eye gazes in-
sanely at the space between her eyebrows, while his left eye is fixed
upon some vague spot behind her. An instantaneous photograph of
such a maneuver, taken at the moment of incidence, would probably
turn the stomach of even the most romantic man, and force him, in
sheer self-respect, to renounce kissing as he has renounced leap frog
and walking on stilts. Only a woman (for women are quite devoid of

æsthetic feeling, as their choice of mates shows) could survive so damning a picture of the thing she venerates.

But the most embarrassing moment, in kissing, does not come during the actual kiss (for at that time the sensation of suffocation drives out all purely psychical feelings), but immediately afterward. What is one to say to the woman then? The occasion obviously demands some sort of remark. One has just received (in theory) a great boon; the silence begins to make itself felt; there stands the fair one, obviously waiting. Is one to thank her? Certainly that would be too transparent a piece of hypocrisy, too flaccid a banality. Is one to tell her that one loves her? Obviously, there is danger in such assurances, and beside, one usually doesn't, and a lie is a lie. Or is one to descend to chatty commonplaces—about the weather, literature, politics, the war? The practical impossibility of solving the problem leads almost inevitably to a blunder far worse than any merely verbal one: one kisses the cutie again, and then again, and so on, and so on. The ultimate result is satiety, repugnance, disgust; even the girl herself gets enough. . . . I lament that Dr. Sturgeon discreetly dodged all such inquiries. His book will please the mushy, for it is full of saccharine evasions; but it is quite worthless as a contribution to psychology.

Portrait of a Tragic Comedian

I

The preface to Frank Harris' two-volume biography of Oscar Wilde bears date of 1910, and on the title page the author appears as his own publisher and even as his own printer. A curious proof of the potency of prudery in the Anglo-Saxon countries! For six years, it would seem, this highly dramatic and significant story of a first-rate artist's rise and fall has been seeking a publisher on both sides of the Atlantic, and now at last, despite the dignified position of the author and his obvious competence to write such a book with discretion and understanding, he is forced to print it privately and from a house in Washington Square! Strange tales go about of its adventures in New York. One publisher, after others had failed, accepted it and had it set up—but when he submitted the sheets to those who have authority in such matters he was warned that its publication would land him in jail. He thereupon had the work revised, and with all passages taken out that could reasonably offer offense to even the most prudish, it was submitted again. He was then plainly given to understand that its publication in any form would expose him to prosecution, and so he was forced to abandon it. Harris himself seems to look forward to some sort of Puritan attack, and in preparation for it rehearses the reasons which moved him to write and print the book—his long and intimate friendship with Wilde; the importance of the man, not only as an individual artist but also as an influence in English letters; the palpable inaccuracy and inadequacy of the existing studies of him; the need of a simple and truthful account of his grotesque mock trials in the English courts; the growth of a huge body of fantastic fables about him and particularly about his last days; the sound principle that even the worst of offenders deserves to have his case presented by one who is not his sworn foe. He might have added, in further defense of his boldness, his own unusual charm as a writer, for his book is not only the most comprehensive and informative volume on Wilde that has yet appeared, but also, and by long odds, the most skillfully written. It is, indeed, an excellent biography, intimate, sympathetic and yet rigidly honest, and whatever its theoretical shortcomings in moral eyes it at least stands up as a piece of writing.

Smart Set 50, No. 1 (September 1916): 280–86.

And why have the publishers been so reluctant to publish it, and the guardians of the public rectitude so eager to suppress it? For the life of me I can't make out. Saving one chapter, I can find nothing in it to lift the eyebrow of any sane adult, and even there Harris does no more than allow Wilde to say a few words (they are empty and unconvincing enough, surely) in his own cause. The truth is told, but it is told cleanly, reticently, with due reserve. I myself, after having read every word of the two volumes, come away in complete ignorance of the precise act for which Wilde was condemned to such barbaric tortures in prison. It may have been one thing, or it may have been some other and quite different thing—both disgusting enough, in all conscience, but neither a penal offense in most civilized countries, and neither so rare in our own land that we can afford to go through any hocus-pocus of holy horror. In my native State, not six months ago, the leader of the vice crusade, a Methodist clergyman in high standing, was taken in such *schweinerei* in the central lamasery of the Young Men's Christian Association, and had to be spirited out of the jurisdiction by his fellow apostles of purity. But when the newspapers, scenting a smutty trial, set up a demand for his indictment and extradition, it was found, to everyone's astonishment, that the offense of which he was accused was not indictable, and so the State Legislature rushed through a special prohibitory act, that the recreant clergy and laity might be better handled hereafter. It was for this indecency, or for something substantially equivalent to it, that Wilde was given two years in solitary confinement, and one long year of it without books, without writing implements, without decent medical attention, and even without sufficient food. It is Harris' offense, if he has committed any offense, that he went to Wilde's rescue when the burdens of his punishment grew maddening and intolerable, that he helped him through the cruel difficulties of the years following his release, and that he now puts himself into jeopardy to tell the man's story as he knows it, carefully and completely, concealing nothing that is salient and significant, and yet making no cheap show of what is merely nasty.

That story, I need scarcely say, is anything but edifying. One rises from it, indeed, with the impression that the misdemeanor which caused Wilde's actual downfall was quite the least of his onslaughts upon the decencies—that he was of vastly more ardor and fluency as a cad and a poltroon than ever he became as an immoralist. No offense against what the average civilized man regards as proper and seemly conduct is missing from the chronicle. Wilde was a fop and a snob, a toady and a social pusher, a coward and an ingrate, a glutton and a grafter, a plagiarist and a mountebank; he was jealous alike of his superiors and of his inferiors; he was so spineless that he fell an instant victim to every new flatterer; he had no sense whatever of monetary obligation or even of the commonest duties of friendship; he lied incessantly to those who showed him most kindness, and tried to rob some of them; he seems never to have forgotten a slight or remembered a favor; he was as devoid of any notion of honor as a candidate for office; the moving spring of his whole life was a silly and obnoxious vanity. It is almost impossible to imagine a fellow of less ingratiating character, and to these endless defects he added a physical body that was gross and repugnant, but through it all ran an incomparable charm of personality, and supporting and increasing that charm was his undoubted genius. Harris pauses more than once to hymn his capacity for engaging the fancy. He was a veritable specialist in the amenities, a dinner companion *sans pair,* the greatest of English wits since Congreve, the most delightful of talkers, an artist to his finger-tips, the prophet of a new and lordlier æsthetic, the complete antithesis of English stodginess and stupidity. Born out of his time, as he himself was fond of saying, he was even more an exile from his true country. The London of the eighties was as immovably hostile to such a man as the Germany of the seventies was to Nietzsche. It could see him only as an extravagant buffoon, a preacher of the fantastic and dubious, one to be regarded with a wary eye; and so it was very quick, in the old old Puritan way, to explain his strangeness in terms of villainy, and to fall upon him, once the chance offered, with an enthusiasm almost religious. Wilde was guilty without a doubt; we have, indeed, his plain confession in this book; but all the same he was not tried but lynched, and no gabble about substantial justice will ever rub out that discreditable fact.

Harris tells us that he was personally convinced of Wilde's innocence until after the first trial. It is the hardest thing in the book to believe, for surely no one else in the London of that day labored under any such delusion, and Harris himself mentions many anterior circumstances that gave him suspicion. The point, however, is scarcely worth making. The important thing is the light that the confession threw upon Wilde's character. Harris had already advised him to flee to France, knowing full well the impossibility of breaking a high tide of Puritan indignation; he now renewed his arguments with all the persuasiveness he could muster, for he saw clearly that, at the second trial, Wilde would fall an easy victim to the prosecution's lawyers, and that the jury's disagreement in the first trial would not be repeated. In order to facilitate the proposed escape (Wilde was out on bail), he borrowed a steam yacht from a friend, and anchored it with steam up at Erith on the lower Thames. More, he had a carriage in waiting, and made arrangements which practically amounted to official connivance. But Wilde could never get up sufficient courage for the enterprise. Once he was actually in the carriage, but at the last moment an astounding cowardice seized him, and he demanded to be taken to his brother's house. "I would as soon take you to prison!" exclaimed Harris. But Oscar stood to his decision. His mood was one of utter inertia; he preferred waiting and doing nothing to the easy way to freedom. Later on, Harris tackled him again, but with equal lack of success. Fear had reduced him to a pitiable state, indeed; he could do nothing save bury his head in the sand; the days of his trial and conviction, and even the first days of his penal servitude, passed over him as in a dream; it would be difficult to imagine a picture of more pathetic weakness.

The story of Wilde's two trials and of the cruelties rained upon him in prison give a serious shaking up to all our old notions of English justice and decency. Both trials were tragic farces. Notorious rogues and blackmailers were admitted as witnesses, a half-witted young man was solemnly put upon the stand, and the newspapers inflamed the jury with extraordinary denunciations of the accused, many of them, as Harris shows, inspired by persons as guilty as the prisoner. Notwithstanding all this clamour for his blood, the first jury disagreed. But the second was more responsive to opinion, and so Wilde was railroaded to prison. On the day after his sentence forty well-known men about town sat down to a public banquet in celebration of the event— "a feast," as Harris says, "to celebrate the ruin and degradation of a man of genius." The leading spirit in this great moral banquet was Charles Brookfield, the present English censor of plays. Brookfield was the author of "Dear Old Charlie," the most indecent comedy seen on the London boards in years. But he constituted himself the unofficial prosecutor of Wilde, and gathered the highly dubious evidence on which he was convicted. Later on, when Brookfield was rewarded with the censor's post for his high services to public morality, some humorous London manager revived "Dear Old Charlie," and it had a hilarious run. The piece had been licensed by Brookfield's predecessor, and he was unable, under the law, to withdraw the license. But poor Wilde was dead before ever this last act of the tragic farce was played out.

Despite the fact that a Royal Commission had already protested against the penalty as barbarous and unreasonable, Wilde was condemned to two years' penal servitude, and the first of them was spent in what was virtually solitary confinement. The prison food was revolting and insufficient; silence was enforced by severe punishments; the prisoner was forbidden to read or to write. His health broke down under this drastic régime and he lost forty pounds in weight; but the governor of the prison and the prison doctor refused him any relief. Harris, meanwhile, was in South Africa. On his return he visited Wilde, and then lodged a protest with Sir Ruggles Brise, the head of the Prison Commission. Brise turned out to be a humane man, and at once ordered a relaxation of the killing discipline. Wilde was given pen, ink and paper, and soon began work on "De Profundis." Brise went still further. He told Harris that he was in favor of reducing Wilde's sentence, and that he would urge the Home Secretary to reduce it if it were not for fear of Puritan objections in Parliament. To meet this situation Harris suggested that a petition be prepared, signed by the leading authors of England. Brise jumped at the suggestion, and proposed George Meredith as the first signer. But when Harris approached Meredith the latter curtly refused. So did Professor Churton Collins. So, it appears, did Swinburne. Harris went from door to door. He found them all closed against him. There was no Christian charity on tap in England. Worse, there was no courage. Most of these magnificoes based their refusal frankly on the ground that it would be dangerous to hold out a hand to Wilde, with the state of public opinion what it was. Harris himself and Professor Tyrrell, of Trinity College, Dublin, seem to have been the only ones with valour enough to face that storm—not forgetting the Rev. Stewart Headlam, "who was an English clergyman, and yet, wonder of wonders, a Christian."

So Wilde served his two years, not escaping a single day. Once he was released the Puritan rage against him revived, and he went to France. Had he been given, in those days, a helping hand, it is highly probable that he would have pulled himself together and spent the rest of his life in diligent and valuable work. To a few relatively happy months of this period, indeed, belong his best writings—"The Ballad of Reading Gaol" and parts of "De Profundis." But what he actually got, save from a few faithful friends, was contumely of an unmeasured and almost unbelievable sort; he was firmly lodged in the Puritan valhalla of devils, and no extravagance of hatred was too much for him. The result was that, after a gallant new start, he slipped back into his old associations, and presently he was living in squalid idleness in Paris, drunken, dirty and indecent. It was then that all the worst weaknesses of the man came out. He borrowed money right and left, wasted his days in filthy debauchery, and played ingrate and traitor to his best friends. The experience of Harris was perhaps typical. During his Paris days Wilde devised an excellent scene for a play, but found himself unable to complete it. He proposed to Harris that they collaborate on it, and after long negotiations, during which Wilde's unfitness of the task became manifest, Harris ended by buying the idea from him for £50. The money paid, Harris went back to London, completed the play—it was called "Mr. and Mrs. Daventry"—and sold it to Mrs. Patrick Campbell. Wilde, hearing of this, now demanded more money, and Harris, to pacify him, gave him another £50. But the worst was to come. The moment the play was announced, various actors and actresses came forward with the claim that Wilde had sold his idea to them, and investigation showed that he had actually done so, and on a large scale. Mrs. Brown Potter, Beerbohm Tree, George Alexander and Ada Rehan were among these claimants; some had paid Wilde as much as £100. Worse still, he acknowledged the swindle without shame, and even denounced Harris for depriving him of "a certain income"!

After this curious episode he went downhill rapidly, and was soon quite unable to do any work at all. His sole means of support was the charity of his friends, and to the business of wheedling money out of them he devoted all of his surviving energies. The end that now rapidly approached was of a sort to delight the Puritan heart. Wilde had suffered a fall in prison and one of its results was an abscess of the ear. In addition, he was in the last stages of chronic alcoholism, and beside, was victim to an unmentionable disease, the product of his vices. He died in a little hotel in a by-street, with only two friends, Robert Ross and Reginald Turner, at his side. The death-bed scenes were full of horror; he seemed doomed to go out of life in abominable filthiness. The body was buried in quicklime, like that of the hanged man in "The Ballad of Reading Gaol." Years later Ross went to Paris with Wilde's son to have it reinterred in Père Lachaise. When it vas dug up it was found that the quicklime had failed to act; the features were still recognisable. "At once Ross sent the son away, and when the sextons were about to use their shovels, he ordered them to desist, and descending into the grave, moved the body with his own hands into the new coffin in loving reverence."

So much for the life and death of Oscar Wilde. Harris gives no space to a criticism of his books, and I follow his example. Thanks to the labors of Ross, they are now to be had in an excellent complete edition of fourteen volumes. Innumerable other editions exist (some of them boldly pirated), but that of Ross is better than all the rest. Much that is hollow and feeble is in those fourteen volumes—epigrams that strain and creak, poems that are all a brittle sounding, an æsthetic theory that floats upon the surface and is chiefly borrowed to boot. But there are other things, and rare and precious things—the best wit that England has produced since the Restoration, three or four incomparably amusing plays, the noblest ballad in English, some essays that have left their mark, a story or two of the first rank, an endless stream of good writing. Wilde, beyond all things, was a stylist, and perhaps the greatest of his time. His epigrams may lose their tang, his plays may go out of fashion, even "De Profundis" and "The Ballad of Reading Gaol" may cease to move, but so long as there is an art in our resilient and glowing English speech, he will live as one who knew pre-eminently how to use it. The charm of his style is in the very least of his writings—his squibs, the speeches in his plays, his letters to the newspapers. He could no more put words together without making music than he could face a temptation without yielding to it. Our depressing Puritan philosophy is against such men. It distrusts the artist with a great distrust; it sees in him a prophet of that innocent gusto, that pagan joy in life, which is its chief abomination; it is always ecstatically eager to discover him a criminal, and to fall upon him with the utmost rigors of its savage justice. Wilde was in the wrong century and the wrong time. The Irishman of genius should not go to England, but to France.

Harris, as I say, has done a good job in this life of his friend, no matter how much specialists in righteousness may belabor it with incomprehensible objurgations. He has told the truth about Wilde's stupendous weaknesses, but he has also managed to convey some understanding of the man's unquenchable attractiveness. There was never another quite like Oscar. His very grotesqueries somehow brought him friends, and not all his rogueries and indecencies could ever drive them away. "One can be sure," says Harris, speaking of Ross' last services, "that the man who won such fervid self-denying tenderness, had deserved it, called it forth by charm of companionship, or magic of loving intercourse." Harris' book is yet another proof. It is a grim and unsentimentalized record, but there is shot through it the enchantment of a personality that, after all, must have had something fine and inspiring in it—of a man who, for all his vileness, was at least far better than the Pecksniffs who tore him to pieces.

II

An era of pamphlets seems to be upon us, with the war diligently helping its advent. Scarcely a day passes that I do not receive three or four. Usually, true enough, they are set up in large type and palmed off upon the public as books, but this is merely one more count in the indictment of publishers. Covers or no covers, they yet remain pamphlets, and some day some miraculously intelligent publisher will see the advantage of putting them out in paper and at twenty-five cents, and so cabbage a lot of dollars. The causes of this late flowering of an old plant are not far to seek. The newspapers, falling more and more into the hands of mere stockjobbers and shopmen, have sunk to such an abyss of imbecility that nothing approaching an intelligible discussion of public problems is visible in their columns. The days when a Hamilton, a Madison or a Jay turned to them is long past; they no longer invite the man who has anything worth hearing to say; their sages and soothsayers are such empty platitudinarians as Dr. Frank Crane, Edwin Markham, Arthur Brisbane and Herbert Kaufman. Turn to the best of them and you will see plainly what a falling off there has been since the heroic age. The discussion of great questions, even in such pretentious gazettes as the Boston *Transcript,* the New York *Evening Post* and the Philadelphia *Ledger,* seldom arises above the level of a lecture by a fresh-water college professor; they are almost incredibly ill-informed and as unbrokenly sophomoric and humorless; two-thirds of them are even written in school-boy English. The New York *Sun* (God rest its soul!) offers a measure of the decline. Imagine the journal made great by Charles A. Dana in the hands of Frank A. Munsey, author of "Afloat in a Great City," "The Boy Broker" and "The Boy Pirates of the Hudson"!

Hence the pamphlet. Hence, too, such phenomena as the *New Republic,* a gallant effort but lacking the requisite of brains. All of the *New Republic* young men are pamphleteers, and as undergraduates go, some of them are not bad ones. I reach into the pile and draw forth a work that, if it hasn't actually appeared in those virtuous pages, at least smells of them sweetly. Its title is "Reclaiming the Ballot," and its author is Ward Macauley (*Duffield*). What seminary this Mr. Macauley adorns I do not know, but the ardour of Politics IV is still plainly in him, and if he doesn't really get very far beyond the newspaper editorial writers in his ideas, he at least writes much better English. His theory is that the ballot is the palladium of our liberties, but that we have fatuously permitted birds of evil plumage to roost upon it, thus besmirching its façade. To save it, he proposes that we abandon the custom of voting in saloons, barber-shops and harness-stores, and erect "a permanent building, properly equipped for the important work to be undertaken," in each "election precinct." This building, he says, would at once become a center of neighborhood discussion and righteousness. There proposed laws would be threshed out by the communal Bryans and Hampdens. There recreant aldermen would be called sternly to account. There the uplift would be pumped up perennially. There the gentry and commonalty of the parish would meet on election night to witness in person the counting of the ballots.

Alas, for Dr. Macauley: I greatly fear that his Remedy must be ranked with all the other sweet perunas—the Initiative, the Referendum, the Recall, the Short Ballot, the City Manager, the Voting Machine, etc., etc. Let him go out in the world a bit and he will lose his faith in Sure Cures. There is, in fact, only one way to get good government, or even reasonably decent government, under a democracy, and that is to get rid of the democracy. The mob man is never going to be purged of his weaknesses by shortening or lengthening his ballot, or by giving him new clubs over legislators and judges, or by erecting fantastic temples to Demos on the corners now occupied so comfortably by seductive kaifs. Let those temples be ever so high, he would still steer clear of them when honest men sawed the air in them, and still pack them to the doors when their pulpits were held by mountebanks. He has, in fact, an incurable liking for such performers, and for the rogues who exploit and debauch him no less. It would give him no joy to see the corruptible put on incorruption; it would take away his hopes; he would see a career shut its doors to him. Nay, let us have done with this madness of trying to cure the evils of mob rule with more mob rule—of dosing the patient endlessly out of the very jug that brought him his horrendous snakes. The one way to get men of truth and honor into public office is to restrict the ballot to those citizens who know what truth and honor are. The cure for democracy is not more democracy, but a dashed sight less democracy. . . . Behold, I myself preach a peruna. I, too have a sovereign balm. Well, why not? I am an American, and hence a believer in perunas. Say what you will against me and mine, you must at least grant that I offer it free of charge—that I do not bellow for reform, as it were, with one lung and pant for a job with the other.

III

A kind lady in Syracuse, N. Y., favors me with the suggestion that these monthly discourses would be of more spiritual benefit to the extant illuminati and of greater delight to posterity if I gave over the reviewing of current books and devoted my space to the consideration of the higher and most lasting problems of literature. The notion intrigues me; it promises less work and a greater elbow-room. Nothing could be more fatiguing and dispiriting, indeed, than the business of reading such stuff as now commonly goes for beautiful letters in America. The passing fiction grows worse and worse, and the so-called serious books are marked more and more by a hollow platitudinousness. No decent biography has been printed in the United States for five years. Before the war, though the native novels were chiefly very bad, there were at least a few decent English reprints every month, but now all of the English novelists save one or two have gone to pot, and the current work of such men as Bennett and Wells is of more interest to the psychologist than to the critic. Why wade through such drivel? Why waste time reading it and writing about it when there are so many more appetizing fish to fry? The Syracuse blue-stocking asks the question, and I echo it as in duty bound. What is the pleasure of the sodality? Let me hear your voices, ladies and gentlemen. I shall be bound by the majority vote.

Many sapient and uplifting articles suggest themselves. For one thing, I'd like to do, some day before I am embalmed, a full-length dissertation upon "Huckleberry Finn," pointing out the qualities which rank it with "Don Quixote," "Tom Jones" and the comedies of Molière. For another thing, it would divert me to tell the whole truth (its first time in print) about the late August Strindberg, the Swedish Dowie. Again, I think I could amuse myself profitably with a treatise upon the stealings from Nietzsche in latter-day American literature, beginning with "The Strenuous Life." Yet again, there is the pleasant job of doing homage to George Ade, undoubtedly the greatest of American humorists next to Mark Twain. Yet again, a review of the American newspaper reviewers, with specimens of their handiwork, would probably startle the judicious. Yet again, there is room for a formal article on the poetry of Lizette Woodworth Reese, whose one sonnet, "Tears," is worth all the doggerel written by gifted Harvard boys since Vol. 1, No. 1, of the *Transcript*. Yet again, there is a scientific inquiry into the total absence of anything approaching a civilized literature south of the Potomac River. Yet again—but it would be easy to make a list a foot long. I slip in an article on the literature of the New Thought, and retire to the ante-chamber. Let the voice of the constituency be the voice of God.

The Creed of a Novelist

§1.

The similarity between the fundamental ideas of Joseph Conrad and those of Theodore Dreiser, so often exhibited to the public gape in this place, is made plain beyond all shadow of cavil by the appearance of Dreiser's "A Hoosier Holiday" (*Lane*), a volume of mingled reminiscence, observation, speculation and confession of faith. Put the book beside Conrad's "A Personal Record" (*Harper,* 1912), and you will find parallels from end to end. Or better still, put it beside Hugh Walpole's little volume, "Joseph Conrad" (*Nesbit*), in which the Conradean metaphysic is condensed from the novels even better than Conrad has done it himself: at once you will see how the two novelists, each a worker in the elemental emotions, each a rebel against the prevailing cocksureness and superficiality, each an alien to his place and time, touch each other in a hundred ways.

"Conrad," says Walpole (himself a very penetrating and competent novelist), "is of the firm and resolute conviction that life is too strong, too clever and too remorseless for the sons of men." And then, in amplification: "It is as though, from some high window, looking down, he were able to watch some shore, from whose security men were forever launching little cockleshell boats upon a limitless and angry sea . . . From his height he can follow their fortunes, their brave struggles, their fortitude to the very end. He admires that courage, the simplicity of that faith, but his irony springs from his knowledge of the inevitable end." . . . Substitute the name of Dreiser for that of Conrad, with "A Hoosier Holiday" as text, and you will have to change scarcely a word. Perhaps one, to wit, "clever." I suspect that Dreiser, writing so of his own creed, would be tempted to make it "stupid," or, at all events, "unintelligible." The struggle of man, as he sees it, is more than impotent; it is meaningless. There is, to his eye, no grand ingenuity, no skillful adaptation of means to end, no moral (or even dramatic) plan in the order of the universe. He can get out of it only a sense of profound and inexplicable *dis*order, of a seeking without a finding.

There is not only no neat programme of rewards and punishments; there is not even an understandable balance of causes and effects. The

Smart Set 50, No. 3 (November 1916): 212.

waves which batter the cockleshells change their direction at every instant. Their navigation is a vast adventure, but intolerably fortuitous
and inept—a voyage without chart, compass, sun or stars . . .

So at bottom. But to look into the blackness steadily, of course, is
almost beyond the endurance of man. In the very moment that its im-
penetrability is grasped the imagination begins attacking it with pale
beams of false light. All religions, I dare say, are thus projected from
the soul of man, and not only all religions, but also all great agnosti-
cisms. Nietzsche, shrinking from the horror of that abyss of negation,
revived the Pythagorean concept of *der ewigen Wiederkunft*—a vain and
blood-curdling sort of comfort. To it, after a while, he added explanations almost Christian—a whole repertoire of whys and wherefores,
aims and goals, aspirations and significations. Other seers have gone
back even further: the Transcendentalists stemmed from Zeno of Elea.
The late Mark Twain, in an unpublished work, toyed with a characteristically daring idea: that men are to some unimaginably vast and incomprehensible Being what the unicellular organisms of his body are
to man, and so on *ad infinitum*. Dreiser occasionally dallies with much
the same notion; he likens the endless reactions going on in the world
we know, the myriadal creation, collision and destruction of entities, to
the slow accumulation and organization of cells *in utero*. He would
make us specks in the insentient embryo of some gigantic Presence
whose form is still unimaginable and whose birth must wait for eons
and eons. Again, he turns to something not easily distinguishable from
philosophical idealism, whether out of Berkeley or Fichte it is hard to
make out—that is, he would interpret the whole phenomenon of life as
no more than an appearance, a nightmare of some unseen sleeper or of
men themselves, an "uncanny blur of nothingness"—in Euripides'
phrase, "a tale told by an idiot, dancing down the wind." Yet again, he
talks vaguely of the intricate polyphony of a cosmic orchestra, cacoph-
onous to our dull ears. Finally, he puts the observed into the ordered,
reading a purpose in the displayed event: "life was intended as a spectacle, it was intended to sting and hurt" . . . But these are only grop-
ings, and not to be read too critically. From speculations and
explanations he always returns, Conrad-like, to the bald fact: to "the
spectacle and stress of life." The bolder flights go with the puerile solu-
tions of current religion and morals. Even more than Conrad, he sees
life as a struggle in which man is not only doomed to defeat, but de-
nies any glimpse or understanding of his antagonist. His philosophy is
an agnosticism that has almost got beyond curiosity. What good
would it do us, he asks, to know? In our ignorance and helplessness,
we may at least get a slave's comfort out of cursing the gods. Suppose
we saw them striving blindly too, and pitied them?

§2.

The function of poetry, says F. C. Prescott, in "Poetry and Dreams" (a book so modest and yet so searching that it will be years before the solemn donkeys of the seminaries ever hear of it), is to conjure up for us a vivid picture of what we want, but cannot get. The desire is half of the story, but the inhibition is as plainly the other half, and of no less importance. It is this element that gives its glamour to tragedy; the mind seizes upon the image as a substitute for the reality, and the result is the psychical *katharsis* described by Aristotle. It is precisely by the same process that Dreiser and Conrad get a profound and melancholy poetry into their books. Floating above the bitter picture of what actually is, there is always the misty but inordinately charming picture of what might be or ought to be. Here we get a clue to the method of both men, and to the secret of their capacity for reaching the emotions. All of Conrad's brilliant and poignant creatures are dreamers who go to smash upon the rocks of human weakness and stupidity—Kurtz, Nostromo, Lord Jim, Almayer, Razumov, Heyst, even Whalley and M'Whirr. And so with Carrie Meeber, Jennie Gerhardt, Frank Cowperwood and Eugene Witla. They are not merely vivid and interesting figures; they are essentially tragic figures, and in their tragedy, despite its superficial sordidness, there is a deep and ghostly poetry. "My task," said Conrad once, "is, by the power of the printed word, to make you hear, to make you feel—it is, above all, to make you *see*." Comprehension, sympathy, pity—these are the things he seeks to evoke. And these, too, are the things that Dreiser seeks to evoke. The reader does not arise from such a book as "Sister Carrie" with a smirk of satisfaction, as he might from a novel by Howells or James; he leaves it infinitely touched . . .

Mr. Walpole, in his little book, is at pains to prove that Conrad is neither realist nor romanticist, but an intricate combination of both. The thesis scarcely needs support, or even statement: *all* imaginative writers of the higher ranks are both. Plain realism, as in the early Zola, simply wearies us by its futility; plain romance, if we ever get beyond youth, makes us laugh. It is their artistic combination, as in life itself, that fetches us the subtle projection of the muddle that is living against the orderliness that we reach out for—the eternal war of aspiration and experience—the combat of man and his destiny. As I say, this contrast lies at the bottom of all that is vital and significant in imaginative writing; to argue for it is to wade in platitudes. I speak of it here simply because the more stupid of Dreiser's critics—and what author has ever been hoofed by worse asses!—insist upon seeing him and denouncing him as a realist, and as a realist only. One of them, for example, has lately printed a long article maintaining that he is blind to the spiritual side of man altogether, and that he accounts for his characters solely by some incomprehensible "theory of animal behaviour." Could one imagine a more absurd mouthing of a phrase? One is almost staggered, indeed, by such critical imbecility, even in a college professor. The truth is, of course, that all of Dreiser's novels deal fundamentally with the endless conflict between this "animal behaviour" and the soarings of the spirit—between the destiny forced upon his characters by their environment, their groping instincts, their lack of courage and resourcefulness, and the destiny they picture for themselves in their dreams. This is the tragedy of Carrie Meeber and Jennie Gerhardt. The physical fact of their "seduction" (they are willing enough) blasts them doubly, for on the one hand it brings down upon them the conventional burden of the pariah, and on the other hand the worldly advancement which follows widens their aspiration beyond their inherent capacities, and so augments their unhappiness. It is the tragedy, too, of Cowperwood and Witla. To see these men as mere melodramatic Don Juans is to fall into an error almost unimaginably ridiculous. The salient fact about them, indeed, is that they are *not* mere Don Juans—that they are men in whom the highest idealism strives against the bonds of the flesh. Witla, passion-torn, goes down to disaster and despair. It is what remains of the wreck of his old ideals that floats him into peace at last. As for Cowperwood, we have yet to see his actual end—but how plainly its shadows are cast before! Life is beating him, and through his own weakness. There remains for him, as for Lord Jim, only the remnant of a dream.

§3.

With so much ignorant and misleading criticism of him going about, the appearance of "A Hoosier Holiday" should be of service to Dreiser's reputation, for it shows the man as he actually is, stripped of all the scarlet trappings hung upon him by horrified lady reviewers, male and female. The book, indeed, is amazingly naif. Slow in tempo, discursive, meditative, it covers a vast territory, and lingers in far fields. One finds in it an almost complete confession of faith, artistic, religious, even political. And not infrequently that confession comes in the form of somewhat disconcerting confidences—about the fortunes of the house of Dreiser, the dispersed Dreiser family, the old neighbors in Indiana, new friends made along the way. As readers of "A Traveller at Forty" are well aware, Dreiser knows little of reticence, and is no slave to prudery. In that earlier book he described the people he encountered exactly as he saw them, without forgetting a vanity or a wart. In

"A Hoosier Holiday" he goes even further: he speculates about them, prodding into the motives behind their acts, wondering what they would do in this or that situation, forcing them painfully into laboratory jars. They become, in the end, not unlike characters in a novel; one misses only the neatness of a plot. Strangely enough, the one personage of the chronicle who remains dim throughout is the artist, Franklin Booth, Dreiser's host and companion on the long motor ride from New York to Indiana, and the maker of the book's excellent pictures. One gets a brilliant etching of Booth's father, and scarcely less vivid portraits of Speed, the chauffeur; of various persons encountered on the way, and of friends and relatives dredged up out of the abyss of the past. But of Booth one learns little save that he is a Christian Scientist and a fine figure of a man. There must have been much talk during those two weeks of careening along the high-road, and Booth must have borne some part in it, but what he said is very meagrely reported, and so he is still somewhat vague at the end—a personality sensed, but scarcely apprehended.

However, it is Dreiser himself who is the chief character of the story, and who stands out from it most brilliantly. One sees in the man all the special marks of the novelist: his capacity for photographic and relentless observation, his insatiable curiosity, his keen zest in life as a spectacle, his comprehension of and sympathy for the poor striving of humble folks, his endless mulling of insoluble problems, his recurrent Philistinism, his impatience of restraints, his suspicion of messiahs, his passion for physical beauty, his relish for the gaudy drama of big cities, his incurable Americanism. The panorama that he enrolls runs the whole scale of the colors; it is a series of extraordinarily vivid pictures. The sombre gloom of the Pennsylvania hills, with Wilkes-Barré lying among them like a gem; the procession of little country towns, sleepy and a bit hoggish; the flash of Buffalo, Cleveland, Indianapolis; the gargantuan coal-pockets and ore-docks along the Erie shore; the tinsel summer resorts; the lush Indiana farm-lands, with their stodgy, bovine people—all of these things are sketched in simply, and yet almost magnificently. I know, indeed, of no book which better describes the American hinterland. Here we have no idle spying by a stranger, but a full-length representation by one who knows the thing he describes intimately, and is himself a part of it. Almost every mile of the road travelled has been Dreiser's own road in life. He knew those unkempt Indiana towns in boyhood; he wandered in the Indiana woods; he came to Toledo, Cleveland, Buffalo as a young man; all the roots of his existence are out there. And so he does his chronicle *con amore,* with many a sentimental dredging up of old memories, old hopes and old dreams.

Strangely enough, for all the literary efflorescence of the Middle West, such pictures of it are very rare. I know, in fact, of no other on the same scale. It is, in more than one way, the heart of America, and yet it has gone undescribed. Dreiser remedies that lack with all his characteristic laboriousness and painstaking. When he has done with them, those drowsy villages and oafish country towns have grown as real as the Chicago of "Sister Carrie" and "The Titan." One sees a land that blinks and naps in the sunshine like some great cow, udders full, the cud going—a land of Dutch fatness and contentment—a land, despite its riches, of almost unbelievable stupidity and immobility. We get a picture of a typical summer afternoon; mile after mile of farms, villages, little towns, the people sleepy and empty in mind, lolling on their verandas, killing time between trivial events, shut off from all the turmoil of the world. What, in the end, will come out of this over-fed, too happy region? Ideas? Rebellions? The spark to set off great wars? Or only the silence of decay? In Ohio industry has already invaded the farms; chimneys arise among the haystacks. And so farther west. But in Indiana there is a back-water, a sort of American Midi, a neutral ground in the battles of the nation. It has no art, no great industry, no dominating men. Its literature, in the main, is a feeble romanticism for flappers and fat women. Its politics is a skeptical opportunism. It is not stirred by great passions. It knows no heroes. . . . What will be the end of it? Which way is it heading?

§4

Save for passages in "The Titan," "A Hoosier Holiday" marks the high tide of Dreiser's writing—that is, as sheer writing. His old faults are in it, and plentifully. There are empty, brackish phrases enough, God knows—"high noon" among them. But for all that, there is an undeniable glow in it; it shows, in more than one place, an approach to style; the mere wholesaler of words has become, in some sense, a connoisseur, even a voluptuary. The picture of Wilkes-Barré girt in by her hills is simply done, and yet there is imagination in it and touches of brilliance. The sombre beauty of the Pennsylvania mountains is vividly transferred to the page. The towns by the wayside are differentiated, swiftly drawn, made to live. There are excellent sketches of people—a courtly hotelkeeper in some God-forsaken hamlet, his self-respect triumphing over his wallow; a group of babbling Civil War veterans, endlessly mouthing incomprehensible jests; the half-grown beaux and belles of the summer resorts, enchanted and yet a bit staggered by the awakening of sex; Booth *père* and his sinister politics; broken and forgotten men in the Indiana towns; policemen, waitresses, farmers, country characters; Dreiser's own people—the boys and girls of his youth; his brother Paul, the Indiana Schneckenburger and Francis Scott Key, author of "On the Banks of the Wabash"; his sisters and brothers; his beaten, hopeless, pious father; his brave and noble mother. The book is dedicated to this mother, now long dead, and in a way it is a memorial to her, a monument to affection. Life bore upon her cruelly; she knew poverty at its lowest ebb and despair at its bitterest; and yet there was in her a touch of fineness that never yielded, a gallant spirit that faced and fought things through. *Une ame grande dans un petit destin:* a great soul in a small destiny! One thinks, somehow, of the mother of Gounod. . . . Her son has not forgotten her. His book is her epitaph. He enters into her presence with love and with reverence and with something not far from awe. . . .

In sum, this record of a chance holiday is much more than a mere travel book, for it offers, and for the first time, a clear understanding of the fundamental faiths and ideas, and of the intellectual and spiritual background no less, of a man with whom the future historian of American literature will have to deal at no little length. Dreiser, as yet, has not come into his own. In England his true stature has begun to be recognized, and once the war is over I believe that he will be "discovered," as the phrase is, in Germany and Russia, and perhaps in France. But in his own country he is still denied and belabored in a manner that would be comic were it not so pathetically stupid. The college professors rail and snarl at him in the *Nation* and the *Dial;* the elderly virgins of the newspapers represent him as an iconoclast, an immoralist, an Anti-Christ, even a German spy; the professional moralists fatuously proceed to jail him because his Witlas and his Cowperwoods are not eunuchs—more absurdly still, because a few "God damns" are scattered through the 736 crowded pages of "The 'Genius.'" The Puritan fog still hangs over American letters; it is formally demanded that all literature be made with the girl of sixteen in mind, and that she be assumed to be quite ignorant of sex. And the orthodox teachers sing the hymn that is lined out. In Prof. Fred Lewis Pattee's "History of American Literature Since 1870" (*Century*), just published, there is no mention of Dreiser whatever! Such novelists as Owen Wister, Robert W. Chambers and Holman F. Day are mentioned as "leaders"; substantial notices are given to Capt. Charles King, Blanche Willis Howard and Julian Hawthorne; five whole pages are dedicated to F. Marion Crawford; even Richard Harding Davis, E. P. Roe and "Octave Thanet" are soberly estimated. But not a line about Dreiser! Not an incidental mention of him! One recalls Richardson's "American Literature," with its contemptuous dismissal of Mark Twain. A sapient band, these college professors!

But the joke, of course, is not on Dreiser, but on the professors themselves, and on the host of old maids, best-seller fanatics and ecstatic Puritans who support them. Time will bring the Indianan his revenge, and perhaps he will yield to humor and help time along. A Dreiser novel with a Puritan for its protagonist would be something to caress the soul—a full-length portrait of the Eternal Pharisee, a limning of the Chemically Pure, done scientifically, relentlessly, affectionately. Dreiser knows the animal from snout to tail. He could do a picture that would live. . . .

§5.

Of the novels that have reached me since our last session not many have beguiled me. With paper so costly and the thoughts of the people solicited by so many more important concerns, one might reasonably expect the publishers to scrutinize manuscripts with an extra-careful eye; but the truth is that, though the gross output of fiction is less than it was two years ago, the relative proportion of shoddy writing remains at its old mark. That is to say, nine out of ten of the new novels are without any merit or value whatever. Such a piece of trade goods, for example, as "The Pride of a Moment," by Carolyn Wells (*Doran*) is not only artificial and empty; it is downright tedious, and reading it is a hard business. "The Unspeakable Perk," by Samuel Hopkins Adams (*Houghton-Mifflin*), is almost as bad. In substance it is an attempt to get into one small volume the theatrical romance of Zenda, the sentimentality of Henry Sydnor Harrison, and the quasi-scientific quality of the same author's earlier book, "The Health Master." The result is nearly complete failure. The thing is so badly nailed together that it squeaks like a windjammer in a gale. Mr. Adams' successive difficulties with fiction should have convinced him long ago that the didactic novel is not for him. It is a pity that he does not go back to that unadorned exposition which, in "The Great American Fraud," he managed with such force and skill.

I pass over "Trail by Fire," by Richard Matthews Hallet (*Small-Maynard*); "Big Timber," by Bertrand W. Sinclair (*Little-Brown*); "The White Pearl," by Edith Barnard Delano and Samuel Field (*Duffield*); "Tish," by Mary Roberts Rinehart (*Houghton*); "Petty Simmons at Siwash," by George Fitch (*Little-Brown*); and "Ten Beautiful Years," by Mary Knight Potter (*Lippincott*)—the first three, conventional best-sellers, full of villains, bare-chested heroes, stolen gems, beautiful heroines, and all the other usual lumber; the last three collections of well-written but uninspired magazine stories. Nor can I find anything save an endless ingenuity in "The Red Stain," by Achmed Abdullah (*Fly*), an author capable of very much better writing, as readers of THE SMART SET well know. Nor in "Love in Youth," by Frank Harris (*Doran*), a romance very commonplace (almost, indeed, Williamsonian) in plan, though with oases of agreeable observation and speculation. One looks for originality in Mr. Harris, and automatically resents the descent to millionaire heroines and handsome chauffeurs. Perhaps the story is a brick heaved satirically at the compounders of department-store fiction. The late Frank Norris played that trick in "Blix." Deriding the sentimentality of his time, he had been accused of spurning sour grapes. His answer was "Blix," a tale as sentimental as the best of them, and an excellent piece of writing to boot. "Love in Youth" is also a good piece of writing, but its content is scarcely worthy its investiture.

"Three Sons and a Mother," by Gilbert Cannan (*Doran*); "The Family," by Elinor Mordaunt (*Lane*), and "The Prisoner," by Alice Brown (*Macmillan*), are marked by far more ambitious effort. They are, indeed, character studies on a rather large scale, and all of them show dignity of conception and care in the writing. Of the three, I have found "The Family" most interesting. It offers a picture of the gradual decay of an English provincial family, and has an air of assurance in it that somehow carries conviction. . . . "Magdalen," by J. S. Machar (*Kennerley*), is the first of a series of Slavic Translations to be made by Dr. Leo Wiener, of Harvard. The choice of this tale for the opening volume was unfortunate, for on the one hand it is written in a style that must inevitably strike the American reader as stilted, and on the other hand the life that it shows in a small Bohemian town is more Teutonic than Slavic. The Bohemians, indeed, have been Teutonized almost as effectively as the Wends, despite their sentimental glances toward the East. Dr. Řehák in the story, rising to denounce Austrian domination, can't do it without using German words: he pays a fine for the crime. What could be more German than Pilsner? Who hates a Croat, a Slovene, a Serbian, more than he hates an Austrian? Alas, for Bohemia, that charming land! . . .

Two novels remain, and by long odds the best of the boiling. Of "Casuals of the Sea," by William McFee (*Doubleday*), you have doubtless heard news; the daily papers have granted much space to it, and Huneker has given it two solid columns in the *Sun*. A disorderly and uneven story, and yet an astonishingly fresh and vivid one. As for me, I refuse to believe that it is the work of a sheer beginner. It is too sophisticated for that, too plentifully flavored with the tricks of the trade, too consciously clever. But all the same, it is plainly the work of one who has but lately got his stride; it has an air of newness; its people come from first-hand observation; there is a total absence of the marking time of the old novelist. I think you will like it. . . . The other book is

"Windy McPherson," by Sherwood Anderson (*Lane*), a first novel that holds out unmistakable promise. The figure of Sam McPherson, financier and romanticist, dominates it from the first page to the last; all the other characters, though some of them are very deftly drawn, are unimportant save as they react upon him. We follow him from his boyhood in a little Iowa town, overshadowed by the drunkenness and clownishness of his father, to his youth as a pushing young business man in Chicago, his maturity as a manipulator of men and money, and into the psychic break-up his middle age. As in Dreiser's "The Titan" the essential conflict of the drama is within the man himself. On the one hand there is his homeric energy, his determination to get on, the sheer clang and rattle of him, and on the other hand there is the groping sentimentality that beats him at the height of his success. He and his wife fall out almost absurdly: she can't have a child. But behind that bald fact one senses a dream that is grand and even noble, and it is the harsh awakening from it that shakes McPherson out of his world, and sets him adrift at forty, a waster, a drunkard and a chaser of chimeras. This catastrophe, it seems to me, is managed weakly. An air of unreality, even of improbability, gets into it. Nevertheless, one somehow picks up something of the author's own belief in it, and at bottom, I daresay, it is soundly enough imagined. Turn to Crile, and you will find much the same picture of the devastating effect of an accumulation of violent impressions and sensations, a too rapid gathering of experience. But whatever its fault here, the book at least lifts itself far out of the common rut. It is written forcefully, earnestly, almost passionately. There is the gusto of a true artist in it. I suspect that we shall hear much more about this Mr. Anderson.

The Omission

By Owen Hatteras

In the days of the Calif Abdul Hamid (related Scheherazade) there dwelt in Bagdad a man known to his neighbors as John Jones Ali. And the father of Jones kept a kahn for merchants, but to such a bourgeois vocation the son had no tendency. And this did not disappoint, but made proud rather his parent. When he would discover his progeny poring over some great folio he would swell with a tingling satisfaction, for the sons of his friends read not at all, or if they did, perused only obscene legends from the Arabian Nights.

John Jones learned many things as a youth and as he drew close to manhood a definite ideal shaped itself in his consciousness. But he never stated it to anyone and did not even whisper it to his father as the old kahn-keeper lay on his bed in death, but secretly he had determined to become the wisest man in the world. And having the means through his father's will undividedly to attend his ambition, he began first to study philosophy.

And he read Confucius and Laotse and the book of the Christians and of course the tomes of the teachings of Abu Hanifah and Al-Schafei. And coming from the Persian mystics to the Greeks, he devoured Pythagoras, Zenophanes, Heraclitus, Anaxagoras, Epictetus and Plato on Socrates. And after this he delved into Berkeley and Kant and Leibnitz and Hegel and Schopenhauer and Hume and Herbert Spencer and Haeckel and Bergson. And he even read some G. B. Shaw in a philosophic connection because he had once perused an article (by Shaw) setting forth the information that Shaw was a philosopher. And presently he knew everything about philosophy. But the thought assailed him, "I am an ignoramus in science."

So Jones began with zoology and he learned exhaustively concerning the protozoa, the metazoa, the coelenterata, the echinoderma, the arthropoda, et cetera. He went into bacteriology and imported agar-agar to stew into culture media and carried germs in tubes in his coat pocket to incubate them. Furthermore, he attacked the science of physics and committed to memory the laws of motion, heard of Pascal and saw a

Smart Set 50, No. 3 (November 1916): 212.

voltaic pile. From this he went to chemistry and the eighty odd elements and such names as sodiumparadimethylaminoazobenzenesulphonate. And presently he knew everything about science. But he mused, "In literature I am an ignoramus."

So Jones cast his energies upon the dramatists and it would be folly to attempt a summing up of the playwriters he read. So thorough was his study that to him the playwrights Augustus Thomas and Earl Derr Biggers were as familiar as William Shakespeare and Eschylus. And he read the novelists and did not omit "Pollyanna" or "Their Yesterdays." And following, the essayists and the poets and the miscellaneous writers. And . . .

But before he could learn any more—and he was beginning to wonder what there would remain to learn—the stocks which he held in the Bagdad Railway became worthless and he was left penniless. So in the course of two weeks, because from his erudition he had omitted one item, he starved to death.

He had forgotten to learn how to make a living.

Professors at the Bat

I

On page 41 of his treatise "On the Art of Writing" (*Putnam*), Sir Arthur Quiller-Couch, M.A., King Edward VII Professor of English Literature in Cambridge University, makes a thumping ass of himself—the best of all proofs, perhaps, of his professorial fitness and dignity—a devastating answer to those prudes who railed against the appointment of a second-rate novelist to so august a chair. "A professor of Greek," said Dr. Johnson, "is one who knows little Greek, and nothing else." The official pundits, God knows, show folly enough in their own gardens; when they cross the fence they debauch the fancy with the ferocity of their imbecilities. Here the professor of English literature takes a hack at pathology. Observe:

> I was waiting the other day, in a doctor's anteroom, and picked up one of those books—it was a work on pathology—so thoughtfully left lying in such places. . . . I found myself engaged in following the antics of certain bacilli generically described as "antibodies." I do not accuse the author (who seemed to be a learned man) of having invented the abominable term; apparently it passed current among physiologists and he had accepted it for honest coin. I found it, later on, in Webster's invaluable dictionary: Etymology, "body" (yours or mine), "anti," up against it; compound, "antibody," a noxious microbe.

I leave the joke to your own sapience. On second thoughts, I briefly explain it. It lies in good Sir Arthur's clownish assumption that "bacillus" and "antibody" are synonyms, that they mean the same thing. As a matter of fact, they mean two quite different things, for a bacillus is an alien (and usually hostile) invader of the organism, whereas an antibody is a substance formed in the blood to combat it, or, more precisely, to neutralize the toxins it so copiously spews forth. How the gifted sage managed to extract his preposterous etymology from Webster I can't imagine. Can it be that the last edition of old Noah actually defines an antibody as "a noxious microbe"? Nor can I imagine how so bald a howler passed unchallenged at Cambridge, where, in the midst of all the dons, there must surely be half a dozen educated men. Re-

Smart Set 50, No. 3 (November 1916): 280–86.

member, this infantile bosh was spouted from the rostrum at a public and well-attended lecture, that it was repeated a few weeks later at a second lecture, that both lectures were reported in the newspapers, that they caused no little discussion, that the author (see his preface) carefully revised the manuscript, that the ensuing book was printed last year in England, that the antibodies guff eluded all the reviewers, that it is now reprinted unchanged in the United States, and that this is the first (and will probably be the last) discovery of it! . . .

Do I make a mountain out of a molehill, fatuously seeking to air my own bacteriological parts? By no means. I select this curious imbecility as no more than a salient example of what the book shows in general. It is, indeed, a fine specimen of professorial criticism at its worst—donkeyishly pedantic, labored in style and often extremely shaky in its facts. There is, of course, the characteristic and inevitable hymning of a neglected genius—the oldest of all devices for getting a name for originality and learning. In this case the hero is Sir Thomas Wyat, lover of Anne Boleyn and chief contributor to Tottel's Miscellany (1557). That Wyat was a pioneer maker of English lyrics is known to every sophomore, but that he was a great poet it remained for Quiller-Couch to discover. Here is one of his songs, solemnly brought forward in proof:

> Is it possible?
> For to turn so oft;
> To bring that lowest that was most aloft:
> And to fall highest, yet to light soft?
>   Is it possible?
>
> All is possible!
> Whoso list believe;
> Trust therefore first, and after preve;
> As men wed ladies by license and leave,
>   All is possible!

This masterpiece is cited, not only to demonstrate Wyat's genius, but to help prove the sagacious knight's main thesis in his book, to wit, that English literature is not Anglo-Saxon in origin, but Latin. From end to end he harps upon it, and from end to end all he manages to show is that English literature, like all other European literature, was given a tremendous impetus by the Renaissance. When he argues that English poetry, as we know it today, stems clearly from the Italian through Wyat and the other Sixteenth Century imitators of Petrarch, he throws overboard the whole of early English balladry, and reads such men as Blake, Kipling, Rossetti, Masefield and even Tennyson out of meeting as English poets. The dangers of riding a hobby could be made no plainer. His eye on mere forms, Quiller-Couch seems to forget spirit almost entirely—and now and then he even gets befogged as to forms. By the very same process of reasoning one might make a Latin of Klopstock, whose "Der Messias" was an imitation of Milton, who imitated Dante. It would be quite easy, indeed, to prove by the Cambridge doctor's syllogisms that German literature is not Germanic but Latin. His entire argument is fanciful and tortured. If that sort of criticism passes for profound at Cambridge, then it is no wonder that Cambridge did not establish a chair of English literature until 1910.

In his manner, as in his matter, Quiller-Couch is strained and un-convincing. Plentifully begauded a book professedly devoted to the teaching of English composition one comes upon such specimens of high-school preciosity as this:

> Bethink you how deeply Rome engraved itself on this island and its features. Bethink you that, as human nature is, no conquering race ever lived or could live—even in garrison—among a tributary one without begetting children on it. Bethink you yet further of Free-man's admission that in the wholesale (and quite hypothetical) gen-eral massacre, "the women doubtless would be largely spared." . . .

And so on, and so on. A book of unconscious humor all compact. A book whose substance, more than once, reduces its title to a charm-ing absurdity. . . .

Another denizen of the academic shades, Prof. Fred Lewis Pattee, comes forward with a work of much more sense, but still one that ex-hibits a professor's habits of mind. It is called "A History of American Literature Since 1870" (*Century*), and it runs to nearly 500 pages of small print. What Prof. Pattee says of the authors he discusses is often perfectly sound and true, and sometimes it is original and penetrating, but in choosing candidates for discussion he follows schoolroom ideas of importance very closely, and so his work, despite a certain inde-pendence of judgment, is conventional and lopsided as criticism. He suggests a man making very creditable music on a fiddle defectively tuned. It is not the literature in being that most interests him, but that literature which is no more than a pale imitation of old artificialities, a thing of inane respectabilities—for example, the essays of Agnes Rep-plier and Paul Elmer More, the fiction of the New England spinster school. He gives several chapters to the poets, and pronounces verdicts upon such modest ones as Maurice Francis Egan and Ina Donna Cool-brith—and then forgets Lizette Woodworth Reese altogether! He mentions E. S. Martin with respect and credits Brander Matthews with adding a "brilliant chapter to the sum of American criticism"—but the name of W. C. Brownell is not in his index! He has a word for Hamilton Wright Mabie, and another for Jeannette L. Gilder—but not one for James Huneker! He gives five whole pages to F. Marion Crawford, and many more to the dialect mongers, male and female, of the 90's—and then passes over Dreiser without a line!

True enough, there is an excuse for some of these omissions in his preface. He says that he confines himself to "those authors who did their first distinctive work before 1892." But he is constantly breaking through that rule. Frank Norris' "McTeague" was not published until 1899. If it is worth discussing—and it undoubtedly is—then why isn't "Sister Carrie," which came less than a year later, worth discussing also? If Richard Harding Davis is fit meat for a solemn judgment, then what of Edith Wharton? If Owen Wister, Alice Hegan Rice and Robert W. Chambers are seriously to be listed among American novelists, then why not Mrs. Watts? . . . But let us not press the professor with too many such questions. After all, he was free to make his book as he pleased. You will find in it, in the midst of many timorous ifs and buts, some excellent valuations of such men as Howells, Lafcadio Hearn and Bret Harte. And you will find in it, too, some curious outbursts of college town smugness and nonsense—for example, in the pages on Frank Norris, with their characteristic confusion of representative art and moral purpose. . . . Altogether, a very creditable volume—for a professor. It lacks anything approaching true force; it shows no understanding whatever of the streams of national literature that now run; it is, in general, pallid and scholastic; but it at least shows a certain fluency and ingenuity within its limits, and it is not ill written.

II

In various other solemn tomes of the month one encounters strange and savoury doctrines. For example, in "The Truth About the Bible," by Sidney C. Tapp (*Pub. by the author*), there is the doctrine that all the horrors of life are due to sex, and that any man who favors a pretty girl with a kiss is risking hell. I am old enough, alas, to begin reading such books, but not yet old enough to begin believing them. . . . In "From Doomsday to Kingdom Come" (*Small-Maynard*), Seymour Deming imitates Gerald Stanley Lee in style and Major-General Roosevelt in the voracity of his appetite for perunas. He has a ready gullet, it would seem, for all of them, from prohibition to vice crusading and from mothers' pensions to the initiative and referendum—for all, that is, save preparedness. For this saving grace much thanks. I have observed the militia at their exercises and begin to lose stomach for world conquest. . . . In "Ventures in Worlds," by Marian Cox (*Kennerley*), we are made privy to the news that Germany has been ruined by music. Fleeing from Europe when the war broke out, the author met Siegfried Wagner at Bayreuth, and found him drinking beer and eating white radishes. His conversation staggered her. "Since then," she says, "I have placed the musicians, the militarists and the millionaires all together as the makers of our modern predatory civilization." In another essay she argues against modern marriage on the ground that it forces man and wife to live together, and so takes the edge off their romance. They become, in fact, like fellow-boarders or partners in business, even like brother and sister, and thus their marriage grows incestuous. I use the fair essayist's own word. She is lavish with her parts of speech and even more so with her heresies. A book to bounce you a bit. A headlong rush of ideas, some of them amusing. Tempo: *Vivacissimo con fuoco.*

III

The novels of the month show the usual badness. The best of them, "These Lynnekers," by J. D. Beresford (*Doran*), is immeasurably below the same author's "Early History of Jacob Stahl." The Lynnekers of the title are a provincial English family, respectable in blood and proud of the fact, and the tale concerns their fortunes during a period of twenty or more years. The father, cure of a stupid parish on the outskirts of a cathedral city, passes through the agonies of genteel indigence into the serenity of a somewhat empty old age, with a gallant death, albeit in bed, to glorify him in the end. The eldest son marries a fat girl of means and influence, and settles down as a minor canon. The second son contracts an alliance with a dubious widow considerably his senior. One of the daughters runs off with a neighboring carpenter, vastly scandalizing her snobbish brothers. The other daughter falls into acrid spinsterhood, consecrating herself to suspicion. The mother, after a financial transaction as questionable as Nora Helmer's, takes refuge in an amiable imbecility. There remains the youngest son, Richard, an odd one, what the biologists call a sport. Floored by Greek at school, he goes into a bank, attracts the attention of a City magnate, retires with a competence at twenty-seven, resists a bishop's efforts to make a parson of him, dallies with agnosticism in its milder forms, and passes from the scene as an amateur astronomer. This Richard is the central figure of the chronicle, and should be the most vivid of them all. Unluckily, Mr. Beresford makes him precisely the least vivid. One wonders, at the end, why so many persons of importance—*e. g.*, a rich cousin, the City magnate and the bishop—

should have been attracted to him so strongly, and aroused to such interest in the state of his fortunes and soul. We hear that they found
him remarkable but we never find out why, As he is presented to us he
never rises above a commonplace sort of cleverness; surely nothing that
he ever actually says or does is of the slightest distinction. Even in detail Mr. Beresford contrives to make him incredible. For example, we
are asked to believe (page 385) that after five years in the City of London he hasn't "got either a tail coat or a pot hat in the world." What
nonsense is this? Has anarchy descended upon Threadneedle street?
Have London financiers turned Goths and Huns? . . . Altogether, a
third-rate novel, though by a novelist at the threshold of the first class.
The war has played the devil with Britain's fictioneers. Not a single
book worth talking about has come from them in two years. Wells,
Bennett, Locke, Walpole, Chesterton, Snaith, Merrick, George, Kipling, Beerbohm, Moore, Galsworthy—one and all they show the strain.
Even Conrad seems to be marking time.

The native novels are chiefly machine-made. "The Heritage of the
Sioux," by B. M. Bower (*Little-Brown*), is the usual slap-stick melo-
drama of the cow country. "Cap'n Gid," by Elizabeth Lincoln Gould
(*Penn*), is a boarding-house comedy. "Clover and Blue Grass," by Eliza
Calvert Hall (*Little-Brown*), is a book of Kentucky short stories, partly
in dialect, by an author cursed by the praise of General Roosevelt.
"The Girl at Big Loon Post," by George Van Schaick (*Little-Brown*), is
another of the endless romances of the Hudson Bay country, with the
inevitable brave Englishman and the inevitable dusky heroine. "Chloe
Malone," by Fannie Heaslip Lea (*Little-Brown*), is a Southern love story of the school of Henry Sydnor Harrison. The rest I spare you,
jumping swiftly to "The Hausfrau Rampant" (*Doran*), for which E. V.
Lucas, the maker of anthologies, stands sponsor. The book is made up
of translated selections from Dr. Julius Stinde's series of German comic
sketches, "Die Familie Buchholz," a work as familiar and as popular in
Germany as the tales of Bret Harte and O. Henry used to be in this
country. It by no means belongs to the grand literature of Kaiserdom;
it is not mentioned in Friedrich Kummer's "Deutsche Literaturges-
chichte des neunzehnten Jahrhunderts," nor in the last edition of
Gotthold Klee. But all the same there is some capital buffoonery in it,
and I have snickered over Frau Buchholz since the days of my earliest
struggles with the almost-impossible-to-learn-and-never-to-be-
sufficiently-dashed German language. Mr. Lucas has got a good deal of
this effective if somewhat behemothian humor into his book, though
the effort to boil down four volumes to one naturally leads him into
occasional snares, and every devotee of the original will probably seek
in vain for some favorite scene. It is curious how little the excellent

comic writing of Germany is known in England and America. We hear far too much about Treitschke, Eucken and other such owls, and far too little about such merry fellows as Otto Julius Bierbaum, Ludwig Thoma and Roda-Roda. Most of these literary scaramouches have revolved around Munich, and kept their arteries filled with its incomparable brews; its comic papers, enriched by their work, make *Life, Puck* and the rest of our barber-shop weeklies seem poor indeed. The dozen or more volumes of Bierbaum offer a rich mine to any translator who will explore them. His "Irrgarten der Liebe" (which had sold 50,000 copies at the time of his death in 1910) contains some of the best humorous verse I have ever encountered, and his prose tales and travel sketches are full of excellent stuff. The late Percival Pollard, whose "Masks and Minstrels of New Germany" (*Luce*) gives a good account of all these wags, formed the plan of translating the whole of the "Irrgarten," and employed me as a hack poet to help him. We had done no more than a dozen of the poems when Pollard's sudden death put an end to the enterprise. I nominate Louis Untermeyer and Franklin P. Adams as executors and assigns. They could do the job to perfection.

There remains "The Woman Gives," by Owen Johnson (*Little-Brown*), in which the old theme of redemption by woman's love appears in a Bohemian setting. The hero, Daniel Garford, is so floored by the discovery of his wife's infidelity that he changes his name to Dangerfield and takes to *vin rouge*. From this wallow he is dragged by the devotion of Inga Sonderson, a girl with black hair and a face as brown as an Indian's, and in the end he gets upon his legs again and becomes a famous artist. Inga, however, marries another man. The rest of the characters of the tale are rather conventional caricatures of the sort of jitney geniuses one meets in Greenwich Village, with a rough diamond, a mysterious Frenchman and other old friends added. These persons show little vitality; their stereotyped cavortings in the first half dozen chapters grow heavy and wearisome. The latter half of the story, in which Dangerfield and Inga come to grips, is vastly better written. It shows, indeed, some of the fine skill which Mr. Johnson got into his Lawrenceville stories—now almost put out of memory by his successive boob-shockers and best-sellers. One sheds a banal but none the less sincere tear upon the swift vulgarization of so many young writers of sound promise. Robert W. Chambers is the archetype of them; all his gaudy novels, stacked sky-high in the department stores between the talcum and the corset-coven, are not worth one of his early short stories. The cheap magazines snare them with gigantic offers, the book publishers merchant their work like soap, and that is the end of them.

IV

Of the books that remain, "The Book of the Dance," by Arnold Genthe (*Kennerley*), is the most intriguing, for it contains but a page and a quarter of text, and thus gives a holiday to my eyes. Nay, more than a holiday: a sweet massage—for its pages are filled with Mr. Genthe's. excellent photographs of dancers, and some of them are very charming damsels. Genuine action often appears in these pictures; the photographer has transfixed movement without losing it. Among the performers employed as models are Maud Allan, Isadora Duncan, Loie Fuller, Anna Pavlowa, Ruth St. Denis and Lady Constance Stewart-Richardson, the last-named rolling her eyes to the limit of physiological oscillation. A few of the ladies, their names politely withheld, appear in a state of virgin innocence. No doubt a special edition for the helplessly concupiscent will appear later, with every leg in an overall and the star-spangled banner draped around every middle. This is a chemically pure republic; the moral must be protected from their blushful imaginings.

Two other books, "The Memoirs of a Physician," by Vikenty Veressayev (*Knopf*), and "Impressions and Opinions," by Havelock Ellis (*Houghton-Mifflin*), I reserve for more extended notice later on. Dr. Ellis, in particular, deserves a whole article. He is a man of extraordinary industry, originality and versatility, and his five or six volumes upon the psychology of sex are the first in the English language to treat the vexed subject with resolute courage and comprehensive learning. It goes without saying that these books are under the ban of the professional pornophobes; they expose too mercilessly the pious nonsense of the current "sex hygiene" literature to go without challenge; every now and then some bookseller is jailed for keeping them in stock. But Dr. Ellis is by no means a narrow specialist. His volume on Spain is a delightful piece of writing; his study of dreams is as searching as the work of Freud; in addition he has edited two such widely different series of books as the Mermaid Series of old English dramatists and the Contemporary Science Series—each absolutely the best in its own field. His present volume is made up of extracts from his private daybook, and the variety of its contents shows the intellectual scope of the man. We are here introduced, indeed, to the rich stores of one of the first intelligences of England; I hope to describe some of its achievements on a future day.

Three books of plays—"The Locust Flower and The Celibate," by Pauline Brooks Quinton (*Sherman-French*); "Duty and Other Irish Comedies," by Seaumas O'Brien (*Little-Brown*), and "The Poor Little Rich Girl," by Eleanor Gates (*Arrow*). The last-named you have probably seen in the theatre; it was a great success a season or two ago. In book-form it is preceded by a foreword by my brother in the sacred sciences, George Jean Nathan, who says of it, and quite accurately, that it is "at once a work of genuine fancy and sound art." (The rest of the learned gentleman's remarks are by no means clear. Some of his snarls of speech, indeed, leave me quite squeezed. For example, ". . . the quality of fanciful imagination is of the catalogue no (or at best, small) part." Again:

> As against the not unhollow symbolic strut and gasconade of such over-paeaned pieces as, let us for example say, "The Blue Bird" of Maeterlinck, so simple and unaffected a bit of stage writing as this—of school dramatic intrinsically the same—cajoles the more honest heart and satisfies more plausibly and fully those of us whose thumbs are ever being pulled professionally for a native stage less smeared with the snobberies of empty, albeit high-sounding, nomenclatures from overseas.

Our old *bierbruder,* the Henry James complex. I turn to the date of this inextricable fugue, and the mystery vanishes. It appears as February 8, 1916. On the evening of February 7, 1916, beginning at 11 P. M., Allah Council, No. 7, of the Knights of St. Stanislaus, held its annual oyster roast at the Café des Bozart. . . . Nevertheless, it would pay my eminent colleague, after cannibalism upon his own compositions, to pursue his reading seven pages further. "Follow the judicious," says K'ung Fû-tze, "and learn to be like them." . . . The other playbooks interest me less. In Miss Quinton's two pieces there is much preciosity and straining for effect. The Irish comedies of Mr. O'Brien are in the manner of Lady Gregory's, and two of them, "Duty" and "Jurisprudence" are well done. In the latter, by the way, Mr. O'Brien makes bold use (page 44) of a word still waiting in the ante-room of polite English, to wit, *alright.* This word seems to be struggling hard to get in; I encounter it constantly in manuscripts, and one of the leading American novelists is very fond of it, though his publisher's proofreaders keep it out of his books. Will it become respectable? The analogy of *already,* which was two words, *al* and *redy* in Middle English, indicates that it will. As for me, however, I still sniff at it. It strikes me as clumsy, uncouth, too grossly New Yorkish. It carries with it something of the vague unpleasantness of *tho, thru* and the other one-legged abominations of the Simplified Spelling Board. It is a word for persons who have nothing to say, and who wish to say it as economically as possible. It is a harsh word, a mongrel word, a word without a soul. Let it be damned.

V

My report, in the September number, of a petition received from a fair reader in Syracuse, N. Y., to the effect that I give over the reviewing of current books, chiefly bad, and devote my space to literary essays of a more general and lofty character—this report has brought me many letters from estimable constituents, and their voice, in overwhelming majority, is in support of the Syracusan. The plan accords with my secret yearnings; I presented it, in fact, in an ingratiating manner; I shall adopt it as soon as the books now on my wharves are worked off. This will be about January 1, and the first monograph under the new dispensation will be printed in the March number. The subject I reserve *in petto*. But it will have its roost, you may be sure, in the higher strata of beautiful letters, and its discussion will make for virtue and enlightenment at the domestic hearth.

Let this be sufficient warning to the publishers that I shall not consider myself bound, after January 1, to review the books they send to me. I may add a few brief notices to my discourse each month, but then again I may not. This "sufficient warning," of course, will never reach the Barabbases; no self-respecting publisher ever reads reviews; the business of clipping them and filing them, like that of distributing review copies, is intrusted to the janitor. Three times during the past year I have given formal notice that I do not review war books—that each new one reaching me goes into my hell-box unopened. In the August number I rehearsed this notice at great length. Also, I ventured the prophecy that no publisher would read it, and that I would receive at least thirty war books during the thirty days following its publication. The actual number was twenty-eight. My ashman, an intelligent Belgian refugee, has read them all. He reports that they have made him pro-German.

VI

Next month, *Deo volente,* a session with the poets. In the past I have dedicated the month of May to them, but this year they are too numerous and pressing to be put off. The output of poetry, indeed, seems to be augmented rather than decreased by the war. All other tribes of authors are a bit chastened, but the minnesingers whoop and burble as never before. Let us, then, spit on our hands and make ready for them.

Chanson d'Amour à la Carte

By Owen Hatteras

My love is like a chocolate *soufflée,* delicate, sweet, soft, pure, an enchantment to the eye.

Her cheeks have the caressing tenderness of a well-cooked *ris de veau braisé Jardinière.*

She has at once the ethereal charm of *Gervais crême* and the solid goodness of *jambon grillé aux oeufs.*

When she is sad I see in her eyes the vasty, melancholious depth of *legierte Geflügelkleinsuppe.*

When she smiles the heavens rain *potage de volaille Camerani.*

I love this sweet and succulent wench. She reminds me of *crême Bavaroise aux fraises.* Of *champignons madère.* She has the reserve and aloofness of a *salade de concombres* and the glorious warmth of *Rinderbrust mit Meerrettich.*

I esteem her greatly. I almost prefer her to a *pilau* of lamb *à la Turque.*

Smart Set 50, No. 4 (December 1916): 128.

The Literary Shambles

§1

The strained and tedious manner of "The Magazine in America," by Prof. Algernon Tassin, of Columbia University (*Dodd-Mead*), is almost enough to conceal the interest of its matter—almost, but fortunately not quite. The learned pundit writes with all the dullness of his flatulent order, and, as usual, he is most horribly dull when he is trying most kittenishly to be lively. I spare you examples of his writing; if you know the lady essayists of the United States, and their academic imitators in pantaloons, you know the sort of arch and whimsical stuff he ladles out. But, as I have hinted, there is something worth attending to in his story, for all the defects of its presentation, and so his book is not to be sniffed at. He has, at all events, brought together a vast mass of scattered and concealed facts, and arranged them conveniently for whoever deals with them next. The job was plainly a long and laborious one, and rasping to the higher cerebral centers. The professor had to make his mole-like way through the endless files of old and stupid magazines; he had to read the insipid biographies and autobiographies of dead and forgotten editors, many of them college professors, preachers out of work, prehistoric uplifters and bad poets; he had to sort out the facts from the fancies of such incurable liars as Griswold and Poe; he had to hack and blast a path across a virgin wilderness. The thing was worth doing, and, as I say, it has been done with commendable pertinacity.

It is astounding, considering the noisiness and nosiness of the American magazines today, to glance back at the timorous and bloodless quality of their progenitors. All of the early ones, when they were not simply monthly newspapers or almanacs, were depressingly "literary" in tone, and dealt chiefly in stupid poetry, silly essays and artificial fiction. The one great fear of their editors seems to have been that of offending someone; all of the pioneer prospectuses were full of assurances that nothing would be printed which even "the most fastidious" could object to. Literature, in those days, was almost completely cut off from life. It mirrored, not the struggle for existence, so fierce and dramatic in the new republic, but the flaccid reflections of feeble poet-

Smart Set 50, No. 4 (December 1916): 138–44.

asters, self-advertising clergymen, sissified "gentlemen of taste," and other such donkeys. Poe waded into these *literati* and shook them up a bit, but even after the Civil War the majority of them continued to spin pretty cobwebs. Edmund Clarence Stedman and Donald G. Mitchell were excellent specimens of the clan; a lone survivor is to be found in William Winter. The "literature" manufactured by these tear-squeezers, though often enough produced in beer cellars, was frankly aimed at the Young Person. Its main purpose was to avoid giving offense; it breathed an empty and idiotic piety, a snug niceness, a sickening sweetness. It is as dead today as Baalam's ass.

The *Atlantic Monthly* was set up by men in revolt against this reign of mush, as *Putnam's* had been a few years before, but the business of reform proved to be difficult and hazardous, and it was a long while before a healthier breed of authors could be developed, and a public for them found. "There is not much in the *Atlantic*," wrote Charles Eliot Norton to Lowell in 1874, "that is likely to be read twice save by its writers, and this is what the great public likes . . . You should hear Godkin express himself in private on this topic." *Harper's Magazine,* in those days, was made up almost wholly of cribbings from England; the *North American Review* had sunk into stodginess and imbecility; *Putnam's* was dead, or dying; the *Atlantic* had yet to discover Mark Twain; it was the era of *Godey's Lady's Book.* The new note, so long awaited, was struck at last by *Scribner's,* now the *Century* (and not to be confused with the *Scribner's* of today). It not only threw all the old traditions overboard; it established new traditions almost at once. For the first time a great magazine began to take notice of the daily life of the American people. It started off with a truly remarkable series of articles on the war; it plunged into contemporary politics; it eagerly sought out and encouraged new writers; it began printing decent pictures instead of the old chromos; it forced itself, by the sheer originality and enterprise of its editing, upon the public attention. American literature owes more to the *Century* than to any other magazine, and perhaps American thinking owes almost as much. It was the first "literary" periodical to arrest and interest the really first-class men of the country. It beat the *Atlantic* because it wasn't burdened with the *Atlantic's* decaying cargo of Boston Brahmins. It beat all the others because it was infinitely and obviously better. Almost everything that is good in the American magazine of today, almost everything that sets it above the English magazine or the Continental magazine, stems from the *Century.*

At the moment, of course, it suffers a sort of eclipse, and the newspapers but recently reported its owners as at odds. The thing that injured it was mainly the yellow magazine of the *McClure's* type—a variety of magazine which surpassed it in the race for circulation by exaggerating and vulgarizing all its merits. Dr. Tassin seems to think, with William Archer, that S. S. McClure was the inventor of this type, but the truth is that its real father was the unknown originator of the Sunday supplement. What Dr. McClure did was to apply the sensational methods of the cheap newspaper to a new and cheap magazine. Yellow journalism was rising and he went in on the tide. Hearst was getting on his legs at the same time, and I daresay that the muck-raking magazines, even in their palmy days, followed him a good deal more than they led him. McClure and the imitators of McClure borrowed his adept thumping of the tom-tom; Munsey and the imitators of Munsey borrowed his mush. *McClure's* and *Everybody's,* even when they had the whole nation by the ears, did little save repeat in solemn, awful tones what Hearst had said before. As for *Munsey's* at the height of its circulation, it was little more than a Sunday "magazine section" on smooth paper, and with somewhat clearer half-tones than Hearst could print. Nearly all the genuinely original ideas of these magazine Napoleons of yesteryear turned out badly. John Brisben Walker, with the *Cosmopolitan,* tried to make his magazine a sort of national university, and it went to pot. Ridgway, of *Everybody's,* planned a weekly to be published in a dozen cities simultaneously, and lost a fortune trying to establish it. McClure, facing a situation to be described presently, couldn't manage it, and his magazine got away from him. As for Munsey, there are many wrecks behind him; he is forever experimenting boldly and failing gloriously. Even his claim to have invented the all-fiction magazine is open to caveat; there were probably plenty of such things, in substance if not in name, before the *Argosy*. Hearst, the teacher of them all, now openly holds the place that belongs to him. He has galvanized the corpse of the old *Cosmopolitan* into a gigantic success, he has distanced all rivals with *Hearst's,* he has beaten the English on their own ground with *Nash's,* and he has rehabilitated various lesser magazines. More, he has forced the other magazine publishers to imitate him. A glance at *McClure's* today offers all the proof that is needed of his influence.

Dr. Tassin halts his story at its most interesting point, for he says nothing of what has gone on since 1900—and very much has gone on since 1900. For one thing, the *Ladies' Home Journal* has seen the rise of a swarm of imitators, many of them very prosperous. For another thing, the all-fiction magazine of Munsey *et al.* has degenerated into so gaudy a confection that Munsey must blush every time he thinks of it. And for a third thing, the muckrake magazine has blown up, and is no more. Why this last? Have all the likely candidates been muckraked? Is there no longer a taste for scandal in the vulgar? I have heard endless discussion of these questions and many ingenious answers, but all of them fail to answer. In this emergency I offer one not hitherto put forward. It is this: that the muckrake magazines came to grief, not because the public tired of muckraking, but because muckraking succeeded. That is to say, the villains so long belabored by the Steffenses, the Tarbells and the Phillipses were eventually all deprived of their old power, and in their places sweet and virtuous reformers were set up. The muckrake magazines, having bellowed for the setting up of these reformers, were now compelled to praise and anoint them—and the public straightway lost interest in the matter. And why? Simply because the public always gags at praise. What it wants is denunciation. It delights in scandal, cannonading, whooping, a good show. It chortled and read on when Aldrich, Boss Cox, John D. Rockefeller and the other bugaboos of the muckrakers were being beaten to death; it promptly sickened when Ben B. Lindsey, Jane Addams and the rest of the brummagem saints began to be hymned. This, I believe, is the true cause of the decay of the muckraking magazines; it was not that they muckraked too long, but that they stopped muckraking altogether. Hearst has never fallen into any such error; he takes on a new bugaboo the moment an old one grows wobbly; he never commits the folly of praising anyone, save perhaps himself. It astonishes me that he has never embraced the opportunity so plainly before him. Why doesn't he start a magazine devoted to muckraking the muckrakers?

§2

Condensation is carried to such a fine point in "The Creative Will," by Willard Huntington Wright (*Lane*), that the reader long accustomed to the stuffed and flabby books of commerce will probably find it as strange a fare as caffeine C.P. or ninety-eight per cent. alcohol. A whole æsthetic theory is here reduced to 251 paragraphs, and some of them are so short that they are little more than apothegms. But for all that relentless conciseness, the ideas of the author are stated with the utmost clarity, and many of them are ideas which penetrate to the heart of a much-belabored and very difficult subject. It will be curious to see what the orthodox art critics make of the volume. In it all of their pretty generalities and sentimentalities are thrown overboard, and an effort is made to set up standards of beauty that are, to some extent at least, scientific and exact. Here and there the very sweep of theory is apt to knock the reader off his feet, and make him reach out desperately for the criteria demolished, but on the whole it must be granted that Mr. Wright establishes his notions with excellent plausibility and address, and that his work rises immeasurably above the feeble, impressionistic twaddle that passes for art criticism in the United States. He may be wrong in details, but he is headed the right way, and the amount of hard and original thinking that he has got into this small volume is really quite amazing. There is material in it, given the usual style of wordy writing, for a dozen books of its size.

Readers of the author's former work, "Modern Painting" (*Lane*), know the general direction of his ideas in the matter of the graphic arts. It is his contention, in brief, that the programme in painting or sculpture is just as false and befogging a thing as the programme in music, and that its seductions are responsible for most of the confusion which reigns in æsthetic discussion. Practically the whole of contemporary art criticism is corrupted by this pre-occupation with non-æsthetic significances. Such a picture as Millet's "The Angelus," for example, is commonly estimated, not by the æsthetic reactions it awakens, but by the sentimental emotions it evokes. It is pretty, it is pious, it is sweet, it is affecting. Saying so much, its admirers think that they have also said that it is a great work of art. But the truth is that a work of art must stand or fall by quite different standards, which have nothing whatever to do with sweetness, or piety, or mere prettiness. It may be, in fact, quite devoid of any representative meaning or associative suggestion, and still make a powerful appeal to the sense of beauty. And it may, on the contrary, arouse the emotions like a bugle call, and yet be as inconsiderable æsthetically as the wallpaper in a hotel room. In music it is easier to find examples than in painting, for music has been better emancipated from mere illustration than any other art, despite the continued existence of the slum area of opera. Brahms' Fourth Symphony has no sentimental significance; it is empty of all piety, patriotism and amour; it represents no object or idea; it symbolizes no recognizable emotion. And yet, as everyone knows, it is a superb work of art, and its appeal to the æsthetic centers is almost overpowering. Contrariwise, Sibelius' "Finlandia" awakens the emotions like a call to arms. In it there is revolt, heroism, the cry of an oppressed people; it stirs the heart as effectively as Schubert's "Ständchen" caresses the lachrymal glands. And yet, at bottom, it is a cheap and insignificant piece of work, without either novelty in design or ingenuity in execution. It belongs, in brief, to that debased and sentimentalized order of art of which "The Angelus" is a prime example, just as Brahms' symphony belongs to that pure and noble order of which Michelangelo's "Slave" is a prime example.

But if a work of art is not to be judged by its emotional or intellectual content, then what standards are we to apply to it? It is Mr. Wright's business in his book to answer this question, and he has carried the condensation of his answer to such a point that it would be folly to try to condense it further. He begins by describing the elements of æsthetic response as they appear in bodily movements and impulses, and he proceeds to show how these movements and impulses tend to fall into rhythms, and how these rhythms are synchronized into complex and yet coherent designs. First setting forth the nature and effect of such simple one-dimensional designs as the unaccompanied melody and of such two-dimensional designs as the flat drawing, he enters upon a detailed discussion of those larger forms which occupy three dimensions, and of the arrangement and inter-relations of their parts. As I say, it would be impossible to summarize this discussion clearly. Disdaining superficialities, it strikes down into the very heart of the æsthetic problem. It is painting, of course, that chiefly interests the author. His most original and convincing contributions are to the question of composition on flat surfaces, sad to that of color, particularly as a means of overcoming the flatness. But he draws upon all the arts to reinforce his arguments, and he displays a wide and sound knowledge of their aims and difficulties. The book, indeed, is packed with penetrating reflections, shrewd judgments and arresting turns of thought and phrase. It lifts itself vastly above the common run of critical works. It is an attempt to get down to the fundamentals of æsthetic form and organization, and of æsthetic response no less, and I commend it to all who see in art more than a mere reinforcement of sentiment. It blows a clean wind through the fogs and obfuscations of the immemorial pundits.

§3

It is not sufficient to pile praises upon Frank J. Wilstach's "Dictionary of Similes" (*Little-Brown*); I am almost tempted to the indecency of greeting it with three cheers. The motto on the title page, out of George Moore's "Vale," tells the story. "It is hard," says George, plaintively, "to find a simile when one is seeking for one." Hard is far too mild and empty a word. Make it cruel, horrible, damnable, *scheusslich*. Who, putting words together to the glory of God, has not been halted, tortured, stumped by the quest? Who, living by the apt and savoury phrase, has not searched the libraries and the second-hand book stores for a dictionary of similes as good as Soule's dictionary of synonyms—and all in vain? And who, of all this harassed clan, will not fall upon the fat volume of Dr. Wilstach with joy? It is the fruit, one need not be told in the preface, of years and years of labor—of meticulous spouting into endless books, of herculean searches for authorities, of truly staggering sorting, weighing and indexing. All the known and unknown similes in all the European tongues seem to be there, from such common ones as "as hard as nails" and "as hot as the hinges of hell" to such rare flowers of fancy as Irvin Cobb's "no more privacy than a goldfish"—surely one of the most pungent similes ever devised. The learned thesaurist has swept the whole field of English literature, from Malory to Wallace Irwin, and has borrowed in addition from the literatures of many other countries. Shakespeare and the Bible contribute thousands of specimens; hundreds come from Balzac, Byron, Emerson, Rabelais, Carlyle, Kipling. Swinburne seems to have been a fertile maker of similes: his name appears very often. So does that of Thomas Moore. So does that of Oliver Wendell Holmes. Many familiar specimens, of course, are credited to Anon.; they go back, in some cases, to the childhood of the race. But many others have been tracked to their sources. "As flat as a pancake," it appears, was first used by Ludvig Holberg, the father of modern Danish literature, who lived in the early eighteenth century. "Lean as a lath" is credited to Thomas Heywood, the contemporary of Shakespeare. "Fleet as an arrow" is first found in a poem by Firdausi, a Persian poet of the tenth century. "As happy as the day is long" comes from an old Scotch proverb. "As high as heaven" is from the Bible. So is "as hot as an oven." "As merry as a marriage bell" is out of Byron. "As mild as a dove" is from Shakespeare.

Very few similes in anything approaching general use seem to have been missed. One that I note is "as sound as a bell." Another is "as fresh as a fish," which is very common in Northern Europe, and is to be encountered in the first act of "A Doll's House." But these omissions, as I say, are not many. Dr. Wilstach has done his work with relentless thoroughness; his nets have dredged all the oceans. Moreover, he has arranged his specimens according to a handy and intelligent plan, so that they may be consulted with the minimum of labor. Finally, he has added a learned and interesting preface upon the history of similes in all ages, and has digested and summarized the scant literature of the subject. Altogether, a book of such obvious value that it needs no encomium. In six months every aspiring author will have it at his elbow. Need I say that the gifted author is a native of Indiana, the Attica of our fair republic? And need I add that his work has been long in circulation in manuscript among the literary genii of that super-literate commonwealth? Indianapolis should rear a shaft to him in the shank of Main Street, and keep it bathed in roses and lilies forever.

§4

The novels of the autumn, in the main, are so dull that I can't get through them. A brilliant exception is "Somewhere in Red Gap," by Harry Leon Wilson (*Doubleday-Page*), an extension of the chronicles of that "Ma" Pettingill who was a saucy and Molièresque figure in "Ruggles of Red Gap." Mr. Wilson is one of the few living American novelists who actually know how to write. Seduced, like all the rest, by the cheap magazines, he yet manages to keep from stooping to their level. Instead, he pulls them up to his. The comic novel, perhaps the most difficult of all novels to write, is his oyster. He concocts it with the most amazing skill; he gets genuine characters into it; he makes it a work of art. You will go wrong, indeed, if you miss the hard merit of his "Somewhere in Red Gap." . . . But what other fictioneer comes near it? Alas, it is hard to find one. Machine-made situations, wooden characters, hollow bosh and rhodomontade, feeble sentimentality— little else is to be encountered in such trade goods as "The Wall Street Girl," by Frederick Orin Bartlett (*Houghton*); "The Power-House," by John Buchan (*Doran*); "Miss Theodosia Heartstrings," by Annie Hamilton Donnell (*Little-Brown*); "The Breath of the Dragon," by A. H. Fitch (*Putnam*); "The Hampstead Mystery," by Watson and Rees (*Lane*); "The Daughter Pays," by Mrs. Baillie Reynolds (*Doran*); and "The Tortured Soul," by Estelle Z. Huselton (*Sherman-French*). The very names of most of these tales give them away. And if the names were not enough, there would be the canned reviews and the pictures on the slip covers—chromatic portraits of homeric heroes and startlingly beautiful heroines, scenes of hair-raising dramas, sugary sentiment in wash. As for me, I find reading them a hard business. If you are interested in them, better subscribe for the New York *Times*.

Nor do I get very far into such things as "The Average Woman," by W. Dane Bank (*Doran*); "From the Housetops," by George Barr McCutcheon (*Dodd-Mead*); "The Towers of Ilium," by Ethelyn Leslie Huston (*Doran*); "Pincus Hood," by Arthur Hodges (*Small-Maynard*); "To the Minute," by Anna Katherine Green (*Putnam*); "The Sins of the Children," by Cosmo Hamilton (*Little-Brown*); "The Triumph of Tim," by Horace Annesley Vachell (*Doran*); "The Cross of Heart's Desire," by Gertrude Pahlow (*Duffield*); "Skinner's Dress Suit," by Henry Irving Dodge (*Houghton*), and "The Wandering Dog," by Marshall Saunders (*Doran*). Here there is better writing than in the worst, but after all, only better writing. One searches in vain for an idea, a new point of view, an arresting method of approach. It is all commonplace, usual, empty, tedious. A hundred such novels would not be worth one "McTeague," or one "Heart of Darkness," or even one volume of fables by George Ade.

I offer you a few better things, but without enthusiasm: "Love and Lucy," by Maurice Hewlett (*Dodd-Mead*); "Barnacles," by J. MacDougall Hay (*Doran*); "Olga Bardel," by Stacy Aumonier (*Century*), a very promising first novel by a writer introduced to America by THE SMART SET; "Leather-Face," by the Baroness Orczy (*Doran*); "The Beloved Son," by Fanny Kemble Johnson (*Small-Maynard*); "The Green

Alley," by Eden Phillpotts (*Macmillan*); "The Romance of Martin Connor," a brisk tale of adventure by Oswald Kendall, a newcomer (*Houghton-Mifflin*); "Dead Yesterday," by Mary Agnes Hamilton (*Doran*), and "Mr. Britling Sees It Through," by H. G. Wells (*Macmillan*). The Wells story, a tale of the war, is much better than most of the other things he has done of late, but it still falls far below "Tono-Bungay" and "The History of Mr. Polly." "Dead Yesterday," another war story, is perhaps the best of the whole lot. There is some bad writing in it, but there is at least no cheap sentimentality. The Hewlett book makes one weep for the old days of "The Forest Lovers" and "Brazenose the Great." The new Locke novel, "The Wonderful Year," makes one reach despairingly for the hemlock. The rest is silence . . .

§5

Christmas books begin to show themselves in such endless number that it is quite impossible to notice all of them, or even the twentieth of them. I pass over the cheap things for the department-store trade, with their banal texts, their quasi-leather bindings and their hotel decorations, and reach expectantly into the pile of more appetizing works. The first volume to reward the prehensile digit is "The Mystery of the Hated Man," by James Montgomery Flagg (*Doran*), a collection of capital comic pictures, with indifferent humor filling the spaces between them. Mr. Flagg, I fear, will never stagger humanity at the typewriter; the play of his fancy is reminiscent of all the barber-shop weeklies that ever were; he seldom achieves a wheeze that is new, or squeezes fresh juices from an old one. But when he turns from writing to drawing he is immediately full of a lively and genuine jocosity. His pictures have measurably mitigated the horrors of my existence. I offer his little book as a good one to present to that estimable gentleman of God, your pastor . . . The next tome that emerges from the bin would probably cause him to lift an eyebrow and cock an ear, but all the same I venture to guess that it would give him no small delight in secret. It is "The Fighting Man," by William A. Brady (*Bobbs-Merrill*), the manager of Jim Corbett and of many theatrical troupes. The volume, in a sense, is an apology for the author's life. He seeks to make it clear that fate rather than inclination turned him to the prize-ring; his private tastes, he says, run to dramatic art in its loftier phases, and particularly to Shakespeare. But all this, after all, is beside the point. The simple fact is that Mr. Brady managed his sluggers with the greatest skill and gusto, and that his retirement was a great loss to an ancient and noble sport. He tells his story in a vivacious manner, and it is well worth reading.

Various other likely Christmas books show themselves, among them "Midsummer Motoring in Europe," by De Courcey W. Thom (*Putnam*); "Beethoven: the Man and the Artist," by Friedrich Kerst (*Huebsch*); "Told by the Sandman," by Abbie Phillips Walker (*Harper*). Mr. Thom's charming chronicle makes a welcome break in the stream of war books by college boys, trained nurses, connoisseurs of atrocities and out-of-work English novelists, for it deals with the Europe that blew up in August, 1914, and so there is something of the romance of history in it. His tour took him through Belgium, Normandy, Brittany, Switzerland and South Germany, and he seems to have paused very often to buy photographs, for he presents a great many good ones. Unluckily, he also appears to have wasted a lot of time writing poetry, and some of it he rashly prints.

"Told by the Sandman" is an excellent collection of little stories to be read aloud to children. Mrs. Walker has written hundreds of these tales during the past five or six years, and they have attained to an enormous popularity in a syndicate of newspaper. They are simple enough to lie within the comprehension of a child too young to read itself, and yet there is a constant ingenuity in them, and they do not cover the ground of the classical fairy stories. It is surprising that they were not put into book covers sooner. . . .

1917

Suffering among Books

Politeness must be mingled delicately with criticism in dealing with "The Leatherwood God," by William Dean Howells, for it is the work of a man of eighty, and much high striving is behind him, and not a little sound accomplishment. On the whole, a superficial novelist, and not to be mentioned in the same breath with such men as Clemens, Dreiser and Norris, Dr. Howells has yet concocted three or four novels that belong to the top of the third rank, and at least one, "The Rise of Silas Lapham," that is a valuable and permanent contribution to our national literature. On the whole, a somewhat romantic and unintelligible critic, with a great gift for discovering bogus geniuses, he has nevertheless done some useful pioneering, notably for Turgenieff and Dostoievsky, and, to come nearer home, for such men as E. W. Howe, author of "The Story of a Country Town." And on the whole, an essayist of an empty and kittenish variety, he has still managed to be mildly entertaining, and to develop a style that often shows the pungent charm of the unexpected.

Americans always judge their authors, not as artists, but as men. Edgar Allan Poe, I daresay, will never live down the fact that he was a periodical drunkard. Mark Twain, the incomparable artist, will probably never shake off Mark Twain, the after-dinner comedian, the flaunter of white dress clothes, the public character, the national wag. As for Dr. Howells, he gains rather than loses by this confusion of values, for he is a highly respectable gentleman, a sitter on solemn committees, an intimate of college presidents and reformers, a man vouched for by both the *Atlantic Monthly* and the *Ladies' Home Journal,* and the result is his general acceptance as a member of the literary peerage, and of the rank of earl at least. For twenty years past his successive books have not been criticised, not even adequately reviewed; they have been merely hymned and fawned over. The dean of American letters in point of years, and in point of published quantity, and in point of public prominence and influence, he has been gradually enveloped in a web of superstitious reverence, and it grates harshly to hear his actual achievement discussed in cold blood.

Nevertheless, all this merited respect for an industrious and inoffensive man is bound, soon or late, to yield to a critical examination of the artist within, and that examination, I fear, will have its bitter mo-

Smart Set 51, No. 1 (January 1917): 266–72.

ments for those who naïfly accept the current Howells legend. It will show, without doubt, a first-rate journeyman, a contriver of pretty things, a clever stylist—but it will also show a long row of uninspired and hollow books, with no more ideas in them than so many volumes of the *New Republic,* and no more deep and contagious feeling than so many reports of autopsies, and no more glow and gusto than so many tables of bond prices. The profound dread and agony of life, the surge of passion and aspiration, the grand crash and glitter of things, the tragedy that runs eternally under the surface—all this the critic of the future will seek in vain in Dr. Howells' urbane and shallow volumes. And seeking it in vain, he will probably dismiss all of them together with fewer words than he gives to "Huckleberry Finn" . . .

Intrinsically, "The Leatherwood God" is little more than a stale anecdote, and the dressing that Dr. Howells gives it does not lift it very far above this anecdotal quality. The central character, one Dylks, is a backwoods evangelist who acquires a belief in his own buncombe, and ends by announcing that he is God. The job before the author was obviously that of tracing the psychological steps whereby this mountebank proceeds to that conclusion; the fact, indeed, is recognized in the canned review, which says that the book is "a study of American religious psychology," and by the fair critic of the New York *Times,* who praises it as "a remarkable psychological study." But an inspection of the text shows that no such study is really in it. Dr. Howells does not *show* how Dylks came to believe himself God; he merely *says* that he did so. The whole discussion of the process, indeed, is confined to two pages—172 and 173—and it is quite infantile in its inadequacy. Nor do we get anything approaching a revealing look into the heads of the other converts—the saleratus-sodden, hell-crazy, half-witted Methodists and Baptists of a remote Ohio settlement of seventy or eighty years ago. All we have is the casual statement that they are converted, and begin to offer Dylks their howls of devotion. And when, in the end, they go back to their original bosh, dethroning Dylks overnight and restoring the gaseous vertebrate of Calvin and Wesley—when this contrary process is recorded, it is accompanied by no more illumination. In brief, the story is not a study at all, but simply a story—as I have said, an anecdote. Its characters reveal only what a passing glance would reveal; its dialogue is tedious; its well-made sub-plot is pointless; it skims the skin. There is not even the charm of good writing. Dr. Howells forgot his style as he forgot his psychology. Any fifth-rate novelist might have put the thing together as well; there are dozens of American novelists who would have done it far better. . . . I surely hope I have been polite.

But what an invitation is in the subject! What a great novel is there! The United States, from the earliest times, has swarmed with just such jitney messiahs as Dylks—some of them even more self-deluded than he was, some of them plain rogues. Joseph Smith, Schlatter, Mary Baker C. Eddy, John Alexander Dowie, the prophets of the Shakers, the Holy Rollers, the Holy Ghost and Us maniacs, the Seventh Day Adventists, the various Mennonites, the nigger Methodists—the list is a long and juicy one. The spectacle of a Billy Sunday assaulting Pittsburgh, Philadelphia, Baltimore, Kansas City and Boston is not new; there have been periodical outbreaks of this same religious savagery ever since the Great Awakening of 1734, and before that time the colonies were full of heretic-hunters, and the politics of some of them was chiefly a combat between theologians. To be an American, indeed, means to carry a depressing cargo of religious balderdash; the great-grandfathers of two-thirds of us thought that hell was yawning for them, and were willing to believe anything in order to escape. It is thus always easy to get a hearing for theological ideas in the United States; they enter into our very laws and customs, and are heard with a gravity that it would be hard to match anywhere else in Christendom. Democracy, Puritanism, Philistinism—they are sisters under their skins—nay, they are one and the same. And yet how little the latter-day Puritan appears in our literature—how seldom he has been studied objectively, and his quirks platted. A penetrating and admirable small sketch appears in a book I have already mentioned: E. W. Howe's "The Story of a Country Town." But Howe had other fish to fry; he slapped in his Methodist hound of heaven brilliantly, and then passed on to melodrama and the pains of young love. I advocate a novel by Dreiser, to be called "The Puritan"—a full-length study, in all his relentless meticulousness, of the sort of fellow who contributes money to Billy Sunday funds, and believes that all will go to hell who are not purged by total immersion in water, and opposes Sunday baseball and moving-pictures, and whoops for prohibition, and delights in vice crusades, and has, perchance, an eye for a shapely leg. In New York this gladiator of the gospels tends to disappear; save when some new Parkhurst or Comstock heats up his fires, he is seldom heard of. But in the hinterland he rages so steadily that he may be almost accepted as the normal American type. And there is an endless supply of mad mullahs, all divinely inspired and impassioned, to keep him snorting. Few of them, in these later days, actually claim to be God, but all of them claim to be on intimate and confidential terms with Him, and all of them launch thunderbolts of anathema on every man who ventures to hoot at their revelations.

§2.

Of the other fiction of the current boiling the best, and by long odds, is to be found in several volumes of short stories, and the best of these short stories are not properly fiction at all but two-thirds fact. They are in a book called "The Further Side of Silence," by Sir Hugh Clifford, K.C.M.G. (*Doubleday-Page*). This Clifford, if he is not actually the man who discovered Joseph Conrad, is at least the man who first set Conrad on his legs. A glance at his own writing shows why he was so alert to the merits of the great Pole. He is, in fact, a writer of very considerable skill himself, and in these Malay sketches he is writing of a people and a country that he knows intimately, for he went out to the Federated Malay States as a boy in his teens, and he remained there, off and on, until he became their Governor. Here he presents vivid and intensely interesting pictures of the Malay in all the situations of daily life—hunting, fighting, thieving, marrying, dying. There is a truly capital account of a running amuck, and another of the intrigues at a petty Malay court. The gusto of a true story-teller is in all of the sketches; their half-savage people live and breathe; one need not be told that Clifford knows his little brown brother from head to heels, and has an old affection for him. No better reading is in the month's books.

"Tales of the Pampas," by W. H. Hudson (*Knopf*), leaves me cold, as his "Green Mansions" did. This Hudson is now enjoying a boom, with John Galsworthy thumping the tom-tom for him, and great combers and breakers of over-praise beating 'round him. His present stories deal with the Argentina of sixty or seventy years ago, before the railroad broke the immense loneliness of the pampas. A supernatural touch is in them; one hears of women turned into birds, and other such doings. But I am unable to find any noticeable skill in the way they are told; even the style, indeed, lacks the music that relieved the dullness of "Green Mansions." Nor do I find anything comparable to "Silence" or "The Seven Who Were Hanged" in "The Crushed Flower," by Leonid Andreyev (*Knopf*), a volume made up of five short stories and three novelettes. Andreyev is undoubtedly a fictioneer of very high talents, but he, too, has his bad moments, and some of them overtook him when he was writing "The Crushed Flower." As for "The Turtles of Tasman," by Jack London (*Macmillan*), it contains seven poor stories and one good one. The good one is "Finis," a tale of the Klondike. Needless to say, it is devoid of those banal "ideas" with which Dr. London so often corrupts his fiction. When he sits him down to tell a simple tale, he usually does it with great success, but when he grows scientific or expository he quickly becomes tiresome. Finally, there is "The Whale and the Grasshopper," by Seumas O'Brien

(*Little-Brown*), a book of fantastic fables, many of them very amusing. But I'd rather see a volume of Mr. O'Brien's longer stories, already grown familiar in the magazines. They have loud laughs in them, they are Irish farce at its best; they rescue the Irish literary renaissance from its prevailing melancholy.

§3.

In the remaining fiction there is little to arrest the exploratory eye. Perhaps the best of it is to be found in "Royal Highness," by Thomas Mann (*Knopf*), a story dealing very minutely and often very amusingly with the life of a German grand ducal family. It was written before the war, and is thus free from the current fustian. "The House of Luck," by Harris Dickson (*Small-Maynard*), is a tale of love, gallantry and villainy in the Vicksburg of the thirties, and curiously enough, considering the usual liveliness of the author, it is written in a stilted and tedious style. "Filling His Own Shoes," by Henry C. Rowland (*Houghton-Mifflin*), is a stupid confection in the W. J. Locke manner, with a shoe clerk for hero; it would be difficult to imagine anything more incredible, either as to characters or as to incidents. "Dr. Nick," by L. M. Steele (*Small-Maynard*), is a piece of sentimentality running to 439 pages, with an immigrant boy and girl as hero and heroine. "Betty at Fort Blizzard," by Molly Elliot Seawell (*Lippincott*), and "The Romance of a Christmas Card," by Kate Douglas Wiggin (*Houghton-Mifflin*), are sheer mush; both ladies seem to lose their old cunning as year chases year. "A Drake, by George!" by John Trevena (*Knopf*), is a highly labored and not often intriguing farce, with a story-book sea captain for its chief personage. "The Emperor of Portugalia," by Selma Lagerlöf (*Doubleday-Page*), is quite the worst tale by this author so far translated. It tells how an old Swedish peasant, when his only daughter disappears into the maw of a large city, turns to the delusion that she has married an emperor, and that he himself is an emperor, too. Not a bad idea; its opportunities, indeed, are many and obvious. But Mlle. Lagerlöf quite fails to make anything of it. "Quaker-Born," by Ian Campbell Hannah (*Shaw*), "The Old Blood," by Frederic Palmer (*Dodd-Mead*), and "Told in a French Garden," by Mildred Aldrich (*Small-Maynard*), all deal with the war and all are bad, with Dr. Palmer's story leading them as worst.

§4.

"The average actor," says Arthur Hornblow, in "Training for the Stage" (*Lippincott*), "holds the mirror up to nature and sees in it only the reflection of himself. . . . In France they call an actor a *M'as-tu-vu*, which, anglicised, means a Have-you-seen-me." . . . The learned critic, so far sound, evades plumbing the psychological springs of this astounding and almost invariable vanity, this endless bumptiousness of the mime, this hall-mark of the *cabotin* in all climes and all ages. His one attempt is banal: "a foolish public makes much of him." Nonsense, my dear Herr Kollege! The sprouting Coquelin is full of hot and rancid gases long before a foolish public has had a fair chance to make anything of him at all, and he continues to emit them long after it has tried him, condemned him and bidden him be damned. There is, indeed, little choice in the virulence of their self-respect between the Broadway star who is slobbered over by press agents and fat women and the poor ham who plays thinking parts in No. 7 road companies. The two are alike charged to the limit; one more ohm, or degree, or molecule, and they would burst. Actors begin where professional dancers, Fifth Avenue rectors and Chautauqua orators leave off; the most modest of them (barring a few unearthly traitors to the craft) matches the conceit of the solitary cutie on a slow ship. In their lofty eminence of pomposity they are challenged only by negro bishops and grand opera tenors. I have spoken of the danger they run of bursting. In the case of tenors it must sometimes actually happen; even the least of them swells visibly as he sings, and permanently as he grows older. . . .

But why are actors, in general, such blatant and obnoxious asses, such arrant posturers and wind-bags? Why is it as surprising to find an unassuming and likable fellow among them as to find a Greek without fleas? The answer, for all its stumping of Dr. Hornblow, is really quite simple. To reach it one needs but consider the type of young man who normally gets stage-struck. Is he, taking averages, the intelligent, alert, ingenious, ambitious young fellow? Is he the young fellow with ideas in him, and a yearning for hard and difficult work? Is he the diligent reader, the hard student, the eager inquirer? No. He is, in the overwhelming main, the neighborhood fop and beau, the human clothes-horse, the nimble squire of dames. The youths of more active mind, emerging from adolescence, turn to business and the professions; the men that they admire and seek to follow are men of genuine distinction, men who have actually done difficult and valuable things, men who have fought good fights and are respected and envied by other men. The stage-struck youth is of a softer and more shallow sort. He seeks, not a chance to test his mettle by hard and useful work, but an easy chance to shine. He craves the regard, not of men, but of women. He is, in brief, a hollow and incompetent creature, a strutter and poseur, a popinjay, a pretty one. . . .

I thus beg the question, but explain the actor. He is this silly youngster grown older, but otherwise unchanged. An initiate of a pro-

fession requiring little more information, culture or capacity for ratioc-
ination than that of the lady of joy, and surrounded in his work-shop
by men who are as stupid, as vain and as empty as he himself will be in
the years to come, he suffers an arrest of development, and the little
intelligence that may happen to be in him gets no chance to show itself. The result, in its usual manifestation, is the average bad actor—a
man with the cerebrum of a floor-walker and the vanity of a fashionable clergyman. The result, in its highest and holiest form, is the actor-
manager, with his retinue of press-agents, parasites and worshipping
wenches—perhaps the most preposterous and awe-inspiring donkey
that civilization has yet produced. To look for sense in a fellow of such
equipment and such a history would be like looking for serviettes in a
sailors' boarding-house.

By the same token, the relatively greater intelligence of actresses is
explained. They are, at their worst, quite as bad as the generality of actors. There are she-stars who are all temperament and balderdash—
intellectually speaking, beggars on horseback, servant girls well
washed. But no one who knows anything about the stage need be told
that it can show a great many more quick-minded and self-respecting
women than intelligent men. And why? Simply because its women are
recruited, in the main, from a class much above that which furnishes its
men. It is, after all, not unnatural for a woman of considerable intelligence to aspire to the stage. It offers her, indeed, one of the most
tempting careers that is open to her. She cannot hope to succeed in
business, and in the other professions she is an unwelcome and much-
scoffed-at intruder, but on the boards she can meet men on an equal
footing. It is, therefore, no wonder that women of a relatively superior
class often take to the business. . . . Once they embrace it, their superiority to their male colleagues is quickly manifest. All movements
against puerility and imbecility in the drama have originated, not with
actors, but with actresses—that is, in so far as they have originated
among stage folk at all. The earliest Ibsen pioneers were such women
as Madame Modjeska, Mrs. Fiske and Janet Achurch; the men all hung
back. Ibsen, it would appear, was aware of this superior alertness and
took shrewd advantage of it. At all events, his most tempting acting
parts are feminine ones. . . . The girls of the stage demonstrate this
tendency against great difficulties. They have to carry a heavy handicap
in the enormous number of women who seek the footlights merely to
advertise their real profession, but despite all this, anyone who has the
slightest acquaintance with stagefolk will testify that, taking one with
another, the women have vastly more brains than the men and are ap-
preciably less vain and idiotic. Relatively few actresses of any rank marry actors. They find close communion with the strutting brethren

psychologically impossible. Stock brokers, dramatists and even theatrical managers are greatly to be preferred.

In committing to print these few modest and moderate observations upon actors, I make the usual reservation. That is to say, I admit specifically that there is a small minority of actors who approximate in good manners and sound intelligence the average of civilized men. But I hasten to add that this minority is very small, indeed, and that within my personal range of observation, it includes no more than four or five men. Many years ago Channing Pollock revealed to me that he had discovered the existence of an actor who was neither vain nor noisy, and proposed that he entertain me with a marvel by introducing me to the fellow. I proposed in reply that the introduction be postponed for six months in order to make sure. Three weeks later this actor was slugged by a stage hand for his gross and intolerable bumptiousness during a rehearsal, and before the expiration of the six months his manager had kicked him out and he returned to England. Since then, so I am informed, he has died decently in the trenches. It is thus possible, after all, that Pollock may have been essentially right. But I don't think so, and neither, I believe, does Pollock.

§5.

If I were younger and less immersed in obesity, I should like to write an article on the books that have quite failed of achieving their original purposes, and are yet of respectable use and potency for other purposes. For example, the Book of Revelation. The obvious aim of the learned author of this work was to bring the early Christians into accord by telling them authoritatively what to expect and hope for; its actual effect during eighteen hundred years has been to split them into a multitude of camps, and so set them to denouncing, damning, snitching on, jailing and murdering one another. Again, consider the autobiography of Benvenuto Cellini. Ben wrote it to prove that he was an honest man, a mirror of all the virtues, an injured innocent; the world, reading it, hails him respectfully as the noblest, the boldest, and gaudiest liar that ever lived. Again, turn to "Gulliver's Travels." It was planned by its rev. author as a devastating satire, a horrible piece of cynicism; it survives as a story-book for sucklings. Yet again, there is "Hamlet." Shakespeare wrote it frankly to make money for a theatrical manager; it has lost money for theatrical managers ever since. Yet again, there is Cæsar's "De Bello Gallico." Julius composed it to thrill and inflame the Romans; its sole use to-day is to stupefy and sicken school-boys. . . . Which brings us, by a drop of 10,000 metres, to "Doreen and the Sentimental Bloke," by C. J. Dennis (*Lane*), a book written wholly in rhyme, and hence obviously intended to be poetry. If the obvious is the true, then the author's intent fails, for the thing is mawkish, tedious and idiotic. But though the book thus misses its apparent purpose by a mile, it very effectively achieves a very different purpose, for it is an excellent compendium of Australian slang, and the study of that slang will interest every connoisseur of the English language and its dialects.

Mr. Dennis's protagonist is a Melbourne loafer, and the tongue in which the volume is written is the modified Cockney of the Melbourne docks. One notes immediately the battle that is going on down there between English slang and American slang, with an ambitious native slang occasionally taking a hand. The basis of the new dialect is plainly the Cockney speech of the Thames-side; the low-caste Australian, indeed, is as fond of *blimed* and *lydy* and as uncertain of his *h's* as a London costermonger. In his vocabulary, as in his pronunciation, there are numerous reminiscences of England. He is full of such words as *bloke, beak* (for magistrate), *cove, quid, toff* and *fag.* But to them he has added so many Americanisms that his brothers at home would probably find it hard to follow his discourse. He has borrowed, for example, scores of such verbs as *to kid, to plug along, to back and fill, to beef, to bluff, to cop out, to fade away, to jolt* and *to rile,* and scores of such adjectives as *rattled, snide, dead* (as a superlative), *square* and *tough* (e.g., to qualify *luck*). Many characteristic phrases have gone over from American into Australian; *to chew the rag, to go chase yourself, to take a tumble, to get it in the neck, knock-out-drops, for keeps, to get wise, up to me.* Many others (and single words with them) have gone over with changes in meaning. *To mug,* in Australia, does not mean to photograph, but to kiss. The *conk* (conch) is not the head, but the nose. *Leery* does not mean sophisticated, suspicious, but vulgar, low. The words *tom* and *tart,* applied to a girl, seem to have no disparaging significance in the antipodes; Mr. Dennis' bloke is always referring to his sweetheart as a *tart.* Moreover, certain familiar American words and phrases have been borrowed in substance, but changed in form. *On the level* appears as *on the straight. All in* has become *all out. Gazabo* has been shortened to *gazob. Going some* has been turned into *going strong.* But *nerve, peach, splice, scrap* and *stunt* have gone over unchanged.

Of native Australian slang Mr. Dennis offers a number of interesting specimens. *'Ead serang* is obviously by Cockney out of Malay. *Bonzer,* perhaps, may be traced to *bonny,* for it signifies charm or excellence, and is often applied to a girl. But what of *spruik,* which means a showman's speech and is apparently synonymous to the American *spiel?* And what of *ribuck,* an interjection indicating assent? And what of *chiack,* signifying banter? *To crack a boo* is easily understandable. It means primarily to betray emotion, and by metaphor to divulge a secret. To be gloomy is *to have the joes.* A spoil-sport is a *nark.* *To run the rabbit* is exactly equivalent to the American *to rush the can.* A *squiz* is a brief glance. *To smooge* is to flatter (perhaps from the Yiddish *to schmoos*). *To snuff it* is to die. A steady job is a *lurk.* Anything that is bogus is *slanter.* A gullible fellow is not a *sucker,* but a *punter.* To court a girl is *to track with her.* . . .

Altogether, a rich and racy slang. The English and American strains, coalescing, seem to be producing a native stock that is ingenious and interesting. Unluckily, it is impossible to deduce any of the rules of Australian grammar from Mr. Dennis' stanzas. His sentences, though made up chiefly of slang, are usually conventional in structure. In the *Volkssprache* of the United States gradual changes in the conjugation of the verbs and the declension of the pronouns have been going on for a century past, and there has been so vast an enrichment of the vocabulary that the language is now quite unintelligible to an Englishman. I have in manuscript a grammar of this national tongue and shall probably publish it in a year or two. So far as I know it has never got any attention from the academic grammarians. They continue, professorlike, to teach a grammar that is exotic and artificial, and a syntax that no ordinary American, save at times of conscious pedantry, ever so much as bows to after he leaves school.

The Rough-House on Parnassus

§1.

The war has gone to the heads of the poets, and they gyrate, snort and roll their eyes like Russian dancers. A fearful din arises; it comes in great waves and breakers of sound, like the bellowing of the saved at a Methodist revival. And cutting through it, like a sharp knife through a hog's neck, shrills the appalling superwhoop of Poet Peter Golden, author of "The Voice of Ireland," and the loudest, wildest, most death-and-devil-defying, most ear-to-a-semi-liquid-jelly-reducing minnesinger of them all. Thus, arising trombonally above the rest, his blood-curdling song of hate to his recreant fellow-Gael, the Hon. John E. Redmond, P. C.:

> Beside your heaped-up monumental shame
> Iscariot's will be an honored name;
> Dermot MacMurrough, Corydon or Keogh,
> For all their treason never sank so low.
> O Arch Assassin of your land and race,
> Long may you live to dodder in disgrace;
> And when they lay your carcass in the clay,
> *The very worms, ashamed, will turn away!!!*

I add a few screamers to bring out the bounce of it. Atop it, under the curiously modest title of "A Request," he piles this one:

> When Britain is securely bound
> And 'round her fast Fate's web is wound,
> Lord God in Heaven, I ask one prayer—
> Grant me the glory to be there!
>
> Give me the great boon to be nigh
> When 'round her neck the noose they tie,
> And send her shrieking in the air!
> Grant, grant, O God, that I be there!

Smart Set 51, No. 2 (February 1917): 394–400.

This, mark you, is hot stuff. But hotter still is in the book—hotter, indeed, than I would dare transcribe to the pages of a great family magazine. England is denounced as a harpy, as a harridan, as a "vile, diseased old harlot," as a "perjured, pandering prostitute." She is accused of murder, mayhem, piracy on the high seas, lying, sheep stealing, rebating, seduction under promise of marriage, passing bad cheques, violations of the Mann Act. And thus, in high, astounding terms, she is challenged to do her darndest:

> You have planted your flag upon every crag
>   Where the winds of the world do blow;
> Your ships they sail before every gale
>   Where the world's waters go;
> You have conquered the races near and far,
>   From the sun's rise to its set;
> But, oh we fling it in your face—
>   We are not conquered yet!
>
> By the higher things you could never feel,
>   By the dreams you could never know,
> We will fight to the end of the glorious fight,
>   O hated and ancient foe;
> And we pledge you our hate, our deathless hate,
>   Till the stars from their course are driven,
> And the very ends of the earth itself
>   Asunder are rent and riven!

Well, well, let us not cackle over Professor Golden. No doubt it is quite natural for a patriotic Celt to feel a certain heat when he thinks of England, just as it is natural for a Belgian to feel a certain heat when he thinks of Germany. Moreover, this fevered bard of the Irish-German-Austrian-Hungarian-Bulgarian-Turkish cause is surely but little more absurd than most of the hymnalists of the English-French-Belgian-Russian-Portuguese-Italian-Japanese-Rumanian cause. One and all the war poets quack and gargle dismally; their strophes turn to fustian quickly; they will be buying up their war stuff and hiding it in their garrets in two or three years. So far, in fact, though I have read them literally by the thousand, I have encountered but two war poems of any genuine merit. One of them is a sonnet by the late Rupert Brooke, and the other is a German poem called "I Have An Old Mother," or something of the sort—a very beautiful, and even noble piece of writing. The French poets are all at the front, and hence benevolently silent; the English poets, and particularly their American echoes and valets, seems to be trying desperately to surpass the bosh and bluster of the German "Hassgesang gegen England." Even the mildest of the jongleurs takes to grotesque monkey-shines when he writes of the war. For example, Charles Hanson Towne, whose "Today and Tomorrow" (*Doran*), in the midst of very pretty lyrics, contains half a dozen hysterical war poems. They resemble nothing so much as doggerel versions of headlines in the *Evening Telegram*. Worse, they are antagonistic in sentiment. In one sonnet the gifted rhapsodist denounces the United States for standing clear of the unpleasantness, and in another he tells William Watson (who has apparently asked him about the matter) that neutrality is a sweet thing and a proof of piety. As for Walter Conrad Arensberg, he descends in "Idols" (*Houghton-Mifflin*) to theological and psychopathological balderdash; it will make truly astonishing reading when the show is over. Wilfrid Wilson Gibson does even worse; he makes the Mother Goose songs his model, as in "The Bayonet":

> This bloody steel
> Has killed a man.
> I heard him squeal
> As on I ran.
>
> He watched me come
> With wagging head.
> I pressed it home,
> And he was dead.
>
> Though clean and clear
> I've wiped the steel,
> I still can hear
> That dying squeal.

The school, obviously, of "Hickory, Dickory, Dock." Poetry to be inscribed upon school-house walls. . . . Quite as bad are the noisy roars of Lewis Worthington Smith in "The English Tongue" (*Four Seas*), a sophomoric imitation of Kipling at his cheapest, and the pious rumble-bumble of Grace Fallows Norton in "What Is Your Legion?" (*Houghton*), a book of dithyrambs in the "Maryland, My Maryland" manner. Such stuff is certainly not poetry. It belongs, roughly, to that strident sub-department of beautiful letters which also includes the George M. Cohan song, the Presidential harangue of acceptance and the college yell. In Ruth McEnery Stuart's "Plantation Songs" (*Appleton*) war verse drops a cellar further, and becomes indistinguishable from the inspirational rubbish of the newspapers. For example:

If first and best are sacrificed
    And epileptics thrive,
Begetting by their feeble strain
In pale successors of the slain
Whose sons within their loins have lain
In soldiers' trenches—whence again
    Will virile men arrive?

Why not send idiots to fight?
    Conscript the leper camps?
Wipe out the White Plague on the field?
Soldiers of courage it would yield!
Perhaps our murderers might be healed
By overwork—and kindly shield
    From prisons' glooms and damps.

Ding-dong "poetry"—and a belated suggestion. As a matter of fact, the French have sent all their Apaches, actors and poets into the forefront of the fray, the Germans have thus got rid of thousands of Socialist orators, and the Russians have depopulated Siberia in freedom's cause. Even the English, perhaps the least sharp-witted of civilized peoples, have had sense enough to give the Irish good seats at all performances. . . . From such platitudinous piffle one turns with relief to a few war poems of a measurably better sort. Some of them are to be found in "London, One November," by Helen Mackay (*Duffield*), and others in "A Song of the Guns," by Gilbert Frankau, R.S.A. (*Houghton*). Both of these poets run to *vers libre;* Mrs. Mackay even abandons initial capitals. Much guff is in their books, but in the midst of it there is also an occasional line of beauty, a stray picture that flashes and lingers. But the best of all the war poetry, it seems to me, is in Carl Sandburg's "Chicago Poems" (*Holt*). Here, at all events, one finds restraint and self-respect. Sandburg does not try to scare the Kaiser to death with tall talk, nor does he slobber the old, old slobber over the Belgians (who probably tire of it sorely, and would greatly prefer better rations), nor does he argue that the United States is a fair vestal among the nations, and devoid of all the hoggishness, imbecility and hypocrisy of the rest. What he does say, of course, is more or less self-evident, for so much has been said about war that scarcely anything remains to be said, but he at least spares us his sobs. . . .

Curiously enough, many of these bad war poets do excellent work in other fields. In Mr. Arensberg's book, for instance, there is a three-liner which throws up a brilliant and agreeable image. He calls it "The Voice of One Dead," and it is as follows:

> Of the relented limbs and the braid, O lady,
> Bound up in haste at parting,
> The secret is kept.

Here speaks one of decent restraints, a fellow to be trusted and respected, a gentleman. But when he turns to carnage Mr. Arensberg blubbers. So with the excellent Towne. Some of his short lyrics— "After," "Love Can Die," "Mysteries," "The Quiet Years"—are pure bursts of song. So, too, with Mr. Gibson. His one-act plays in blank verse are the best in the current harvesting. As for Mrs. Norton, she prints a whole book of pretty verses, by name "Roads" (*Houghton*), and save for a few bad war songs at the end, it lifts itself well clear of the fustian of "What Is Your Legion?" . . . I wish I could say as much for Mrs. Stuart, but the fact is that her "Plantation Songs" are almost as bad as her war songs. Her method of manufacturing a negro song is the simple one of first writing a fourth-rate poem, and then translating it into imperfect dialect. The result a gross misrepresentation of negro ideas, and even of the negro vocabulary. An example from the poem called "Wash-Day":

> When de dusk brings out de edges
> O' de west'ard growin' hedges,
> An' each gou'd-flower on de stable is a sun,
> F'om de fiel' beyon' my bleachin'
> Comes a cow-song, so beseechin'
> Dat I fools aroun' untel de milkin's done.

Imagine a plantation darkey using such an adjective as "westward-growing," or talking of suns (in the plural), or perceiving anything "beseeching" in a cow-song! Such stuff is machine-made and without merit. It is sentimental and bogus. The sub-Potomac lutanists would do well to cease writing it.

§2.

Let us make no truce with bad poets. The art is incessantly invaded by aspirants with no more talent for its tricks than I have for those of diplomacy, and no more capacity for its emotions than George Nathan has for those of the Holy Rollers. Let us, as politely as possible, bounce them off Parnassus. . . . What rights, for example, has a poet to assault Christendom with so huge and unpleasant a projectile as Sarah Taylor Shatford's "Birds of Passage" (*Sherman-French*)—a book of no less than 425 bad poems, 510 pages of buncombe and bathos, more than a pound and a half of tosh. I open the vast tome at random and encounter this:

> A young girl dreaming of last night's joy,
> When her hand was won by a handsome boy,
> Gazes with loving and steady *glare*
> On a beautiful diamond solitaire!

Note the rapt damsel's "glare"! And then turn twenty pages to:

> It you marry for companionship,
>   You may eat your crust alone;
> You may wander as the guest of God,
>   If you marry for a home.

> If you'd weld with gold the marriage bond,
>   You may sweat to earn your bread;
> There is one cause, and one only,
>   Which will bless the marriage bed.

Go further, and fare worse! Encountering it in such heroic doses one longs fretfully for the Zeppelins. Let the chute be greased for "Birds of Passage," Rudolph, and notify the hyenas in cage No. 7 that it is coming down. . . . Give them warning too, of "Songs of Daddy-hood," by Albert Edmund Trombley (*Gorham*), a far thinner but still most damnable volume of sloppy sentimentality, a sugar-teat for push-ers of perambulators, a maudlin piece of goods, by Allah's chinners! . . . And of "Journeys of a Soul," by Nathan Appleton Tefft (*Gorham*), a sweet brew of piety and patriotism. . . . And of "Ad-em-nel-la," by Ethan Allen Hurst (*Hudson*), a doggerel version of a Kaw legend, with a preface in which the author talks of a time "when the race shall have been advanced to the grade of susceptibility where it can receive and enjoy the beauty of his work." . . . And of "Random Verse," by F. W. B. (*Badger*), and particularly of the lines on page 42:

> I am American, am I
> And not a being can
> Say he is on a plane more high;
> I'm good as any man.

And of "The Garden of Abdullah," by Adolph Danziger, not forgetting this:

> A happy man is good and clean,
> For others' gladness makes him glad;
> A wretched man is bad and mean,
> For others' glances make him sad.

And of "Law and Love," by E. J. V. Huiginn (*Badger*), and of "The Arcades," by Lollie Belle Wylie (*Caldwell*), and of "The Long Way," by Gilbert Moyle (*Four Seas*), and of "Ballads and Lyrics," by Eldredge Denison (*Sherman-French*)—dull, sentimental, maudlin stuff, with no more poetry in it than a Salvation Army hymn-book. It rolls endlessly from the presses; it is a panoramic monument to human vanity and folly. Measurably better, but still vapid and uninspired, is the poetry of such bards as Arthur Ketchum, Newbold Noyes, Caroline Stern, Glenn Ward Dresbach and May Stranathan. In Noyes' "Echo" (*Sherman-French*), for example, one finds all the ancient rubber stamps; velvet feet, sunkissed landscape, falling dusk, happy heart, golden voice, sorry knave, whispering birch—a vast emission of the obvious and commonplace. I spare you further examples. There are publishers who specialize in pursuing these half-poets with their blandishments, and the result is the endless stream of their books. Let a passable lyric appear in a magazine, and its author is straightway approached with an offer to print a book, chiefly at his own expense. Such subtly flattering invitations are forever passing through magazine offices; scarcely a week passes that I do not receive an inquiry from some newly hatched poet or other, asking if this or that firm is reputable. The answer is simple: so far as I know, all of them are reputable. That is to say, they do what they promise to do; they print the book and send it out for review. It gets, as a rule, a few formal notices. Some fair critic in Dubuque or Charlottesville, working her way through high school by writing for the local gazette, perhaps hails it as sweet and soul-filling. The product is another bad poet in the ring, another versifier turned loose. . . .

I do not speak from remote and arctic heights, sniffing disdainfully. When I was young and full of gas I printed a book of verse myself, and paid a clipping bureau $5 for the seventeen ensuing clippings. Fifteen of them were politely complimentary; the other two told the bitter truth, and in harsh terms. Once I got over the first shock of it, I began to be grateful to those two unknown truth-tellers, and I have been grateful to them ever since. Had they been lazier, or politer, or more humane to young poets, I might have gone on concocting bad poetry for three or four more years, and so remained cadaverous and moony and a nuisance to my betters. Some philanthropist should subsidize a critic to round them up and do execution upon the novices every year. It would clear the libraries of many worthless books, and the poets themselves, in the end, would erect a shaft to their benefactor. . . .

§3.

Alas, the harpists of harder and longer service stand in almost as much need of the corrective slapstick—at least this autumn. I open "Including You and Me," by Strickland Gillilan (*Forbes*), spouting with appetite for another "Finnegan," another "Ode on the Antiquity of Microbes." All I find is a collection of inspirational rubbish of the farm-paper variety, with here and there a saving touch of humor. In "Heart Songs and Home Songs," by Denis A. McCarthy (*Little-Brown*), there is only the rubbish. For example:

> Month of flowers, month of bowers,
> Month of happy sunlit hours!

Turn now to "Lundy's Lane," by Duncan Campbell Scott (*Doran*) a poet praised by William Archer. I find only the usual stuff, the formal stuff, the hollow stuff—cold, precise stanzas without the slightest glow or gusto—poetry as devoid of passion as a syllogism. Nor do I get a single thrill out of "The Great Maze," by Hermann Hagedorn (*Macmillan*), a rhapsodist of very respectable accomplishment in the past. His long title poem leaves me chilly and lonesome, and his play in blank verse, "The Heart of Youth," is such heavy going that I have not got to the end of it. Nor am I lifted up by Edwin Arlington Robinson's "The Man Against the Sky" (*Macmillan*). On what theory could a sane man maintain that there is poetry in such a composition as his "Llewellyn and the Tree"? Or in his imitations of Browning? . . . But Robinson, at all events, has his moments. In the midst of his vast dreariness I happen upon this:

> His fame, though vague, will not be small,
> As upward through her dream he fares,
> Half clouded with a crimson fall
> Of roses thrown on marble stairs.

I hail the one rose on the poet's marble stair. . . . I find another in Amelia Josephine Burr's "Life and Living" (*Doran*), or, perhaps more accurately, a whole sheaf: the poem called "Poppies" is full of a fine sincerity, a simple eloquence, an unmistakable beauty. But with it come many things that fall below it a million miles. . . .

The tried and tested poets, in truth, make a rather sorry showing this autumn. The books they offer are chiefly interesting, not because of their contents, but because their authors are well known. This is particularly true of John Masefield's "Good Friday and Other Poems" (*Macmillan*). The drama in verse which fills the half of it is a competent piece of work, but almost wholly lacking in the divine fire. If it had been written by some beginning *poétereau* no one would pay any attention to it. Mr. Masefield's sonnets, perhaps sixty in number, are scarcely more arresting. If it be true, as the canned review says, that they are "held by critics to rank with the best in the English language," then there are critics at large who deserve to have their credentials examined by the *polizei*. Lloyd Mifflin, in his day, wrote better ones; I could name four or five by Lizette Woodworth Reese that belong to an altogether higher order. . . . Nor do I think that Edgar Lee Masters, in his "Songs and Satires" (*Macmillan*), reaches the level of "The Spoon River Anthology." The best thing in the book, it seems to me, is "In the Cage," a searching discussion of the relations between man and woman—but after all, a discussion, not a poem. The same thing may be said of "The Cocked Hat," a philippic against the late William Jennings Bryan, a celebrated politician of the last age. I find such things as "Rain in My Heart" and "When Under the Icy Eaves" rather formal and empty. But one thing, at least, may be said of Mr. Masters: he is never downright dull. As eager and agile intelligence is visible in everything he does; if he is not actually a first-rate poet he is at all events a sharp-witted and interesting man. . . .

I pass over various dispiriting things: "Laodice and Danaë," a labored play in blank verse by Gordon Bottomley (*Four Seas*), almost devoid of poetical thought: "Five Men and Pompey," by Stephen Vincent Benét (*Four Seas*), an experiment in character portrayal which works out but clumsily; "There Was a Time," by Anne Murray Larned (*Badger*), a thin book of children's poems; "The Tragedy," by Gilbert Moyle (*Four Seas*), a scenario in imperfectly poetical form; "Poems of Panama," by George Warburton Lewis (*Sherman-French*), the chief of police down there. And so to "Advent Songs," by Simon N. Patten (*Huebsch*), a butchery of old hymns in the name of the uplift. Mr. Patten explains in a long introduction that those hymns are archaic and abhorrent. They express the theological ideas of dead generations; they are full of a fiery faith, and what is worse, of resignationism; what they need is a dash of Service. "The Christ of today," he says, "is not the shepherd counting the stars and guarding the lambs. He is the fireman who rushes pell-mell to save the cottage." So much for the theory. Here, in "Onward, Christian Soldiers," is the practise:

> Onward, earnest people,
>   Spreading Christian lore;
> Greet thy erring brother,
>   Harmony restore.
> Feud cannot divide us,
>   Nor can foe dismay;
> Ours a faith of promise,
>   Bright the coming day.

Let me be frank: I prefer the original.

§4.

We come to sweeter strains. In "Turns and Movies," by Conrad Aiken (*Houghton-Mifflin*), in the midst of much heavy piling up of conventional lines, there is more than one distinct lifting of the mood—for example, in "Discordants," a group of very fair songs, and in "Evensong," a simple and eloquent piece of writing. The thing that Mr. Aiken has yet to master is the fine art of selection; he is still a bit too prodigal with his parts of speech; his inspiration is spread out, so to speak, over too great an area. The worst of his offending, however, seems to be over. At the end of his book he gives plain notice that he will add no more to the inextricable coils and convolutions of "Earth Triumphant," a poem praised by the Boston *cognoscenti,* but really very poor stuff. I have a feeling that he can do much better, and it is supported by certain passages in the present volume.

He will have to go pretty far, however, before he overtakes Bliss Carman and Francis Ledwidge, the former of whom offers a thin little book called "April Airs" (*Small-Maynard*), and the latter a larger tome called "Songs of the Fields" (*Duffield*), with an introduction by Lord Dunsany. Mr. Carman is so tried a poet that his work does not need to be described. In the latest volume, as in those gone before, it is marked by the great qualities of simplicity, directness, clarity. It often seems so transparent, indeed, that the fine skill put into it is apt to be lost sight of. Do not, belovéd, fall into that blindness. It is vastly more difficult to make such austere and shining little lyrics, each so unadorned and yet so full of charm, than to manufacture whole cantos of rhetorical fustian. Mr. Carman sings of modest and familiar things—the lovely round of the New England year, with its mild spring, its well-behaved summer, its melancholy autumn, its long and quiet winter. He gets a touch of magic into the least of his stanzas, and a touch of wistfulness. It is not poetry to inflame the cortex and race the pulse, but it is sound and honest poetry none the less.

As for Ledwidge, he makes a series of brilliant pictures of the Irish countryside—the vivid greens, the poor cottages, the weed-grown road., the lonely and sinister mountains. Simple words, simple measures—and yet all lighted up with images like this:

> And like an apron full of jewels
> The dewy cobweb swings.

It is almost impossible to believe, as Lord Dunsany says, that Ledwidge is no more than an inspired clodhopper, a peasant miraculously gifted with song. I have no belief in such miracles. The business of writing English verse is a craft as well as an art; it has its tricks and mysteries; it must be learned laboriously, just a. book-keeping or fiddle-playing must be learned. I suspect that this Ledwidge, in the intervals of his clod-hopping, gave many a fevered night to the study of Keats and Shelley.

More good verse out of Ireland is in "Poems of the Irish Revolutionary Brotherhood," edited by Padraic Colum (*Small-Maynard*). The poets represented are Thomas MacDonagh, P. H. Pearse, Joseph M. Plunkett and Roger Casement, all now done to death, alas, for their parts in the Irish rebellion. Here we have the poetry, not of English poets accidentally of Irish birth, but of genuine Irishmen, and hence mystics. The winds of old romance sigh through their stanzas: one sniffs old pagan altar fires in the midst of Christian songs; the wonder of ancient Erin is there.

§6.

The Imagists, judging by their latest volumes, seem to be petering out. I can find nothing in such collections as Mary Aldis' "Flashlights" (*Duffield*), Robert Alden Sanborn's "Horizons" (*Four Seas*), Richard Aldington's "Images Old and New" (*Four Seas*), and John Gould Fletcher's "Goblins and Pagodas" (*Houghton-Mifflin*), save a somewhat tedious straining for effects that are never actually reached. Mrs. Aldis is the least competent and effective of these revolutionists. Her opening poems, "The Barber Shop" and "Love in the Loop," are simply highly improbable anecdotes in stumbling lines; there is no more poetry in them, no more conjuring up of images, no more exaltation of the spirit, than in so many editorials in the Boston *Transcript;* they are weak, flat and foolish. Mr. Fletcher, in his color symphonies, succeeds rather better. Here and there a picture takes form; there is brilliance in detail; the thing shows a certain worthy earnestness. Moreover, Mr. Fletcher prefaces his book with a clear and interesting exposition of his poetic ideas—ideas often erroneous, but still not insane.

But the best of the current Imagist burbling is to be found in Donald Evans' "Two Deaths in the Bronx" (*Brown*), and Carl Sandburg's "Chicago Poems" (*Holt*), and particularly in the latter. Mr. Evans broke out as a prosodic anarchist several years ago, and performed various atrocities in two thin books. He is now a bit more sedate, and a bit more persuasive. At all events, he gets atmosphere into his poems; they have individuality; they are anything but commonplace. I give you "Two Modern Lovers," "Valley of Desire" and "Infidelities" as examples of his talents. . . . Mr. Sandburg's book is thick and in parts it is padded, but half a dozen of the compositions in the first section—the Chicago section—make it worth while. A volume of Chicago lyrics, or even of Chicago sonnets, would be, perhaps, an absurdity. One can scarcely imagine the half-medieval clang and gusto of that overgrown cow camp put into meticulously measured lines. Here the thing is done in its own spirit. Here one gets something of the rattle—and something of the great hope and striving, too. It is an experiment well carried out.

The Books of the Irish

I

The Irish talent for impossibilities reveals itself fully in beautiful let-ters. The tasters of books tell us that romance is dead; the Irish re-vive the corpse and set it to dancing. They tell us that the grip of the epic is gone; the Irish resurrect Diarmuid and Grania, Naisi and Deir-dre, and make them as real as Tom Jones. They tell us that symbolism passed with "When We Dead Awaken"; the Irish fill their poems with overtones and their very plays with spectral shapes. They tell us that no great literature is ever written in a tongue foreign to its makers; the Irish invade the language of the conqueror with Gaelic idioms and Gaelic modes of thought, and make a new English that is as sonorous and as savory as Marlowe's. They tell us that letters cannot prosper in the turmoil of politics; the Irish turn from the land laws to prosody without batting an eye, and stop a peasant comedy to shoot a red-coat, and face a firing-squad with sheaves of sonnets under their arms.

A people of fantastic and almost unearthly quality; a race that nev-er was on land or sea! Its literature is at once the oldest and the young-est in Europe. Its grand tales of enchantment antedate the Niebelungenlied; its new tales of wonder postdate Walter Pater. The heirs of the scholars who taught Christendom how to write Latin verse in the fourth century now teach Anglo-Saxondom how to write Eng-lish prose. Where is there another land with so fabulous a literary his-tory—a history so high in its peaks at beginning and end, and so low in its dark valleys between? A hundred years ago, even sixty or seventy years ago, no one read a genuinely Irish book. The literature of the country, in so far as it was known at all, was dismissed as barbarous and contemptible; it seemed no more than a mess of picaresque ballads and wild fairy tales, not always in good taste. But today, thanks to the labors of a few learned and devoted men, the old epics loom up in all the glow and majesty of the Odyssey, and out of the inspiration of the heroic past there has arisen a new literature that is as fecund, as various and as unmistakably national as any in Europe. Yeats and Dunsany are miles apart, and yet both are as Irish as Paddy's pig. Lady Gregory and AE. are separated even farther, and yet the essential Gaelicism of the

Smart Set 51, No. 3 (March 1917): 138–44.

one is as plain as the Gaelicism of the other. A school? A movement? Bosh! As well try to put Zola and Ellen Key, or Nietszsche and Tolstoi into double harness. What we have here is not merely a school or a movement, but a literature.

As I say, you will search far before you find parallels for its paradoxes. Perhaps there is one in Flanders, with Maeterlinck and Verhaeren writing French to match the French. Perhaps there is another in Norway, with Danish turned upon the Danes by Ibsen and Björnson. But in both cases literature had to wait until the turmoils of politics had died down, and men began to forget that their tongue was the tongue of a foreign foe. In Ireland there has been no forgetting. The fathers of the new literature, indeed, were political agitators almost more than they were literary pioneers. They essayed to dethrone England, English, the English and all Englishdom. They turned to the ancient demi-gods as to inspiring heroes of nationality; they called upon the Gael to be a Gael once more. One and all, they learned Gaelic, thought in Gaelic, made Gaelic at once their symbol and their weapon. But the forces they faced were too sturdy for them. The English language engulfed them in its gigantic and irresistible tide; they were forced, willy-nilly, to yield to it; they ended by making it their own. No stranger surrender has ever been seen, and no stranger conquest by the conquered. The neo-Celts, pumping not only their materials, but even their forms out of Gaelic, have emptied into English the most lavish stream of new idioms and new rhythms that it has received since the days of Elizabeth. The style of such writers as Yeats, AE., Lady Gregory, Dunsany, and above all, Synge, is not merely a development of old styles, a refinement of Wilde and Pater, a tickling up of Arthur Symons; it is something quite new under the sun and as golden and gorgeous as the music of trumpets. He who has inner ears must needs rejoice in it forever; it is a debauch of lovely phrases; there is in it a ripple of endless surprises. No man who is genuinely an artist will ever write English hereafter without giving an ear to it, and borrowing from it, and owing inspiration to it.

As *cognoscenti* are aware, this grand revival of letters in Ireland has not gone unsung. It has, in fact, had processions of brass bands to whoop up its progress. Its chief protagonists, especially Yeats, George Moore and Lady Gregory, have revealed a fine gift for *réclame;* they have got into the newspapers of all the world, and made themselves talked of. It has provoked bitter and profitable animosities; the glare of politics has been thrown upon it from time to time; even the huge slaughter of the war has contrived to augment its romance. More important still, it has been fortunate enough to bring out, almost by accident, two or three talents of the very highest consideration, and the noise that these talents have made has directed attention to the whole movement. The natural consequence has been a great deal of writing about it—books, pamphlets and articles; polemics, expositions and interpretations; defenses and denunciations; bosh and tosh unending. On the dramatic side alone it has engendered three times as much criticism as drama.

But until the present there was no single book that told the whole story of the revival in a coherent and accurate manner—that traced its origin and growth with sure knowledge, and discussed its leading figures with any understanding of their real purposes and relations, and separated the facts about them from the chaff of report and surmise. That lack is now supplied, in part, by "Literature in Ireland," by Thomas MacDonagh (*Stokes*), and in completeness by "Ireland's Literary Renaissance," by Ernest A. Boyd (*Lane*). The book of MacDonagh covers the field of neo-Celtic poetry, and, by an easy transition, the field of neo-Celtic prose style; the book of Boyd covers the whole progress of the new literature, from its beginnings in the translations of Mangan, Ferguson and O'Grady to its flowering in the tales and plays of Dunsany, the plays and travel sketches of Synge, the imaginary histories of George Moore, and the poems of Yeats, Colum, Hyde and MacDonagh. Boyd brought to the business exactly what it required, for he had behind him not only a thorough acquaintance with the whole body of the new literature, down to its most inconsiderable journalism, but also a personal intimacy with most of its leading spirits, and a sound comprehension of the remainder. His volume is judicious, sympathetic, informative and readable; it strikes the right middle course between punditic tediousness and gossipy garrulity. It puts him into equal fellowship with the best of the new Irish poets, dramatists and novelists, for he is the first historical (at opposed to polemical) critic that the movement has produced, and his first book is so intelligently done that it will be a difficult thing for his successors to surpass it. . . .

Much misleading writing has resulted from the confusion of the Irish literary renaissance, as we know it today, with the original neo-Celtic movement, which still survives among the intransigeants, and has been much prospered by the rebellion of last Easter. The two, despite their common sources and their possession of many principles and champions in common, are really quite distinct, for most of the new writers, while not forgetting their debt to Gaelic, accept the accomplished fact that Gaelic is dying out, whereas the more furious of the neo-Celtic patriots still cherish a hope of reviving it, and look to Irish freedom to get it on its legs again. The latter are thus not only not in accord with the former, but even in antagonism to them, for they see in the acceptance of English an abandonment of one of the most precious of Irish heritages. But this antagonism, after all, is more academic than real, for more than once, with Hibernian versatility, the same man has belonged to both camps, and the leader about whom the Gaelic movement chiefly revives, Dr. Douglas Hyde, is also the father of the Gaelicized English in which the best works of the revival are written. Mr. Boyd gives an example of Dr. Hyde's pioneering in his "Love Songs of Connacht" (1893):

> If I were to be on the brow of Nefin and my hundred loves by my side, it is pleasantly we would sleep together like the little bird upon the bough. It is your melodious wordy little mouth that increased my pain and a quiet sleep I cannot get until I shall die, alas!

Here, obviously, is the pattern that Synge and Lady Gregory followed—the pattern brought to a perfection of design in the speeches of Christy Mahon and Pegeen Mike in "The Playboy of the Western World," in the gabble of the old paupers in "The Workhouse Ward," and, above all, in the unforgettable phrases of Maurya in "Riders to the Sea." Mr. MacDonagh discusses its genesis at great length, and shows its dependence upon the idioms of Gaelic; Mr. Boyd traces its growth after Hyde's discovery of its possibilities. Synge, perhaps, did not borrow directly from Hyde, but he at least borrowed Hyde's trick of listening to the people of the countryside. Here we have, not an exact rendering of Gaelic idioms in a foreign tongue, but an effort to set down and preserve the peasants' difficulties with and blunderings in that tongue. It is thus from the true Irish, the countryfolk of Ireland, that the new dialect derives. There is as much of their naif mysticism and their homely humor in it as of their actual speech. It is racy of the soil. But there has been added to it an element that the soil never could have produced, and that is the element of conscious artistry, of æsthetic sensibility and sophistication. The new Irish are genuine artists. They hear and feel the most delicate overtones of speech. Their ears are as sensitive as Elizabethan ears to the slightest whisperings of beauty in words.

Of the two books now in court, Boyd's and MacDonagh's, you will find Boyd's by far the more informative and useful. MacDonagh confines himself to a relatively narrow field. It is Irish verse that chiefly interests him, for he was a poet himself and a good one, and his execution after the Easter rebellion was a heavy loss to letters. To appreciate him to the full, perhaps, one must be an Irishman; his very criticism is full of a Celtic twilight; he never proceeds by direct statement when he can proceed by allusion. There is a charm in all that, and Boyd misses it, but he makes up for it by marshaling his facts clearly and by writing in a straightforward and understandable manner. His book is particularly valuable for its illumination of the days of beginning. The greater part of new Irish criticism has concerned itself with end products, and especially with end products in the theater. Boyd avoids this false emphasis, and keeps the dramatic writings of the movement in their proper place. They are, of course, important; they include some of the best stuff that Young Ireland has given forth. But they have got so much attention that there is danger of forgetting the Irish poets and novelists and essayists, and the work of the dramatists themselves in other fields. These lacks are met by the two volumes before us. They are interesting and valuable books. . . .

II

I nursed a secret hope that last month's article would bring me a wreath of ivy from the Authors' League of America, or, at all events, an invitation to guzzle *vin rouge* with the Poetry Society, for it was not only intrinsically meritorious, but it also had a certain historical and military interest, for it was my one hundredth mensual discourse in this place. No such celebration of the anniversary having been forthcoming, I herewith recall it myself. It is not often, on this bleak western front of civilization, that a critic holds a trench so long. The hazards of the trade are numerous and flabbergasting. The authors one puts to the torture have a habit of making furious and unexpected reprisals; the publishers undertake countless counter-offensives; there come fearful squawks from Old Subscribers when their prejudices are violated or their pet fictioneers are nailed to the wall; even the best of editors, in the midst of such a din, grows skittish at times, and wonders if a change of critics would not help his digestion. All in all, a harsh and forbidding life, and yet, after eight and a third years, I still pursue it, and if all goes well I hope to print my thousandth article in February, 1991. In those eight and a third years I have served under four editors, not including myself; I have grown two beards and shaved them off; I have eaten 3,086 meals; I have made more than $100,000 in wages, fees, refreshers, tips and bribes; and I have written 510,000 words about books and not about books; I have received, looked at, and thrown away nearly 3,000 novels; I have been called a fraud 700 times, and blushed at the proofs; I have had more than 200 invitations to lecture before women's clubs, chautauquas, Y. M. C. A.'s, chambers of commerce, Christian Endeavor societies, and lodges of the Elks; I have received 150 pounds of letters of sweet flattery; I have myself written and published eight books, and reviewed them all favorably; I have had seventeen proposals of marriage from lady poets; I have been indicted by grand juries eight times; I have discovered thirty bogus geniuses; I have been abroad three and a half times, and learned and forgotten six foreign languages; I have attended 62 weddings, and spent nearly $200 for wedding presents; I have gained 48 pounds in weight and lost 18 pounds, and have grown bald and gray; I have been converted by the Rev. Dr. Billy Sunday, and then recanted and gone back to the devil; I have worn out nine suits of clothes; I have narrowly escaped marriage four times; I have had lumbago and neuralgia; I have taken to horn-rimmed spectacles; I have eluded the white-slave traders; I have fallen downstairs twice; I have undergone nine surgical operations; I have read the *Police Gazette* in the barbershop every week; I have shaken hands with Dr. Wilson; I have upheld the banner of the ideal; I have kept the faith, in so far as I could make out what it was; I have loved and lied; I have got old and sentimental; I have been torpedoed without warning.

Ah, the wonder and glory of life! The precession of the equinoxes! The mystery of tears and laughter! The toxic gurgle of a kiss! The way flowers shoot up, and horned cattle gambol in the fields! Eight and a third years seems a short while, and yet it has fetched me out of youth into middle age, and left my heart as bulged and battered as a gladiator's ear. Eight and a third years ego "Floradora" was still the rage, and the *New Republic* was unheard of, and Pilsener came in by every ship, and the muckrakers yet drove a fine trade, and Dr. Wilson was happy and untempted at Princeton, and Major-General Roosevelt was a simple colonel of cavalry d. R. a. D., and Diaz was on deck in Mexico, and beefsteak was still 23 cents a pound, and God was in His heaven, and all was well with the world. Where are the charming young authoresses who came to THE SMART SET office in the autumn of 1908, the cuties who tripped in with their ingratiating smiles and their manuscripts under their arms; the sweet ones who were startled to find that a critic of the bozart could be so toothsome a youth, and so beautifully polite? Married, thirty, fat, sour, abhorrent! Where are the poets who sent in notice that I was a *schuft,* and that their dithyrambs would survive my snickers? Dried up, blown away, forgotten, accursed! Where are the new geniuses who inflamed the skies that year—the revolutionary novelists, the novel soothsayers? Done, desolated, damned! Where are all the Great Thinkers that Col. Roosevelt used to introduce with such loud whoops—the faunal naturalists, the Pastor Wagners, the Warrington Dawsons, the exotic poets? Passed on, alas, passed on! I remember great vogues, excitements, turmoils—for Bergson, for W. B. Trites, for Eucken, for Gorky, for Maeterlinck, for Arnold Bennett, for Leonard Merrick, for Chesterton, for Mathilde Serao, for Synge, for H. G. Wells, for William James, for Alfred Noyes, for Robert W. Service, for Signorina Montessori, for Ellen Key, for Chekoff, for Dr. Cook, for

that poetizing jail-bird out West (I have even forgotten his name!) . . .
Dominus dedit, Dominus abstulit! Mais où sont les neiges d'antan! . . .
Wein nicht, Süsschen, 's giebt gar kein Use! . . .

I glance back through my first compositions for this sodality and
find some strange things. For example, this in the initial article: "Mary
Roberts Rinehart is a new writer." Again, a solemn tirade against the
platitudinousness of Upton Sinclair: evidently news in 1908. Yet
again, good counsel to Mlle. Marie Corelli: "I should advise her to
spend six months in the chorus of a Broadway operetta." Operetta?
They still existed eight and a third years ago! . . . In No. 2, a long
hymn to Joseph Conrad, the opening anthem of a cantata yet going
on. Conrad, in 1908, was scarcely more than a name on this side of the
water, and only a hushed whisper on the other side. All of his greatest
stories had been written, but they had dogged about from publisher's
office to publisher's office, and each successive book had come out
with a new imprint. Run your eye down the list: Macmillan, Appleton,
Dodd-Mead, Scribner, Doubleday, McClure, Putnam—seven different
publishers for his first seven books! He was a long time getting down,
but down he went in the end. Today his works are offered to cognoscenti in an elegant series of navy-blue, limp-leather volumes: very
roycrofty, indeed. I am almost tempted to lay in a set. Not only does it
soothe the cultured eye, but it would also save wear and tear of the
first editions, which are now soaring in value. My natural sagacity,
which functions in profane affairs as well as in *belles lettres,* led me to
accumulate them while they still sold at par, and they now fortify me
against the *Canis lupus.* "Almayer's Folly," published at six shillings, is
worth from $25 to $35, according to your passion for it. "The Nigger
of the Narcissus," in good condition, would probably bring more.
Even so recent a book as "Some Reminiscences," published in 1912,
carries a premium of $10 or $12. The whole set was offered a year or
so ago for $150. I doubt that it could be brought together today for
less than $225. The graft of book reviewers, if they have foresight, is
thus seen to be very fair. A forward-looker, I have acquired wealth, and
eat and drink, perhaps, more than is strictly decent.

And Dreiser! Back in 1908 only "Sister Carrie" was behind him,
and even "Sister Carrie" was but little known, for the first edition had
been suppressed by a snuffling publisher, and the second edition had
but recently reached the book-stalls. That first edition is now so rare
that collectors bid against one another for every stray copy that shows
itself. It would be a good idea to hunt up the old plates and print a
forgery; nine collectors out of ten have been pleasantly deceived by the
forged first edition of Thackeray's "Second Funeral of Napoleon."
Such risks add to the charm of book collecting, for every professor of

the art believes firmly that he himself is beyond being fooled, and so it joys him to think of the swindles perpetrated on the other fellow. Incidentally, I know a dealer who lately bought a fine copy of the original "Sister Carrie" for twenty-five cents. He found it in a junk-shop, and leaped from the place like an archdeacon stung by wasps the moment the transaction was closed. Human-like, he couldn't help boasting about his coop, and so I was able, on juridic grounds, to beat him down to a couple of dollars for the prize. I in my turn then emitted oxygen, whereupon a kind friend, unsuccessful in his own hunt for the book, affably accepted it from me as a present. I had, of course, another copy. I shall leave it to some orphan asylum when I die, and so help to save Dreiser from hell. The Comstocks, as I write, bawl for his blood on the ground that Eugene Whitla, in "The 'Genius,'" is a mammal, and occasionally looses a big, big damn. By the time this article is printed, he may be safely roosting in some kindly jail, with leisure to read his own books. If he gets more than six months he will have time to finish them. Then, perhaps, he will fall to work upon a novel in strict accord with the prevailing Methodist canon—a novel whose males confine their carnalities to sly glances at servant girls, and to fighting their way into Billy Sunday meetings "for men only," and to the diligent study of such literature as "What a Girl of 45 Should Know," and II Samuel, xi, 2–77. . . .

I am often asked if I enjoy my job, and reply frankly that I do. There is, at all events, constant variety in it; a surprise is always around the corner; that is a dull month which doesn't produce two or three genuinely interesting books. I glance back over eight and a third years and recall such things as Sudermann's "The Indian Lily," and Anatole France's "The Revolt of the Angels," and Lord Dunsany's "The Book of Wonder," and Arnold Bennett's "The Old Wives' Tale," and Dreiser's "The Titan," and H. G. Wells' "Ann Veronica," and Mrs. Wharton's "Ethan Frome," and Max Beerbohm's "Zuleika Dobson,"* and Conrad's "Victory"—I glance back and decide at once that my time has not been wasted. It is a superlative pleasure to dredge such glowing and memorable books out of the stream of drivel and commonplace, the endless avalanche of balderdash by the Oppenheims and the Chamberses, the Bindlosses and Hall Caines, the Corellis and Phillpottses, the jitney Richard Harding Davises and second-table O. Henrys. Sound literature, indeed, is being produced in this, our age. The rate of emission of good books is more rapid than ever before. Moreover, it seems to me that discrimination is increasing, despite the flood of shoddy wares. There is still a vast market for such sentimental slobber as one finds in the "Pollyannas" and "Bambis," but it is no longer mistaken for great art, as was done with the slobber of Dickens. We have as many boob-thrillers and mountebanks as ever before, but we do not revere Hall Caine as Bulwer-Lytton was revered. We yet have rages for sensational poets, but they do not last as long as the rage for Byron, nor do so many folk succumb to them. Puritanism still wars upon all art among us, but its arm grows weak and the devices on its banners are laughed at. I doubt that any truly first-rate book has gone unrecognized for twenty years past; I doubt that any first-rate book has gone unpublished. If a new Samuel Butler should print a new "Erewhon" tomorrow, even the *Nation* would be aware of it within a year.

The United States, of course, produces relatively little sound writing of its own, but it has at least grown eagerly hospitable to the sound writing that is produced elsewhere. Our thirst for foreign novelties, in truth, it almost as avid as the Germans'. Scarcely a month goes by that some new Selma Lagerlöf or Leonid Andreyieff or Emil Verhaeren or Mathilde Serao or Henri Bergson is not discovered, devoured and hymned. The Americanos got down Ibsen long before the English; the first performance of an Ibsen play in English, indeed, was given in Louisville back in 1882. They embraced Synge while the Dublin mob was yet heaving benches at him. They saw the first adequate performances of Shaw. They were bemused by the moonshine of Maeterlinck before France gave him a thought. They are hot for English novelists who are scarcely heard of at home . . . One of the causes of this alacrity of welcome, perhaps, lies in the somewhat appalling mediocrity of our domestic produce in beautiful letters. Our books, in the main, lack genuine distinction; they just miss arousing the imagination. The country, for example, is full of novelists who have shown promise and then failed. Robert Herrick is one. He began auspiciously, but today he wallows in claptrap. His trouble is plain enough: he is clever, but not profound; he has facility, but he lacks ideas. Edith Wharton is another. She rose to the peak of "Ethan Frome" and then settled down into a valley of fustian. A third is Robert Grant. He flew all the signals of great talent—and then hauled these in. Howells, James Lane Allen, John Luther Long, Hamlin Garland and the rest of that elder company have run their race. Churchill has succumbed to the national platitudinousness. Miss Cather and Mrs. Watts have yet to strike twelve. Stephen French Whitman, Ernest Poole, Henry Milner Rideout, Owen Johnson and a dozen others of their quality seem to be done for; the lure of the *Saturday Evening Post* has finished most of them.

But let us not wail and gnash our teeth. We still have Dreiser, and despite "The 'Genius',", he will probably do his best work hereafter. He is the one novelist among us who shows no response whatever to the variable winds of public favor; he hacks out his path undeterred by either praise or blame; a sort of blind fury of creation seems to move him. And we still have two or three other men who are sound artists, and yet as American as trading stamps or chewing gum: Booth Tarkington, George Ade, Harry Leon Wilson. All have yielded themselves to temptation: all have stooped for the shekel. And yet, when everything has been said, Ade's "Fables in Slang" come near being the best comic writing of our time in any language, and Tarkington's "Penrod" is a book that will long outlive Tarkington, and Wilson has done things in "Bunker Bean" and again in "Ruggles of Red Gap" that belong to satire at its best, and hint clearly at what he could do on a larger scale if he would only spit on his hands and make the effort.

I speak only of novelists. Of poets and other such lesser fauna, I shall discourse, perchance, at some later conference.

The Infernal Feminine

I

The women, woven, built and kneaded up
Of hydrogen, of azote, oxygen,
Of carbon, phosphorus, chlorine, sulphur, iron,
Of calcium, kalium, natrum, menganese.
                                   —*John Davidson.*

W. L. George is not only the cleverest, and by long odds, of the younger English novelists of the moment; he is also a specialist in the soul of woman, and has written many a fair pamphlet, leading article and dithyramb upon it. And yet, in his new book, "The Intelligence of Woman" (*Little-Brown*), he seldom proceeds, for all his skill, beyond that facile shocking of the respectable which consists of stating platitudes loudly and scandalously. The trick is an old one, and always works. Take it away, and nothing would remain of the works of George Bernard Shaw save a smell of brimstone and a few paltry stealings from Ibsen and Sardou. George Moore uses it; Anatole France uses it; Maximilian Harden uses it; Nietzsche used it. Dropping a thousand metres, I myself use it constantly, and shall put it to service in this present article; without it I would be a dull ass, indeed, and almost fit for the pulpit. As for George, he achieves a thumping platitude in his very title, for the fact that women are intelligent is so horribly patent that it takes all of their intelligence to make us forget it.

The *intelligence* of women? Go to, my dear Mon Chair! As well argue that Scotchmen are stingy, that Puritans have dirty minds, that cats are feline, that Jews are Jews. Women are not only intelligent; they have almost a monopoly of the harder and more valuable sorts of intelligence; the Thing In Itself is as feminine as rouge and cruelty. Men are brave. Men are strong. Men have sentiment. Men are romantic, and love beauty. Men can sweat and endure. Men are damphools. But in so far as they are intelligent they are feminine—in so far as they show a sharp and penetrating sense they are still nourished by the milk of their mothers. "Human creatures," says Dr. George, borrowing from Weininger, "are never entirely male or entirely female; there are no men, there are no

Smart Set 51, No. 4 (April 1917): 266–72.

women, but only sexual majorities." Find me an intelligent man, a man free from sentimentality, a man hard to fool, a first-rate man—and I'll show you a man with a wide streak of woman in him. The good traits and qualities of the male, the marks of the unpolluted masculine, are at the same time the marks of the numskull. The caveman is all muscle and mush; without a woman to boss him and think for him, he is a truly pitiful spectacle, a baby with whiskers, a libel on God.

So far as I can make out by experiments on dogs and guineapigs, there is no biological necessity for this superiority of the frescoed sex. That is to say, it does not lie in any anatomical or physiological advantages. Women, in fact, have smaller brains than men, though perhaps not in proportion to weight. There are quite as many low, epicycloid brows among them. Their ears stand out as absurdly. They suffer from the same adenoids, gastritis, cholelithiasis, gastrectasis, nephritis—from the same pathological conditions that produce sentimentality, religion, patriotism, messianic delusions, alcoholism, the worship of baseball players, intrigues with servant girls and the other typical neuroses of men. They have, in essence, the same appetites and weaknesses, the same fits of emotion, the same vanities. . . . Nay; their superiority is not a gift of the gods; it is a cultivated acquirement; their greater intelligence is an effect of use. Its springs are to be found, not in any inherent mental advantage, but in an obvious physical *dis*advantage—in the inferiority of their frames, their relative lack of brute strength. In the beginning, two things made them physically weak; first, the expensive imbecility of the process whereby they bring forth offspring, and secondly, the egoistic desire of men for mates of apparent inferiority and docility. And in the end, one thing has made them mentally strong: the dire necessity of counterbalancing this physical weakness by craft, their sheer need of brains. The Jews got their intelligence by the same enforced process; Nietzsche has described it at great length. The English have lost theirs by a contrary process; the Americans are going the same route.

That anyone should seriously doubt the intelligence of women, even enough to give excuse for a book demonstrating it, is one of the mysteries of human psychology. All the evidence upon which the doubt is grounded is evidence that is utterly worthless. What men mistake for lack of intelligence in women—and, as I shall show, very few men who actually know women ever honestly make this mistake—is merely a lack of technical proficiency. Two great forces keep them from acquiring that vast mass of small intellectual tricks, that complex of petty knowledges, that collection of cerebral rubber-stamps, which constitutes the chief mental equipment of most men. The first of these forces is the social necessity that has kept them pinned down, at least until lately, to a round of trivial duties in the home, and to a cloistered seclusion therewith. The second is the great social convention that, despite their new revolt against it, still holds up marriage as the most honorable career open to them—as the gaudiest prize, in fact, that the practice of their conventional virtues can hope to win for them. The result is that women have neither the opportunity to acquire the jingling facility that passes for intelligence in men, nor the time. A woman's apprenticeship is too short, and she is too much distracted from its business by the more important enterprise of snaring a husband. Unintelligent women—I here speak comparatively, for no woman, not downright insane, may be reasonably called unintelligent—are commonly more successful in this pursuit than more intelligent women, if only because the latter have a keener sense of its absurdity; but their very success, by giving them a chance to gloat, enables them to exert pressure upon their superior sisters, and so we see both classes chasing men as hotly as ever an archbishop chased the devil. Hence their prevailing deficiency in technical equipment—in the little talents that serve the world in place of intelligence. Before the stenographer of 21 can master a tenth of the idiotic "knowledge" in the head of the male bookkeeper of 30, she has married the boss—or perchance the bookkeeper himself—and so tries to forget it as soon as possible. Before the girl cook picks up a fourth of the culinary subtleties that are commonplaces even to the negro chefs on Pullmen dining-cars, she has caught a man and need bother about them no more, for he has to eat, in the last analysis, whatever she sets before him, and his lack of intelligence makes it easy for her to meet and shut off his academic criticisms.

For these reasons women sometimes take on a superficial and very deceptive air of stupidity. Because they cannot do all the puerile tricks that men can do—because they cannot add up a column of figures correctly, or understand baseball batting averages, or boss a gang of sandhogs, or set a rat-trap, or understand the doctrine of the atonement, or distinguish between the platforms of two groups of job-seekers, or read with straight faces an editorial in the New York *Evening Post*— because they are incapable of such petty feats it is assumed that they lack brains. But the truth is that their very incapacity in these matters is a proof of their superior intelligence. Their minds disdain so mean a virtuosity; their habitual mental dealings are with far more profound and respectable things; they inhabit a world above the world of trivial artifices. And what theory thus urges, the common experience of mankind bears out. No sane man would consult his wife about hiring a clerk, or trimming his cuffs, or voting for Assemblymen, or getting his shoes shined; but by the same token no sane man would *fail* to consult his wife about taking a partner into his business, or growing a moustache, or running for office, or sailing for Europe in time of war, or marrying off his daughter, or choosing his son's college, or combating a blackmailer, or joining a church. Such things are genuinely important; they lie at the foundation of well-being; an error in deciding about them has permanent and serious consequences. Here is where the superior mental grasp of women comes in; here is where they rise above the insignificant axioms and formulæ of men; here is where they get elbowroom for the exercise of what is called their intuition.

Intuition? Bosh! Then it was intuition that led Darwin to the hypothesis of natural selection. Then it was intuition that composed "Die Walküre." All this intuition of which so much is gabbled is no more and no less than intelligence—intelligence so keen that it can penetrate appearances and get at the substance within. Women decide all the great questions of life correctly, not because they are good guessers, not because they are divinely inspired, not because they have some occult power, but simply and solely because they have sense. They see things at a glance that most men could not see with searchlights and telescopes; they grasp the essentials of a problem while men are still debating its mere externals. And the reason, as I have said, is not far to seek. Their experience of the world, and especially what may be called their inherited experience, has forced them to be clear-headed and sharp-witted; above all, it has rid them of that vast burden of sentimentality which roosts upon the cerebrum of men. Thus they estimate persons and ideas, not in the terms of what would be pleasant, or in terms of what ought to be, or in terms of what must be if this or that insane assumption is sound, but in terms of what actually is. They are the supreme realists of the race. Apparently illogical, they are the exclusive possessors of a rare and subtle super-logic. Apparently unobservant and easily fooled, they see with bright and horrible eyes. Apparently the slaves of delusion, they are as alive to the indubitable fact as so many foxes. . . . Men, of course, also show a certain intelligence—rare men all the time, lesser men now and then. Men, too, sometimes have brains. But no man, I venture, is ever as steadily intelligent, as constantly sound in judgment, as little deceived by appearances, as the average woman of forty-eight. . . .

II

I have said that women are not sentimental. The doctrine, I daresay, will cause a protest. The theory that they are is itself a juicy sentimentality; one sentimentality will be brought up to establish another. But an appeal to a few obvious facts will be sufficient to hold up my contention. Turn to the field in which the mental processes of men and women are most dramatically brought into conflict and contrast—

to the field, to wit, of marriage. Surely no long argument is needed to establish the superior acumen and strategy of women in this business. The very fact that marriages occur at all is a proof, indeed, of their possession of greater intelligence than men, for it is plainly to a man's interest to avoid marriage as long as possible, and as plainly to a woman's interest to make a favorable marriage as soon as possible. The intelligence of the two sexes is thus directed, in this capital concern of life, to two diametrically antagonistic ends. Which intelligence commonly wins? I leave the verdict to the jury. All men fight it off; some men are successful for relatively long periods; a few extraordinarily intelligent and resourceful (or perhaps merely lucky) men escape altogether. But in the long run, as everyone knows, the average man is duly married and the average woman gets a husband. In the long run the majority of women, in this clean-cut duel, demonstrate their enormous mental superiority to the majority of men.

Not many men, worthy of the name, gain any valuable thing by marriage. Even assessing its benefits at their most inflated worth, they are palpably overborne by crushing disadvantages. When a man marries, indeed, it is no more than a sign that feminine strategy—*i. e.,* feminine intelligence—has forced him into a more or less abhorrent compromise with his own honest desires and best interests, and whether that compromise be a sign of his stupidity or of his cowardice it is all one. In the first case, he marries because he has been clearly overcome in a combat of wits; in the second case he chooses marriage as the safest of all forms of liaison. In both cases his inherent sentimentality is a powerful weapon in the hands of his antagonist. It makes him cherish the fiction of his enterprise, and even of his daring, in the very midst of the military operations against him. It makes him accept as real the play-acting that women always excel at, and at no time more than when stalking a man. It makes him, above all, see a glamour of romance in a transaction which, even at its best, contains as much of gross trafficking as the sale of a mule. The man never wants *all* that marriage offers and implies; he wants, at most, no more than certain parts; he wants, let us say, a cook but not a mother-in-law, a representative in society but not a prying partner in his business, a beautiful mistress but not a sharer of his bathroom, theology, income and secret ambitions. But in order to get the thing that he wants, he has to take a lot of things that he doesn't want—that no sane man, in truth, could imaginably want—and it is to the business of forcing him into this disastrous bargain that the woman of his "choice" addresses the best efforts of her superior intelligence. Once the game is fairly set, she searches out his weaknesses with the utmost discretion and pertinacity, and plays upon them with all her resources. He is at a disadvantage from the start. His sentimental and unintelligent belief in theories that she knows quite well are not true—*e. g.,* the theory that she shrinks from him, and shies at marriage itself—gives her a weapon against him that she drives home mercilessly. The moment she discerns that sentimentality bubbling in him, he is hers to do with as she will. Save for acts of God, he is forthwith as good as married.

This sentimentality in marriage is seldom, if ever, observed in women. Their choice of mates is made with the brain and not with the heart, and quite naturally, for they have as much to gain by marriage as man has to lose, and is it any wonder that they seek to enter upon it on the most favorable terms possible, and with the minimum admixture of disarming emotion? Men get their mates, in the common phrase, by falling in love. That is to say, they account for the act of marriage, after feminine intelligence has made it practically inevitable, by enshrouding it in a maze of sentimentality and romance. Their defeat is thus made glorious; they clank their shackles with proud and even boastful shouts. Women are more cautious about embracing the conventional hocus-pocus of the situation. They never acknowledge that they have fallen in love, as the phrase is, until the man has formally avowed the delusion, and so cut off his retreat. With them, falling in love thus appears as a sort of afterthought, or, perhaps more accurately, as the spread of a contagion. The theory is that the love of the man has inspired it; that it was non-existent until the heat of his own flames set it off. This theory, it must be admitted, has a certain element of fact in it. A woman, once the man of her choice is safely snared, not infrequently unbends a bit herself, and throwing off her intelligence and its inhibitions, indulges in the luxury of a more or less forced and mawkish sentiment. But it is almost unheard of for her to descend to this banality before the sentimental intoxication of the man is assured. To do otherwise—that is, to confess, even *post facto,* to an anterior descent—would bring down upon her the scorn of all her sisters. Such a confession would be an admission that sentimentality had got the better of her intelligence at a critical moment—and in the eyes of women, as in the eyes of the small minority of intelligent men, no treason to the higher cerebral centers could be more degrading.

This disdain of sentimentality in the chief business of their lives, and even of that higher form of sentiment which passes over into æsthetic sensibility, is well revealed by the fact that women are seldom bemused by mere beauty in men. Save on the stage, the handsome fellow has no advantage with the fair over his more Gothic brother. In real life, he is viewed with the utmost suspicion by all women save the most stupid, and their matrimonial enterprises are almost always directed toward men whose lack of pulchritude is accompanied by a counterweighting lack of vanity, and who are thus easier to bring down, and what is more, easier to hold subject. The weight of opinion among women is decidedly against the woman who falls in love with an Apollo: she is regarded, at best, as a silly creature, and at worst, as one pushing bad taste to the verge of indecency. Such weaknesses are resigned to women approaching senility, and to the more ignoble sort of women laborers. A shop girl, perhaps, may fall in love with a moving picture actor; a half-idiotic old widow may succumb to a college boy with shoulders like the Parthenon; but no woman of self-respect, even supposing her to be temporarily flustered by a lovely buck, would yield to that sort of madness for an instant, or confess it to her dearest friend. To do so would be to become a hissing and a mocking. Women know how little such purely superficial values are worth; they choose their husbands as intelligently as they traffic in the marts; the voice of their order, the first taboo of their freemasonry, is firmly against making an æsthetic recreation of the serious business of marriage.

That men show no such sagacity is too well known to need demonstration. The baits they swallow most greedily are not edible and nourishing baits, but merely bright and gaudy ones. They fall for a pair of black eyes, a synthetic complexion, a graceful figure, or a shapely ankle, without giving the slightest thought to the fact that a whole woman is there, and that within the cranial cavity of the woman lies a brain, and that the habits and capacities of that brain are of vastly more importance to their future well-being than all imaginable physical stigmata combined. In brief, they estimate women, and hence acquire wives, by reckoning up their external aspects, which is just as intelligent as estimating an egg by its external aspect. Worse, they do not get at the realities even here; they judge by a mere glance, and are thus easily deceived by the most abominable frauds. Many a man never really sees his wife—that is, as her God sees her, and as the embalmer will see her—until after they have been married for years. A trained nurse tells me that even when undergoing the extreme discomforts of parturition, the great majority of women continue to sophisticate their complexions with pulverized dyes, and to give thought to the discreet arrangement of their hair. These transparent devices reduce the psychologist to snickers, and yet it must be obvious that they entrap and make fools of men. If a man has a noticeably sensible wife, he is almost apologetic about it; the ideal of his sex is always a pretty wife, and the vanity and coquettishness that so often go with prettiness are erected into charms. In other words, men play the love game so unintelligently that they often esteem a woman in proportion as she conceals her native intelligence. Women seldom, if ever, make that blunder. What they esteem most in men is not beauty or social graces, but that complex of small capacities which makes up masculine efficiency and passes for masculine intelligence. This intelligence, at its highest, approximates their own. They thus respect it, and seek it out.

III

I have accused Dr. George of retailing platitudes—an accurate charge, but still an unfair one. The indubitable, it must be admitted, is not always the obvious. His case needed no proving, but he proves it with noble skill. His book, indeed, is one of the most competent and persuasive that I have encountered for a long while, and he is particularly convincing in his discussion of feminism and of the future of marriage. In these remote outposts of civilization it is common to confuse feminism and woman suffrage. They are really no more closely related than a dog and its fleas. The suffrage movement is the intellectual slums of feminism; it attracts only those women who are almost as stupid as men; its central doctrine, that one sovereign peruna will suffice to ease all the belly-aches of humanity, is typically masculine in its sentimental imbecility. Of like sort are the male manias for prohibition, the initiative and referendum, the short ballot, preparedness, and the direct election of Senators. The sort of woman who believes in such nonsense is precisely the sort of woman who yearns to wear pantaloons and be a man—the sort who envies the oafish stupidity and hoggishness of men, and wishes she could put off her feminine intelligence and take on a masculine mushiness and boorishness.

In particular, the suffragette is one who is jealous of a definite masculine privilege—to wit, the privilege of promiscuity in amour. Read the books of the chief suffragette wild women, and you will find running through all of them an hysterical denunciation of what is called the double standard of morality. The existence of this double standard seems to drive the poor girls half frantic; they bellow raucously for its abrogation, and demand that the frivolous male be visited with even more idiotic penalties than oppress the frivolous female; some even advocate gravely his punishment by surgery. All this, of course, is hocus-pocus. What the principal lady crusaders actually desire is not that the male be reduced to monogamy by sumptuary laws, but that his franchise of dalliance be extended to themselves. The most elementary acquaintance with Freudian psychology exposes their secret animus. Unable to snare males under monogamy, or, at all events, unable to ensnare males worthy the respect of other women (for the suffragette husband, in all candor, must be dismissed as a truly horrible creature), they leap to the theory that they would be more successful if the rules were easier. Nothing could be more absurd. If the rules were easier, they would find it even more difficult to get husbands than it is to-day, for, to paraphrase George Bernard Shaw, every sane man would prefer a stray kiss or two from a genuinely attractive woman to the whole devotion of the average suffragette. Thus the theory of the whoopers and the snorters of the cause, in its esoteric as well as in its public aspect, is unsound and imbecile. They are simply women who, in intellect, are two-thirds men—and this fact explains their failure to achieve presentable husbands quite as well as it explains the ready credence they give to political and philosophical absurdities, What the more sensible sort of men esteem in women is not a hollow and booming quasi-masculinity, but unmistakable femininity—*i. e.*, a decent reserve and self-respect—*i. e.*, the sort of intelligence which holds the emotions in check—*i. e.*, the highest sort of intelligence. The suffragettes are hopeless simply because they show no such reserve and self-respect, and hence no such capacity for inhibiting emotion, and hence no such intelligence. They are simply donkeys—as noisy and as stupid as men.

The feminists are a far more delicate and intelligent breed, which is the same as saying that they are far more feminine. The thing they ask for is not the privilege of being as blatant and emotional as men—*e. g.*, in politics—but freedom from those ancient conventions which force them to conceal and sophisticate their superior intelligence in order to flatter men's vanity. In brief, what they want is free opportunity in the world—opportunity to meet men on equal terms, without any need to encase the steel of their intellect in the velvet of etiquette and superstition. This end they will undoubtedly attain. Women might have attained it in any age of the world's history; in more than one age they actually did attain it; if they are still short of it today it is only because they have been seeking it but a brief time, and are still somewhat defectively organized and led. In detail, if not in gross, they have scored easy and innumerable victories. In the matter of property rights, they have come to full equality with men; in many of the American States, in truth, the wife is now favored above the husband. In the professions they have made steady progress in all directions where genuine intelligence is required—*e. g.*, they have conquered nursing, which requires quick and accurate thought, but failed in the law, which requires only a vehement disregard of sense. In business, they have completely broken down the old delusion of romance in sex, and so got their freedom quickly; not even the barber-shop weeklies gabble any more about stenographers seducing their bosses, and not even policemen seriously believe that shop-girls are sold into white slavery by theirs. And in the broader field of social relations they have gone quite as far, for divorce is now as easy in all civilized states to the woman as to the man, and the woman who has charm enough can adopt the masculine end of the double standard with impunity, and suffer no more actual damage than she would suffer by having a tooth knocked out. . . .

The end? Who knows? As for me, I anticipate (and even hope for) a sort of revival of the matriarchate, a reinstatement of woman to the position that her superior intelligence entitles her to. Once on an equal footing with man, once completely emancipated from convention, she will not stop with equality. More, she will not be able to stop; her natural superiority will make it impossible for her to brook the pretensions of her inferiors. And why should she? Our theory that men should rule the world is, after all, no more than a theory; if we cling to it fanatically it is only because we love set ideas, fixed forms, anything to save us thinking; we may see it overturned as we have seen other apparently immutable principles overturned. What are men doing to deserve their kingship? Observe their performance in politics, the chief business of civilization. Here in the United States they have chosen from among their number one who is put forward as the man most fit, among all American men, to run the state. And what do we find when we examine this gentleman? We find a wholesaler of notions so infantile that they must needs disgust an intelligent suckling—an endless geyser of fallacies and sentimentalities, a cataract of unsupported assumptions and hollow moralizings, a man whose noblest flights of thought are flattered when they are called intelligible. This is the male champion. I do not venture upon the cruelty of comparing his preposterous ideas to the ratiocinations of a woman of like fame and position; all I ask of you is that you weigh them, for sense, for shrewdness, for respect for facts, for intelligent grasp of relations, with the idea of the average midwife. . . .

Nay, I do not fear feminism. Feminism is the hope of intelligence. Feminism will save us from romance and superstition, from sobs and slobber, from guff and gush.

Shocking Stuff

§1

Mark Twain, dead, promises to stir up the animals even more joyously than Mark Twain, living. The old boy left his best jokes to the last; from his tomb issue sparks that set the hair of the virgin reviewers afire. "The Mysterious Stranger" (*Harper*) is already exposed; there will come, soon or late, I daresay, a public edition of "What Is Man?" now bringing fancy prices in private; in the end, perhaps, we shall get a glimpse of that appalling piece of satire mentioned by Albert Bigelow Paine in his biography—that tale of the microbes who inhabit a man's veins, and worship him as their god, and employ priests and bishops to present their suits to him, and imagine him as dreadfully concerned about their ultra-microscopic souls, hopes, sins, aspirations and theology. . . .

How criticism in America has misestimated this colossus! How the cackling of literary wenches, male and female, has resounded around the one indubitable giant of our literature! First they sought to dismiss him as a hollow buffoon, a brother to Josh Billings and Petroleum V. Nasby. Then they made a sort of national Peck's Bad Boy of him, an ambulent Punch and Judy show for banquets and chautauquas, a William Jennings Bryan armed with a slapstick. And finally, sensing his greatness dimly, they erected him into an apologetic kind of equality with Thomas Bailey Aldrich and William Dean Howells, and issued an impertinent amnesty for the errors of his youth. What will these donkeys now answer to "The Mysterious Stranger"? What, with their grudging *imprimatur* flung into their faces, will they say of such stuff as this:

> . . . a God who could make good children as easily as bad, yet preferred to make bad ones; one who could have made every one of them happy, yet never made a single happy one; who made them prize their bitter life, yet stingily cut it short; who gave his angels eternal happiness unearned, yet required his other children to earn it; who gave his angels painless lives, yet cursed his other children with biting miseries and maladies of mind and body; who mouths justice and invented hell—mouths mercy and invented hell—mouths Golden

Smart Set 52, No. 1 (May 1917): 394–400.

Rules, and forgiveness multiplied by seventy times seven, and invented hell; who mouths morals to other people and has none himself; who frowns upon crimes, yet commits them all; who created men without invitation, then tries to shuffle the responsibility for man's acts upon man, instead of honorably placing it where it belongs, upon himself; and finally, with altogether divine obtuseness, invites the poor, abused slave to worship him! . . .

Here, indeed, is food for the college professors who pipe for Optimism and a Brighter World, and denounce Dreiser for his harsh truth-telling, and apply the criteria of the Sunday school to beautiful letters. Here, having taken the viper reluctantly to their bosoms, they are stung damnably. Here a bomb goes off in the sanctuary. . . . And loaded with what? With platitudes, of course. "The Mysterious Stranger" shocks by the very process I described and exemplified last month: it turns the obvious into the scandalous by stating it plainly. The preface to "What Is Man?" dated February, 1905, puts Mark himself on the stand in confirmation:

> The studies for these papers were begun twenty-five or twenty-seven years ago. The papers were written seven years ago. I have examined them once or twice per year since and found them satisfactory. I have just examined them again and am still satisfied that they speak the truth. Every thought in them has been thought (and accepted as unassailable truth) by millions upon millions of men—and concealed, kept private. Why did they not speak out? Because they dreaded (*and could not bear*) the disapproval of the people around them. Why have not I published? The same reason has restrained me, I think. I can find no other.

More, the same reason still halted Mark at the brink of his new resolve. He printed "What Is Man?" but only in a private edition, limited to 250 copies, and never offered for sale. The book, in fact, is still unpublished. Stray copies of the private edition, coming into the second-hand book-shops, fetch $45 or $50. Even a pirated English reprint, issued by the Rationalist Press Association in 1910, now brings $10 or more. Mr. Paine tells us something about the inner springs of this diffidence. Mrs. Clemens was a very religious woman, and Mark hesitated to violate her pruderies; after her death he was equally disinclined to forget them. The rest he tells himself. He knew how hard his fight for position had been; he knew how long it had taken him to live down the sacrileges of his youth; he knew what direful penalties outraged orthodoxy could inflict; in the Gorky case both he and Howells turned tail discreetly, and a memorandum given by Paine shows what he was afraid of.

But, dead, he is safely beyond the gabble, and so, after a prudent interval, Paine begins the printing of the works in which, writing knowingly for posterity, he could set down his true philosophy without fear. That philosophy, thus displayed, is all that was needed to make his position secure. It shows that a coherent and understandable idea was underneath all his grotesqueries; that he was by no means the empty *enfant terrible* a pious legend has sought to make him; that he saw human life, not as a pleasant comedy, but in all the naked horror revealed to Rabelais and Swift; in brief, that the sharp egos of a first-rate artist were in his head. "Your race, in its poverty," says the nephew of Satan in "The Mysterious Stranger," "has unquestionably one really effective weapon—laughter. Power, money, persuasion, supplication, persecution—these can lift at a colossal humbug—push it a little— weaken it a little, century by century; but only laughter can blow it to rags and atoms at a blast. Against the assault of laughter nothing can stand. You are always fussing and fighting with your other weapons. Do you ever use that one? No; you leave it lying rusting. As a race, do you ever use it at all? No; you lack sense and the courage." . . . The sense was there—and the grave has supplied the courage. Here, indeed, is a dead man who tells a tale. . . .

As I say, "The Mysterious Stranger" will probably knock the breath out of all the literary girls, and return old Mark once more to the *index expurgatorius* of the Carnegie libraries. In the books of vapid "criticism" by college professors he will again suffer the pious deprecation that was his portion in the days of "A Tramp Abroad" and "Huckleberry Finn." Tears will be shed over his "morbidness," as they were once shed over his "flippancy." But all this braying of the long-eared will take no more from his stature as an artist than the ranting of Methodists will take from the stature of Dreiser. Mark is quite safe, professors or no professors. He is not only not shrinking; he is growing year by year. More and more the fact becomes plain that he was one of the first-rate men of his time, that his place as a literary artist was, and is, beyond that of any other American; that he stood head and shoulders above all the Holmeses and Lowellses and Emersons who admitted him to their sodality so grudgingly, and patronized him so absurdly, and made asses of themselves so beautifully. Put the best work of the best of these men beside "Huckleberry Finn." It is like ranging Mendelssohn's Scotch Symphony beside Beethoven's C Minor, or a landscape by an English academician beside Rubens' "Chateau de Stein." Mark was simply beyond them. And he is beyond the stupidity of their heirs and assigns today.

§2

When Carl Van Vechten's first book, "Music After the Great War," was published a year or so ago, I lifted a modest hymn in praise of it, and at the same time denounced the other music critics of America for the fewness of their books, and for the intolerable dulness of that few. Nine-tenths of all our tomes upon the tone art have to be imported from England, or clawed from the baffling Deutsch. Our native Hanslicks—or, at all events, all save Huneker—either confine themselves to punditic trivialities in newspapers and concert programmes or write books so leathery and preposterous that only music teacher can read them. And even Huneker, in these later years, seems to be neglecting music for the lesser arts. His last full-length book of musical criticism was his "Overtones," dated 1912, and "Overtones" was pieced out with discourses on Flaubert and Nietzsche. Hence my rejoicing at first sight of this Prof. Van Vechten, for his maiden volume was full of interesting ideas and sound information, and it was written in a style that made reading very pleasant.

Now comes his second book, "Music and Bad Manners" (*Knopf*)— thicker, bolder, livelier, better. In it, in fact, he definitely establishes a point of view and reveals a personality, and both have an undoubted attractiveness. In it he proves, following Huneker, that a man may be an American and still give all his thought to a civilized and noble art, and write about it with authority and address, and even find an audience that is genuinely interested in it. Huneker got his first breath in Philadelphia, and still, I believe, swears off his taxes there, and keeps the family pew at St. Ostendorf's. Van Vechten, despite his Knickerbocker name, comes from an even remoter outpost—to wit, from Cedar Rapids, Iowa, in the saleratus and osteopathy belt. A strange hatching for such a nest! But nevertheless, a bird of very bright plumage, and, after Huneker, the best now on view in the tonal aviary.

The worst thing in "Music and Bad Manners" is the chapter which gives the book its title—a somewhat banal collection of anecdotes about tenors with the manners of Duroc-Jerseys and concerts made gay by rough-house, almost fit for the long-winter-evening pages of *The Musician* or *The Étude*. His second chapter, made up of idle spoofing on moving-picture music, is nearly as bad: it might have been printed in *The Outlook*. But in Chapter III he spits on his hands, as it were, and settles down to business, and the result is a long, a learned and a very instructive dissertation on modern Spanish music—a school of tone so little understood, and even so little known, that it gets but twenty lines in Grove's Dictionary, and is elsewhere scarcely mentioned at all. Here is useful pioneering; here is also good criticism, for it arouses the curiosity of the reader about the thing described, and makes him want to know more about it. And following it come four chapters upon various aspects of that new music which now causes such a pother, with its gossamers of seconds and elevenths, its wild, niggerish rhythms, and its barbaric Russian cadences. The Slavs are at the bottom of it; its chief prophet is Igor Strawinsky and its plenipotentiary in New York is Leo Ornstein. Dr. Van Vechten constitutes himself its literary agent, and makes out a very plausible case for it. It outrages, as yet, the ear trained in the three B.'s—but the ear grows tougher as year chases year. Who cannot remember the time when even "Til Eulenspiegel" was denounced as cacophony? Nay, there are critics alive today, and drawing pay from New York papers, who got their start bellowing for more tunes in "Die Wälkure." Under the musical bridges the water rushes like a mill-race.

I shall not attempt a summary of Van Vechten's exposition. It deserves a first-hand reading, and besides, I am still but imperfectly converted to all these new prodigies of tone, and so I might distort the tale in the telling. Long hours over the piano score of Strawinsky's "Zhar-Ptitsa" have left me in a somewhat muddled state of mind. My fingers come to grief in the very introduction; there is a rhythm in the seventh measure which, so far at least, they have failed to convey to the keys. Again, I trip over the tonality at the beginning of the first tableau, "Zakoldovann'ii Sad Kashcheia": the signature is C major, but the actual key seems to be G sharp major, with a lowered third. In the third measure it fades into D major, and then into G minor, and then back into D major. Yet again, what a damnable thing is the dance of the fire-bird, *allegro rapace*. The flutes, I suppose, bear the weight of the curse in the orchestra; in the piano score there is a continuous flutish cadenza on a separate staff. God help the flutes! Yet again, how does one play the series of trills in the section called "Nastuplenie Utra?" Strange things, indeed, are in this ballet. Trills resolve themselves into ear-splitting double organ points in seconds. In one place there is a quintuplex shake on all five tones of the chord of the ninth, with the seventh lowered. Chords of the eleventh and thirteenth are piled upon one another; an ordinary discord sounds like a steal from Haydn; at one place, where Strawinsky actually borrows a whole figure from S. Coleridge Taylor's setting of "Many Thousands Gone," one gets the effect of a swallow of Pilsner after a hard day's work. Amazing stuff, indeed! But idiotic, unimaginable, *unmöglich*? Please, gents, no leading questions! I have not said so! By the Spring of 1920 it may all sound as flat and unprofitable as the whole-tone scale. The ear mellows. Who, today, can actually grasp the fact that Mozart was denounced for harmonic anarchies? Who can even *hear* the successive fifths in the minuet of the Jupiter symphony?

Van Vechten, as I have said, writes bouncingly and entertainingly. But like all critics he suffers from a literary disease: perhaps the critical frenzy itself is a pathological state. In his case it is the custom of putting a large part of the discourse into parentheses. His essay on Spanish music, for example, runs to 75 pages, and upon every one of them save ten there is a parenthesis, and sometimes half a dozen. He puts whole sentences within the curved lines; sometimes even whole paragraphs. A few days on Blackwell's Island would cure him of this malady; uncorrected, it puts clumsiness into what is otherwise a very graceful style . . . The book is bound in boards of a staring pea-green. At first blush the color seems gratuitously strident, but second thoughts bring it into harmony with the music discussed within. The taste of Mr. Knopf, the publisher, is usually to be trusted. He is bold, but he always seems to know what he is doing. His career, by the way, deserves watching. In little more than a year of independent publishing he has brought together a formidable list of interesting books, and many of them appear to be selling. The publishing business has room for a man of his enterprise and intelligence. Most of the older and richer houses are run by old women in pantaloons; there is no great trade in America, indeed, which shows a vaster imbecility. Reflection and discrimination seem to have been almost completely divorced from publishing; books are printed for any and all reasons save the reason that they are worth printing. Some of the largest houses in the country devote themselves chiefly to merchanting garbage that should make any self-respecting publisher blush. If it were not for the influence of the big English publishers things would probably be even worse. They at least send over a few dozen fairly decent books every month and so save the face of the trade.

§3

One of Knopf's enterprises is the publication of a series of plays, original and translated, to be called, somewhat absurdly, the Borzoi Plays. Number one of the series is a translation of Michael Arzibashef's "War"; number two is "Moloch," by Beulah Marie Dix; number three is a translation of Ludwig Thoma's "Moral," and number four is a new translation of Nicolay Gogol's familiar Russian comedy, "The Inspector-General." Of these, the most interesting is the Thoma piece—a sharp and racy comedy, well Englished by Charles Recht. The piece should have even greater success in the American theatre than it has had on the Continent, for the situation it deals with is far more American than European. In brief, it sets forth the results of an anti-vice

campaign in a German city. When, at the hot behest of certain vocifer-
ous virtuosi of virtue, the police raid the leading bagnio of the town,
they capture, among other things, the diary of the estimable landlady,
one Mme. d'Hauteville. They have grasped, alas, a lion by the tail, for
the diary contains a minute record of calls made upon the good lady by
most of the dignitaries of the place, including the chief howler of the
Sittlichkeitsverein, or Society for the Suppression of Vice. Worse, a very
high personage, a *Hoheit* no less, is also on her books. . . . The end
may be guessed. With the evidence against their prisoner complete, the
police have to let her go, and what is more, to silence her. In this business the local Comstock lends an important hand; he steals the diary
from the police and so saves his own and many another goose-fleshed
neck. The closing scene shows him receiving a decoration for his services to public morality.

A pungent and excellent play. A little masterpiece of irony. That
Thoma remains almost unknown on this side of the ocean is quite
amazing. The late Percival Pollard hailed "Moral" at least seven years
ago, and there is a whole chapter upon the piece in his book, "Masks
and Minstrels of New Germany" (*Luce*), published in 1911. Thoma
has been editor of *Simplicissimus,* the greatest of all comic papers since
1899, and has contributed hundreds of sketches and stories to its pages, chiefly under the *nom de plume* of Peter Schlemiehl. A Rabelaisian
capacity for burlesque is in him; he reaches an almost screaming absurdity in his *"Lausbubengeschichten"* (tales of boyhood) and his *"Brief-
wechsel eines bayrischen Landtagabgeordneten"* (letters of an illiterate
member of the Bavarian Lower House). Here the humor is laid on
with a shovel; the very ribs of the reader are made to ache. But in
Thoma's plays there is a finer method. In "Moral" he reaches genuine
satire, and in two other pieces, *"Die Lokalbahn"* (The Local Railway)
and *"Die Medaille"* (The Medal), he comes near to the same achievement. In his *"Kleinstadtgeschichten"* (Tales of a Small Town) one finds
the precise idea of George Bernard Shaw's "O'Flaherty, V. C." Many
of his other ideas have been quietly borrowed by scriveners in the vul-
gate, but so far as I know, "Moral" is the first of his works actually to
be translated. His peasant comedies, of course, defy the translator.
Much of their humor depends upon vagaries of dialect, and the rest is
grounded upon customs and habits of mind that would be wholly unintelligible to Americans.

Thoma is 50 years old and was born at Oberammergau, the home
of the Passion Play. His father was a Chief Forester in the Bavarian
highlands, and the boy grew up amid the icy heights of the eastern
Alps. He was destined for the parental profession and in 1886 he entered the School of Forestry at Aschaffenburg. But he found that the

new science of forestry, as imparted at that academy, had far too much science in it and far too little hunting and camping-out, and so he transferred himself to the law—obviously a senseless exchange, for he found the law even worse, and though he got his doctorate in 1893 and hung out his shingle at Dachau, he was never happy at the bar. Politics interested him more: it offered the best substitute for the wild life that he loved. He became a spell-binder for the National Liberal party and began to write political pamphlets and pasquinades. The dismissal of Bismarck, he says, filled him with the utmost bitterness against the throne. In 1897 he moved to Munich, and two years later became editor of *Simplicissimus*. There he has remained, and since the death of Otto Julius Bierbaum, in 1910, he has been accepted as the first of German humorists. We have no one in America precisely like him. Our comic writers, almost without exception, show a naif and somewhat provincial character. Even in Mark Twain and George Ade one constantly glimpses a peasant making fun of the great world; in the eternal battle between the Davidsbündler and the Philistines, they frankly take the side of the Philistines. Thoma is more European, more Continental, more a man of the world. In his wildest grotesqueries, as in those of Bierbaum, Roda Roda and Anatole France, one always finds an air of sophistication, an undeniable grace, a keen critical sense. Bierbaum dedicated his comic poems and sketches to such men as Franz von Lenbach, Hugo von Hoffmansthal and Richard Strauss. Imagine Ellis Parker Butler dedicating a book to Sargent, or to Percy Mackaye, or to Walter Damrosch! There is a difference!

§4

Various other interesting plays are among the month's books. For example, "Six Plays of the Yiddish Theatre," translated by Dr. Isaac Goldberg (*Luce*). The authors represented are David Pinski, Sholom Ash, Perez Hirschbein and Solomon J. Rabinowitsch. Dr. Goldberg's selections are excellent; they range from a biblical drama by Pinski to a rough farce by Rabinowitsch and an extraordinarily effective little folk-play by Ash. The last-named piece is the best in the book; there is in it, indeed, something of the unfathomable mystery and poetry of the Synge plays; it is astonishing that none of our Little Theatres has discovered it. Ash himself is the chief present hope of the Yiddish theatre; he alone, among all the Yiddish dramatists, deserves to be called a first-rate literary artist. Ten or twelve years ago, during the height of the late Jacob Gordin's fame, the East Side theaters were producing some of the best plays to be seen in New York. But since then their audiences have become gradually Americanized, and as a result their taste has been debauched by the trade goods of Broadway. Such stupid bosh as "The Lion and the Mouse" has been translated and its influence grows painfully visible. The most popular Yiddish playwrights of today are not the Ashes and Pinskis, but makers of tin-pot melodrama like Rocoff and Zolatorefsky and tear-squeezers like Libin. It is no longer a pleasant adventure to enter the garlic belt on a winter night and grapple with the difficulties of Slavic-Syraic-German. In the palmy days of Gordin it was common for the Yiddish theatres to do plays by Ibsen, Hauptmann and the Russians. One of the best performances of *Nora* that I remember was given by Mme. Kaminsky, a very beautiful Russian Jewess. It was in those days that new Nazimovas and Kaliches were being discovered in the Ghetto weekly, and all the Broadway critics were in a sweat of enthusiasm. But now the vernacular playhouses devote themselves chiefly to rough operettas and idiotic melodramas. The more civilized Jews no longer go to their own theatres. Instead, they swarm to Irving Place.

Another play-book of much interest is the volume of "Three Plays" by Padraic Colum (*Little-Brown*). The pieces in the collection are "The Fiddler's House," "The Land" and "Thomas Muskerry." All of them were printed half a dozen or more years ago in the famous Abbey Theatre Series of plays, but the thin little volumes of that series now bring a premium, and so it is good to see them done again, and in so dignified and sightly a volume. Most devotees of the printed play, I daresay, have read them; they rank among the best things the Irish Literary Renaissance has given to the theatre. . . . Two other interesting volumes follow: "Read-Aloud Plays," by Horace Holley (*Kennerley*), and "The Fruit of Toil," by Lillian P. Wilson (*Bobbs-Merrill*). In both there is an effort to widen the field of the drama—to make it include, not only plays of definite organization, but also modest dialogues of episode and mood. The two authors approach the problem from widely separated points, but both achieve good results. . . . As for "The Woman Who Wouldn't," by Rose Pastor Stokes (*Putnam*), it suffers from a too hortatory tone, and also from the fact that its chief dramatic situation was exhausted four years ago by Stanley Houghton in "Hindle Wakes." . . . As for "King Saint Olaf," by Gustav Melby (*Badger*), it is a clumsy attempt at a drama in verse, and so dull that it grows unbearable. . . . As for Miles M. Dawson's new translation of Ibsen's "Brand" (*Four Seas Co.*), it is made useless by the fact that all four of the previous translations—by C. H. Herford, F. Edmund Garrett, William Wilson and J. M. Olberman—are decidedly better. Here is a specimen of Dr. Dawson's uncouth jingling:

BRAND

Would you a hundred dollars give,
That she might pass away in peace?

THE PEASANT

Yes, priest!

BRAND

Two hundred?

THE PEASANT

As I live,
Her from her terrors to release,
My house and homestead would I sell.

§5

An American playwright who takes his craft seriously and knows what he is about is George Middleton, author of "The Road Together" (*Holt*). This is his sixth or seventh play-book, and in every one of them you will find intelligent human problems intelligently worked out. Not that Mr. Middleton is a mere dramatist of the chair, with his eyes always on the library and never on the stage; far from it, indeed. He has written successful acting plays for such popular stars as Julia Marlowe, Robert Edeson and James K. Hackett; he even had a hand in so gaudy a confection as "Hit-the-Trail-Holliday." But beside trade goods, he also writes pieces with ideas in them, and he maintains those ideas with considerable plausibility and address. In "The Road Together" his aim is to establish the plain fact, so seldom heard of in the drama, that marriage is far more than a hope and an emotion. His protagonists, *Wallace* and *Dora Kent,* come to a connubial *débâcle. Dora* discovers that *Wallace* is anything but the heroic young reformer she has imagined him; *Wallace* discovers that Dora has been warming up an old affair with another gentleman. A fine chance for big scenes, rhetoric, ranting, pistols for two, fustian *à la* Bernstein. But Mr. Middleton takes a more moderate view of it. *Wallace* and *Dora* have been married for several years; they have got used to each other; more, they have unconsciously come to depend on each other. Very easily and convincingly, the truce thus established in little things stretches out to take in big things. Instead of throwing up everything and making a wreck of his life, *Wallace* turns to new schemes for making money; instead of rushing off to Reno, *Dora* goes on keeping house. They shake hands. The old illusions are gone, but, after all, it is still pleasant to have a home.

Needless to say, Mr. Middleton leaves out of this situation all its customary clap-trap. *Wallace* doesn't sob upon the library table; *Dora* doesn't let down her hair. There is no prattling infant to toddle in in its nightie. Dora doesn't discover herself *enceinte*. Nay; this Mr. Middleton has no traffic with such machinery. His play, I daresay, will be a long while getting to Broadway. But meanwhile he is doing sound and honest work.

The Genius

by Owen Hatteras

When Professor Phineas Phildoodle finished his reading from the works of Anakananda Raspore, the famous Indian poet, the members of the Smithville Literary Society made manifest their approval of the Oriental's genius by applauding loud and long.

The handclapping having somewhat abated, Samuel Bunker, president of the society, arose and spoke as follows:

"Fellow members: I wish to say that it has rarely been my privilege to listen to poems so replete with the rich philosophy of the Orient and at the same time so permeated with such singular beauty of phrase. Doubtless all of Professor Phildoodle's auditors feel, as do I, that they have received a message from one of the world's great, transcendent geniuses!"

As the meeting broke up a mighty chatter arose concerning the place in literature of the great Raspore. It seemed to be the consensus of opinion of the members that the Indian poet was the premier mystic of the world.

Fifteen minutes later Professor Phildoodle was escorted in a Pullman on his way back to Boston.

"Either I am a genius or else I have proved my contention that there is considerable bunk involved in this sudden craze for Oriental literature," said the vendor of knowledge. Then, with a chuckle, he added: "And to think! It only took me an hour and a half to write the whole darned lot of it!"

Smart Set 52, No. 2 (June 1917): 76.

The Plague of Books

I

When, in the year ten of this damndest of centuries, there appeared a book by a college professor in which it was openly admitted that Mark Twain was a greater writer than Oliver Wendell Holmes, I hymned the prodigy as one full of exhilarating portents and anointed the good professor himself with lavish cataracts of cocoa butter, vaseline, neats' foot oil and curve grease. His name was William Lyon Phelps, A.B., A.M., Ph.D.; he was Lampson professor of English language and literature in Yale College. I hailed him as the first herald of the academic enlightenment, the bold forerunner of a new renaissance, the pioneer of intelligence in the professorial chair. Let me now, with a wry face, withdraw and swallow the great bulk of those unguents. Let me take back and purge myself with those caressing pomades. Down, down they go! I was honest, brethren, but I was somehow wrong. The Phelps of 1917 has gone back to orthodoxy and the stale fruits of the scholastic grove. A mugwump and iconoclast no longer, he now chants the standard liturgy of Harvard and of Yale, of Princeton and of Columbia, of literary embalmers and of his witless order, of heavy platitude and of pious gosh. His book of 1910, "Essays on Modern Novelists," had novelty and the breath of life in it; there was more than one show of independence in its judgments; it rang clear. His book of 1917, "The Advance of the English Novel" (*Dodd-Mead*), is a flat reboiling of old respectabilities, a hack job for literary ladies and college boys, a mass of mush. It might have been written by Hamilton Wright Mabie or Edwin Markham, even by Brander Matthews, even by that fair Ella (I forget her last name) who interprets literature to the women's clubs out in Chicago. It might have run serially through the paleozoic columns of the Boston *Transcript;* one can even imagine it following Dr. Mabie's "White List of Books" in the *Ladies' Home Journal.* In it the estimable professor goes back to the tasteless herbs of his New England youth; once more he is the pedagogue who edited "The Poetry and Prose of Thomas Gray" and "The Best Plays of Chapman" for sweating and god-forsaken school-boys. In it, after that memorable

Smart Set 52, No. 2 (June 1917): 138–44.

aberration at forty year, he returns to his drowsy bath in the academic Lethe, there to await the last, sad bugle-call.

Et tu quoque, my dear Mon Chair! . . . Do I bawl and snuffle? Do I call the professor names? Then consider what a blow has found my ribs. For seven years I nursed this serpent. For seven years I cried him up as one who had drunk at college pumps and yet lived. For seven years, in season and out of season, I kept a spotlight on him, displaying him to the nobility and gentry as a college professor shaken free of the class-room, a pundit emancipated from superstition, the White Hope of the seminaries. And now he turns upon me and sets fire to the deck beneath my feet. Now he adopts the criteria of the Literary Supplement of the New York *Times.* Now he is sicklied o'er with the pale cast of Harvard and the *Nation.* . . . I assume the black cap and proceed to issue judgment upon him in due form of law. May his work be tagged and chewed up for posterity, when his time comes to die, by his successor as Lampson professor of English at Yale. May his books be adopted as texts in all the fresh-water colleges west of the Wabash, and may generations of plowboys learn to venerate him between Dr. Robertson Nichol, the Methodist Taine, and Dr. Mabie, the Hannah More of Summit, N. J. May he find no books to read in the purgatory of professors—a deep and roaring hole, I surely hope—save the novels of James Fenimore Cooper and the critical works of Paul Elmer More. May he live to see his verdicts solemnly accepted by readers of books, and O. Henry put above Frank Norris, and Owen Wister above Theodore Dreiser, and Charles D. Stewart invested with the late toga of Mark Twain, and W. J. Locke revered as a great Christian moralist. To the calaboose, Mr. Catchpoll! Out, out! . . .

In detail, it is hard to deal with this curiously hollow and uninspired book. It proceeds upon no intelligible plan; it is incoherent and uninforming; it is prejudiced and ignorant; its valuations are often preposterous, and sometimes almost fabulous. What is one to think of a critic who devotes a whole page to a discussion of H. G. Wells's "The Wife of Sir Isaac Harmon," and then fails to mention "The New Machiavelli" at all? Of one who hails Mrs. W. K Clifford's "Love Letters of a Worldly Woman" as a "masterpiece," and then forgets to name a single work by Hugh Walpole, J. S. Beresford or W. L. George? Of one who describes O. Henry as a "genius" who will have "abiding fame," and then rigorously avoids any mention of Dreiser, or Robert Grant, or Thomas Nelson Page? Of one who speaks seriously of the "highest reaches" of the "art" of Henry Bordeaux, the French Harold Bell Wright? Of one who gravely accepts General Lew Wallace as a first-rate novelist? Of one who signs his name to the doctrine that "the American novelist most worthy to fill the particular vacancy caused by the death of Mark Twain is Charles D. Stewart"—the author of a volume of vaudeville anecdotes called "Finerty of the Sandhouse"? Of one who—but there is no need to multiply examples. A few such judgments are sufficient. Worse, they are accompanied by a lot of puerile moralizing, an endless dallying with the notion that the aim of art is to perfume and sweeten the beholder. The Encyclopedia Britannica's astounding discovery that "A Mummer's Wife" is a tract against gambling is gone one better by the discovery that "Esther Waters" has "a nobly ethical tone" and makes the reader "feel a moral stimulation." (God help poor old Moore! Imagine the *Stammvater* of the literature of Texas as an evangelist!) Samuel Butler's "The Way of All Flesh," we are told, will be "of real service to Christianity." (O, shades, liver and lights of Shaw!) Joseph Conrad's "The Point of Honor" is "an allegory of the struggle between good and evil, with the triumph of good." W. J. Locke, since "The Morals of Marcus Ordeyne," has been converted to Christianity, and is "an ethical philosopher," and his "Simon the Jester" is "illumined with deep religious feeling" . . . Pish, tartuffery, cant! It reaches its climax in a passage on Zola. "He was found, in the morning, lying half out of bed, his face on the floor buried in his own vomit. . . . An excellent illustration of the limits of his art." . . .Ah, the sweet, the savory, the "moral" Puritan!

Enough, and too much! What must the English think when they read contemporary American criticism—such piffle as Mabie's pious prattle for high-school girls, More's staggeringly ignorant "criticism" of Nietzsche, the late "History of American Literature Since 1870," by Professor Fred Lewis Pattee, the reviews in such journals as the *Times* and the *Outlook,* such lame and pointless stuff as is in Dr. Phelps's present volume? One of the amusing characteristics of the books by professors is their unanimous failure to so much as mention Dreiser. The thing, indeed, takes on the aspect of an organized movement; the fellow becomes a sort of bugaboo to the rev. pundits, to be put into Coventry with Beelzebub. It will be curious to see how long this moral exile lasts. Already the British violate its terms. The London *Academy,* taking the professors from the rear, calls "Sister Carrie" the greatest of American novels. The *Fortnightly,* the *Spectator,* the *Saturday Review* and the *Athenaeum* heap praises upon its successors. Arnold Bennett, H. G. Wells, W. J. Locke, Frank Harris and others of their kidney venture upon the atrocity of putting Dreiser above Howells—a blasphemy, but by experts, ladies, by experts! Over all roars the voice of Theodore Watts-Dunton, surely a respectable man! . . . Let us reserve our snickers until the day the first drover of rah-rah boys swallows the bilious Indianan, as Dr. Phelps swallowed old Mark in 1910. Let us

see what university sends its "professor of English language and literature" to do that noxious job. Let us stay our guffaws a bit longer. . . .

A sad, sad lot, these Yankee tasters of beautiful letters—but stay! A
few months ago, taking the air in Fifth avenue, I dropped into one of
the stores given over to marked-down books. On the 50-cent counter
reposed a volume entitled "The Spirit of American Literature," by
John Macy (*Doubleday-Page*). The name of this Macy was known to
me; I had received reliable reports from my Boston agents that he was
a man of sense. Nevertheless, his publishers had not thought it worth
while to send me his book when it was published in 1913, and it now
reposed upon the bargain counter, among a lot of other forlorn "re-
mainders." I bought it, steered for Lüchow's, sent Gustav for a *seidel* of
Hoboken malt, and inquired within. . . . What I found was a first-class
book of criticism, a book sparkling with the ideas of a well-read and
intelligent man, a book by a genuine lover of books, a true joy and delight. Not a trace of academic fustian! Not a line of flapdoodle! Not a
hint of the college professor! Here was sharp and shrewd judgment.
Here was clear and independent thinking. Here was enthusiasm unashamed and contempt undisguised. Here, above all, was sound writing—a graceful flow of sentences, a stock of new phrases, a piquant
and intriguing style. No book of criticism that I have read in ten years
has given me more pleasure. No book has set my own notions to bubbling more furiously. None has left me with a more vivid sense of vigorous and worthwhile intellectual experience. . . . I recommend it to
you without qualification. Macy is the antidote to the pedagogues. He
will be discovered, I daresay, in fifteen or twenty years. But once discovered, he will not be quickly forgotten.

II

Have I laid an interdict upon the professors, damning them all,
one and every, in the name of the great Jehovah and the Continental
Congress? Then let me except and apologize to Prof. Ludwig Lewisohn, A.M., Litt.D., second in command of a department in the Ohio
State University at Columbus. The syndics of the Ohio State University had better keep a watchful eye upon this Lewisohn; he has written
two or three very excellent books, and before long there will be academic White Slave traders on his trail, seeking to lure him to some
larger seminary, and the fatter honoraria thereof. His volume on "The
Modern Drama," published in 1915, is the sanest and most illuminating discussion of dramatic currents since Ibsen in the language. And
his new book, "The Spirit of Modern German Literature" (*Huebsch*),
sweeps a wide field with so sure and practised a glance that every hill-

ock and hollow of it is measured at once. A small book, even a meagre book, but a book packed full of sharp and sound criticism. With its subject matter I profess a good deal more than the average college professor's acquaintance; I have written a whole book upon one small subdivision of it, and at least five kilometres of articles upon other parts. But I had not read twenty pages of Lewisohn before I saw clearly that this was a man who knew infinitely more about it than I did, and, what is more, a man who had the rare faculty of reducing his vast knowledge to order and simplicity, and of making it not only clear, but also interesting. His English style, in truth, is a model of transparent and dignified writing; he says what he has to say with the utmost directness and clarity. . . . But surely this is not his last word upon the subject. He must do the thing over and at length; he must make a thorough job of it. One of the chief of the worth-while enterprises after the wounds of the war are bound up will be that of interpreting the people on one side to the people on the other. In particular, the Germans and the Americans must be made to put away their present prejudices and stupidities, and to see each other as they really are—as the only two nations whose future looms up as magnificently as their past. We err in judging the Germans by their jingoes, by their Junkers and by the fifth-rate *bourgeois* who constitute their chief contribution to our own population. And the Germans err in judging us by our political mountebanks, our newspapers and our social pushers. What is durable, and genuine, and profound, and significant in each nation is concealed from the other. Think of the childish gabble that goes on in the United States about Nietzsche—or, to adopt the American spelling, Nitsche, Nietzshe or Neitzshy! And think how the Germans would open their eyes if the Boston Symphony Orchestra should play in the Gewandhaus! . . .

The remaining books of criticism interest me less. "Pencraft," by William Watson (*Lane*), is no more than the mooning of a bad poet. I am unable to discern any ideas in it. Its one coherent contribution to criticism is a proposal to "divide literature into three kinds or orders, and to call them the cantative, the scriptive and the loquitive." What we have here, of course, is no more than a fresh outbreak of the old labelling mania, so dear to *MM. les professeurs*. A new set of tags, and presto! we have a new theory, a new armament of criteria, a new philosophy! With all due respect to an honest jingler, Poosh! . . . As for "How to Read," by J. B. Kerfoot (*Houghton-Mifflin*), my much-esteemed colleague on *Life*, the fault of it is that it takes too many words to state a few sound but in no wise remarkable ideas. What Dr. Kerfoot says is always perfectly true, but he supports it with such an excess of elaborate illustration and example that he is often lost in his own storm of words. As an article, or even as a pamphlet, his volume would have been capital. But perhaps I here lose sight of his chief purpose, which was plainly to engage and educate the reader who has never given any thought to the process of reading at all. This reader, perhaps, needs all that elaboration of explanation, and that hortatory note no less. At worst Kerfoot shows plainly that he has given sober and profitable thought to his business, and that his competent reviewing of books, for long so popular a feature of *Life,* is undertaken seriously, and with a correct understanding of its principles. Why doesn't he print a book of his reviews? It would be shrewd, succinct, unbiased, discreet and highly profitable.

III

As it remained for Dr. Frank J. Wilstach to write the first usable dictionary of similes in English (I reviewed it in high, astounding terms in this place last December), so it remained for his brother, Dr. Paul Wilstach, to write the first intelligible book on Mount Vernon, a place so charming that it is surprising it has not attracted a whole brigade of authors. Frank is the more deep and learned of the Wilstachii; it took him twenty-five years to hatch his tome of similes; for almost a generation he brooded upon it in Pullman cars, on the station platforms of remote hamlets, and in the gaudy bridal chambers of hinterland hotels. A work of illimitable industry, of huge fixity of purpose, of endless value to the literati. The name of Wilstach is embalmed in amber. Paul, the younger brother, has tackled easier jobs, but done them all well. His *opi* include five or six plays, the best life of Richard Mansfield, and many ingenious critical compositions. It was he, I believe, who first prepared a literary map of the United States, showing the fat cluster of genii in the vicinity of La Fayette, Ind., the seat of the Wilstach family, the site of Schloss Wilstachburg, and the capital of the bozart in These States. His book on Mount Vernon is characteristically thorough and entertaining. Into it he has got everything about the noble old estate that is worth knowing, and particularly everything that the writers of guidebooks leave out.

Have you ever been there? If not, you have missed the most charming pilgrimage that America offers. Don't make the trip down from Washington by trolley; it is abominable. And don't make it by boat; you will miss Alexandria. Hire a motor-car and go in state, as befits a patriot making a journey of piety to the one indubitable national shrine. Begin at the Washington monument, proceed along the lovely sweep of the Speedway, cross the long bridge, and then plunge into Virginia. Virginia is a state of poor white trash and bad roads, but the road to Mount Vernon is an exception, for it was built by Uncle Sam for military purposes, and a multitude of big army signs, designed to keep the artillery from wandering off into the swamps, point the way clearly. Five or six miles of dips and curves, and you are at Alexandria, a sleepy old Southern town that is still struggling out of the eighteenth century. I know of no more charming one north of Charleston, save only Annapolis. On the main streets, true enough, one sees signs of a garish, amateurish sort of progress, but in the side streets the ancient colonial houses still stand in all their dignity of faded brick, and there are great trees along the kerbings, and nigger boys play marbles in the gutters, and fat old wenches, turbaned as in "Uncle Tom's Cabin," swap Baptist scandal over the rickety yard-rails. Alexandria has age; it has distinction; it has the thing vaguely called atmosphere. More, it has reserve and dignity; it seems to be a town of ladies and gentlemen. Old George was there often in his day. He passed through a dozen times a year, and went to church there and to dances, and sometimes took aboard a military cargo of strong waters, and once, when the hostess of the evening offered tea, he made a satirical note of it in his diary, and no doubt pleaded his wounds and albuminaria the next time he was invited. Imagine him in the Virginia of today—a Paradise of tin-pot evangelists, "dry" and "pure," a commonwealth run by cads!

Once out of Alexandria, there is a long bridge to cross, and then one plunges into the pleasant Virginia countryside, and goes up and down a long series of hills, with now and then a gorgeous glimpse of the Potomac to the left. The river, between Washington and Mount Vernon, must be at least a mile wide. At all events, there is a majestic sweep to it, and light mists float upon it, particularly in the morning, and make it seem grand and faraway, even when one is directly before it. Ten or twelve miles of this and a sudden turn brings one to the gates of the old estate. Outside, a clutter of eating-houses a park of automobiles, a horde of solicitous darkeys. Within, the calm and stateliness of a hundred and twenty-five years ago. I can imagine nothing more grave, more imposing, more beautifully simple and charming. Long rows of box hedges. Magnificent old trees. An incomparable stretch of lawn. A group of old and lovely houses, white, clean, regal. The home of a man of mark, a man of self-respect, a cultured and reposeful man, a gentleman. Go to the front of the house and look up and down the Potomac. The solemn serenity of the panorama will make you catch your breath. Nowhere else in the East, not even on the Hudson, is there a more lordly site for a house. And nowhere is there a house that fits more perfectly into its surroundings. George himself designed it as it stands today, and he made it exactly right. One cannot imagine improving it in the slightest. It mirrors the man as not even his portrait mirrors him—precise, laborious, a lover of the amenities, hospitable, generous, well-groomed, touched with imagination. One could reconstruct Washington from this, his home. He loved it as he loved nothing else. Fighting his forlorn and desperate fights five hundred miles away, it was forever in his thoughts. It was his anchor to windward, his retreat and refuge, the hub and center of his whole adult life. A glance at it to-day tells more about him than all the books.

The Mount Vernon Ladies' Association, a *verein* of dutiful dames, keeps it up in a truly admirable manner. The grounds are cared for *con amore;* the old flowers still grow in the gardens; the house itself is spick and span; the explanatory placards are really explanatory; the attendants are silent and polite. But why, having gone so far, do they not go farther? Why not supply civilized nourishment to the strangers within the gates, and so promote their happiness and turn an honest penny? There is a delightful open-air restaurant at Versailles; there is another in the Schloss garden at Heidelburg; why not one at Mount Vernon? The place is too beautiful to be rushed through; one wants to linger all day, and in the middle of the day one hungers. Thus seized on a late visit, I resorted to a public eating-house without the gates—and went home bilious and full of curses. This eating-house announced a Virginia chicken dinner at three shillings; it turned out to be the worst ever admitted to my œsophagus—a horrible complex of stringy, half-raw rooster, soggy mashed potatoes, stale bread, clammy sliced tomatoes and boot-leg coffee—in brief, a meal for stevedores and dumb brutes. Why heap such insults upon the pilgrim? The Ladies' Association, I dare say, has no control over the eating outside; but why not set up good eating *in*side, and so blast those external ordinaries with decent competition? I present the idea for what it is worth. The up-keep of Mount Vernon is expensive; the Ladies' Association has to charge a quarter at the door; why not offer honest meals to patriots, and so gain both their gratitude and more of their cash?

Wilstach, in his book, does not enter into such problems, but contents himself with describing Mount Vernon as it is and as it used to be. Washington, in his day, led almost the ideal life down there. He had plenty of land, he had a fine house, he had a corps of contented slaves, and he had a rich wife. It was the money of this wife that paid for the improvements he was constantly making; the Washingtons themselves were land poor, and most of them were second-raters. They did not like the *chatelaine* of Mount Vernon. Very few of them, indeed, ever visited the place during her lifetime. Washington's own mother kept away. But there was an endless stream of other visitors. Before the war the General, then a Colonel, entertained many a party of British officers from the ships of war that came up the river, and after the war he was beset by hordes who yearned to feast their eyes up-on him. It was a long journey and there were no inns nearby; in con-sequence, all callers had to be fed, and not a few of them had to be entertained overnight. The dinner hour was three o'clock and the Gen-eral, when in residence, always sat at the head of his table. According to one chronicler, "he sent the bottle about pretty freely after dinner." Tea was served a couple of hours later, after which Washington retired to his study, and devoted himself to his interminable letters, diaries and accounts. (He left a whole wagon-load when he died.) Supper was at nine o'clock, but he did not partake of it. Instead, he went to bed. The old four-poster is still there. A roomy and comfortable couch indeed, and in a most pleasant room. . . .

I commend "Mount Vernon" (*Doubleday-Page*) to your kind atten-tion. It is an ingratiating and agreeable book. It tells a lot that is worth knowing about the greatest man the New World has ever seen.

IV

The remaining tomes of the month offer little of interest. "A Handy Guide for Beggars," by Vachel Lindsay (*Macmillan*), contains some pretty sketches of the high-road, but is marred by preciosity and affectation, just as the author's poetry is. He strains and tortures his parts of speech; he seeks effects by elaborate means and then fails to achieve them at all. And in his philosophy, no less than in his writing, there is a plentiful buncombe.

On "Golf for Women," by some anonymous fair one (*Moffat-Yard*), I cannot report at all, for I am neither a woman nor a golfer, but my *blanchisseuse,* who is both, tells me that it is very instructive. The illustrations depict various ladies in the act of clouting golf balls—a series of truly appalling poses, and highly destructive to the charm of those who happen to be of matronly habit. "What's the Matter With Mexico?" by Casper Whitney (*Macmillan*), also eludes me, for I find it difficult to dredge up any interest in the crime and aspirations of the Mexicans, or in the political mountebankery that issues from their do-ings here in the United States. I lament, of course, that the proposed war with them failed to come off, for it would have taken Major-General Roosevelt into the field and so filled the world with joy, but further than that, to borrow old Friedrich's phrase, I consign them to statistics and the devil. Neither am I able to report upon "Creative Evolution," by Cora Lenore Williams, M.S. (*Knopf*), for it opens with a quotation from Henri Bergson, the parlor philosopher, and then in-troduces Edwin Markham, the laureate of the New Thought, and then goes sky-hooting into the interstellar spaces of the Chautauqua metaphysic. . . . Two books remain. "More Wanderings in London," by E. V. Lucas (*Doran*), needs only a line of notice; all of us know how well Mr. Lucas does that sort of thing. The full-page drawings in color by H. M. Livens add much to its value. In Joseph Pennell's "Pictures of the Wonder of Work" (*Lippincott*) the drawings are much less satisfactory. Some of them seem to be reproduced badly, but others—for example, the pictures of the Alberta oil wells—are intrinsically pointless and unbeautiful. Good photographs, in many cases, would have been far better. But mingled with these uninspired designs are a few very vigorous and impressive ones, and Mr. Pennell's text, at all events, is always spicy and amusing. The magazines of to-day, he says, have gone to pot; "there is scarcely an art editor left." . . .

V

Next month, I fear, another bout with the poets. I used to get rid of them in one article a year, but of late their books begin to multiply so horribly that I suppose it will soon take two. The output of books of all other sorts was greatly diminished by the war. This was particularly true of novels; for the first six months or so, indeed, I received but two or three a week, and so enjoyed an intellectual vacation, and greatly improved my mind. But the poets were not halted an instant. All they did was to stop burbling about their souls and hussies and begin gurgling about the lamentable strife overseas. I estimate that 100,000 war poems were composed and uttered in the United States between 4 o'clock P. M. of August 1, 1914, and noon of January 1, 1917. I would be glad to trade the whole lot, I am sorry to say, for a box of paper collars and the works of Flavius Josephus. Not a poem among them! Not a noble line!

Rosemary

BEING SELECTIONS FROM
A ROMANTIC CORRESPONDENCE

By Owen Hatteras

Dear Gus:
    . . . Then there was the box of cigar-lighters, each a thin, flat strip of some sort of white soft wood, perhaps white pine or *Populus tremuloides*. When you had lighted your cigar with one of them you stuck it into a receptacle filled with sand. The floor in front of the counter was always covered with the charred ends of these lighters. . . .

When you opened the store-door a bell on a spring gave a loud clang; also, the odor of an exotic soup came to you from the living quarters beyond. The place was kept by Mr. Jacob Holzapfel, but Mrs. Holzapfel always attended to customers in the mornings. Jacob himself never appeared until noon.

The popular price in those days was six-for-a-quarter, and Mrs. Holzapfel always recommended a certain brand by assuring you that it was "a nice free-smoker."

In the rear of the store a part was fenced off for manufacturing purposes—a sort of cage of chicken netting ran all the way to the ceiling—but no one ever saw a cigarmaker at work in it. At night Jacob would take in the huge sign advertising Battle Ax plug, and hang it on this cage, so that customers would not disturb the evening session of the Franz Abt Penochle and Social Club. . . .

Don't forget: it was a segar store, not a cigar store . . .

No; you're wrong. The Positively No Checks Cashed sign didn't appear until young Julius, the son of the house, took over the business. In old Jacob's day there was a hand-written placard above the mirror that simply said No Trust!

During July and August all the mirrors in the store were soaped by young Julius, whose filigrees and scrolls gave promise of a great future in the arts. The mirror nearest the door was further embellished with the words Please Call Again. They started in the southeast corner—say

Smart Set 42, No. 3 (July 1917): 60–62.

at a point near Tallahassee, Florida—and ran uphill to Duluth, Minnesota.

Of course, I needn't remind you of the wooden Indian outside, or of the rickety Welsbach burners in the window, or of the picture of the Hoffman bar (lithographed on tin), with a key to the personages shown in it on the back. Even you, who have no sentiment in you, must remember and cherish these. Also, the old dark-brown spittoon in front of the case of pseudo-meerschaum pipes—a thing at least fourteen inches in diameter, with a removable top in the form of an inverted cone. Also, the stove in the rear, with a guard around it made of tin, brightly shined by Mrs. Holzapfel. Also, the cinnamon cigarettes that Jacob sold to the young—he was virtuous and refused to sell Recruits or Sweet Caporals to boys in knee-breeches.

I challenge you to add a single detail—that is, a major detail. Don't think you can surprise me by mentioning the huge watch that Jacob wore, or by recalling that he always wore a straw hat in the store, even in winter. I remember these things, too. I also remember his varicose veins. I haven't heard of anyone having varicose veins for twenty years, but Jacob had them, and was always talking about them. He felt them every year—whether it was in Spring or in Autumn I don't remember—and he would sigh and say: "Yes, that's what I got for serving my time in the army."

Don't tell me that the money was kept in a till under the counter, or that the till played "The Chimes of Normandy" every time it was opened, or that young Julius knew how to fix it so it wouldn't, or that the store closed on Summer afternoons when the Schuetzenverein met at Händel and Haydn Park. I remember, my boy! I remember!

Also, I remember Yolande Wallace, and how one picture of her, in the days of Allen & Ginter, was worth two Lillian Russells, three Della Foxes or four Marie Jansens.

I seize the opportunity, M. le Ambassadeur, etc., etc.

BILL

II

Dear Bill—

I grant you all you say, but do you remember Nina Farrington? Frankie Bailey was a mere Charlotte Greenwood compared to Nina. I was in love with her from Christmas, 1890, to the early Spring of 1891, and would have gladly run off with her and married her. Moreover, do you remember May Waldron? There's one on you, my venerable friend! And Helen Dauvray? And Queenie Vassar? And Delia Stacy? (What was that thing that Powers and Daly did? Was it "A Straight Tip"?) And Sylvia Thorne? And Helen Redmond? And Lottie

Gilson? And Isabel Coe? And Kate Castleton? (Now tell me you would have thought of *her!*) And Jennie Weathersby? And Sandol Milliken? And poor Bettina Gerard? And Elsie Leslie? (Own up: you loved her, too, and would rather have been the Pauper with her than the Prince without her!) And Katherine Florence? And Vashti Earl? And Lizzie MacNichol? And Selma Herman? How about it, old Polonius? . . .

I'll bet you have forgotten them all. Moreover, I'll bet you haven't thought of Fanny Rice these ten years past. Or of Phroso. Or of Perdicarus. Or of Florence Burns. Do you recall Palmer Cox and his Brownies? Or Sockalexis? Or Caesar Young? Or Sylvester Schofield? Or the old *Etruria*, once queen of the seas? Or Bosco—"he eats 'em alive!"? Or the days when people used to come to New York to see the Eden Musée, the Aquarium and the Brooklyn Bridge? Or St. Jacob's Oil? Or Maceo? Or the Yellow Kid? Or Evangelina Cisneros? Or the Banda Rossa? Or Salvator? Did you belong to a bicycle club and take century runs? Did you ever see Kiralfy's "The Fall of Pompeii"? Do you remember the Seeley dinner? Or the Bradley Martin ball? Or the McCaull Opera Company? Or "The Corsican Brothers"? Or "The Still Alarm"? Or "Ta-ra-ra-boom-de-ay!"? Or Little Egypt? Or Youssuf, the Terrible Turk? Or Colonel Waring? Or Howe & Hummel? Or Tom Gilsey? Or Louise Hepner? (There's one to beat Vashti Earle!) Or Johann Hoff? Or the Lexow committee? Or Hannah Elias? Or Pony Moore? Or Kid Lavgne? Or the Seven Sutherland Sisters? Or the Six Little Tailors? Or "Sam'l of Posen"? Or Radway's Ready Relief? Or Etienne Girardot? Or Gladys Wallis? Or Ted Marks' sacred concerts? Or the Harlem Coffee Cooler? Or "Bingen on the Rhine"? Or Captain Putnam Bradlee Strong? Or Lion Coffee? Or Kirk Munro? Ivory Starch? Luetgert, the sausage man? Monarch bicycles? Cushion tires? "Just as the Sun Went Down"? George Dixon? Selina Fetter? Turtle spittoons—you stepped on the head of the turtle and the lid flew back? Also cuspidors with "Locksley Hall" and "Enoch Arden" pictures enameled on them in colors? Isadora Rush? Beer bottles with tin foil around the necks and with wire around the corks? O. N. T. thread ? James Means' shoes? Piso's Cough Syrup? "In the Baggage Coach Ahead"? Sagwa Indian Tonic? "Harper's Young People"? "The Ben Hur Chariot Race March"? Star Pointer? "She's Only a Bird in a Gilded Cage"?

Do you remember when there were still men who wore cuffs as round and as large as stove-pipes, and fastened them with flat, square cuff-buttons as big as postage stamps? Did you ever wear a Nelly Bly hat, or a polo cap? Did your father wear Congress gaiters, and haul them off with a boot-jack? Did your Uncle Clarence use a meerschaum cigar-holder, so made that its stem seemed to be tied in a knot? Did your Aunt Petunia wear black satin to funerals? Did your Uncle Hugo ever sing "Wait 'Till the Clouds Roll By, Nellie!"? Did you ever hear the Allen G. Thurman March? If not . . .

As ever,

Gus.

III

Dear Gus—

. . . Of course, you must remember the Palmer House bar, with its floor of silver dollars. And Palmer House rolls. And the Brothers Byrne's "Eight Bells." And the Royal Blue express on the B. & O. And Helen Lord. And Adelaide Hermann, wife of "The Great," in the levitation trick. And General Shafter. And Charles H. Yale's "The Devil's Auction." And Connie Mack. And Breitenstein. And Hanlon's "Superba." And the cerise glass globe with the lumps on it that used to adorn the chandelier in the vestibule. And Zimmer's baseball game. And the Ouija board. And Sam Jones, the evangelist. And Bid McPhee. And "Siberia." And Bert Coote. And "The Soudan." And Lord 1Dunraven. If not, then you are a child, indeed.

But do you remember the days when all self-respecting men wore white boiled shirts, with bosoms as stiff as boards and little tags at the waist-line? . . . Also, do you remember the gilded shovel and coal-scuttle that stood beside the white marble mantelpiece in the parlor? A pretty pink ribbon was tied to the handle. Then there was the little gilt slipper—I saw one once when I peeped into the servant girl's bedroom*—with a thermometer on it. At the top was a velvet pin-cushion, always stuck full of black jet pins. Also, there was the plaster of paris Venus de Milo with a small clock, always out of order, where the umbilicus should have been. And then there was the sea-shell on the mantel—you must remember how it would roar when you held it to your ear. And the moustache-cup—God bless me, I almost forgot it!—with Father's name on it in gilt letters of Old English. And the lambrequin of fringed chenille—always red!—with pansies embroidered all over it, or maybe daisies. . . .

Moreover, you forget Caroline Miskel. Can I ever forgive you for that!

Yours,

Bill.

IV

Dear Bill—

. . . Forgot Caroline Miskel? Avaunt! It was too precious a memory to dredge up. When she married Charlie Hoyt, 700,000 hearts were broken. If I live to be a hundred I'll never forget her. . . . Nor Jessie Bartlett Davis. Nor Ruth Peebles. Nor, for that matter, old Hen Barnabee. . . .

. . . Nor Verona Jarbeau? Nor Christine Blessing? Nor Nellie Rosebud? . . . Do I beat you here? . . .

Gus.

* *That's none of your business.*

Bluebeard's Goat

By William Drayham

If all the things that Richard Hoof had said to women since the time he passed his thirteenth birthday were collected and expurgated they would make a wonderful book. What sparkling pages, what luxurious nuances, what exquisite modulations would this book contain! Rabelais and Verlaine, Shaw, Moore and La Fontaine, Goethe and Balzac and Louys and Grimm could not have written this book in the finest maturity of their genius. Its profundities, its melodious extravagances, its fantasy and grotesquerie, its pathos, sorrows and despairs—but enough of it. This Baedeker of Love, this Apocalypse of passion does, not exist. Its contents are a part of the four winds, the seven seas and four score seven memories. They will never be collected. The book will never be written.

Henrietta, the waitress of the Queen's Girdle, is dead, and with her two chapters have vanished. Marguerite is married, fugit another two chapters. Gladys and Mabel and Helen, Chloe and Myrtle and their sisters and their cousins and their aunts and their mothers have danced and motored and repented at least ten other chapters out of their foolish heads. The Bishop's wife would have to be placed on the rack before she yielded the four and a half rare chapters which are hers.

Ditto the Salvation Army leader and the patriotic grandmother who organized the great Allied Bazaar.

And then there are the chapters in the little odd ugly corners where no one ever looks for them, pages upon pages which live a fugitive if indelible existence among a little army of Magdalens and chambermaids.

Richard Hoof sauntered down the bright avenue swinging his cane lightly and smiling an aimless smile upon the panorama of Spring. The wind careened over the gay pavements, spanking the hurrying ladies and revealing incidental poems in shoecraft, tragedies in ankles, melodramas in legs and here and there a hole-proof illusion. But Richard, he of the Great Unwritten Book, was meditating further chapters and his eyes were upon his soul. Now and then a greeting came from the passing crowd and Richard answered mechanically, albeit brightly.

Smart Set 52, No. 3 (July 1917): 94–96.

SMART SET • 1917

His work was done for the day. He had written his three editorials, one on the War, one on the Wheat Crop and the third on the Immigrant of Tomorrow.

He had absorbed three glasses of Bock according to his long time honored notion of drinking the health of every grave fulmination which left his pen. He had given his spirit over to the promptings of love and Spring, and in his mind was the name of a woman and the address of her home.

II

Another man than Richard, in his place, would have found but little to smile about, even aimlessly. Rather would this other fellow have worn a dubious and tragic air. Rather would his heart have been heavy and his thought bitter. But for Richard the sorrows of life were the joys of art—and love was his art. And then, perhaps, the smile was only a mask, as the old songs have it. Indeed, as he approached the address in his mind, his steps grew slower, his face somewhat serious.

What a queer woman. Her eyes were always circled with light. Her fingers were slender and restless. He had made progress. But there had been, to think of it bluntly as a man should when alone, no surrender. Was it that he had forgotten how? At thirty-five one forgets many things. He rehearsed in his mind the five months of defeat, delightful months, to be sure, months full of secrets and tender elations. But the secrets were too thin, the elations too tender. At twenty-five they might have been victory. At thirty-five they were defeat.

Growing somewhat more serious, he thought of the fact that never before had the Siege endured five months. He had a record of twenty-five minutes which was shared by the wife of a Methodist parson. But those others were different. He waved a vague mental hand at them in disparagement. Either was unique. Perhaps it was her youth. She was only twenty. But Mildred was only eighteen—and that was a year ago. It could not be her youth. He was conscious of the fact that by "her youth" he was adroitly referring to his own age.

And no, he had not forgotten. He had tried then all, all of the paraphernalia of Eros, the wiles, the sincerities and insincerities, the despairs and brutalities, the hot and cold sweats, the fencings, approaches, retreats, the epigrams, the stupidities, the innocences, the spiritual Half Nelsons, the Toe Holds, the Hammerlocks, dope needles, drugged cherries, Uplift dramas, Naturalism, Symbolism, breathing of prayers and laying on of hands—and at their conclusion on this merry day in Spring was inscribed the word defeat.

Yes, had the Great Book been written, Esther might have served as the Great Scintillating Synopsis.

He recalled the scene in the conservatory just four months ago—when victory had seemed like a plum at his finger tips. His brain had been clear even though his heart beat out the usual call to charge.

"I will call you Esther," he said, "and we will be friends. I have always wanted a real friend. We will not fall in love. I would rather always think of you at a distance than forget you in an embrace. If you give me happiness I will not seek to bury it in the beautiful grave of your lips. I will confess to you, I have known love. I have known what it is to stimulate your eighty-seventh kiss with the memory of your first. Not that I do not believe in love. Santa Claus and Cupid are phantoms which no wise man will ever deny. I told them very previous. (*Smile*) (*Debonair sigh*) But when the stars appear hereafter I am content to gaze on them. I do not desire to put them in my pocket. Is it agreed, that we do not pocket the stars?"

He watched her as he talked. It had been a solemn pact. He did not expect twenty to smile at what he said. Thirty—perhaps.

For Thirty there would have been another beginning. Yes, he remembered it as a good get off. She had placed her hand in his and he had lifted it to his lips gravely. No, the memory did not inspire him with a desire to kick himself. Everything to its time and place. Love, like God, to the true believer is incapable of the absurd.

And the other scenes—perfect all of them. He thought back slowly, impartially, weighing things with the deliberation of a connoisseur. Every link was there—but there was no chain. At the end of five months Esther was an unstormed lady and he a somewhat serious, unrequited Knight.

His heart contracted suddenly as he stopped in front of her house. He felt dimly that things were being taken out of his hands. The Editorial on The Immigrant of Tomorrow had come hard. He had even left the third Bock unfinished.

He pressed the doorbell. There was one way left. He smiled to himself. Of course, that was it—the one way he had overlooked.

III

He entered the house and found her in the familiar room which somehow. faded from his eyes as he beheld her. She was Spring at twenty, and he felt as he held out his hand to her that he was reaching across the gulfs of many things. But his eyes lighted at the smile of tier face, at the enthusiastic play of her features, as she greeted him. She said she was glad he had come, that she was thinking of him, and feeling somewhat lonely—the afternoon was so bright and—and—

She looked at him for a word.

Be was silent.

There was one way left, the way of the heart. He would not act. He would not pose. He would let this queer, gasping sensation in him guide him. So he remained silent, and yet full of unspoken things. Like a boy, he hoped and then blushed at his duplicity. He must not think.

They talked of friends and a book. Between his answers—for he was mostly answering—he seemed abstracted, ill at ease. He said nothing clever. His sentences contained no sting or twist. He only smiled a little, and yet he did not frown. Gradually he seemed to grow more preoccupied, a bit nervous, even shy. He arose and walked up and down the room once.

An hour passed and the talk grew slower. Esther's animation died away. At last she stared out of the window at the sky that was growing a trifle dim and the day that was a trifle tired. She was beautiful and her eyes were circled with light and her fingers were restless. There was silence.

A hurdy-gurdy—the gods were good—a hurdy-gurdy started up playing far away a song of the streets, a little thing of a rollicking sadness. They listened together. It was a homely overture to Spring, as delicate as the silence in the room, full of wistful joys.

He leaned forward and took her hand in his. His fingers trembled and were moist. His lips were dry. He felt breathless, unsteady.

"Esther," he said softly, "I love you. I—I love you with my whole heart."

The hurdy-gurdy played on in the slow sunset—and the world had become a wonderful obbligato.

"I love you."

He drew her to her feet and embraced her. His kisses sought her lips and queer, broken, impetuous words came with them, the words, it seemed, of a man learning a new language.

"Tell me, please, tell me!"

She moved from him. As through a haze splintered with the clanging of a barrel organ, he saw her standing in the distance. She was crying, and talking, too. Her hands were to her cheeks, her lips were parted.

"I'm sorry," he heard her say, "oh, so sorry. I like you so much. But there's someone else. Oh, Richard, please forget, please! Let us be as we started . . . as you promised. The stars, Richard . . . in our pocket. . . ."

IV

He stood outside her house in the twilight. The world seemed changed. Was it only an hour or so ago he had walked down the bright avenue, swinging his cane, or another time, another age? He closed his eyes and being a man, of a sort, smiled.

And then he turned and looked at the house.

Was she still crying? He felt hungry for her, a strange swift hunger that yet left him quiet and sorrowful. He would never see her again. She was to marry in June. The thought of this other brought another pain to him.

What could he have done to have won her? He shook his head. After all—he had had his share of . . . of . . . things. But, he smiled again, how different this would have been, how new and fresh, like beginning to live.

He looked at his watch and started. It was late . . . dinner. He hurried to the corner and bought a bunch of violets and then with a brisk step hurried on home to his wife.

The Conclusions of a Man of Sixty

By Owen Hatteras

Men's clubs have but one intelligible purpose: to afford asylum to fellows who haven't any girls. Hence their general gloom, their air of lost causes, their prevailing acrimony. No man would ever enter a club if he had an agreeable woman to talk to. This is particularly true of the married men. Those of them that one finds in clubs answer to a general description: they have wives too unattractive to entertain them, and yet too watchful to allow them to seek entertainment elsewhere. The bachelors, in the main, belong to two classes: (*a*) those who have been unfortunate in amour, and are still too sore to show any new enterprise, and (*b*) those so lacking in charm that no woman will pay any attention to them. Is it any wonder that the men one thus encounters in clubs are dull and miserable creatures, and that they find their pleasure in such stupid sports as playing cards, drinking highballs, shooting pool, and reading the barber-shop weeklies? . . . The day a man's mistress is married one always finds him at his club.

II

A civilized man's worst curse is social obligation. The most unpleasant act imaginable is to go to a dinner party. One could get far better food, taking one day with another, at Childs'; one could find far more amusing society in a bar-room or in a bordello, or even at the Y. M, C. A. No hostess ever arranged a dinner without including at least one intensely disagreeable person—a vain and vapid girl, a hideously ugly woman, a veteran of some war or other, a man who talks politics, a follower of baseball. And one is enough to do the business.

III

Democracy: the navigation of the ship from the forecastle.

Smart Set 52, No. 3 (July 1917): 117–18.

IV

The theory that man hath a soul gives great comfort to many men, and particularly to those who consider the mental superiority of a chimpanzee and the moral superiority of a dog.

V

The common belief of women to the contrary, fully ninety-five per cent. of all married men are faithful to their wives. This, however, is not due to virtue, but chiefly to lack of courage. It takes more initiative and daring to start up an extra-legal affair than most men are capable of. They look and they make plans, but that is as far as they get. Another salient cause of connubial rectitude is lack of means. A mistress costs a great deal more than a wife; in the open market of the world she can get more. It is only the rare man who can conceal enough of his income from his wife to pay for a morganatic affair. And most of the men clever enough to do this are too clever to he intrigued.

I have said that ninety-five per cent. of married men are faithful. I believe the real proportion is nearer ninety-nine per cent. What women mistake for infidelity is usually no more than vanity. Every man likes to be regarded as a devil of a fellow, and particularly by his wife. On the one hand, it diverts her attention from his more genuine shortcomings, and on the other hand it increases her respect for him. Moreover, it gives her a chance to win the sympathy of other women, and so satisfies that craving for martyrdom which is perhaps woman's strongest characteristic. A woman who never has any chance to suspect her husband feels cheated and humiliated. She is in the position of those patriots who are induced to enlist for a war by pictures of cavalry charges, and then find themselves told off to wash the general's underwear.

VI

Marriage is apparently the safest form of intrigue, but actually it is the most dangerous. Men are forced into it by cowardice; they are forced out of it by the courage of the cornered rat.

VII

Beware of first impulses: they are nearly always honest!

VIII

The moralist's notion that a stern repression will divert sex activity into socially useful channels has a good deal of plausibility in it. Such sex activity, actually diverted, is at the bottom of most æsthetic effort, and most altruistic effort, and even a good deal of intellectual effort. All art, at bottom, is a love song; man, like the peacock, spreads his plumage when his eye grows amorous. But the trouble with this repression theory is that repression doesn't always repress. The sex activity attacked is not changed into something else, but into a debased and worse form of itself. Read Freud and you will understand the process; look around you and you will see it. The gusto of sex, denied normal satisfaction, is transformed into an irresistible and horrible obsession, a sort of madness. The machine-made ascetic, presumably purged of all thought of sex, is actually unable to think of anything else. Hence the sex-crazy Puritans, the smutty old maids, the snouters into filth.

IX

The safest philosophy, because the most comforting, is not that of hope and faith, but that of disdain. One subscribing to it escapes the great curse of indignation: he is never disappointed or dashed. He disdains even the devils who get him in the end. . . . Safe and comforting, but difficult, difficult! Not many men have the talent for it.

The Cult of Dunsany

I

When George Nathan and I took over the editorship of this great family magazine, in the summer of 1914, the first author we invited to invade its pages was Edward John Moreton Drax Plunkett, Baron Dunsany. Since then we have been hymned more than once, in public prints, as his discoverer, and Nathan, to this day, exhibits himself in Broadway pothouses in that character. All buncombe, my dears! We no more discovered Dunsany than we discovered the precession of the equinoxes. Two of his books of tales, "Time and the Gods" and "The Book of Wonder" (*Luce*), were actually in print in America a full year before we trained our siege guns upon him, and at least one of them had been in print in England since 1905. Moreover, three of his plays had been produced at the Abbey theatre in Dublin, two had been put on with success at the Haymarket in London, one had toured Russia, another had been done in Manchester, and still another had actually seen the light in Buffalo, N.Y. (One is reminded here of the first production of an Ibsen play in English—in Louisville!) And in the meantime no less than four further volumes of his tales had been got into type across the ocean.

Dunsany was thus anything but a newcomer; on the contrary, more than two-thirds of his work was already behind him. But for some reason that remains unfathomable as the doctrine of infant damnation he was still almost, if not quite unknown. In London the *Saturday Review* printed a few of his shorter stories, and a few connoisseurs of the fantastic occasionally mentioned him; in the United States he was not even a name. If you don't believe it, turn to Cornelius Weygandt's "Irish Plays and Playwrights" (*Houghton*), a bulky and possibly exhaustive tome, published in February, 1913. The name of Dunsany, in small type, appears twice in a list of plays produced by the Abbey Theatre, but there is not a word about him in the body of the book, and he is not even mentioned in the index! Search the whole critical literature of that year, and of the next year no less, and you will find no more. The Little Theatre movement was already in full swing; the jitney Frohmans were combing the ninth-rate playhouses of Vienna, Ber-

Smart Set 52, No. 3 (July 1917): 138–44.

lin, Paris and Budapest for new one-acters. But not one of them had
ever heard of Dunsany. Nor had any of the Forty-second Street Haz-
litts. Nor had any of the Taines, Brandeses and Max Beerbohms of the
literary weeklies.

Wherefore, when the noble lord was introduced into the pages of
this great moral periodical, he went off, as it were, like a bomb. In two
months all the corn-fed literati were gabbling about him; in two
months more even the women's clubs had become aware of him; by
the spring of 1915 he was produced on the East Side, and the Broadway Walkleys braved the garlic to inspect him, to announce him, to
whoop for him. What followed was characteristic, and a bit humorous.
The dramatist who had been overlooked for five or six years, standing
in plain view all the while, suddenly became the rage, and all the managers of Little Theatres and Portmanteau Theatres and Vestpocket
Theatres and Demi-Tasse Theatres and Short-Order Theatres began
loading the cables with offers for his plays. The production of "A
Night at the Inn," in May, 1916, brought the climax. This adept and
creepy melodrama, as William Winter would say, knocked New York
cold. The newspapers flamed with the news of its success; great cara-
vans of limousines rolled down Grand Street nightly, knocking over
hundreds of pushcarts, maiming thousands of children; even Brander
Matthews and Diamond Jim Brady went to see it. By the end of the
year Dunsany got to Broadway. Since then he has been the reigning
favorite of all those New Yorkers who love and venerate art, vice
Vernon Castle and Charlotte Greenwood, retired. . . .

Eheu, a sad fate for a great artist! To be pawed by millinery buyers
from Akron and St. Louis! To be praised in the *Evening Telegram!* If,
despite my caveat, I had any part, however small, in setting off this
clapper-clawing I apologize to Dunsany with tears in my eyes, and
promise to sin no more. For here, undoubtedly, is one who belongs to
the small company of first-rate men; here is one who has heard the authentic sirens sing; here is a true priest of romance; here, after Synge
(and perhaps *not* after him), is the finest poet that Ireland has produced in five hundred years. There is something in his work so delicate, so simple, so childlike, that he seems one with the makers of fable
in the nonage of the world. It is with sure instinct that he sets his
scenes in antique mists and peoples them with folk out of fallen and
forgotten empires; he has no more to do with the life of today, or with
the passions of today, or with the rouged and simpering beauty of to-
day than Peter Pan. He has the magic to conjure up what has been
long gone and out of mind, and to make it live again, and to make us
sorry that its day is done. He is a visionary whose visions transcend
space and time. He has brought back into English letters a fragile and

precious thing, so ancient that it seems quite new . . . And behold how fate rewards him. His fancies out of dead heavens and hells soothe the distended stomachs of carnivora who weep when the band plays "Dixie." He himself inhabits a ditch in some French cabbage field . . .

A Dunsany literature begins to spring up. There is an excellent estimate of his plays in "The Contemporary Drama of Ireland," by Ernest A. Boyd (*Little-Brown*), a book that I shall notice at length on some other day. There is a larger study in "Dunsany the Dramatist," by Edward Hale Bierstadt (*Little-Brown*), and, what is more, a clear statement by Dunsany himself of some of his chief ideas. Better still, his own writings appear in new editions, convenient, cheap, complete. Before me, for example, lie five uniform volumes of the tales: "The Gods of Pegana," "Time and the Gods," "The Sword of Welleran," "A Dreamer's Tales," "The Book of Wonder" and "The Last Book of Wonder" (*Luce*)— an admirable edition, indeed, with all the amazing illustrations by S. H. Sime. It is time to be laying in Dunsany. It is time to be discovering him as a great artist, as well as a Broadway sensation and a star of the magazines. His work has something in it that is rare and potent and infinitely charming. He can fetch up moods and images that belong to other literatures and other ages. . . .

II

I arise from "I, Mary MacLane" (*Stokes*) with the one thought: what a ghastly thing it must be to be a Puritan, and fear God, and envy the wicked, and flee from carnal joys! The truth about the Butte Bashkirtseff comes out at last, and it is simple and pathetic. When, at nineteen, she shocked the Sunday-schools with "The Story of Mary MacLane," it was still left obscure; the monkey-shines of her flapperhood, so to speak, distracted attention from it and concealed it. But now, at thirty-five (she herself says "thirty or so"), it emerges crystal-clear; she has learned how to describe her malady accurately, though she still wonders what it is. And that malady? That truth? Simply that a Scotch Presbyterian with a soaring soul is as cruelly beset as a wolf with fleas, a zebra with the botts. Let a spark of the divine fire spring to life in that arid corpse, and it must fight its way to flame through a drum fire of wet sponges. A humming bird immersed in *Kartoffelsuppe*. Walter Pater writing for the *London Daily Mail*. Lucullus traveling steerage . . . A Puritan wooed and tortured by the lewd leers of beauty. Mary MacLane in a moral republic, in a Presbyterian diocese, in Butte . . .

I hope my figures of speech are not too abstruse. What I mean to say is simply this: that the secret of Mary MacLane is simply this: that the origin of all her inchoate naughtiness is simply this: that she is a Puritan who has heard the call of joy and is struggling against it damnably. Remember so much, and the whole of her wistful heresy becomes intelligible. On the one hand the loveliness of the world enchants her; on the other hand the fires of hell warn her. This tortuous conflict accounts for her whole bag of tricks; her timorous flirtations with the devil, her occasional outbreaks of finishing-school rebellion, her hurried protestations of virginity, above all her incurable Philistinism. One need not be told that she admires Major General Roosevelt and Mrs. Atherton, that she wallows in the poetry of Keats. One knows quite as well that her phonograph plays the "Peer Gynt" suite, and that she is charmed by the syllogisms of G. K Chesterton. She is, in brief, an absolutely typical American of the transition stage between Christian Endeavor and civilization. There is in her a definite poison of ideas, an æsthetic impulse that will not down—but every time she yields to it she is halted and plucked back by qualms and doubts, by the dominant superstitions of her race and time, by the dead hand of her kirk-crazy Scotch forebears.

It is precisely this grisly touch upon her shoulder that stimulates her to those naif explosions of scandalous confidence which make her what she is. If there were no sepulchral voice in her ear, warning her that it is the mark of a hussy to be kissed by a man with "iron-gray hair, a brow like Apollo and a jowl like Bill Sykes" she would not confess it and boast of it, as she does on page 121 of her new tome. If it were not a Presbyterian axiom that a lady who says "damn" is fit only to join the white slaves, she would not pen a defiant Damniad, as she does on pages 108, 109 and 110. And if it were not held universal in Butte that sex passion is the exclusive infirmity of the male, she would not blab out in meeting that—but here I get into forbidden waters and had better refer you to page 209. It is not the godless voluptuary who patronizes leg-shows and the cabaret; it is the Methodist deacon with unaccustomed vine-leaves in his hair. It is not genuine artists, serving beauty reverently and proudly, who herd in Greenwich Village and bawl for art; it is precisely a mob of Middle Western Baptists to whom the very idea of art is still novel, and intoxicating, and more than a little bawdy. And to make an end, it is not cocottes who read the highly-spiced magazines which now burden all the book-stalls; it is sedentary married women who, while faithful to their laborious husbands in the flesh, yet allow their imaginations to play furtively upon the charms of theoretical intrigues with such pretty fellows as Francis X. Bushman, Enrico Caruso, George Jean Nathan and Vincent Astor.

An understanding of this plain fact not only explains the MacLane and her gingery carnalities of the chair; it also explains the better part of latter-day American literature. That literature is the self-expression of a people who have got only half way up the ladder leading from moral slavery to intellectual freedom. At every step there is a warning tug, a protest from below. Sometimes the climber docilely drops back; sometimes he emits a petulant defiance and reaches boldly for the next round. It is this occasional defiance which accounts for the periodical efflorescence of mere school-boy naughtiness in the midst of all our oleageinous virtue—for the shouldering out of the *Ladies' Home Journal* by magazines of adultery all compact—for the provocative baring of calf and scapula by women who regard it as immoral to take Benedictine with their coffee—for the peopling of Greenwich Village by oafs who think it a devilish adventure to victual in cellars, and read Krafft-Ebing, and stare at the diabetic and corset-scarred nakedness of decadent cloak-models.

I have said that the climber is but half way up the ladder. I wish I could add that he is moving ahead, but the truth is that he is probably quite stationary. We have our spasms of revolt, our flarings up of peekaboo waists, free love and "art," but a mighty backwash of piety fetches each and every one of them soon or late. A mongrel and inferior people, incapable of any spiritual aspiration above that of second-rate colonials, who seek refuge inevitably in the one sort of superiority that the lower castes of men can authentically boast, to wit, superiority in docility, in credulity, in resignation, in morals. We are the most moral race in the world; there is not another that we do not look down upon in that department; our confessed aim and destiny as a nation is to inoculate them all with our incomparable rectitude. In the last analysis, all ideas are judged among us by mortal standards; moral values are our only permanent tests of worth, whether in the arts, in politics, in philosophy or in life itself. Even the instincts of man, so intrinsically immoral, so innocent, are fitted with moral false-faces. That bedevilment by sex ideas which punishes continence, so abhorrent to nature, is converted into a moral frenzy, pathological in the end. The impulse to cavort and kick up one's legs, so healthy, so universal, is hedged in by incomprehensible taboos; it becomes stealthy, dirty, degrading. The desire to create and linger over beauty, the sign and touchstone of man's rise above the brute, is held down by doubts and hesitations; when it breaks through it must do so by orgy and explosion, half ludicrous and half pathetic. Our function, we choose to believe, is to teach and inspire the world. We are wrong. Our function is to amuse the world. We are the Bryan, the Billy Sunday among the nations . . .

As for the MacLane, to return to her upon her Montana Alp, she is typical in her character as philosopher, but assertively untypical in her character as artist. The thing that is the matter with her is the thing that is the matter with all the literati of the current (and so vain!) revolution; her point of difference lies in her vastly greater skill at revealing her symptoms. She is, in fact, a highly competent performer with the stylus—so competent that she manages to conceal her competency almost completely. On the surface her book is all school-girl naughtiness and innocent prattling; beneath there is a laborious artificiality which must needs evoke professional commendation. One fancies her painfully concocting her phrases, testing her effects, planting her bombs for the boobs. I do not hesitate to say that I admire the lady, let the chips fall where they may. She is one of the few damsels of letters in this republic of the moral and damned who actually knows how to write English, the other being Lilith Benda. She senses the infinite resilience, the drunken exuberance, the magnificent power and delicacy of the language. She knows words; she has the style . . . But Mary MacLane the stylist is not the Mary MacLane who sells so copiously in the department stores and is touted in the newspapers. Nor is that best-selling, eyebrow-lifting Mary quite the moral American I have descanted upon, the Presbyterian stripped. Nay, the Mary whose works hide under boarding-school pillows is no more than a humble shocker, an American Glyn, a lady Chambers. That Mary of the vulgar adoration, I hope and believe, does not actually exist in Butte. The real Mary, at bottom, is a genuine artist, and there must be in her something of the artist's fine earnestness and self-respect. Her followers must needs disgust her; she must needs laugh at the Philistines who are even further down the ladder than she is herself . . . Oh, the irony of it! To feel the thrill of words, to be lured and caressed by beauty—and to be doomed to play *agent provocatrice* to moony flappers and lascivious fat women! . . . I almost hope I am wrong.

III

In "Misinforming a Nation" (*Huebsch*) Willard Huntington Wright performs an unpalatable job with admirable skill and diligence. The nation he refers to in his title is our own and the misinformation he so vigorously belabors is to be found in the eleventh edition of the Encyclopedia Britannica, perhaps the strangest piece of intellectual goods ever handed to the American public. I daresay a hundred thousand Americans have paid stiff (though curiously variable!) prices for this work; maybe ninety-five thousand of them innocently accept it as a compendium of all the information that is worth having in stock. It is Mr. Wright's aim in his little book to show them that they are wrong—that the Britannica's is really a fifth-rate performance, ignorant, prejudiced, disingenuous and incomplete—that the culture it so ostentatiously pumps into our barbarism is really no culture at all, but merely the superficial quasi-culture of the English middle-classes—of Grub street hacks, journalistic moralists, university pedants, and all sorts of pious bounders. A frankly commercial undertaking, designed to wring shekels from the Yankee peasantry, it does not even deign to flatter its targets. One finds in it, from end to end, no more than a long hymn to English genius, and when genius runs out, to English dog-gedness, and when even doggedness is exhausted, to English respecta-bility and stupidity. No Englishman who has ever been heard of at all, however faintly, is spared his bath of unguents. But when it comes to Americans, the learned editors immediately begin to hesitate and for-get. When I tell you that such men as Jacques Loeb, Ethelbert Nevin, Simon Flexner, Luther Burbank, Richart Hovey, Ambrose Bierce, G. Stanley Hall, George W. Crile and the Wright brothers are denied bi-ographies, you will begin to get some notion of the studied deficiencies of this highly imperfect reference book.

Wright's exposé, of course, comes at an unpropitious time. On the one hand the promoters of the Britannica have but recently finished a lush advertising campaign in the newspapers, and so he may confident-ly look for a big crop of unfavorable and even indignant reviews. And on the other hand the circumstances of the war naturally incline the public mind toward Anglomania. But the war can't last forever, nor is the current Anglomania very deep-seated. Soon or late there must be a reaction against our intellectual servitude to England, and particularly to all that is most hollow and meretricious over there. There is an Eng-lish leadership that we might follow with profit and self-respect; it is the leadership of that small minority of Englishmen who are intelligent and gentlemen. But what we actually run after is the sort of leadership that even Englishmen themselves gag at; the leadership, for example, of such upstart vulgarians as Northcliffe, and such adroit sophists as Bryce, and such nonconformist wizards as Sir Oliver Lodge, and such feeble moralists and sciolists as many of the contributors to the Britan-nica. Such men arise inevitably under a democracy; we have a gigantic crop of our own. The thing for us to do, in crossing the ocean for en-lightenment, is to differentiate between these noisy pretenders and the men who genuinely represent the highest culture of Britain.

A point to be remembered here is that scholarship, in England, has never attained to quite the same dignified position it holds on the Con-tinent, and that it thus attracts a less virile and capable body of men to its service. England, for nearly three hundred years past, has been es-sentially a commercial nation, and the chief national energies have been devoted to the extension of trade, and hence of the empire. This enter-prise has attracted, in one way or another, most of the first-rate men of the nation. The applied sciences, because of their social utility, have caught something of the glow, but in the pure sciences, in the arts and in general scholarship the English have lagged behind. The result is that scholarship, in the England of today, is almost as cheaply estimated as it is in the United States, and the second result is that it attracts, in the main, only second and third-rate men. Examine any typical body of English scholars—for example, the critical faculty of the Britannica—and you will find that it is largely composed of men without any civilized tradition behind them, and with no capacity for that austere detachment of spirit which is necessary to the competent performance of their work. They are not primarily scholars; they are primarily Christians, or "good citizens," or "right-thinking Englishmen," or sectarians of some other absurd sort, and scholars only secondarily. This explains the suburban mugginess and cocksureness that Mr. Wright finds in the Britannica; it explains, too, the moral obsession, for moral certainty and enthusiasm are the exclusive possessions of the inferior.

Mr. Wright protests, and with justice behind him, against the endeavor to unload this cargo of national prejudices and superstitions upon a different, and, in many respects, far superior people. Some of the examples that he points out, of insularity, of ignorance, of downright imbecile distortion of facts, are really quite astounding. In the article on the Drama, running to nearly seventy columns, the new Irish drama, perhaps the richest and most significant national drama of our time, is dismissed in twelve lines! In the department of painting, such tenth-rate English daubers as Steer, Orchardson and Etty are given special biographies heavy with encomiums, and such important foreigners as Van Gogh and Cézanne are without biographical mention! In literature the crying up of English nonentities is even more staggering. Mrs. Humphry Ward gets four times as much space as George Moore; Joseph Conrad gets but a third of the space given to Marie Corelli, and Hermann Bahr, Romain Rolland, Otto Julius Bierbaum, Hugo von Hofmannsthal and Lady Gregory are not discussed at all. Altogether, a shameless exhibition of cheap national prejudice, of booming ignorance, of childish affectation. The Germans, curiously enough, are relatively well treated; the discussion of them is often inadequate and sometimes stupid, but there is little show of downright ill-nature. But when it comes to the Irish, the French, and above all, the Americans, criticism takes to flight and patriotic tub-thumping has its place. Yet this is a work that Americans are asked to accept as authoritative, as exhaustive, as fair and square!

Mr. Wright, though he will collide with the colonial spirit, now so ludicrously evident in more than one quarter, deserves commendation for a laborious and extremely difficult piece of work. His book is small, but it represents almost incalculable industry and painstaking. I have alluded only to the chapters on the arts; he is equally comprehensive and convincing when dealing with the sciences and with philosophy. To discover an American of broad enough culture to achieve so hydra-headed a task, not only adequately but well, is in itself an event of no little significance. Can it be that we begin to produce critics who really know something?

IV

In the novels of the season—they run to almost fabulous num-bers—I find a laudable display of technic, but little else. That is to say, they are competently put together, but almost wholly uninspired; not one of them has moved me or will stick in my mind. It is the merit of a truly first-rate novel that it leaves a brilliant and inerasible impression behind it, that one carries away from it a memory well-nigh as vivid as that of experience itself. So one rises from "Henry Esmond," from "Sister Carrie," from "Anna Karenina," from "Germinal," from "Lord Jim," from "Sister Teresa," even from "The Old Wives' Tale." There is gusto in such tales; there is an emotional momentum that is, so to speak, contagious; there is a profound appeal to sympathy and feeling. But in the second-rater there is only a trick well performed. One may greatly admire that trick, but once it is done it is done. When I look back over many years of novel reading I find that my memory auto-matically sieves out the good from the bad. I remember the former without an effort, and in detail. I remember Johan Boyer's "The Power of a Lie," and Edith Wharton's "Ethan Frome," and Frank Norris' "Vandover and the Brute," and Hugh Walpole"s "The Gods and Mr. Perrin," and many a book by Conrad, Dreiser, Bennett, Wells, Andrieff and Anatole France; in each of them there was some magic that left its mark, some idea that went home. But when I try to remember the in-numerable books that came out with them and were read with them, I am completely lost. I can't even remember their authors' names . . .

Nothing before me, I am convinced, will remain long after my scavenger takes the physical corpse away. I have got through "Mi-chael," by E. F. Benson, with tolerable amusement—but it is fading already. Not a trace of the infectious joy of "Mrs. Ames"; not a trace of the fiery brilliance of "Dodo." A sound novel, but no more. Mr. Ben-son is an accomplished workman; he is a civilized man—the reviewer of the New York *Times* notices it and is "amazed" by it—; he usually has something to say. But when he wrote "Michael" the divine frenzy was not in him . . . Nor was it in W. B. Trites when he wrote "Brian Banaker's Autobiography" (*Knopf*), another suave piece of work, but as cold as an aunt's kiss and as hollow as a jug. One feels constantly that most of it is left untold, that the important is sacrificed to the trivial. On page 300 it not only ends; it dies . . . Nor in Hugh de Sélincourt when he wrote "A Soldier of Life" (*Macmillan*), an attempt to depict the collapse of nerves following an experience of the war. Sélincourt starts out bravely. He sets his stage skillfully. But the transactions that follow quickly descend to sentimentality and the obvious . . . He began too soon. The war novels must wait the end of the war.

Dulness, dulness: in "Changing Winds," by St. John G. Ervine (*Macmillan*); "Mendel," by Gilbert Cannan (*Doran*); "The Chaste Wife," by Frank Swinnerton (*Doran*); "The Wonder," by J. D. Beresford (*Doran*); "Edith Bonham," by Mary Hallock Foote (*Houghton*); "The Shifting Spell," by Leslie Probyn (*Duffield*); "Madame Prince," by W. Pett Ridge (*Doran*). Here we have a vast writing against space; a dreadful piling up of claptrap; ideas rolled out like noodles. Mr. Beresford has an excellent notion for a satirical novelette; he makes a third-rate novel of it. Mr. Ervine swathes an anything but acute study of cowardice in such trappings that it suffocates. The rest flounder in their own fogs. It is difficult for the mind to fix itself upon such vapidity; there is no drama in it, no purpose, no passion. Its very assumption of significance begins to irritate in the end. One turns with something not unlike relief to the frank tear-squeezing of such things as "The Road to Understanding," by Eleanor H. Porter (*Houghton*); "Little Mother," by Ruth Brown MacArthur (*Penn*), and "Joan and the Babies and I," by Cosmo Hamilton (*Little-Brown*), or to the undisguised melodrama of "Greenmantle," by John Buchan (*Doran*); "Lost Endeavor," by John Masefield (*Macmillan*); "Sea Plunder," by H. De Vere Stacpoole (*Lane*); "Under the Big Dipper," by D. George Dery (*Brentano*) and "Fleming Stone," by Carolyn Wells (*Lippincott*). Here, at least, there is no pretension to profundity; here there is balderdash unashamed.

The Charmed Circle

By William Drayham

CHAPTER I

So good an authority as Virgil, whose verse another poet has called "the stateliest measure ever moulded by the lips of man," remarked one day, possibly to his friend Horace, that "the shrubs and humble tamarisks have not their charms for all."

Almost two thousand years later another Horace, this time resident near Buffalo in the State of New York, came upon this aphorism and felt his life justified by classical precedent.

Horace Blackwell thought in terms of rich and rare orchids. When he thought of music it was Grand Opera that concerned him. The heroines of his dreams wore splendid stuffs of silk and velvet bought in far countries and about their white arms these dim princesses wore strange bracelets of carven jade greener than the distant sea.

Had he been enabled to choose the lot in life that he would have liked, Horace Blackwell would have dwelt in an old castle, gray with memories, and walked over springing turf that had shaken beneath the weight of armored knights and chargers in a day when there were courts of love, and tournaments were the diversions of the rulers.

Horace, therefore, at a small town near Buffalo which was a collection of factories rather than an eligible site for homes, felt the oppression of his lot more than most men. It is true the house of his aunt in which he had been brought up was the best house in the town. And it was true that this estimable lady had money which would be his. But there were drawbacks he could not overlook.

Smitten with the belief that work inevitably ennobles, Mrs. Blackwell had insisted her nephew enter one of the factories that encircled her pleasant home. She preferred that he take a dinner pail and work from the bottom up. The lower rungs taught so much more of the real and lasting values of life, she explained.

Horace listened to her patiently. He was newly come from a small college and intolerant of provincial advice, but he knew so little of the life commercial that he supposed she was right in what she said.

Smart Set 52, No. 4 (August 1917): 3–28.

But he grew agitated when he understood that she expected him to work as a common laborer so that when he arrived at her age he would be a partner in a factory which turned out so many millions of bottle openers a year.

"How old are you?" he demanded.

Mrs. Blackwell admitted being sixty-three. It seemed that her natal year had been marked by unprecedented calamities in the neighborhood, disasters by fire and flood, so that she could not possibly be mistaken.

"And I am twenty-three," he mused, "so that if I live forty years more I can own a part interest in a factory."

His aunt was disconcerted by an aimless question je flung at her with almost an appearance of anger. "And what sort of hands shall I have when I am your age?"

"Hands?" she cried. "What has that to do with it?"

He knew better than to tell her what was in his mind. He had beautiful hands for a man, long, white with tapering fingers and carefully kept nails. Many and many a time he had seen in imagination these hands of his enclose in their own the tinier ones of some beautiful woman of rank and fashion in the world to which he had no right of entry. Forty years of bottle opening industries would make them gnarled and horrible. He could only contemplate such a disaster by assuring himself that if it were to come he would wear gloves night and day.

"I'm not built for that sort of work," he said at length. His aunt had a neat little property and she must not be wounded; also he rather liked her.

"What work are you built for?" she demanded.

"I will think it over and let you know," he said seriously.

"That's your father all over," she grumbled. "That man might have owned this town if he'd had a mind to." She snorted. "He used to collect flowers and ferns and went chasing butterflies and bugs on Sunday when the others were in Sunday school."

He looked at her with enthusiasm. So far he had only heard that his father was a failure from a business point of view. This was his progenitor in a wholly new light. He saw in him one who had also rebelled at the narrow circle. His aunt disapproved of the sudden light on interest.

"Chasing butterflies on Sunday afternoons!" she sneered. "I suppose you feel you'd like to do that?"

"I should like to chase them back to the rainbow from where they came," he said extravagantly.

In the end Horace chose, since he must obey his aunt, to become a bookkeeper. For five years he labored at this devitalizing work, and had the span of life permitted him to toil at it for five hundred years his skill would never have brought him to owning a factory.

But during those five years he had learned something of the life for which he longed. A girl from the co-educational college he had attended taught him much. She had been a governess in a wealthy household and assured him that knightly manners and stately graces belonged to a day that was dead.

"You've got to be a man of the world," said this sapient maid. "People don't write verses to their lovers any more; they take them to Tiffany's and let them pick out what they want.

"And," she continued a trifle vaguely, "you've got to have charge accounts everywhere."

The little book of verse that Horace had hoped some day to be a stepping stone to cherished love was laid aside reluctantly but instantly. Some of the stanzas had merit but most had not, so the world was little the poorer. His new ambition was to be a man of the world. Others have wrecked themselves in such attempts, but there was a streak of caution inherited either from his mother or acquired in the bookkeeping department of his factory.

He kept this ambition to himself, but went twice a week to Buffalo and patronized the spoken drama. Men of the world always did this, he knew. And there was the need, too, for him to understand the ordering of a dinner and the names of wines and liqueurs. Park and Merril's catalogues helped him with the wines, but Buffalo was a poor guide to one who sought knowledge of the gastronomic arts.

Effie Horton, the governess with ideas on modern society and the newer chivalry, was a great aid to him at first in shaping his nebulous ambitions. She was a pretty girl, her figure was svelte and charming, and he called to mind certain evenings of June, now three years gone by, when he had kissed her with all the relish that first love creates. There was a warmth, too, in her hair and caresses that many of his fellows would have appreciated more than he. She was the only girl whom he had kissed since he was emancipated from the stupid kissing-games of his childhood parties.

Effie Horton was engaged for the moment in endeavoring to aid two daughters of a Buffalo banker to pass their entrance examinations to a fashionable college. She met Horace often in Delaware Park near her employer's residence, and told him of her life in New York, where she saw, if she did not mix with, the bearers of names that counted for much in the register of social distinction. Occasionally she had lunched with her employer, a lady of expensive tastes, in the really first-class restaurants and hotels. Horace was often a trifle annoyed that she did not remember more of the fashionable gossip she must have heard.

"How funny you are, Horace," she said when he had chidden her for this.

"I don't see that at all," he said stiffly.

"Silly boy," she returned. "What good call it do you? You'll never have enough money to last in that crowd ten minutes, even if you got in, which you couldn't do if you lived to be a million and eight years old. The man in the family I was kept a steam yacht. I've been on it. You could sleep forty guests on board, and it cost him twenty thousands dollars a month to keep it in commission. Then they had a grouse moor in Scotland, a cottage at Newport, a house on the Avenue, a chateau on the Loire, and a place near Aiken."

"And did you go to them all?" he asked enviously.

"I had to," she retorted, "but it was precious little full for me to be on the outside looking in with no decent clothes to wear."

"But men made love to you," he asserted, looking at her appraisingly.

"Not the sort of men I wanted," she answered, "and not in the sort of way I liked."

"I'm afraid you're incurably romantic," he said, "the sort of girl who wants to love one man only till both of you get old and fat."

"It's the best way, Horace," she said earnestly. "The things I learned when I was with those people would make you sick."

"What things?" he asked eagerly.

"Oh, matrimonial mix-tips and misfits. It cured me of thinking I was going to marry a splendid millionaire."

He looked at her keenly. "Then you thought about that once?"

"Fool-girls always do. I was a fool-girl once."

"And what are you now?"

"Just an ordinary girl who will be happy to get a small flat in New York and a man I can love."

"That's an ambition that ought not to be difficult," he sneered.

Hers was a trivial aspiration for one who had heard of Millionaires' Row, longed to know Newport's cottagers and take to the waves from Bailey's Beach.

"You'd like the French and Italian *tables d'hôtes*," she said presently. "One meets all sorts of interesting people there."

"What sort?" he demanded.

"Authors, musicians and artists mostly. At Gollat's one night Lennison, the cartoonist, drew a dandy cartoon on the tablecloth and dedicated it to me."

Somehow this did not appeal very strongly to Horace Blackwell. He doubted the breeding of men who habitually decorated restaurant napery, and the price of the dinner made him doubt the pedigree of the wine. By this time he could have told the inquirer the price of the better known vintages.

Effie looked at him and sighed. She supposed he would never understand how much she cared for him or believe that it was with him as a life partner she had grown so tender to the idea of a small comfortable home in New York. She had realized early that his ambitions overleaped her own and in his presence forgot the admiration other men were eager to proffer.

Plainly Horace Blackwell was not for her. When his aunt died he would have ten thousand dollars and a comfortable home. No great sum of money to support his ambitions, it was true, but riches to the daughter of a poor Episcopalian minister whose God had rewarded him with a dozen children.

A hundred times poor Effie swore she would not see him again and feel herself humiliated by his indifference. But there was a certain magnetism, unconsciously expended on his part, which kept her the companion of his evening whenever her duties allowed it.

"If anything should happen to your aunt what would you do?" she demanded one night at a theater.

He was engaged in observing how society actors took their stage leave of the ladies they loved; whether they turned their back on them or walked away backward as those do who retreat from royal presences and thus imperil bric-a-brac. He was beginning to see that society actors may vary in their interpretation of social graces and these variations puzzled him. He was so much engrossed in a provincial star of the John Drew school that she was compelled to repeat her question.

"If it happened in the right season I should go to Newport. But she'll outlive me," he concluded gloomily. The play was one of high life as the author imagined it to be and his participation in its glories seemed very far away. A moment later he was sorry for the impression he had given. "I hope she will live for years," he said emphatically as he thought of her constant kindness. "She's a dear old creature even if we don't often agree on things."

"She's sixty-two," Effie reminded him.

"That's nothing," he retorted, "she'll see eighty for certain."

Speculation on the span of life is invariably risky. Even as he spoke the poor old lady lay dead in her house. And there was something grimly humorous in the manner that one sparing in her diet should come to her end.

Horace had telephoned from the mill that he was going to dine in Buffalo and go to a theater. And as the night was hot and the ice almost gone she determined to eat the steak he had bought and cooked for him. A piece of this unaccustomed delicacy stuck in her throat and choked her to death ere her condition was observed by the woman who was working in the adjoining kitchen.

The house and ground left to her heir was worth about seven thousand dollars. She begged him not to dispose of it. There would come a time, she said in a letter written not so long before her death and delivered to him by her lawyer, when he would see that the dreams he dreamed were idle visions and would realize that marriage and a home were nearer to happiness. He did not tell Effie Horton that his aunt hoped he would marry her. But he determined to honor her wish not to sell the house, although he might never be able to endure it as a home.

There remained about twelve thousand dollars besides, and with this in cash and a draft on a New York bank he tore himself free of his native town. And his manner of going was as incomprehensible as his whole life had been to those among whom he had moved. He did not even go to the mill to collect the monthly salary of seventy-five dollars that was due had he waited but twelve hours longer. Nor did he make the house to house visits that neighbors paid who were to adventure into distant parts. He left as caretaker the old woman who had waited on his aunt, and told her he would probably never return.

When he had gone they realized that this self-contained, good-looking, friendless son of their own soil was a stranger whom they had never known.

And since loyalty to strangers has never been accounted a virtue, most of them said he would come to a bad end, and many of them hoped it.

CHAPTER II

Horace reached New York during the last week of May and registered at a not too obtrusive hotel. It was not his intention to remain there long, since he had gathered from his researches in the literature of polite society that a bachelor gained more *cachet* if he had two discreet rooms somewhere close enough to Fifth Avenue to regard it as his nearest thoroughfare.

These rooms he obtained without difficulty. He had none of the dislike to getting the most for his money which many young men had whom he had observed upon the stage. There was a cautious strain in his ancestry and he visited many attractive suites before he decided on what he wanted. There was a wealthy young man whose unsympathetic father insisted he should rough it on the western plains for a year as an antidote for an enervating existence in New York. These rooms were to be sublet, furniture and all, and into them without effort Horace Blackwell came. He felt it a piece of amazing luck, for he was enabled to take young Worthington's Japanese valet—a model of silence, courtesy and discretion—and start his career as a man about town within a week of leaving his home.

And so soon as his address had been determined upon he had cards engraved. One reading them would see that Mr. Horace Blackwell's addresses were Marshfield, Erie County, N. Y., and such-and-such a number Fifth Avenue. Marshfield was legitimately his. When he came to read the title deeds to his aunt's house he found it was described therein as Marshfield. That it was situate in the town of Bowlerville was information none need know.

Worthington's rooms were a little too well furnished. The criticism that the old vulgarian Gloster, of Kipling's poem, passed on his son's rooms at college could have been as well exercised on these furnished by the decadent son of a great ironmaster. At that time Blackwell had not made the discovery that he possessed naturally good taste. There were oriental hangings, for example, that Worthington had bought at great cost because he was assured they had decorated the apartments of a sultan's favorite wife. The paintings that he had most admired were of Boucher and his pink and white school of vulgar superficiality. But Blackwell did not like to banish them at first, having no standards of art from which to judge them.

The most important morning of his life dawned with no especial radiance. He was intoxicated with the ease and luxury of his life. At a time when he would formerly have been an hour in the accounting room of the Bowlerville mill, Ito brought him delicious tea and the thinnest of bread and butter and asked him at what hour the bath should be ready and what he desired for breakfast. All his life Horace had wanted pajamas of real silk and bath and dressing robes of delicate texture. They were his now and stamped with the name of a fashionable retailer. The pleasant spring breezes came stealing into his room over window boxes of bright flowers.

The touch of caution in him brought the knowledge that men about town may not indefinitely prolong an existence on twelve thousand dollars; but his money was hardly touched and the life of which he had dreamed lay before him. He had rooms on the Avenue and to them would come no pestering friends of other days. His life had always been a self-centered one. Effie Horton alone knew him well, and she was even now striving with the dull daughters of one of Buffalo's proudest families. Adventures were for the bold. If he had not possessed a faith in his destiny he might well have wondered by what path he should proceed. To take off his hat to a pleasing damsel and try to convince her they had met before was no part of his scheme. Such coarse technique savored too much of the college-boy style to suit him. And once, long ago, he had tried it and not with eminent success.

As it chanced, he had invaded New York at a time when the International Polo matches were but a few weeks distant. Polo was a game he had never seen. He knew it was society's sport, the costliest of outdoor exercises, the most splendid game in which physically fit humanity may engage. His first knowledge of it was gained by that best of polo pony stories, "The Maltese Cat," and he had seen mentions of the game from time to time where fashionable America foregathered, Newport, Lakewood, Point Judith and Narragansett Pier.

Smart America had witnessed in the preceding year a very close contest for the International trophy and was looking forward to almost as spirited a one now. Every day the teams were engaged in practice matches and the papers informed him of the time and place. On the day he determined to see the game at first hand he found that the English team would engage in friendly rivalry one on which two Americans played, besides an English baron and a Spanish duke. The game would be on the private estate of a Westbury millionaire. At the depot a taxi took him to the ground, where he was admitted without question. For the first time in his life he was among members of Long Island's smart hunting set.

The big playing field with its white board border, the pavilion wherein men and women sat chatting, the groups of ponies and stable boys and the men in their polo kit might all have been familiar sights so far as the outward interest he took in them. At heart he was more excited than ever he had been. Here he was in the midst of the only sort of his countryfolk he desired to know, not as one who had paid admission, but a guest of the same benevolent magnate as they were.

Here and there were people of coarser clay whom he supposed to be the inevitable newspaper men, red-faced men with cigars and domestic panamas and a tendency to turn the greensward into a cuspidor. He turned aside from them impatiently and walked over to the stamping ponies, where a group of men were talking to some of the players. The grooms were chubby-faced little English lads, very trim in their bedford cords, and they touched their hats and dropped their "aitches" with equal readiness, and when he asked them told him the names of their famous charges.

Presently someone in authority called out, "Stand back there from the ponies."

A few undesirable people moved back, but the men talking to the players remained as they were. And when the man who had shouted perceived Mr. Horace Blackwell, of Marshfield, catechizing the grooms on the points of the ponies he concluded that he, too, was of the elect and permitted him to remain. This was not lost upon Horace, who from time to time strolled back to the spot and proffered a patronizing remark.

It was when he had come back from this shielded spot that he heard his name called and beheld Effie Horton beaming at him. He betrayed little pleasure at meeting her.

"What brings you here?" he demanded.

"My romantic heart," she laughed. "I could not endure Buffalo without you."

"But the real reason?" he asked.

"A chance to get a newspaper job. I'm on the woman's page of the *Evening Herald*. I was on it a year ago just before I went to Buffalo, but there was a new editor who didn't like my work—or me—and I left. Now the old one is back and sent for me. I saw you long ago, but you wouldn't leave the ponies and they wouldn't let me in. How did you get in there?"

"Just walked in," he said. "Those other men stayed, so I did, too. I had as much right as they."

"Oh, shucks!" she cried. "Listen to Horace talking! That tall man with the blond moustache is Lord Minster, who brought the team over. The one he's talking to is Mr. Harry Payne. Oh, yes, you have just as much right as they do! What team are you playing on today?"

Her bantering was rather pleasing than otherwise. He felt he had made an admirable beginning.

"How do you know what their names are?"

"I've come out here twice before to get the men's names and the women's dresses. I left Buffalo before you did. I've had my job two weeks already."

As she spoke a pretty dark woman passed them with a slight, dark man, and went toward the group about the ponies.

Horace looked at her with a very vivid interest.

To begin with, he thought he had never seen so fascinating a woman. She was above middle height, taller than the man who accompanied her, and walked with a grace and litheness that took his eye instantly. There was a spring in her steps that made her walk seem almost like a dance. She radiated an intense vitality. Her dark eyes were full of flashing colors and her laugh more musical than anything he had heard. He watched her till she was lost in the throng. Then he sighed and presently turned to Effie.

"Who is that wonderful creature?" he demanded.

Effie looked at him in silence. This was a new Horace, startled out of his calm airs of superiority into being an eager, interested man, a tinge of red coloring his usually clear pallid skin. It was the Horace, in fact, which she had often hoped to see awakened to her own charms.

"Who is she?" he repeated.

"I don't know," Effie said a little sullenly. "I can't know everybody who horns into a place like this."

"She belongs here," he said with conviction. "Effie, be sweet and find her out."

He smiled at her for another woman's sake more pleasantly than he had ever done for her own.

"That was a ravishing gown, just the thing to fill your column on the *Evening Herald*."

"And what color was it, pray?" she asked.

"How do I know?" he returned, "I saw her face and that was all. Find out for me, Effie! Please, obstinate little redhead, tell me who she is!"

The tone, almost an endearing one, made her very bitterly disposed toward the radiant woman who had swept past her. How little men understand women, she thought, that this one should use such a tone for such a purpose. Or it might be, and this wounded her all the more, that he was utterly indifferent as to what construction she placed on his moods.

"What for?" she said. "What good will it do you? You can't know her."

"Why not?" he flung back, nettled.

She shrugged her shoulders. He should suffer, too. "What has Meadowbrook in common with Bowlerville?"

"I knew she was Meadowbrook," he cried, and passed over the slur as though its source rendered it unworthy of notice.

"I shall find out. There are other newspaper men and women here besides you." He smiled. "You're bluffing, Effie, you don't know who she is."

"I do," the girl cried. "And I know the man she is with and all about both of them."

"You'd much rather tell me yourself than for me to get it from a rival. Who are they?"

"The man's name is Wolfston Colman, one of the best poloists we ever had. Some people say it's only jealousy that keeps him from the team that's to play the Englishmen next week. He was an internationalist once."

"And her name?" he begged.

"That's Mrs. Hamilton Buxton."

"Are you sure?" he cried.

"Why shouldn't she be?"

"I thought Mrs. Hamilton Buxton was a trifle—well, notorious."

"Just a trifle," Effie returned maliciously. "I interviewed her once and I'm not likely to be wrong. Doesn't she make up well?"

He looked at her indignantly.

"She's no older than you."

Effie was paler than usual. She took out a neat little pad and produced a pencil.

"This is the first opportunity I've ever had," she said, "to interview a man who's suddenly fallen in love for the first time. I shall call it 'The Soul's Awakening.'"

He looked at her angrily. She had never seen him show such sudden passion.

"I hate red-headed women," he snapped, and turned on his heel, and walked toward the playing field where the game was beginning.

CHAPTER III

It was that afternoon of early June when the hopes of the men who wore the red rose were dashed to the ground by the accident to their famous number two.

When a backhand blow by the hard-hitting son of the ground's owner struck the cavalryman full in the face and knocked him from his mount there was consternation among such of the spectators who guessed the possible consequence of the accident.

"What a dreadful, dreadful pity," said a musical voice that brought a thrill to Blackwell. "He was playing at the top of his form and he's such a delightful man, too, isn't he?"

The ex-internationalist to whom she spoke smiled. "I haven't your opportunity for finding out how delightful he can be, but he's the best number two they ever sent out from Hurlingham. It's a damned shame. Minster'll have to play, I suppose."

The two were standing within a few feet from Horace and utterly unconscious of his presence. Once the man glanced at him and the owner of Marshfield felt the look an unkind one. It seemed that the famous player had sensed him as one out of his element. It was a quick sudden scrutiny that ended in a half frown.

As a matter of fact, Colman hardly noticed his face. He was looking at this tall good-looking man who wore the colors of the Tenth Hussars, and wondering who he was. New York tailors had just taken to importing regimental and college colors in the form of neckties, and Horace had been attracted by a combination which informed the initiated that its owner belonged, or should belong if etiquette were observed, to that very famous regiment of King's Hussars.

As it was, Horace misconstrued the look and conceived a sudden dislike to the great horseman and an overpowering jealousy that it should be his luck to escort Mrs. Hamilton Buxton.

The niceties of the play, when it was resumed with a new man in place of the injured one, had little attraction for the lately come to New York. He could only stare at this brilliant and magnetic woman whose matrimonial adventures had come even to the attention of his aunt and merited her severe censure. She looked at him once, a cold hard scrutiny, it seemed, which seemed to confirm Colman's verdict of his social impossibility. In a sense, they looked through him and not at him. He wondered if his tailor had proved false when he declared his new customer's suits embodied the last refinements of the art sartorial. Some of the men watching the game were in riding kit; others had obviously motored up. None had clothes on so extremely new as his own. Wolfston Colman was almost carelessly dressed.

As he gazed at the man he envied he caught sight of Effie regarding him with a supercilious smile. He knew she was by way of being clever and it infuriated him to find her watching his entrance into smart society with frank and ungenerous curiosity. He turned away as he caught her glance and looked out into the field, now free of ponies, since it was one of the intervals between "chukkers."

Not many yards distant he saw the tall blond man she had told him was Lord Minster talking to a pretty woman in white and a slight dark man who looked like a Spaniard. Horace had seen her in the pavilion at the other side of the ground when he entered, and she had crossed the field for the first time. He could hear that they were discussing the lamentable accident to the Hurlingham star.

Horace felt suddenly very remote from the world wherein he wished to move. All the men and women about him seemed to have friends everywhere. They chattered and discussed one another and the finer points of the game as though life were for them—as indeed it was for the majority—a round of pleasure. He cast his eyes on the beautiful Mrs. Buxton, who was now engrossed with a pink and white youth in smart riding kit, a youth with indeterminate features and pale hair. It was well enough that she should talk to Colman. He had made a name and was rich besides, and good looking enough, but this hateful lad with white eyelashes angered him. He was annoyed at the insistence with which the favored youth looked at him. It seemed to Horace to be a stare that said no Bowlerville representative had a right on the private field of a millionaire where polo was in progress and the aristocracies of America and Europe mixed.

The favored youth, so far from resenting Blackwell's presence, was sighing in secret that he lacked his stature and looks. This aloof stranger wearing regimental colors was probably one of the companions of the cavalry officers who had come to lift the cup.

He envied them their superb horsemanship and thought unkindly of a mother who had feared for his safety too much to let him learn the art of equitation until it was too late for him to get even a fair seat. Mrs. Hamilton Buxton followed his sober glances and rested her magnificent eyes on the stranger. He was uncommonly good looking, she thought. Half a dozen years ago, perhaps it was more, there had been a Roman prince who looked like him and had the same rather melancholy eyes and the same beautiful tapering white hands.

"Who is that man?" she asked abruptly.

"I don't know," Duff McGregor answered. "I thought you'd know. You know every good looking man and, fortunately for me, some plain ones. Perhaps he's one of these cavalry fellows. They're swarming over."

"Oh, no," she said. "One can always tell a cavalryman by his walk. He's not bred to the sabre and saddle."

Horace sensed that it was about him they talked and the knowledge brought him little pleasure. In avoiding their glances he caught sight of Effie Horton. He felt he had had enough scrutiny and stopped over the board that guarded the enclosed field to walk to the other side of the grounds.

But as he neared Lord Minster and the two to whom he talked the interval was ended and the grooms led out the ponies. There was no time to cross. He must perforce turn back and meet the unsympathetic eyes of those who judged him hardly. There had always been the dislike in his nature to make a fool of himself. Perhaps that was why his life had been tinged with a certain melancholy. He took a sudden and surprising resolve. He was abreast of the lady in white. Effie was staggered when she saw him raise his hat and address her.

"Is Captain Leslie very badly hurt?" he asked.

The lady to whom he spoke had met so much hospitality since her arrival and was besides related by marriage to several American families that she supposed this was one of the many nice young Americans she had met at a dance or a dinner, at Meadowbrook or Piping Rock, whose name she ought to remember but unfortunately could not call to mind.

"They don't know yet," she answered graciously, "but they're afraid his nose is broken. Isn't it a frightful nuisance?"

He uttered some word of conventional condolence and walked with her to the board, where he raised his hat and bowed to them both, the woman in white and the dark little man with her. That was all. But Effie had seen; and not Effie alone. Mrs. Hamilton Buxton had observed him, and this time she did not look clear through him.

Effie could not keep up her air of dignity when she wanted badly to find out how he had come to know these names already in her list of notables at a distinguished gathering.

"How did you know them?" she demanded.

"Know them?" he repeated.

"Don't you know their names, Horace?"

"You don't," he returned with assumed calm; "you can't bluff me this time."

"She was Lady Minster and the man was the Duke of Penderosa, captain of the Madrid Polo Club. Of course I know them."

"This time you happen to be right," he admitted, and marvelled at Horace Blackwell who had been seen publicly walking with a baroness and a duke.

The baroness had smiled and the duke had raised his hat. He had no desire for Bowlerville to know. They would not understand. They would raise rude voices in raucous laughter. He knew his Bowlerville. And it had all happened because be did not want to seem a fool in having set out to cross a field too late and being compelled to turn back and meet unsympathetic glances.

Standing a little apart he saw Lady Minster greet Mrs. Buxton.

"By the way," the American woman asked, "who was that tall good looking man you were talking to just now?"

"I'm ashamed to say I've forgotten his name, and even where I met him. It was at a dance somewhere, or was it a dinner? No, I think it was at a tennis party. But I've been so splendidly entertained here and met so many charming men that I can't for the life of me remember their names."

This conversation was sufficient to establish Blackwell's eligibility in Mrs. Buxton's mind. Although men in all ranks of life bend to beggar maids—and others—they do not like their women to smile at men of inferior birth. There are lamentable stories in society of valets and men of obscure walks of life who have masqueraded sufficiently well to marry women of rank. It is true they have rarely captured buds; but full-blown flowers have occasionally yielded themselves to such suitors and so confounded high families and scandalized relatives and set lawyers to the making of new wills.

Duff McGregor presently found that Mrs. Hamilton Buxton was taking absolutely no notice of his remarks. He was not sufficiently conceited to find anything strange in this, but he thought she need not have turned the battery of those wonderful eyes on a man whom neither he nor she, nor anyone else, apparently, knew. After a time he became oppressed by the sense of his relative unimportance. He could not accuse the lady he admired of flirting like a shopgirl on a holiday at a cheap beach. She had glanced only a couple of times at the stranger and there was nothing in her gaze that might offend propriety. At least so he thought; and sighed a moment later when it occurred to him that his lack of success might be that he could not properly interpret the signs.

Presently someone told him that his mother sought him and he excused himself and walked away. Colman took his place by the lady's side and was too much interested in the fast and exciting play to talk. Until today the invaders had been matched with comparatively slow teams and their own pace was not called upon. But today they were showing speed and teamwork that made him wonder what would be the issue when they met his countrymen, whom he did not consider to be in equal physical condition.

In all his six and twenty years of life Horace Blackwell had never seen a woman who fascinated him so wholly as this magnificent brunette. She was assuredly one of those princesses of whom he had dreamed. And he cursed fate sullenly that he was placed in an environment where such women did not come. Those rooms of his on the Avenue and his discreet Togo seemed miserably lacking in space and importance when he considered how these people about him dwelt. The great mansion standing a half mile distant from the polo ground had, so Effie informed him, sixty rooms in it, and it was but one of several which the millionaire Phillips owned.

He dared not attempt with Mrs. Hamilton Buxton another such maneuvre as he had successfully carried out with Lady Minster and the Duke.

He edged his way through the people near him and presently stood directly behind her looking down at the tendrils of curling hair that grew about her delicate ears. Once or twice she looked past him as though seeking a friend's face in the crowd. And once she allowed those splendid eyes of hers to dwell for a moment on him; he received, as it were, the end of a smile that had been thrown to a friend a few yards distant. Effie and her sneers were forgotten. There was now with him only one end in life, and that to know this adorable woman.

He had lived too much in books and dreams to have that ready wit and address which on such occasions might carry a more experienced man to the land of fleeting romance. He and she had assuredly no common acquaintances upon whom to draw. Had he been of her world this had been easy enough, but Effie's taunt came back to him. What had Meadowbrook to do with Bowlerville?

As he stood sighing at her heels she looked around again; and this time he received the beginning of a smile whose end was caught by a pretty woman passing by. He argued that she must know he was staring at her and thinking about her. And if she resented it she could annihilate him by a look. Presently she clasped her hands behind her back and he stared down at one half-closed hand. Suppose she was holding it thus so that he could slip his card into it! Then he told himself that no society woman would ever do a thing like that. A moment later he remembered the colonel's lady and Miss O'Grady.

But his desire to know her more than offset the risk he might win. In his fancy he saw himself horsewhipped by grooms, run off the field to the derision of dukes and the sneers of Long Island sportsmen for insulting a woman of position. In that moment Horace found himself possessed of a certain courage upon which there had never been the necessity to draw. It was worth the risk, he decided.

CHAPTER IV

As he slipped the engraven cardboard into those slim white hands they curled over it and their owner made no movement. The danger of assault had apparently passed away, for while holding the card she had equally answered some question of Colman's.

Her lack of action was beginning to unnerve him when, at the end of another "chukker" she turned about and looked at him as though suddenly discovering an old friend. That radiant smile he had seen wasted on others was now for him alone.

"Surely it's Mr. Blackwell," she cried. "When did you come?"

He took her hand, prayed that he was not blushing, and said he had arrived perhaps an hour before.

"Of course you know Wolfston Colman?" she remarked.,

"By sight only," he returned easily as he was introduced. He was relieved to find his apprehension that everyone on the field might be watching him was a wrong one. None took the slightest notice.

"What do you think of the Hurlingham lot?" Colman demanded.

Horace had not been listening to the horseman's critical remarks for nothing.

"If our men are not trained as well as they are we shall lose the cup," he said.

Colman turned to Mrs. Buxton with rather in air of triumph. "You see? That's exactly what I said!" In which, of course, he was right.

After a few moments she dismissed Wolfston Colman with a pleasant little nod.

"I shall see you later," she assured him. "I'm simply dying for some tea."

And with Horace at her side she walked over the ground to where in their scores motors were parked. Where tea was to be found he did not know. He was embarrassed by his ignorance.

"We'll go over to the Philipps'," she said casually. "Do you know them?"

"I've met some of them," he said guardedly.

"Have you your motor here?" she asked.

"I came over with another man in his," he returned, and made a vow that his aunt's money could be well expended in purchasing one on the morrow.

She paused by the side of a big car.

"Here's my husband's. We'll use it. He'll probably be furious." The chauffeur opened the door for her. "I, too, came in another man's."

When for the first time they were free from observation she threw him another ravishing smile.

"Well," she said, "and why did you do it?"

His voice came thickly. Experience had not permitted him to do these things without effort.

"How could I help it?" he cried. "There was never anyone so adorable as you."

Mrs. Hamilton Buxton did not answer for a moment. She was far too experienced to be deceived at the gulp in his voice. A number of men she knew could do that admirably, and none of them would ever see forty again. And she admitted frankly that she was adorable. "I ought to be furiously angry with you!"

"But you are not," he said, growing courageous.

She looked at him curiously.

"That depends."

"On what?" he demanded.

"On you," she told him. "If I am disappointed in you I shall be furious."

He wondered what she meant. How many plays had he not seen and how many novels had he not read where some such remark was made by a heroine. A composite picture of such plays or books would reveal a heroine regarding a hero with a look of pained surprise. And she would say, "We have been such good friends but now, now you have spoiled it all!"

This remark was invariably made when the juvenile lead had tried to kiss her. Was Mrs. Hamilton Buxton warning him to kiss her or not to kiss her? Horace Blackwell had thick and luxuriant hair of which he was rather proud. In that moment he would have preferred a bald dome and sophistication to inexperience and waving locks. For her part the lady was not sure what to make of him. That he took so little advantage of the occasion might mean either that he was experienced or inexperienced. The motor had arrived at the Philipps' before she had been able to determine which.

He was rather pleased to find he was among a set of people who did not carry the custom of introduction to the excess usual among the Bowlerville hostesses. There, when a stranger entered a room he was introduced instantly to everyone. This was popularly supposed to put him at his ease, whereas few ordeals are more unnerving.

He saw a number of people whom he had noticed on the field, and most of the poloists were there. He was a little embarrassed when some women stared at him curiously. Two, obviously, seemed discussing him.

Said one:

"Who is that new man she's picked up?"

"No idea," the other returned, looking at him a little enviously. "Quite nice looking, don't you think?"

"I believe she advertises for them," her friend said viciously. This lady had many intimate friends who were seduced by Mrs. Hamilton Buxton's less matured charms.

"Nonsense," the other retorted. "Millicent hasn't any need for that. What she's been looking for for years is for a young man who has never loved before. Mixed education makes that very difficult, she says. They all fall in love at absurd ages on that account and are spoiled before they're seventeen."

"Her affairs are scandalous," the first speaker replied acidly. She spoke with all the bitterness that a woman who has been an unsuccessful sinner adopts when condemning another who has not failed.

Effie had pointed her out to Horace as the Mrs. Codrington who bred, exhibited and rode her own saddle horses at the big shows. He looked at her with the respect born of her assured position. And as he looked he saw that she made a futile effort to catch the attention of a passing footman. In her hand was an emptied teacup. Instantly he advanced toward her and offered to relieve her of it.

"It would be so charming of you to get me another cup," she smiled.

When he was gone on his errand she turned to the woman at her side.

"Here's a splendid opportunity to find out all about him," she whispered. "Melt into the landscape, dear, when he comes back, and I'll introduce him to you later."

"I wondered why you wanted that second cup," her friend smiled.

"So you came with Millicent?" Mrs. Codrington asked when he found himself sitting at her side.

"What Millicent?" he demanded guardedly.

"Millicent Buxton, of course."

So her name was Millicent. He felt the need of circumspection among these people.

"Yes," he admitted.

"She is one of my dearest friends," Mrs. Codrington told him. "School girls together and sister bridesmaids at all sort of matrimonial farces. Curious I've never met you before if you know her so well. We know the same people as a rule."

"New York is a big city," he said a trifle heavily.

"Not the New York *we* know," she corrected. It seemed to her that he was not anxious to inform her of himself or his acquaintance with Millicent Buxton.

"I am not often in New York," he said quietly, "but often enough to have seen you at the Horse Show."

"You're keen on horses then?" she demanded, her eyes lighting.

He remembered he was in the midst of the famous Long Island hunting set and must be circumspect.

"Naturally," he answered, "I came out to see the ponies as well as the men who played them."

"You must come and see my stable some day," she said graciously. There was no doubt but he was exceedingly good looking and his manners were refreshing after those of the men she usually met. That he must be socially secure was vouched for by his knowledge of Mrs. Hamilton Buxton. There had always been rivalry between these two women for the men they liked, and the victory had almost always been to Hamilton Buxton's wife. This new man probably rode well enough to appreciate her superb seat; and, too, there were pleasant leafy bridle paths around her residence where she had spent many happy hours of flirtation.

"Do you know him?" she asked, indicating a big blond man who smiled at her in passing and stopped a moment later to talk to Millicent.

"I rarely remember names," Horace returned. He felt it would be awkward to pose as one entirely new to the people about him. "Who is he?"

She looked at him with a smile.

"How delightfully discreet you must be. Discreet men are so rare."

He observed that the big blond man was talking almost angrily to the woman who filled his thoughts. And it seemed that they spoke of him. None but a husband would scowl at a woman like Millicent Buxton in a crowd like this. He drew his bow at a venture.

"I prefer his wife," he said easily.

"It's quite impossible to be a friend of them both," she declared. "He is so dreadfully violent at times, but I rather like Hamilton."

Her plans to ask him to call and see her horses were shattered when the man, whose name she did not even know, arose at an imperious gesture from Millicent and left her with a mere word of apology.

"Do you know Ella Codrington well?" Mrs. Hamilton Buxton demanded of him.

"I have spoken perhaps a hundred words to her," he answered. There was something rather abrupt and disconcerting in her manner.

"Have you accepted her invitation to ride in the country lanes with her?"

"I wasn't asked," he said mildly.

"You would have been if you'd spoken a dozen words more. I know Ella rather well. In my acquaintance with women I always begin with a little suspicion and increase it as I know them more."

"She said you were one of her dearest friends," he told her.

"She knows more about me than I do about myself," said Mrs. Hamilton Buxton. "Ella always cultivates the discarded lovers of the women she hates. One can pick up a great deal of inside information that way." She looked at him rather coldly. "By the way, I'm looking for information myself."

He concealed the uneasiness he experienced. There was no doubt in his mind her remark had to do with himself and his fitness for his present surroundings.

"It's hot in here," he asserted. "Come outside and talk there."

"Mr. Blackwell," she said gravely, "I am rarely indiscreet unless I've planned to be. I'm only moved by impulses when I want to be. Of course you know what I mean?"

CHAPTER V

It was perhaps the most gratifying moment of Horace Blackwell's life to find himself wholly at his ease. Here he was set in a most unsuitable gathering; men and women of the world he had dreamed of for years were about him and he seemed to be accepted without question. It was not unlikely that he might be ejected as an interloper by liveried servants. And yet he felt no nervousness. He looked into the lovely face of the woman at his side and smiled. He was not yet aware that his rare smile rendered him singularly handsome.

"If you want me to regret anything I'm afraid I shall have to disappoint you, Mrs. Buxton."

"I want to find out some common acquaintance," she declared. "People have asked me who you were and I haven't known what to say. My husband was almost unpleasant about it. I hoped you were one of Ella Codrington's men, although as a rule I'm not so charitable as that, but you tell me you don't know her. Whom do you know here?"

"The only one I want to," he said steadily, "you."

"That, I suppose, is the obvious answer," she said, "but it doesn't help me."

"You mean that I ought not to have come here knowing nobody?"

"Of course," she said impatiently. "We all know one another here. Just now all these English cavalrymen have enlarged the circle, but we know them in England, so that's all right. I thought you were a friend of theirs. You spoke to Lady Minster and I supposed you knew the Philipps, too."

"So you're afraid I'm a burglar?"

"This house would be a treasure trove for you if you were. No, I don't think you are a criminal, Mr. Blackwell."

"You know I'm not," he said quickly. "If you are a woman you must see exactly how it happened. Directly I set eyes on you I saw you were the only woman in the world." His voice came thickly. "I wish I could tell you how lovely you are. I've always dreamed of meeting just such a woman as you. It was because of the hope I might that I have never bothered with girls. I knew that some day—"

He broke off almost in despair. His words seemed so inadequate a translation of the emotions that surged in in him. And he feared, too, that he was making himself ludicrous in the eyes of a woman of the world.

"Are you always such a passionate pilgrim as this?" she said, smiling.

He looked at her with the tortured eyes that faithful dogs bend on loved owners when they are punished.

"You are laughing at me," he cried.

"One always does that, unless one knows a man is sincere," she answered. "It's a method of protection, and you must remember that the truth is never so convincing as a lie."

"I have no right to be here," he said dully. "I'm going, but you know now why I did what I did."

"You mean that you fell in love with me at sight?"

"Is that so wonderful?" he returned.

"With us love is always a matter of design not accident. No, don't go yet," she added when he rose. "Love is a fascinating subject and one can never study it closely enough. I have always thought that the proper way for two people to approach it would be for one to have experience and the other enthusiasm. Which do you bring?"

"I have never loved a woman until I met you," he whispered.

"Then your part must be enthusiasm," she said, looking at him with her magnificent eyes, "and mine experience. Why do you frown?"

"Because I think of the men who have loved you, and the men you have loved."

"That will prevent me from being dull," she laughed. "The only time I feel sorry for my husband is when I think of the gaucheries of my first love and its absurdities."

She paused a moment and looked at him through long lashes.

"I wonder if you will ever tell that to Ella Codrington?"

For a moment he did not answer. He did not know what she meant him to understand by such a reference. She had declared that Mrs. Codrington sought out her discarded lovers. Was he to be of this number?

Curiously enough, he was conscious of an inability to regard this meeting with Millicent Buxton with the *sang froid* he had pictured when, in his fancy of other days, he had enacted similar scenes. He had longed to sin splendidly in Fifth Avenue. He had hoped to dominate women of the world with his wit and cynical self-possession. Instead he found his heart pounding madly and his brain aflame with jealousy at the knowledge that Mrs. Hamilton Buxton was admittedly experienced in the arts of love.

It was fortunate that he did not convey this impression. Used to a world where passion was unchecked although divorce was rare, Millicent Buxton was not able to believe that he had found in her a first love. She was not taken with his wit; she was susceptible to his good looks. It was because Blackwell had never thought of himself as strikingly handsome that he had none of those intolerable airs that good-looking men usually assume. He had aimed at being a man of the world, whereas his only social asset was his deportment and figure and the splendid melancholy of his fine eyes.

"I shall never think of her again," he declared.

"She deserves pity," the other asserted. "Imagine a woman whose husband finds out all her little affairs and forgives her in public!"

"I wish you'd forgive me," he said softly.

"You must be punished first," she retorted. "You are condemned to entertain me on my way back to New York."

"Do you mean it?" he cried.

"If it can be arranged," she said slowly. "What a pity you haven't a motor."

"I'll get one tomorrow," he answered eagerly.

"My husband will most certainly want his if he thinks I'm likely to ride to town with you. We've heaps of others, but they're in use or the chauffeur's mother is dying or something is wrong with the machinery."

"Couldn't I phone for a taxi?" he asked.

"And ruin this darling gown? One can't ride in those dreadful things unless forced into them. One of the Philipps boys will arrange it. They have dozens of them. I'm dining in town—our house is still open—so nobody will think we have eloped."

She leaned forward and called to Duff McGregor, who was sitting lonely a few yards distant.

"Dear Duff," she said when he was at her side, "be a sweet child and motor back to New York without me. I want a convenient excuse."

Blackwell saw the lad color, bow in obedience to her command, and disappear.

"Do you manage all men as easily as that?" he asked.

"Generally," she told him. "As a rule they like it. I am living in the hope of meeting a man who will make me enjoy being ordered about. Sometimes love comes at the bidding of scourges."

"What a horrible idea," he said hotly. "Love is not like that."

"Is this enthusiasm speaking or experience?" she demanded.

"Conviction," he answered. "I love you and I could never hurt you."

"Then you'll suffer," she returned, "and you must reckon on the fact that we sometimes like to be hurt. A woman can only love a man truly who has the power to make her suffer."

"I wish you were not so hard," he said wistfully.

"I'm not—always," she answered. "In fact, I'm rarely *really* hard. What you are objecting to is only flippancy which is another name for the armour we wear to conceal our hurts. Sometimes, dear child, I'm all melting tenderness and filled with the desire to recapture the sentimental couplets that I mouthed when I was really *ingénue*."

"That was before you were married," he said soberly, recalling the angry face of Hamilton Buxton.

"And sometimes after," she flashed back at him. "Marriage only ends the capacity for loving one's husband. It is the gateway of love and opens one's eyes to much more entrancing prospects. Have you ever been in Rome?"

He shook his head.

"I've never been abroad. Why?"

"It was in Rome that I last melted into the sentimental. There was a man there—a prince of a great house—and I think I loved him more than anyone I ever met."

"I hate to hear you say that," he cried. "I can't bear to think of him."

"And yet but for him you would never be sitting here with me. Except that you are taller you are strangely like him. He had that slow smile and the unhurried way with him that you have." Suddenly she touched his hands lightly. "Have you any idea what beautiful hands you have? Yours are like his. When I saw you today watching the polo I was startled. That was why I stared at you. That was why I spoke. You have the same profile."

He could see that the remembrance of this other man moved her deeply. She looked into the distance, seeing nothing, her thoughts a thousand leagues away from him.

"What days of flame they were," she sighed. "The scent of crushed flowers always comes back to me when I think of him. Hamilton took me to Italy soon after we were married and my prince and I used to follow the foxhounds over the Campagna and lose our way and come riding back in the gloaming to see St. Peter's rising out of the mist."

"I can see he had the power to make you suffer," Blackwell said presently when she had finished and was silent.

"It was part of my education," she answered with a shrug of the shoulders. "You are probably a better man than he, but when did we women go seeking manly virtues?"

He looked at her magnificent beauty, her exquisite coloring, her entrancing vitality and then fell to thinking of the day when these must fade.

"There'll be an end to that sort of education some day," he reminded her.

"The creeping years and so on? Of course. When I can't be loved by men I shall try and be feared by women."

Suddenly she rose to her feet.

"I've changed my mind," she said. "I shall motor home alone. You've started me thinking about my Roman. You would make the unwelcome third."

He made a gesture of despair. It seemed that he had won his paradise only to be turned from it.

"What is it, tragic child?" she demanded.

"How can I ever see you again?" he asked.

"I shall think it over," she told him. "By tomorrow I may have returned from my flight into Italy."

"How does that help me?" he inquired anxiously.

"I can't tell yet. Please don't do anything so splendidly heroic as to call. For some reason or other Mr. Buxton has taken a great dislike to you, and he is so socially secure as to indulge in acts of violence at times. He is horribly strong. At Yale he won boxing championships and consorted with pugilists."

"I'd risk that if I could see you," Horace cried with a child's eagerness.

"But I wouldn't risk ridicule," she smiled, "and no man can be thrashed by Hamilton and retain his dignity."

"Then this is the end?" he said despairingly.

"Or the beginning," she retorted.

"I wish I knew what you meant," he cried.

"Do you suppose," she said in a lower voice, "that I should have taken all the trouble to talk to you and cut the man I was supposed to meet here if I thought this was to be the end? Don't you remember that I said I was only moved by impulse when I wanted to be?"

With that she left him and was lost in the crowd. For almost an hour he sat in a chair on the terrace and thought about her. It was an incredible adventure even if it shattered the dreams he had cherished about his own *savoir vivre*. So far in life he had taken no thought about any emotions but his own. Many girls had made their timid offers of friendship, and even love, to be repulsed because they were not of the high world he coveted. He remembered Effie in particular. Because of a summer day when he had thawed from his customary aloofness she had taken his new interest to be something deeper. And when she stammeringly betrayed herself, he had found himself possessed of a certain contempt for so uncontrolled an emotion.

CHAPTER VI

Now a new man was born in him. An attitude of humility had come. He had thought of himself in those long years of waiting as one to whom beautiful women would minister. Now he found himself anxious to prove his affection.

Visions of the knightly days that were gone brought back with them memories of the chivalrous tasks that knights set themselves to perform for the glory of their ladies. He wished he were physically apt enough to chastise the bully, Hamilton Buxton. He staged a dozen scenes in his mind where he thrashed Buxton and foreign noblemen, especially Roman princes, and won adoration from Millicent's eyes.

He was forced to banish such pleasing fancies when lie saw that most of the guests were leaving. In the great hall most of them were shaking the hands of a kindly lady whom he supposed to be his hostess. And as he hesitated what course to pursue he saw Effie, notebook in hand, standing in the outer hall.

The sight spurred him to bow over the lady's hand and murmur a conventional phrase. Assuming him to be one of her son's friends and harbouring no suspicion as to his good faith, she smiled at him.

Effie's pattering feet overtook him half way down the drive. He looked at her kindly. For the first time he felt he understood her. They were fellow worshippers, although their shrines were different.

"Horace Blackwell," she gasped, "what's come over you?"

"What do you mean?" he returned, gratified at perceiving that her sneering manner was gone.

"How is it you're hobnobbing with the Social Register in a house like that?"

"Was I ever one to be satisfied with Bowlerville?" he retorted.

"I suppose I shan't see you any more," she said a little wistfully.

"I'll call and take you out to dinner some night."

"I wish you'd come and have dinner with me down at the Village tomorrow," she urged. "A lot of us, painters, poets and writers, meet at the Red Lion Inn. Some of the brightest intellects in the city."

"Village?" he queried.

"Greenwich," she told him. "New York's Latin Quarter."

She gave him her address and telephone number. He was not enthusiastic about the prospect. He had always doubted the social qualifications of people who consumed new born wine and made sketches on tablecloths.

Horace was relieved from discovering his ignorance as to the fashionable makes of automobiles. The admirable Togo had a cousin of vast mechanical ability whose temporary avocation was that of a chauffeur. At Sato's suggestion Horace purchased second-hand a very handsome car for three thousand dollars, saving thereby almost an equal sum. There was a coat of arms on it, surmounted by a coronet, which added much to the value of the machine in its new owner's eyes.

To step from a fashionable store into the car's luxurious depths and whirl along the avenue in which he had his rooms was an entrancing occupation. A dozen times during this first afternoon of his ownership Horace passed and repassed the Buxton mansion opposite the Metropolitan Museum. There were motors coming and going constantly. Once he thought he saw Millicent, but found it was another woman of her height and colouring. The only moment in which he felt able to gratify Sato's expectations of him was when a coach-and-four came out of an entrance to the Park and he saw Ella Codrington ribbons in hand. She bowed to him brightly. He wished he were certain that Sato saw.

At seven he called for Effie. It was her tragedy that he never noticed what she wore or the style in which her hair was done. She jumped into the big car, thinking he had hired a taxicab. It was a moment of disappointment but one atoned for when she discovered silver fittings graved with coronets and coats of arms. Her exclamations of astonishment and gratification were not finished when they drew up at the

Red Lion Inn. For the time it was a favorite resort of the villagers. It was said that at times people of talent had been seen within its portals.

Horace frankly disapproved of the men and women he met. That he did not understand their art jargon and literary small talk gave him no sense of inferiority. The only man among them who was well dressed turned out to be in "the advertising" and therefore barely tolerated by those who hoped some day to sell stories. And the only woman who did not seem to him hopelessly vulgar was Effie. A woman on his right, a newspaper woman, Effie whispered, talked birth control at him most of the time, and said she was writing a book of sonnets on free love. She had taken too much of the chemical compound which masqueraded as wine and leaned against him heavily.

The only bright spot in the evening was the evident respect of the advertising gentleman, who, it seems, had enquired of Sato whose car he tended, and shaped his diplomacy accordingly. He was rewarded with a ride to his Harlem home in a coronetted limousine.

When he had been set down Horace turned on Effie with disapproval in his voice.

"How on earth did you get in with such a bunch as that?"

"I like them," she returned stoutly. "I'm only a working woman, remember, and it helps me to mix with them."

"Don't ask me to meet them again," he cautioned her.

"They are as good as you and me," she retorted.

"Nonsense," he snapped. "If I were content with the things they like I should be as good as they, but I'm not. You know I was never like the other people in Bowlerville, Effie. They are not half as good as you are, either."

"Do you know that's the first nice thing you've said to me for years, Horace?"

"Is it?" he said, smiling. "Then let me tell you something else. You were by far the prettiest woman in the place tonight."

"You wouldn't have said that about me yesterday afternoon," she pouted.

"It wouldn't have been true," he said brutally. "There's something about those women in that Long Island set that is like strong wine to me. They go everywhere, know everybody, do everything. They have that perfect poise that an aristocracy alone possesses. That crowd tonight was a mass of affectation, boasting of what it had published or painted or was going to. The people over there at Westbury had nothing of that."

"They don't have to be," Effie cried; "they have everything."

"That's exactly what I mean," he said. "I like people who have everything."

That the girl was silent and almost sulky as they drove to her lodging did not worry him at all. He did not notice it.

Although he went out to Meadowbrook to the Polo International Matches he was not able to get a word with Millicent Buxton. On both occasions he caught a glimpse of her in a box, but she was surrounded by those of her own set and if she saw him gave him no sign of it.

He was depressed at the thought she had finished with him. Through long sleepless night hours he asked himself what he had done or said to bring this about. Once he called up her residence on the telephone and succeeded only in getting a servant, who demanded first his name and business ere he could be connected with members of the family. Not caring to do this for fear Mrs. Buxton might be angry, and cursing himself for his lack of courage, he hung up the instrument.

Togo's nightly desire that he might honorably condescend to take rest was rarely fulfilled. Almost a month had gone by since the memorable day when he had met Mrs. Buxton, and he despaired of meeting her again. Effie, seeing him one day, was shocked at his pallor.

Then came the unexpected telegram. "I am coming to see you to-morrow afternoon." It was signed with the word, wholly incomprehensible to him, "Chisola." It was with an absolute certainty that it was from Millicent Buxton that set him to feverish preparations for her reception.

CHAPTER VII

Togo had different ideas as to floral decoration from his employer. Horace was for masses of orchids. Togo for a few simple flowers skilfully placed. In the end the masses won, and young Worthington would hardly have known his rooms.

It was at about five that Mrs. Hamilton Buxton came. He noted with unhappiness that her manner was less affable than he had hoped to see. It seemed hardly possible that this was the same woman who had whispered such meaning words to him at the Philipps house.

"What amazing indiscretion to take rooms directly opposite a club," she said, looking from the window. "Don't you know the club across the way is called the 'Gossips'?"

"I took these rooms from another man," he explained.

"Teddy Worthington was different," she commented. "He used to boast so much of his conquests that nobody believed him, so he took rooms opposite the Gossips, who confirmed his every impropriety."

"They haven't any of mine to gloat over," he said, a little hurt at her manner.

"I wonder?" she said, looking at him.

By this time Togo had removed the tea equipage and closed the door softly behind him.

"You need not," he returned, "you're the first woman who has come to see me." He glanced at her curiously. "Why should you wonder?"

He was standing at her side as he said it. She rose to her feet and turned to him and put her two hands on his shoulders.

"Do you think I want to share you with other women?" she asked.

When it grew dark they motored far into the country, returning to his rooms for the supper Togo had been bidden to prepare.

In the days of almost incredible happiness that followed Horace discovered in Millicent Buxton a thousand entrancing charms. He had feared her bitter careless tongue but found her instead a creature of infinite gentleness. That his money was dwindling brought him unhappy speculations as to the future. Without money it would be impossible to see her. And the little presents he delighted to offer were far too costly for his means.

And of late he had lost money at cards. Millicent had insisted that Duff McGregor should call upon him so as to be able to introduce him as an acquaintance of his own if the need arose. To a little club, used almost wholly for gambling, McGregor had taken him with results that were disastrous. He had no card sense and he played with men who had trained their natural aptness to an expert skill that seemed uncanny to the visitor.

"You've been losing money lately, Duff tells me," Millicent said one day. "Much money?"

"More than I can afford," he admitted.

"By the way, what money have you?" she demanded.

He flushed when he confessed his poor means.

"You can always draw on me if you want any," she said carelessly.

"Draw on you?" he repeated.

"Yes, dear simpleton," she answered. "Surely that's not unheard of?"

"A man can't accept money from a woman like that," he cried.

"They do," she said drily. "Ella Codrington has to deal in horses to supply her men with money. Inconsiderately her husband has cut her allowance."

"Do you think I'm like that?" he asked, reproach in his tone.

"Do you want me to think you better or worse?"

"Different, different," he cried vehemently. "I'm not asking to be thought better."

"I'm afraid I'm not a very good guide to right conduct either for women or men," she yawned. "If you are hard up take my money. It's my own fortune, not Hamilton's."

"It wouldn't be right," he said sententiously.

"If you knew how dull you are when you moralize," she frowned, "you would never utter another platitude. Your ideas of right and wrong aren't a bit interesting. You're perfectly adorable in some ways, dearest of boys, but unfortunately you don't yet know when."

He put his arm about her and kissed her.

"Yes, I do," he whispered.

She clung to him for a long while without speaking. He sensed that there was something that had gone wrong with her today, some one of the many domestic scenes of which she had occasionally hinted.

"Hamilton's been telling his mother about you and me," she said presently. "Old Mrs. Buxton's one dread is that we should divorce and so separate the family fortunes. His mother thinks you are one of the fascinating young dancing men who are such boons to women of the middle classes and can be hired at so much per dance. I told her you were a harmless poet and that I knew you as a Roman prince in another incarnation."

"I hate that man," he said, frowning. "Can't you ever think of me as *me* and not as this prince of yours. I am always reminding you of him."

"Another may remind me of you," she said, smiling.

"I hate to hear you calmly discussing such things as that. Are all women as brutal? Why do you always laugh when I tell you I shall always love you?"

"Because I don't want to be loved by one man forever any more than I want to love one man for eternity. I'm afraid you've been misled about love by the more popular poets like Tennyson, who typifies it as eternal affection."

"If you cared for me really you wouldn't say that," he cried, wounded at her levity.

He had been aware of late that she was not as contented in his company as she had been at first. Several times she had failed to keep appointments or had allowed him to wait hours for her and had never offered an excuse that seemed reasonable. She had often hinted that her husband's unreasoning dislike of him might terminate their friendship. And now it seemed they had mentioned him at a family council.

"You don't care for me as you did," he said dolefully.

"I am not sure that I care for anyone," she retorted, and smiled to take away the sting of her words. "It may be that I am laying fragrant memories away so as to take them out when I am old and need comforting."

"Do you make fun of everything?" he asked.

"No," she said in a graver tone, "I only sneer at what I can't have—or perhaps at what I have lost."

"I'm sure you have been unhappier than you let me guess," he said.

"I began wrong," she said slowly. "I married wrong. I might have been different if I'd met you years ago in Rome instead of my prince. I wish you had known me then, dear. I've altered since that time. I've coarsened for one thing. Partly my own fault, partly the fault of the men I met and most of all my husband's fault."

He realized with bitterness his sense of impotence in dealing with a woman of Millicent's type. His love for her brought him no ability to guide or help her. If only he had been the man he once thought himself to be he might have understood. As it was he felt a blundering child.

"A woman without children," she went on, "often tells herself that she would have been a great success if she'd had any. Nearly always she lies."

She looked up at him with a smile and put her arm almost caressingly on his hand.

"Hasn't anything warned you that there must be an end of this?"

"Some day, perhaps," he cried, "but not yet."

"This is the last time I shall come and see you. There was a dreadful scene at luncheon today. It seems Hamilton has found out all there is to know about you and he can't forgive you."

"But I've done nothing," he said quickly.

"That's why," she retorted. "Hamilton has not done you the honor to be jealous. He is simply annoyed that his wife should have been talked about with someone employed in a humble capacity in one of his own mills."

"His mill?" Horace gasped.

"He owns it, I'm told. Surely you knew if you were there?"

"It was owned by a New York estate, but I had nothing to do with that part of the bookkeeping."

"He said he'd have forgiven me if you'd been an international crook or something exciting like that, but he couldn't stomach a bookkeeper."

He looked at her reproachfully.

"Can't one be decent and be a bookkeeper?"

"Hamilton doesn't demand decency," she explained. "It would rather bore him than otherwise. Don't you see this isn't a moral question at all but simply one of wounded vanity?"

"And with you, too?"

"With me," she explained, "it is the matter merely of a yachting trip. My father's yacht sails for the land of the midnight sun tomorrow night. The family in council today decreed that I should go. Kismet."

She drew his face down to her and kissed him.

"You're a nice boy," she whispered, "a sort of white moth boy who longs to fly into the sunshine and think it a flame. I've been kinder to you than you will ever guess. You've deceived me twice. Once when I thought you clever and again when I thought you a fool." She sighed. "I wish I were as young in soul and emotional experience as you are; I wish I had the chance to start everything at the beginning as you have."

"This is the end," he said tragically.

"What a child you are," she answered.

"I might have been till I met you," he retorted, "but I'm not now. I've never loved anyone else and I thought you cared for me."

"I did," she declared sincerely, "I do still and I shall have all the happier memories of you because I go before we grow weary of one another."

"May I write to you?" he begged.

"Not a line," she said firmly. "This is the end of a chapter. There are new ones ahead for you and me but there's a different heroine in yours and a new hero for me. Don't be tragic about it. I'm sorry to have to go. I shall sit on deck and think of you and long to be back hearing your dear voice telling me all the sweet things about myself that I wish were true. But I tell you the chapter's at an end."

"Are you thinking of the new one?" he asked bitterly.

"On my honor not yet," she said. "There'll be a dull blank page between the two."

She rose from her chair and put her arms about his neck. He felt her warm kisses on his lips long after she had left.

CHAPTER VIII

Duff McGregor, making one of his infrequent visits, found Horace white-faced and haggard sitting by the window. He had called on the stranger to New York in the first place because Millicent Buxton had commanded him so to do. As time passed he grew to like the man. There was a certain dignity and charm in Blackwell's manner that was not without its attraction. Tonight he had called because he was in town and alone. The season was far advanced and few remained of the men he knew.

"Come out and dine somewhere," he said when he had learned the other had not yet eaten dinner.

"I feel I never want to eat again," Horace said miserably. He felt that the foundations of his whole existence were cut away from under him.

"What's happened?" McGregor demanded.

"She's going away tomorrow. I shall never see her again."

"I knew she was going," McGregor returned, "her father has one of the finest yachts afloat."

"It's quite a sudden move," Horace insisted, "she didn't know herself until today."

"It was in the papers a week ago," McGregor corrected. "She generally goes away about now."

Horace did not answer. So it was not a sudden exigency that took her from him but a planned move. She had lied to him. She had tired of him. She was setting out on new adventures leaving him bankrupt no less in money than emotions.

That his extravagance had brought him almost to the end of his resources did not immediately worry him. He repeated a hundred times to himself that she had deceived him. If it had not been for his visitor's restraining presence he could have wept with ease.

And it was because he knew McGregor would look at him curiously when the room was better lighted he pulled himself together so well that the other was almost. disappointed to find not a broken man he expected but one almost normal.

Togo was, commanded to bring champagne. A stock had been laid in since he was under the impression it was the usual drink of society and he supposed Millicent would expect it of him. She drank none of it. McGregor, dry and dust-filled from a long motor trip, welcomed it. It affected him little. It induced remarkable recklessness in his host. Under its influence he found a certain humor in his approach to poverty.

"I have three hundred and forty dollars," he said, and exhibited the amount, "and an automobile whose sale will about pay my debts."

"I can lend you some if you want it," McGregor told him.

"I'm going to win tonight," Horace declared, "I've lost enough at that club of yours. Luck has got to change some time."

"Don't be a fool," McGregor counselled, "you always lose. Come out for a spin in the car and then go to bed and get some sleep."

They went to the little select gambling club instead. If it had been known that Blackwell had so small a stake he would not have been welcomed. But he had an air of wealth and the man who vouched for him was a millionaire.

He played with small amounts for a little and then, resenting McGregor's insistence that he should leave, left his sponsor and sat down to drink with a group of men he had never seen before.

Later on in the evening he realized that he was a wit and at last appreciated. The men found what he said of so much interest that they hung on his words. He was telling them of what he knew of the inside of smart society. He used great names with an intimate ease that produced a deep impression. All the small talk that Millicent had made about her friends was rehashed for the benefit of this unknown group.

To McGregor, an unwilling listener, there seemed something tragic in the whole thing. As a plain, unattractive man he immensely admired Blackwell for his physical perfection and the natural dignity that was his. He had envied him more than another might know, his friendship with Millicent Buxton. And now under the unaccustomed stimulus of drink the man who had loved her was delighting these strangers with accounts of her doings and sayings, telling them things that should have remained inviolably secret.

A club steward at his request called Blackwell to the telephone.

"Nobody wants you," McGregor hissed at him. "I only want to get you away from those men. Can't you pull yourself together and be decent? Can't you try and be the gentleman you pretend to be?"

"What's the trouble?" Horace demanded with the seriousness of the man whose wit is beclouded with alcohol. "What have I done to you?"

"You are talking about the woman you profess to love to a group of men who may blackmail her on account of it for all I can tell."

Horace put his hand to a throbbing head. All the exhilaration had gone from him.

"I do love her," he protested, "you know I do. I was telling them I did."

"Then leave that gang and lose your damned money at some game or another. They won't let you chatter like a fool in there."

McGregor steered him to one of the card rooms. Then he left. It was the end of his acquaintance with Horace Blackwell.

For this one night of his life blind luck followed him. He knew too little of cards to be interested in them, but the roulette table fascinated him. Here everything he bet on won, it seemed. There were piles of notes before him. People proffered him affectionate friendships but he was suddenly filled with disgust at them. One man whispered to him something about what he could buy for Millicent now. The name from foul lips infuriated him and he struck at the man savagely and cut his face. They were almost instantly separated. It was actually the first blow that Blackwell had ever struck in anger, but it possibly saved him from unpleasant company. Some who had witnessed his winnings and realized that his condition rendered relieving him of the money an easy matter hesitated now when they saw his ugly mood. For all they knew he might be armed.

Outside a girl spoke to him. What she said he did not know. He was striding along on another planet thinking other thoughts than the earth-born. For a time she walked by his side. When he turned into Fifth avenue she fell back. It was raining slightly and there were people abroad. He paused to put on the light coat he carried over his arm. When it fell to the sidewalk he found that it eluded his efforts to pick it up. When he stooped dizziness made him stagger. In the end he let it lie there. His mood was one of splendid recklessness. Someone would find it and make use of it.

Togo was not without experience in the ways of bachelors. He mixed a draught that should induce slumber and alleviate some of the headache that would come on the morrow and put his master to bed.

CHAPTER IX

Horace did not get up until midday. His memories of what had happened were of a nebulous nature. He called to mind a disagreement with McGregor. His head told him he must have drunk enormously. And his emptied pockets told him that if he won another had the spending of his prize.

Togo added to his burdens by bringing a sheaf of bills which must be met. He had not the opportunity of evasion which men had whose financial position was secure. And as Togo received a commission on all goods paid for, he urged prompt settlement.

Sato had found a customer for the car who would take chauffeur as well. When Horace had made laborious calculations he discovered that if this were done and his bills met he would be left with less than a hundred dollars.

He had wasted more in a few weeks than he had earned in his life. He fell into a mood of black despair to be aroused by the entrance of Togo, who betrayed an uncommon agitation.

"Two gentlemen to see you, sir," he said.

"Send them away," he snapped. "I won't see anyone."

"You'll see us," a harsh voice said.

Horace turned his aching head to look into the sneering face of Hamilton Buxton. Although Buxton was a heavy drinker and the victim of fashionable vices, his out-of-door life saved him from the effects of dissipation in a measure. He towered square, strong and forbidding over the man in the dressing gown. With him was a friend whom Horace had seen at the polo games, one Robert Cowley, socially elect and, it was rumored, once a warm admirer of Millicent Buxton.

"What do you want?" Horace demanded.

Buxton glanced at Togo.

"A private conversation here or wherever you like."

"Now," he began, when the servant had gone, "I am going to give you the opportunity to deny a rumor which reached me this morning that you made Mrs. Hamilton Buxton the subject of your conversation at a club last night."

In a flash the whole damnable incident came back. That was why

Duff McGregor had quarrelled with him. He felt himself flushing with shame at the recollection.

"I don't remember," he said lamely.

"You mean you're afraid to admit it. Fortunately I have witnesses enough."

"Get it over quickly," Cowley broke in, "tell him you've come to thrash him, the damned coarse-bred impostor."

It was not so much the dread of a beating that made Horace sink into his chair. It was the acid, contemptuous looks that both men bent upon him. The men of the set he had wanted to win all seemed to despise him. There was the caste idea as firmly fixed with them as in Europe. And that he should be justly brought to book through his drunken babble of a woman who still filled his thoughts made defense impossible. Of course she would learn of it, Buxton would take care of that, and she would feel he did not deserve a kindly thought. In that moment he felt a punishment would be a grateful thing to receive. Dimly he hoped it would help to atone for what indiscretions drink had led him to commit.

"Do you deny it?" Buxton demanded.

"I wish I could," he said.

"That wouldn't help you," the other snapped, "I've had it in my mind to do this for a long while."

"It wasn't for that I wished I could deny it," Horace said, "it was because—" He broke off impatiently as he realized they would never understand what he meant. Gross libertines both and they came as avengers of women!

There was no resistance that a man of Blackwell's athletic skill could make effectively against one of Buxton's type. He was beaten with a walking cane to the contemptuous and derisive comments of Cowley. And when his assailant was tired and had flung him to the floor with a crash he lay there feeling no bitterness was left for him to taste.

Alas, that Togo should have been a timorous Jap. One would like to have found him a valorous disciple of Bushido, proficient at jiu-jitsu, a little slim hero from the Orient willing to array himself against men of an alien culture for the loyalty he bore his employer. Togo entrenched himself in his pantry until he was assured the visitors had gone.

Blackwell was sitting in the same deep chair by the window when Togo stole timidly into the room. There was a cut over his eye where he had been hurled against a table leg. He would not answer the man's questions. He waved him from the room and sat there hour after hour. He was not able to decide what he had better do with the life that was left.

It was borne in upon him that Millicent had never cared for him as he once thought she did. He was an experiment for her and not a very successful one. His venture had been a failure. He knew now that it was not only lack of money that would doom him to failure. It was that he would always be an outsider in the society to which he had aspired, to which he felt himself akin but could never hope to reach. The pain of his bruised back was almost forgotten in his mental agony of depression. He was alone. None understood or cared for him.

When he heard light footsteps in the room he supposed they were those of his valet. He did not look around. But it was Effie, shining-eyed and tremulous, who came to his side. Togo, fearing his moody silence, had telephoned that his master was in dire distress.

He looked at her with a grim smile.

"You!" he cried, "come to tell me you know it would happen?"

"Why do you always like to hurt me?" she cried.

"Do I?" he answered more gently. "I didn't mean to, Effie."

She bathed his wounded face in silence. Her touch was like balm to him. He took one of her cool hands and pressed it.

"I believe I have one friend left," he said.

He was very grateful to her for asking no questions. Her presence brought back to him some ancient memories that soothed him in his black moment.

"You were the first girl I ever kissed," he said presently.

"I wish I were the last," she murmured.

"What a mess I've made of things," he commented later. "Do you realize that I'm penniless?"

He told her how his affairs stood. There was nothing left him but to go back to Bowlerville and occupy part of the house that his aunt left him. What he would prefer to do, he confided, would be to go as far away from New York as possible. Oregon for choice and buy a ranch in the fruit zone. It would not need much, a few thousand dollars to begin with.

"And I think I'd ask you to go with me, Effie," he said. There was for the first time in their relations a certain timidity in his next question. "Would you have gone?"

"We both shall go," she cried, her eyes gleaming with an excitement he could not understand. "Wait a moment."

She darted into the hall to return with a silk-lined coat. It was the one he had left lying on the wet sidewalk last night.

"Last night," she explained, "I telephoned here and Togo told me where you had gone. I felt something was wrong and I waited. When you came out I spoke to you but you wouldn't answer. Then I saw you had left your coat on the sidewalk and I picked it up. Do you know what was in it, Horace? Nearly five thousand dollars! I've got it with me."

The Conclusions of a Man of Sixty

By Owen Hatteras

I

A man sweats and fumes for a solid year to write a symphony in G minor. He puts enormous industry into it, and much talent, and maybe no little genius. Nevertheless, its final value in the open market of the world is a great deal less than that of a fur overcoat, half a Rolls-Royce motor-car, or a handful of hair from the whiskers of Henry Wadsworth Longfellow. . . . This teaches us, beloved, that God's in His heaven and all's well with the world.

II

Say what you will of the Seventh of the Ten crimes, it is at least democratic.

III

It is the misfortune of humanity that its history is chiefly written by third-rate men. The first-rate man seldom has any impulse to record and philosophise; his impulse is to act. Thus the writing of history is left to college professors, valetudinarians, asses. Few historians have ever shown any capacity for actual affairs. Even Gibbon was a failure as a member of Parliament. As for Thucydides, he made such a mess of his military (or, rather, naval) command that he was exiled from Athens for twenty years and finally assassinated. How much better we would understand the history of man if there were more historians like Julius Cæsar! Remembering their rough notes, think what marvelous histories Bismarck and Frederick the Great might have written! Such men, being at the center of events, have the exact facts; the usual historians have to depend on deductions, rumors, guesses. More, the great man knows how to tell the truth, however unpleasant; he lacks the mushy sentimentality of the professional historian. But he is born with

Smart Set 52, No. 4 (August 1917): 43–44.

writer's cramp, and so we have to go on depending upon the pious fiction of the professors.

IV

For thirty-five years I have been accused of being a misogynist. And why? Simply because, during all that time, I have been a monogamist.

V

Let a woman have a good mouth and good eyes, and she is beautiful. The other points are secondary.. One of the most beautiful women I know has a nose like a shoehorn. Another sweet one has hair like wire, A pug nose with good eyes is beauty. A Greek nose with muddy eyes is not. What are good eyes? The prime test, I think, is their appearance of depth. They must be true windows of the soul; not blinds. Long lashes help here. So do dark shadows underneath. So do straight, dark eyebrows over white flashes of skin. The color of the actual eye is immaterial, but it must be transparent. That is why dark eyes, black or blue or gray, are the most beautiful. A china-blue eye seems opaque. So does one of a light, yellowish brown. So does one with any hint of red in it. As for the mouth, its beauty depends upon the teeth. They must be white, regular and a bit transparent—that is, pearly. Dead-white teeth, particularly if they be large, are ugly. The lips? Let them be red and not too bulging, and all the purposes of justice are served. The object of lips is to be kissed. One cannot kiss a fat, shapeless lip, or a colorless one, or one the hue of a mackerel. Lip-rouge is a godsend, not only to women, but to men. It saves many a shiver.

VI

Proposed plot for a modern novel, say by George Moore! Herman is in love with Violet, who is married to Armand, an elderly diabetic. Herman and Violet, who are Christians, await with laudable patience the termination of Armand's distressing malady. One day Dr. Frederick M. Allen discovers his cure for diabetes. . . .

VII

It is often argued against certain books that they depict vice as attractive. This recalls the king who hanged a judge for deciding that an archbishop was a mammal.

VIII

The only permanent values in the world are truth and beauty, and of these it is probable that truth is lasting only in so far as it is a manifestation of beauty. The world is a charnel house of dead truths. What has become, for example, of all the impeccable revelations of the Middle Ages? But everything that was essential in the beauty of the Middle Ages still lives.

IX

Various tests for voters have been proposed in America, but few of them have been either honest or discreet. Those based upon education have failed because they have involved imbecile "interpretations" of the Constitution, which is a puzzle even to lawyers. Those based upon property qualifications have mistaken wealth for intelligence. The combination of the two, the so-called three-class voting system, has failed both in Prussia and in Belgium. I offer a simpler scheme. What I propose is that each prospective voter, when he applies for registration, be asked the following questions under oath:

1. Do you believe that Friday is an unlucky day?
2. Do you believe that Jonah swallowed the whale?
3. Do you believe that you know what truth is, what right is, and what justice is?
4. Do you think you ever fool your wife?
5. Have you ever marched in a parade?
6. Do you believe that George Washington was a democrat?

For more than one "yes," blackball the candidate and set the bloodhounds on him.

The Cynic

by W. L. D. Bell

He was a cynic.

He believed that every woman looked at a man with a view to marrying him.

He believed that no woman could shake hands with him without allowing her soft fingers to linger caressingly in his.

He believed that no woman could look at him without gazing at him out of the corners of her eyes, through lowered lashes.

He believed that no woman could kiss him without parting her lips and pressing herself close to him.

One day he met a woman who looked into his eyes fearlessly, laughed at him when he touched her, and slapped him across the face when he kissed her.

He married her.

*　　　*　　　*　　　*

He is still a cynic.

He has merely changed his idea that all women employ similar methods.

Smart Set 52, No. 4 (August 1917): 72.

The Conqueror

By Owen Hatteras

The soul of Bill Johnson as he entered the Tip Top saloon was filled with a queer unrest. He was going to get drunk. He was to drink seven glasses of beer and seven slugs of whiskey. If he was still sober after that he was going to drink a cocktail. When he had achieved the towering poise of a man who can walk up to a policeman and pull his nose, if he is so minded, he was going home and have a good stiff talk with his wife. It was to be the talk which he had deferred for five years of his wedded six. The first thing Bill was going to say in this talk was to forbid his wife going to church.

The saloon embraced him with its intimate, cordial air. The merry fellowship thrust upon his eyes as he opened the door touched a brave fiber in his heart. At the sight and sound of strong men slapping each other on the back, shaking hands with great flourishes, calling out genial oaths and giving vent to fearsome laughs, Bill drew a deep breath and vowed he would forbid her going to church or know the reason why.

Under the persistent light, which was magnificently reflected by the glory of bottles and glasses arrayed in pyramids behind the long shining bar, freemen harangued each other in grave sonorous tones, praised each other in stintless violent measures, swayed and bellowed and raged in a vast camaraderie that stamped itself upon Bill's soul as a sudden vision Elysium, of things as they should be. A fine Homeric gust flared his spirit and he eyed the scene with a humble thankful eye and commanded a beer.

Something was wrong with the world outside, something devilishly, miserably wrong. There were strange horrible forces at work, forces which Bill could neither grasp nor explain. He had a confused notion that men were going to seed, did Bill, and that women were acting up in a devastating and sinister manner. He had a vague presentiment that unless something vigorous, something cataclysmic was done about it, the world would become a sniveling, mincing, unprintable place with no room in it for a real man or an honest oath. At this point in Bill's

Smart Set 52, No. 4 (August 1917): 114–16.

reasoning, logic executed an inexplicable leap and fastened upon Mrs. Johnson and her church-going idiocy as a solution of the entire affair.

Thus he consumed his beer and hung upon the spectacle of strong freemen about him with a sore and grateful heart. He drank alone, listening with one ear to a bellowing argument at his right elbow which was as music to his finer senses. For here strong men were condemning with great poundings of fists upon the bar one of those strange and horrible forces working ruin in the land. Out of the waves of blistering sound which smote the air Bill caught the words, "white livered ministers and old ladies shuttin' off our rights . . . closin' the saloon an' the theayters . . . damn 'em!"

With his other ear Bill obtained knowledge of the fact that close upon his left elbow were four men who considered each other the salt of the earth, who would stand by each other through Hell and Highwater, and who fought valiantly to keep each other from paying for the drinks.

Bill gazed upon his third glass with a grave, appreciative air. In him high words were beginning to burn. This was the thing—this!

Again he took in with his inner senses the scene around him. Here were no capering, smirking powdered little chickens, giggling and prancing about on skinny legs, no sleek oily youths clinging to them, teasing them with puny caresses, no half-women smoking cigarettes and babbling over pink drinks about politics and scandal. Here were men, good honest men all of them, and Bill suddenly slapped one of those at his left upon the shoulder and commanded him to have a drink.

"On me," said Bill.

The rosy-faced bartender wiped a new space dry on the bar and from the mysterious font beneath him drew forth five brews.

"Live round the corner," said Bill. "Dropped in for a social evening."

"Right-o," said the fattest of the four. "Name's Hume—Joe Hume. Glad meetchu. Boys! Misser Johnson!"

A chorus of joyous sounds arose from the group. Mr. Johnson was pulled into its midst.

"You're a'right," cried one of them, tilting back a derby. "You're awlright!"

Bill drank his fourth beer with a quick warm elation nestling into his heart.

Outside the world was wrong, devilishly, miserably wrong. Men went around rolling their eyes like women, mawkish, simpering men, crushing joyous and fine fellows like himself, turning the universe into a drooling sort of devilish prayer meeting, taking all the stuffing out of life—a lot of blue nosed, hypocritical ringers, grafters, sycophants, fuddy

duddy parsons; a blight upon them! A murrain on them! But here about
him—life still survived, healthy manhood still sat upon its throne. Here
about him people were honest and fearless, truthful and human!

Bill's thoughts were not so coherent or refined as these, but the
gaze he leveled upon his seventh beer, the solemn handshake with Mr.
Hume, the expansive oaths which he showered upon his now friends,
were the scenario of a philosophy to which no pen can do entire justice.

"Whiskey, gentlemen," he announced suddenly, "on me. Fi' whis-
keys, son."

Bill had reached the point of transfer. He perceived that he had
fallen among friends, noble spirits who understood and admired him.
He perceived they were all of them uncommon, virile boys, allies, orators, warriors, ready to defend him against the strange and horrible
forces without. He perceived there was a certain glow, luster, undula-
tion to the very scenery—the bar, the walls, the lights, which reflected
their indomitable natures.

The whiskey struck at Bill Johnson's soul and liberated it. From it
fell the shackles of silence, the weights of woe, the distress of doubt.
From it poured into his brain the great light—and the ghoulish miserable forces stood revealed before him.

As one who towers armed above an array of crippled infants, Bill
beheld the causes of his rage, the great hypocritical swarms of sancti-
monious idiots, stamping out beauty, expurgating life of its color and
substance. He beheld this army whining and whimpering in a petulant
fury, organizing societies to take away from him his pleasures—a pack
of fiendish busybodies, emaciated, driveling, sneaking she-men and he-
women ranting over the earth like a disease. With a supreme gesture he
flung his arm across the back of his friend Joe Hume and spoke from
the heights—

"Wife goes shurch."

Joe Hume sat down his glass with a bang. The four freemen eyed
Bill in silence. He drew himself up and gazed in return upon their faces
with a martyred eye.

"Wife goes shurch havenotherdrink."

The four seized upon their glasses and raised them high.

They crowded round Bill Johnson, pounding him upon the back,
exhorting him in terrible and pointless terms. He slowly felt himself
assuming ferocious proportions. In his brain withering, shattering
phrases boiled. Marvelous oaths saturated his soul. His heart became
great, his sinews massive. He felt the muscles of his body swell and he
perceived that he, Bill Johnson, had been affrighted by a mouse. He
would step forth into this swaying world and steady it. Beneath his
contemptuous eye he saw the walls already trembling, the floor quiver-

ing. . His legs became like whalebone under him, supporting him with an exhilarating elasticity. His soul became a citadel out of which he would loose a wrath which would bewilder and annihilate the foe. A furious upheaval was transpiring about him. He stood with his glass poised, contemplating with a dauntless eye the slopes and sinister angles which the floor was assuming.

He observed with a grim courage the fact that his allies who had promised to defend and assist him were falling by the dozens about him, rolling about on the floor and dropping into terrible chasms. These were the forces at work against him, these bottomless pits opening at his feet, these terrible slopes threatening to crush and upset him. He would march over them, step above them, leap and bound across them. The strength of a hundred men was in him. Joe Hume was captured. He noted him struggling in the grasp of a giant slope and shouting for aid. He would save him! With a cunning yet powerful leap he would vault over the snares to the side of Joe Hume, his friend, his ally.

Gathering himself for the spring Bill Johnson sailed forward. He was surprised to find Joe Hume so near at hand. He was dimly aware of a miscalculation. He fell upon his friend and embraced him with a great swoop. Tears of pity and understanding choked him.

"Wife goes shurch," he mumbled into Joe Hume's ear and in the distance observed that three men were drinking from preposterously little glasses.

But there was evidently something wrong with this Hume man. He was a devil. He had the strength of twenty devils. He forced him, Bill Johnson, to his knees and left him lying on the floor with the slopes rushing upon him and a great wave of purple sound thundering under his feet and over his head. Deserters, traitors—they were fleeing from his side. The world was wrong, all wrong. He would change it. Carefully he framed a brave appeal to these ingrates who were leaving him alone in the combat. He perceived the four of them crawling over a swaying precipice toward a tiny door which spun like a top. Summoning vast powers of articulation from his innermost depths Bill Johnson reared himself to his feet and hurled fiery, bursting phrases after their retreating backs.

The bartender, mopping a new space dry in front of him, looked up and perceived a short, thin man with a disheveled mustache and bald head swaying in the center of the room, staring with a strange intensity at an Elk's head on a far wall and proclaiming, in a quavering hopeless voice,

"Wife goes shurch."

Criticism of Criticism of Criticism

Once the college professors begin pulling whiskers and calling names there will be a chance for something approaching intelligence to creep into American criticism. The first warwhoop of the possible (and so benign) conflict is emitted by Prof. Dr. J. E. Spingarn, late of Harvard and Columbia, in his "Creative Criticism" (*Holt*). Nay, the learned gentleman goes further: he uproots the first spray of actual alfalfa. As witness: "To say that poetry is moral or immoral is as meaningless as to say that an equilateral triangle is moral and an isosceles triangle immoral." Worse: "It is only conceivable in a world in which dinner-table conversation runs after this fashion: 'This cauliflower would be good if it had only been prepared in accordance with international law.'" One imagines the blushful indignation of Prof. Dr. William Lyon Phelps, with his discovery that Joseph Conrad preaches "the axiom of the moral law"; the "Hey! What's that?" of Prof. Dr. W. C. Brownell, the Amherst Aristotle; the furious protest of the editor of the New York *Times Book Review,* freshly risen from his refusal to believe that Mark Twain ever held such heretical views as are set forth in "What Is Man?" Dr. Spingarn, in truth, here performs a treason most horrible, and having achieved it, he performs another and then another. That is to say, he tackles all the varying camorras of campus-pump critics seriatim, and knocks them out unanimously—first the aforesaid burblers for the sweet and pious; then the advocates of unities, metres, all rigid formulæ; then the historical dust-snufflers; then the experts in bogus psychology; then the metaphysicians; finally, the spinners of æsthetic balderdash. One and all, they take their places on his chopping-block; one and all, they are stripped, vivisected and put away in cans. . . .

But what is the schismatic professor's own theory?—for a professor must have a theory, as a dog must have fleas. In brief, what he offers is a doctrine of Benedetto Croce out of Johann Wolfgang Goethe—a doctrine anything but new in the world, even in Goethe's time, but nevertheless long buried by the eruptions of the seminaries—to wit, the doctrine that it is the critic's first and only duty, as Carlyle said, to find out "what the poet's aim really and truly was, how the task he had

Smart Set 52, No. 4 (August 1917): 138–44.

to do stood before his eye, and how far, with such materials as were afforded him, he has fulfilled it." And for poet, of course, read the Germanic *Dichter*—that is, the artist in words, the creator of beautiful letters, whether in prose or in verse. Ibsen always called himself a *Digter*, not a *Dramatiker* or *Skuespiller*. So, I daresay, did Shakespeare. . . . What is the poet trying to do? asks Dr. Spingarn, and how has he done it? This, and no more, is the critic's business. The morality of the work, or its lack of it—that, as Maurice Perlmutter would say, is something else again. Has the poet violated the rules of Aristotle? Has he got a heterodox rhyme-scheme into his sonnet? Is his novel too short or too long? Do his iambics trip? *Hal's Maul, du—Narr!* Every sonnet, every drama, every novel is *sui generis;* it must stand on its own bottom; it must be judged by its own inherent intentions. "Poets," says the professor, "do not really write epics, pastorals, lyrics, however much they may be deceived by these false abstractions; they express themselves, and this expression is their only form. There are not, therefore, only three or ten or a hundred literary kinds; there are as many kinds as there are individual poets." Nor is there any valid appeal *ad hominem.* The character and background of the poet are beside the mark; the poem itself is the thing. Oscar Wilde, a bounder and swine, wrote beautiful prose. To reject that prose on the ground that Wilde was no gentleman is as absurd as to reject "What Is Man?" on the ground that its theology is beyond the intelligence of the editor of the New York *Times.*

This Spingarn theory, of course, throws a heavy burden upon the critic. It presupposes that he is a civilized man, hospitable to ideas and capable of reading them as he runs. Here the professors all come croppers, from Brownell to Phelps, and from Boynton to Paul Elmer More. Their trouble is simply that they lack the capacity for taking in ideas, and particularly new ideas; the only way they can ingest one is by transforming it into the nearest related formula—often a harsh and far-fetched operation. This fact explains the inability of these pathetic pundits to understand all that is most personal and original and hence most forceful and significant in modern literature. They can get down what has been digested and redigested, and so brought into forms that they know, but they exhibit alarm immediately they come into the presence of the unusual. Here we have an explanation of Brownell's feeble chatter for dogmatic standards; of Phelps' inability to grasp Dreiser and his absurd effort to read a Sunday-school morality into Conrad; of Boynton's sophomoric nonsense about realism; of More's enmity to romanticism, which is simply a revolt against the dead hand; of all the insane labeling and pigeon-holing that passes for criticism among the gifted Harvard boys of the *Dial* and *Nation.* Genuine criticism is as impossible to such pompous vacuums as music is to a man who is tone-deaf. The critic, to interpret his poet, must be able to get into the mind of his poet; he must feel and understand the creative passion; as Prof. Spingarn says, true "æsthetic judgment and artistic creation are instinct with the same vital life." This is why the best criticism is written by men who disdain all the meaningless labels of the academy—by men who go to the business with minds open, and without any baggage of classroom learning—to be specific, by such men as Georg Brandes, Hermann Bahr and James Huneker, who know nothing about prosodies and unities and care nothing about moralities, but have within them the gusto of artists and so carry with them the faculty of understanding. Huneker, tackling "Also sprach Zarathustra," revealed its content in illuminating flashes. But tackled by More, it became no more than an obscure student's exercise, ill-naturedly corrected. . . .

So much for the theory of Prof. Dr. J. E. Spingarn, late of Harvard and Columbia. Obviously, it is a better theory than those cherished by the other professors, for it demands that the critic have comprehension, whereas the others only demand that he have learning, and accept anything as learning that has been sonorously said before. But once he has stated it, the learned instructor, professor-like, immediately begins to corrupt it by claiming too much for it. Having laid and hatched, so to speak, his stale egg, he begins to argue that the resultant flamingo is the whole mustering of the critical *Aves*. But criticism, as humanly practiced, must needs be a great deal more than this intuitive re-creation of beauty. For one thing, it must be interpretation in terms comprehensible to the vulgar, else it will leave the original mystery as dark as before—and once interpretation comes in, paraphrase and transliteration come in. What is recondite must be made plainer; the transcendental, to some extent at least, must be done into common modes of thinking. Well, what are morality, trochaics, hexameters, movements, historical principles, psychological maxims, the dramatic unities—what are all these save common modes of thinking, short cuts, rubber stamps, words of one syllable? Moreover, beauty as we know it in this world is by no means the apparition in vacuo that Dr. Spingarn seems to see. It has its social, its political, even its moral implications. The finale of Beethoven's C minor symphony is not only colossal in beauty; it is also colossal in revolt; it says something against something. Yet more, the springs of beauty are not within itself alone, nor even in genius alone, but often in things without. Brahms wrote his Deutsches Requiem, not only because he was a great artist, but also because he was a good German. And in Nietzsche there are times when the divine afflatus takes a back seat, and the *spirochaeta* have the floor.

Dr. Spingarn seems to harbor some sense of this limitation on his doctrine. He gives warning that "the poet's intention must be judged at the moment of the creative act"—which opens the door enough for many an ancient to creep in. But limited or not, he at least clears off a lot of mouldy rubbish, and gets further toward the truth than any of his rev. colleagues. They waste themselves upon theories that only conceal the poet's achievement the more, the more diligently they are applied; he, at all events, grounds himself upon the sound notion that there should be free speech in art, and no protective tariffs, and no *a priori* assumptions, and no testing of ideas by mere words. The safe ground lies between the contestants, but nearer Spingarn. The critic who really illuminates starts off much as he starts off, but with a due regard for the prejudices and imbecilities of the world. I think the best feasible practice is to be found in certain chapters of Huneker. Here a sensitive and intelligent artist recreates the work of other artists, but there also comes to the ceremony a man of the world, and the things he has to say are apposite and instructive, too. To denounce moralizing is to pronounce a moral judgment. To admire the sonnets of Shakespeare is to have some curiosity about Mr. W. H. . . . The really competent critic must be an empiricist. He must produce his effect with whatever means do the work. If pills fail, he gets out his saw. If the saw won't cut, he seizes a club and knocks in the patient's head. . . .

This is the method of my virtuous brother in the sacred sciences, G. J. Nathan, whose latest tome, "Bottoms Up" (*Goodman*), has just come to issue. His scheme is the eclecticism that I have described, and it is based upon the precise ideas that Dr. Spingarn now exhumes from Goethe and Carlyle. That is to say, he first tries to find out what a given dramatic author is trying to say in a given work, and then he pronounces judgment upon it, not in terms of some preconceived theory of technique, or morals, or psychology, but in terms of logical intelligibility and æsthetic organization. If he finds that a respectable work of art is before him, he announces the fact at once, and with due gusto of surprise. He does not forget technique, but he puts it second. He does not forget the other things, but he puts them third, fourth and fifth. The result is what might be expected. In the eyes of the critical pundits, with their gabble about climaxes, *scenes à faire,* national dramas, Hamlet's insanity and Beerbohm Tree's technique, he is an anarchist and an ignoramus, but the returns show that he unearths more sound and living things than any of them and explodes more frauds than all of them put together.

Nathan's apparent iconoclasm is easily explained: he devotes himself to an art that shows a thousand mountebanks to one honest artist. The newspaper critics approach a new drama by a Broadway tripe-

merchant in all seriousness, sweating damnably to fit it into some preposterous theory—of method, tendency or morals. Nathan, recognizing it at once for what it is, announces the truth and has done—not
hotly, in a moral rage, but amiably, in good humor. A work of art?
Then so are your grandmother's false teeth! But two of the buffoons,
after all, are diverting: one clouts the other with a *Blutwurst* that turns
out to be filled with mayonnaise. And one of the girls in the second
row has a very pretty twist of the *vastus medialis*. Let us be happy while
we may! . . .

But anon there is pretense so hollow that it is impossible to find anything to praise in it. Well, then, let us recreate it, touching up a line
here, a color there—the result is burlesque, but burlesque that is the
most searching and illuminating sort of criticism. Who will forget Nathan's demonstration that a play by Augustus Thomas would be better if
played backward? Here in "Bottoms Up" you will find many other such
end-products of his method. He does not denounce melodrama with a
black cap upon his head, painfully demonstrating its contumacy to Ibsen, Scribe and Aristotle; he simply sits down and writes a melodrama
so extravagantly ludicrous that the whole genus collapses. And he does
not prove in four columns of a Sunday paper that French plays done
into American are spoiled; he simply shows the spoiling in six devastating lines. The book is not all *reductio ad absurdum;* it is not even all
theater. But its roots, nevertheless, are in criticism, and that criticism is
sound. It recognizes the plain fact that bad art is not only bad, but of-
fensive. It applies ridicule, deftly and mercilessly, to what is actually ridiculous. There are more ideas in its seventy-three pages than you will
find in the whole works of the stale patterers of empty formulæ. . . .

A college critic waits—Prof. Dr. H. Houston Peckham, of Purdue
University. I open his "Present-Day American Poetry" (*Badger*) at random, and discover on page 48 that Emerson was "no better stylist"
than Hamilton Wright Mabie. I grab again, and find on page 34 that
Alfred Noyes is "the foremost poet of our day." Once more, and on
page 82 I encounter a protest against the theory that "ours is not a
sweet, bright land at all, but a land of crime, adultery, white slavery,
industrial oppression, suicide, domestic infelicity and infidelity . . ."
God help the poor college boys!

II

But if our university tasters of beautiful letters are bad, what adjective is to be applied to the garrulous old women who serve us as music
critics? I extract a sample strophe from "A Second Book of Operas," by
Henry Edward Krehbiel (*Macmillan*):

On January 31, 1893, the Philadelphia singers, aided by the New York Symphony Society, gave a performance of the opera, under the auspices of the Young Men's Hebrew Association, for the benefit of its charities, at the Carnegie Music Hall, New York. Mr. Walter Damrosch was to have conducted, but was detained in Washington by the funeral of Mr. Blaine, and Mr. Hinrichs took his place.

Needless to say, the seminaries have not overlooked this geyser of vapidity: he is an hon. A.M. of Yale. *O Doctor admirabilis, acutus et illuminatissimus!* . . .

Romain Rolland's "Beethoven" (*Holt*) promises more, for Rolland at least has a sense of humor. But the little essay is padded to book proportions with old, old stuff—a dozen or more familiar Beethoven letters; four or five pages of good Ludwig's singularly banal reflections; a dull commentary on the symphonies, sonatas and quartettes by one A. Eaglefield Hull, Mus. Doc. (Oxon), apparently the English Krehbiel; a classification of the piano sonatas "in the order of study" (whose order?); a list of Beethoven's compositions that is no better than any other list of his compositions. Moreover, M. Rolland falls a good deal short of expectation in his essay: the little book of Vincent D'Indy is infinitely more thoughtful and entertaining. Two-thirds of his space is devoted to rehearsing the history of Beethoven's life—a history long since gone over by all of us. The rest he dedicates to the proposition that old Ludwig was an apostle of joy, and that his music reveals his determination to experience and utter it in spite of all the slings and arrows of outrageous fortune.

It seems to me that this notion is inaccurate. It might be reasonably predicated of Haydn or of Schubert, but to predicate it of Beethoven is close to an absurdity. Joy, in truth, was precisely the emotion that he could never conjure up; it was simply not in him. Turn to the *scherzo* of any of his symphonies. A sardonic waggishness is there, and sometimes even a wistful sort of merriment, but joy in the real sense— a kicking up of legs, a light-heartedness, a complete freedom from care—is not to be found. It is in Haydn, it is in Schubert and it is often in Mozart, but it is no more in Beethoven than it is in Tschaikovsky. Even the hymn to joy at the end of the Ninth Symphony narrowly escapes being a gruesome parody on the thing itself; a conscious effort is in every note of it; it is almost as lacking m spontaneity as (if it were imaginable at all) a piece of *vers libre* by Augustus Montague Toplady.

Nay; Ludwig was no leaping buck. Nor was it his deafness, nor poverty, nor the crimes of his rascally nephew that pumped joy out of him. The truth is that he lacked it from birth; he was born a Puritan— and though a Puritan may also become a great man (as witness Herbert Spencer and Beelzebub), he can never throw off being a Puritan.

Beethoven stemmed from the Low Countries, and the Low Countries, in those days, were full of Puritan refugees; the very name, in its first incarnation, may have been Barebones. If you want to comprehend the authentic man, don't linger over Rolland's fancies but go to his own philosophizing, as garnered in "Beethoven, the Man and the Artist," by Friedrich Kerst, Englished by the aforesaid Krehbiel (*Huebsch*). Here you will find a collection of moralities that would have delighted Jonathan Edwards—a collection that might well be emblazoned on gilt cards and hung in Sunday schools. He begins with a naif anthropomorphism that is now almost perished from the world; he ends with a solemn repudiation of adultery. . . . But a great man, my masters, a great man! We have enough biographies of him, and talmuds upon his works. Who will do a full-length psychological study of him?

III

Discussing, at our last session, upon the new novels, I reported them all bad, and some of them bad beyond endurance. This month, as if the gods would make amends, they send a number of good ones, and at least two that lift themselves far above the average, even of the good. These are "A Portrait of the Artist as a Young Man," by James Joyce (*Huebsch*), and "The Good Girl," by Vincent O'Sullivan (*Small-Maynard*). Two Irish fictioneers, but both transplanted, for O'Sullivan, I believe, was actually born in the United States, and Joyce, the last time I heard of him, was in Zürich. The Joyce book I need not describe at length; it came into vogue immediately it was published, and a Joyce cult now threatens, perhaps in succession to the Dunsany cult. These Gaels all bring something into the writing of English that it sorely needed, and that something is a gipsy touch, a rustic wildness, a sort of innocent goatishness. In part it is merely stylistic; open any page of Synge or Dunsany at random and you will see how they have retaught the tone-deaf Sassenach how to write *pour la respiration et pour l'oreille*. But there is also a profounder side to it. They have recast matter as well as manner. They combat English correctness, English formalism, the curious English anesthesia to ideas, with the mental suppleness and eagerness of a more sensitive and imaginative race. Dunsany's tales, in their daring, their brilliance, their beauty, reduce the whole work of such a typical Englishman as Eden Phillpotts to an absurdity. A deer cavorts in the forest, a horn winds, it is the springtime of the world; Phillpotts, by contrast, suggests a cow munching alfalfa in a stall. You will find this new air in "A Portrait of the Artist," and again in Joyce's book of short stories, "Dubliners" (*Huebsch*), some of which have already appeared in this favorite family magazine. The novel is an extraordinarily adept conjuring up of the mystery and agony of youth, sure in its effect and original in its method. There is not the slightest hint in it of the usual structure of prose fiction; it is new both in plan and in detail.

O'Sullivan's book is more conventional in its outlines, but nevertheless there is something savory and exotic in it—the Irish rebellion toned down by French logic, a Gallic brake upon the Gael. The protagonist is a Puritan, even a prig, and it is the business of the story to show his disintegration in the face of a profound emotional experience. Upon a young man of normal sophistication, with his wild oats sprouted in cynical flowers, I daresay that the mature charms of Mrs. Sibyl Dover would have produced no more than a flutter of reaction. He would have marked her, besieged her, taken her, and then gone away laughing at her. But Paul Vendred was a softer fellow, and so her collision with him took on the proportions of a catastrophe. Tentacle by tentacle, she fastened herself upon him, until in the end he collapsed utterly, and there was no more man to drag down. . . . The tale is told with the utmost grace and address. It has a logical design; it moves and breathes; it has rhythm and it has poignancy. Vendred, at first glance, seems almost impossible; an air of the fantastic hangs about him. And yet the author makes him wholly real before the end. So, too, with Mrs. Dover. In her the vampire of melodrama takes on plausibility and becomes an understandable human being. The smaller sketches are no less well done—Dover, the grandiloquent bounder, half pickpocket and half dreamer; his daughter Louise, with her swift tragedy, and even the nameless Frenchman who, like a blind man at fireworks, stands before it without comprehending it. Altogether, a novel of very respectable quality—the work of a civilized and reflective man.

Three other pieces worth reading: "The Confessions of a Little Man During Great Days," by Leonid Andreyev (*Knopf*); "His Family," by Ernest Poole (*Macmillan*), and "The Unwelcome Man," by Waldo Frank (*Little-Brown*). In the first, it seems to me, we get the first intelligible picture of the Russian people under the great afflictions of the past three years—despite all the volumes of sophomoric "interpretations" by newspaper reporters and third-rate English novelists. Here, indeed, the tragedy of bleeding Russia becomes suddenly a real thing, searching, present and intolerable. It is a saturnine and cruel book, but one that leaves a haunting image behind it. . . . The theme of "The Family" is the great gulf that yawns between parent and child, the inability of the one to comprehend the other. Old Roger Gale has three daughters. He remembers them as little children, flesh of his flesh, his soul made visible; he sees them toward the end as vague shadows in a mist, eluding him whenever he seeks to come near them. The tale is projected against a vivid panorama of New York, as carefully pointed up as that in "The Harbor." It is a second novel that does not disappoint; this Mr. Poole is not to be sniffed at. . . . "The Unwelcome Man" is the work of a newcomer. It is an attempt to set forth the effects upon a human being of a hostility that began with birth. Quincy Burt came into the world as a resented accident, an error in technique; his course through it, so long as we follow him, is made up of vain efforts to fit himself into it. He vanishes, finally, somewhat mysteriously; there is no catastrophe. Here, at the end, the story lets down a bit, but in its fore parts there is some excellent workmanship. In particular, the one definite episode in amour is managed skillfully and with understanding. A novel that promises a lot. . . .

Joseph Conrad's "The Shadow Line" (*Doubleday-Page*), of course, belongs at the head of all the month's fiction; it is just as surely first as, in music, a new *Tondichtung* by Richard Strauss is first. Nevertheless, it would be idle to put the story among Conrad's best, or even among his second best. Like "Youth," it is a study of the reaction of young blood to the terrifying, and, like "Typhoon," it is a tale of the indomitable, but somehow it misses the gorgeous poetry of the one and the overpowering drama of the other. Perhaps the last lack lies in the very nature of the story: a ship becalmed is palpably a less thrilling spectacle, whatever the drama aboard, than a ship inordinately battered and thrown about. But aside from this, it seems to me that Conrad has failed to get any genuine glow into it, that he has missed the true Conradean subtlety and gusto, that the thing has the air of an imitation—penetrating, but still an imitation. But let there be no repining! More than once there are flashes of the authentic Conrad—in the portrait, for example, of the grovelling steward of the Officers' Home; again, in the portrait of that other steward, Ransome, of the *Melita;* above all, in old Captain Giles. The story, in brief, is no ordinary story. If it pales now and then, it is because it stands in the blinding light of "Nostromo," "Falk," "Heart of Darkness" and "Lord Jim": it is a moon among suns.

Which brings me to lesser stuff: "The Preacher of Cedar Mountain," by Ernest Thompson Seton (*Doubleday-Page*), a romance which begins with a Wild West show and ends with pious tears; "Second Youth," by Allan Updegraff (*Harper*), a farcical chronicle of amour, with a counter-jumper for its hero; "The Hundredth Chance," by Ethel M. Dell (*Putnam*), a dull tale of a *mésalliance;* "The Man in Evening Clothes," by John Reed Scott (*Putnam*), another of the endless variations on the Raffles theme; "Mistress Anne," by Temple Bailey (*Penn*), a dish of sweets; "Bab, a Sub-Deb," by Mary Roberts Rinehart (*Doran*), an amusing sketch of the American *Backfisch,* a personage strangely neglected in our fiction; "Cecilia of the Pink Roses," by

Katharine Haviland Taylor (*Doran*), a "glad" book (both of these last, by the way, are capitally illustrated by May Wilson Preston); "The Cinema Murder," the latest Oppenheim (*Little-Brown*); "The Definite Object," by Jeffery Farnol (*Little-Brown*), a reboiling of Van Bibber's dry bones; "Enchantment," by E. Temple Thurston (*Appleton*), a book that I have been unable to read, and hence cannot report on; "The Derelict," by Phyllis Bottome (*Century*), a collection of excellent short stories, some of them already printed in these refined pages; "The Humming Bird," by Owen Johnson (*Little-Brown*), an uproarious baseball story; "Jerry of the Islands" and "The Human Drift" (*Macmillan*), by the late Jack London, the one a South Sea tale and the other a collection of essays, sketches and one-act plays, and both falling far below London's best. . . .

But I bore you abominably. Perhaps you will get more out of "The Chosen People," by Sidney L. Nyburg (*Lippincott*), the chronicle of a young Jewish rabbi's disillusionment at the hands of his highly secular flock—a story with the rare quality of irony in it, and several very deft character sketches. Or out of "Louisburg Square," by Robert Cutler (*Macmillan*), a tale of Boston, not without its merits, but made a hissing and a mocking by preposterous illustrations by Elise Ames. Or out of "The Eternal Husband and Other Stories," by Fyodor Dostoevsky (*Macmillan*), the latest of the excellent translations of Dostoevsky by Constance Garnett. . . .

The Window of Horrors

By William Drayham

The little shops nestle elegantly along the bright avenue. The tall buildings preen themselves in the sunlight. Their windows glisten and are like ranks upon ranks of little golden and silver butterflies. The people who stroll in the avenue are also quite elegant. They look idly at the luxurious automobiles which glide back and forth down the street. They seem very happy, as if nothing were wrong with the world, as if a carefully manicured and pomaded God were in his boudoir heaven.

They look at the little shop windows, these strollers; at the windows in which such pretty pictures are for sale, in which bizarre knick-knacks lure the eye.

Sometimes they pause in little polite clusters to gaze upon jewels which lie on black velveted surfaces or to admire the Japanese oddities—those fantastically colored and shaped bird cages and Mandarin gowns, potteries and silks—which make you dream for the moment. But always before the window of the *Maison des Robes* they gather most thickly, they pause most delightedly.

For the window of the *Maison des Robes* is entirely the despair of all the other shop keepers in the avenue. It is a Paradise of windows. It is a window of enchantments. It is a fairyland of chiffons and satins, tulles and. cloths which I cannot name. The women who stroll in the Avenue sigh when they pause before it. Here are other windows which exhibit clothes. But they are not like the window of the *Maison des Robes*.

Here there is something strange, something which fascinates. It has an air, just as a Princess has an air. Even men stop to look into it. They behold Romance and Mystery and a loveliness which pales the effulgence of the sun.

Women behold their dreams herein. Before them float gowns which are to their souls as beautiful thoughts are to the souls of the poets. These gowns are worn by strange inanimate figures which stand remarkably silent, in attitudes so startling, so perfect that men often feel their hearts beat faster when they look at them and women always smile with envy.

Smart Set 53, No. 1 (September 1917): 109–18.

It is not as if these things were real within the window of the *Maison des Robes*. They are beyond reality. They belong in the region of masterpieces, of things which surpass nature and gladden the eyes of the world with visions of the ideal.

The shopkeepers often come to look upon this window and to study it. They search the world for and sometimes find such gowns as Mr. Hugo Blute manages to discover and place in his window. They buy of the best figures and employ the most artistic drapers and window trimmers. But even as Reynolds sought to learn the secrets of Titian by scraping the colors from the Venetian's canvas, even as Wilde sought to untangle the tints of Huysmans, they fail.

You see in their windows only clothes, merely a conventional. beauty which makes you think of money and of corsets. But in the window of the *Maison des Robes* there are things you do not see and you search in your mind for fantasies, you dream of ball rooms and grottos, and the boulevard seems to you for the moment like some elegant and exquisite afreet in an Arabian Night.

II

On the morning of a certain day early in June the *Maison des Robes* was unusually crowded. Usually but a woman or two was to be seen therein beside the very polite and pretty clerks. But this day witnessed twenty-seven women, all of them young, all of them possessed of various beauty. They entered one at a time, surveyed for a moment the grey walls, the costly modulated furnishings, and were approached by a matron with white hair and a regal step.

Thus one by one they were ushered through the sumptuous salesroom past the two great black framed mirrors and into an office which was at the rear. The pretty clerks seemed undisturbed by their advent. They stood. in their places like figures in a stage set for Maeterlinck. At one side a willowy black-haired young woman walked slowly back and forth before the gaze of two customers who had alighted from an electric. The elder customer surveyed the willowy one through a lorgnette. A girl with her watched with intent interest the influx of the twenty-seven.

In the office the twenty-seven found chairs to sit upon and two long benches. Only a few were obliged to remain standing. They had come in answer to a tiny advertisement which had appeared in the columns of the morning newspapers.

The advertisement read:

> Wanted—Six of the most beautiful young women in Chicago to work as manikins. No references required. Foreign girls preferred.

Apply in person to Mr. Hugo Blute,—East Michigan avenue, at 5 p.m., sharp.

The young women who now waited for Mr. Blute to arrive preserved a dignified silence and gazed at each other speculatively. Some were obviously of the *demi monde*—bold and artificial Venuses. Some were less elaborately dressed, but fresher looking and possessed of a reposeful prettiness. A few were remarkable-looking, remarkably featured, with eyes which glowed with violet fires.

They had been waiting less than ten minutes when Mr. Blute entered. There was a hurried shuffling of feet and a stir of great portent.

Mr. Blute was a Paganini of shopkeepers—a dwarf-like Paganini. He was a short man with a large head on which lay a mop of black hair, that gave him an appearance of incongruous ferocity. For otherwise he was an elegantly dressed little man, in an afternoon coat, carefully tapering and pressed trousers, pointed black patent leather shoes and linen quite resplendent.

Yet above this almost doll-like costume arose Mr. Blute's massive head and hair. It was apparent that Mr. Blute gave this part of his person a great deal of attention. His face was carefully massaged, his hair was violently combed. His eyebrows, alas, were slightly stenciled and the swarthiness of his skin was relieved by a faint pink flush of some careful cosmetic.

But despite these things Mr. Blute's nose remained obtrusively large, his lips obtrusively heavy, his eyes glistening and in an inexplicable manner, malignant. His hair remained. likewise moplike. There was something pathetic, in fact, about Mr. Blute when he powdered his nose as he did at frequent intervals, to remove the oily glisten which lay upon his skin.

He entered his office with the dapper step of a man who has small feet. He held a silk hat in his hand and a pair of yellow gloves in the other, together with a black lacquer cane.

The twenty-seven who awaited him eyed him with a kindred emotion. They were somewhat startled. It was always this way. with people who gazed upon Mr. Blute for the first time. There was always something vaguely startling and dwarfish about the man until one became inured to him. People who encountered him suddenly would often feel an impulse to gasp.

"Good evening, ladies," said Mr. Blute, in a thin, sweet voice, and depositing his hat, gloves and cane on top of a large mahogany desk he sat down in the swivel chair and surveyed the twenty-seven beauties his advertisement had brought together.

After his polite salutation he seemed to become all business at once.

He eyed his visitors with a general keenness, as one eyes an ensemble. He announced:

"You will first fill out these blanks which I give you and then return them to me. Come forward one at a time, please."

With an exaggerated restraint the twenty-seven obeyed. As they approached to receive their blanks a queer light kindled in Mr. Blute's little black eyes.

The printed matter on the blanks requested each to state her age, her name, her address, her birthplace, and to give what relatives she had in the city, if any. There was a great scribbling among the twenty-seven, who had removed their gloves and revealed an assortment of beautiful and jeweled hands.

Mr. Blute appeared to wax mysteriously excited. He so far forgot himself as to open a drawer of his desk, extract a small powder puff and powder his heavy nose. He also rubbed his palms together and clucked genially with his tongue. One by one the twenty-seven returned the blanks amid a silence. In this silence Mr. Blute then studied the blanks for fully twenty minutes with an expression of intense absorption on his face. Each one he read carefully and placed in one of three divisions.

Finally he called the names of eight of the young women in the office and added:

"Those whose names I have called may go home."

The eight beautiful women whose names had been pronounced arose frowning and walked with great dignity out of the office.

When they had left Mr. Blute clucked his tongue again and said:

"We can now proceed with more despatch. Will Miss Margaret Swinburne step forward, please?"

A tall blonde detached herself and approached.

Mr. Blute eyed her closely.

"You have no father or mother," he said, waving one of the blanks before him. "You are an orphan, yes?"

Miss Swinburne said, "Yes."

"Good," Mr. Blute chuckled.

He looked at her and bade her turn around.

He studied her features intently and after the pause announced, somewhat inanely, as may be seen:

"Excellent. I am devoted to orphans. I favor them in my shop. I employ them. I will employ you. Your duties, you know, will be only to wear beautiful clothes. Silks and laces. You understand what a manikin is?"

Miss Swinburne nodded graciously.

"To show my fashionable customers how beautiful are my clothes," said Mr. Blute, as if Miss Swinburne hadn't understood.

An excitement again appeared to possess him and as if to contain himself he added abruptly:

"You are accepted, Miss Swinburne. Will you sit over there?"

In this same peculiar and abrupt manner Mr. Blute selected the five others from the group. There were several whom Mr. Blute dismissed reluctantly, gazing with glowing eyes upon their lovely faces and turning them around and around before him.

"Ah—ah—" he murmured each time. "You are what I want—what I desire—but—unsuited. Too bad."

He shook his massive head sorrowfully, clucked dismally with his tongue and waved his hand toward the door. But on the whole the six whom he had chosen were among the most remarkable of the beautiful young women.

When the others had departed Mr. Blute sprang from his chair and announced sweetly.

"So. It is settled. You shall all wear beautiful clothes and receive twenty-five dollars each a week. Hugo Blute is not cheap. No. He is— ha!"

He indulged in a vague trilling little laugh and, paused thus in his praise, he assumed a droll position, his short arms folded across his bulky chest, his large head thrown back.

"But there must be a contract, ladies," he went on. "You must agree to place yourselves in my hands for two days. I will take you to the St. John Hotel and send you my most beautiful dresses to become acquainted with. I wish you to try them on and become used to their lines and able to wear them—magnificently."

Here Mr. Blute indulged in his little trilling laugh again and the six beautiful young women regarded his mysterious amusement with six beautiful smiles.

"You will wear them a long time," he said. "I employ orphans and am kind to them. I employ them as long as they remain beautiful. Your only duties while I employ you will be to show off my exquisite dresses to the fashionable ladies. Do I speak plainly? Am I understood?"

A chorus of "Yesses" answered him.

Mr. Blute became suddenly animate. His short legs seemed to prance. He passed among the six manikins to be and shook hands with each of them, patting them tenderly on their arms and clucking up at them.

"Follow me, young ladies," he added. "My automobile will take you to the hotel. Is there anyone of you will have to notify someone of her absence?"

There was a pause. During this pause Mr. Blute became dark and his face glistened.

He eyed each of the six beautiful young women with an ominous, somewhat aggrieved frown, and waited.

After a brief silence a pretty black-haired girl raised her voice.

"I must tell my uncle," she said.

"What's your name?" Mr. Blute asked curtly.

"Miss Marlow."

"Miss Marlow," said Mr. Blute, "you may go home to your uncle. Now, is there anyone else?"

The dismissed one hesitated. Mr. Blute ignored her. The remaining five then watched Miss Marlow leave the office and appeared slightly puzzled. But when she had gone, Mr. Blute diverted their attention with a violent laugh.

"Very well," he cried. "Follow me."

He led his smiling and elated troupe through the luxurious sales-room to a large green limousine which waited at the curb.

It had grown dark. The avenue glowed in the dusk. Vivid patches of light gleamed over the pavements. Clusters of lamps shone gayly down the line of the curbing. People were still strolling leisurely, elegantly by. But now over the avenue was an air of quest, a spirit of masquerade. The hurrying cabs and motors perforated the gloom, with their long shafts of light.

"Step in," said Mr. Blute to his troupe. "The chauffeur will be here directly. All arrangements have been made."

One by one the five disappeared in to the tonneau. He waited and closed the door upon them. He exuded a joyous politeness, laughing aimlessly, bowing elaborately to the laden tonneau, returning briskly to his establishment. Inside Mr. Blute spoke briefly to two of his pretty clerks who were covering the stock and fixtures preparatory to leaving.

"Run along," he ordered, "and play. Run along, children. Don't waste time. Time is valuable, very valuable to the young. Ah, make the most of life."

He patted the two clerks upon the arm in a happy, paternal fashion and approached the white-haired and regal stepping matron—his bookkeeper.

"Run along, run along, Miss Jones," he said to her.

He waited until his staff had clothed itself and. bidden him good evening, and, as the last one passed through the door, he hurried into his office.

Five minutes later a man in a great black coat wearing goggles and a pointed cap mounted the driver's seat of Mr. Blute's machine. This person clucked with his tongue in a way highly reminiscent of his employer, Mr. Blute, and in fact seemed possessed of another of his habits. For, as he adjusted himself in the seat, he extracted a little powder puff from one of his large pockets and dabbed whimsically at his nose. This tell-tale ritual accomplished, the mysterious chauffeur swung his car into the mass of traffic and spun away in the direction of the St. John Hotel.

III

Mr. Blute, looking tired and slightly disheveled, entered the *Maison des Robes* the following morning. He glanced keenly at his pretty clerks who were standing in a solemn little group near the center of the room and bending over an opened newspaper. Mr. Blute paused, he came near them.

"Too bad, ladies," he said. "It is a terrible thing."

"Oh, we are so sorry," one of them answered, and Mr. Blute, shaking his head, sadly passed on into his office.

He closed the door and drew from his pocket a newspaper and sitting down at his desk read the account of the tragedy which had overtaken five young women and an intoxicated chauffeur.

The newspaper stated the young women had been selected by Mr. Blute as the most beautiful in Chicago and were being escorted to the St. John Hotel in the automobile belonging to the proprietor of the *Maison des Robes*. The chauffeur as he guided the machine had appeared to be intoxicated to at least several crossing policemen who remembered his passing. He had, this diabolical chauffeur, finally ended by crashing through the slight guard at the river's edge and into the river, at Adams street. The bridge at this point had been open at the time. Repairs which were being made on the structure had necessitated the closing of the street and thus it was that the accident had been witnessed by no one. An officer named Maloney was the first to arrive on the scene. He peered into the black water and saw great ripples dancing under the red lights of the bridge. It was eight o'clock, according to Policeman Maloney.

Mr. Blute studied the story closely as he read, rereading several paragraphs.

Pressing a button, he summoned one of his pretty clerks and ordered her to secure him copies of the afternoon papers as soon as they appeared.

As he waited their arrival, two policeman desecrated the interior of the establishment with their heavy feet and loud voices, and ended by being ushered into the proprietor's presence. They informed him that his limousine had been fished out of the river, little the worse for wear, but that the police had been unable to recover the bodies of the five young women.

Mr. Blute listened gravely. He answered their questions freely, telling them of the chauffeur whom he had only hired two days before— and whose first name was Harold.

"It is awful," said Mr. Blute, covering his f ace with his hands. "I had prepared rooms at the St. John Hotel and given the man instructions to go there at once. The tragedy has unnerved me, gentlemen."

"We are draggin' fer the ladies and the chauffeur," said one of the policemen, "and will let you know, Mr. Blute, as soon as we find anything."

To the newspaper reporters who arrived at the *Maison des Robes* as the police were leaving, Mr. Blute announced that he would bestow a sum of $100 upon each of the families of the deceased five young women. He revealed their names, as he had done to the police, described their beauties, dwelt bitterly upon the drunkenness of the miserable chauffeur, wrung his hands and clucked solemnly with his tongue.

For eight days the police continued to drag the river for the bodies of the six victims. During this time, apparently overcome by the disaster, Mr. Blute relapsed into a morose condition. His pretty clerks saw him but little. He called upon the police captain in charge of the search for the bodies daily.

At the end of the eighth day the body of a young woman was found near the mouth of the river. The body was taken to the morgue and there identified by a young man as the remains of Mary Collins, his sister. Miss Collins, it developed at once, was one of the five beautiful women who had been chosen by the discriminating Mr. Blute.

The brother identified the body by means of the clothes the young woman wore and a signet ring which she had borrowed from him only a week before. The features were discolored beyond recognition by the water, seeming also to have sustained certain bruises.

In quick succession during that night four other bodies were recovered from the mouth of the river. Like the first, their faces were disfigured by discolorations and bruises. The coroner and police explained this fact by the theory that the bruises had been sustained in the accident itself, the plunge into the river, and the discolorations had been brought on by the abrasions.

Three of the bodies were identified by landladies. One was a Miss Helen Lowrey. The second, Miss Dorothy Janes. The third, Miss Anna Hyde. The landladies wept and declared the victims had roomed with them when alive. The identifications were made by means of the clothing, of rings, ornaments, shoes and hosiery. Mr. Blute himself established the identity of the fourth, remembering in particular the black and white checked suit in which the body was attired—and the long grey gloves.

An inquest was held and the bodies buried. The search for the drunken chauffeur was discontinued. Mr. Blute reimbursed the brother of one of the victims with his check for $100, and thus two weeks after the evening of the tragedy the matter was forgotten, and business at the *Maison des Robes* was resumed..

Even Mr. Blute appeared to have recovered some of his joyous and paternal air which the incident had for the time taken from him. The elegant people who walked in the avenue passed the window of the famous establishment and soon forgot, as they gazed at the exquisite interior, the story of the five beautiful women, the drunken chauffeur and the open bridge.

The night after the inquest, Mr. Blute walked briskly towards his home. His automobile was still suffering repair. He had ridden to a point within four blocks of where he lived in the street car. It was warm and the promise of a storm was in the sultry air.

Mr. Blute's home was a large red brick house located in a peculiarly dismal part of the city which had once been the center of wealth and society. The mansions which had once lent an air of solid and tasteful affluence to the street now stood with their windows broken, their porches sunken, their stairs overgrown. Large "For Sale" signs painted white, shone out of the darkness. Here and there were some still inhabited.

A stagnation had apparently overtaken the district. To the south furious building activities had converted the almost prairies of twenty years ago into populous resident sections. To the north the avenue had changed the scene into one of glitter and prosperity.

But in this space, where stood the home of Mr. Blute a decay had fallen. The night lay somberly upon it, the sagging outlines of the tumble-down mansions appeared faintly out of the unrelieved gloom.

Before one of the more preserved of these mansions Mr. Blute stopped. A single light burned in an upper window.

Mr. Blute, peering into the darkness about him, suddenly mounted the steps and let himself into the house with a key.

He locked the door carefully behind him.

For a moment he stood still and listened and then he walked to a front window in the large barren room to the right of the hall and dropped to his knees in front of a cracked pane.

He remained thus on his knees for ten minutes, peering cautiously into the street, only his mop of hair and gleaming eyes visible above the ledge.

After gazing into the vacant street in this odd manner, Mr. Blute arose, rubbed his palms together and, smiling, tiptoed gently up the stairs.

The old mansion became full of creakings and groanings as Mr. Blute progressed. But at the top of the flight he paused and the noises ceased.

He paused and peered intently at a door behind which a light burned. Into his eyes came, it seemed, an answering light, a faintly ecstatic gleam.

Mr. Blute inserted a key in the door lock and turned it. The door opened slowly.

The room in front of Mr. Blute was illuminated by a lighted gas jet. Across the walls fell long trembling shadows. He walked directly to the jet and turned on the light fuller. Two cabinets, in which a variety of odd surgical instruments and bottles of colored liquids reposed, came into view. Also ranged across one end of the room there appeared to be five long tables on which lay the bodies of the five young women, who had entered Mr. Blute's automobile one evening two weeks ago.

IV

Mr. Blute, as if remembering something, dashed back to the door and locked it with the key. He then returned to the other end of the room and surveyed the contents of the five tables. Each of them was partially covered with a black cloth.

"Ah, my beauties," said Mr. Blute softly. "Everything is settled. You have been decently buried. And one of you has cost me an extra $100."

He frowned at the middle figure and wagged a reproving forefinger at it.

"Why didn't you mention that brother of yours, eh? Pah! Women are never to be trusted," he growled.

But recovering his good spirits Mr. Blute clucked genially with his tongue, walked to one of the cabinets and proceeded to remove an array of apparatus, instruments and bottles.

As he made these preparations his eyes strayed continually to the bodies on the tables. He kept mumbling to himself:

"Orphans, excellent. Ah, beauties, I have made no mistakes . . . no mistakes."

The proprietor of the *Maison des Robes* then spread out his strange paraphernalia on a sixth and smaller table. His mop of hair became awry, his eyes gleamed and an unlovely oil gradually overspread his face.

But his hands were busy, dexterously busy. They mixed the liquids of the bottles, they lighted little gas burners and cooked little pots. There was an elaborate methodicality about Mr. Blute during these operations. He counted things, he insisted upon laying everything straight and keeping everything clean.

Towards the end of his labors he grew excited, gazing into the bubbling pots, clucking with his tongue and finally prancing up and down and rubbing his palms vigorously together.

It was obvious that Mr. Blute was preparing a solution, a delicate, difficult solution from the intensity of his maneuverings. Having prepared this in at least five different ways—there were five little pots, Mr. Blute filled a long hollow needle-like instrument with the bubbling liquid from one of the pots.

"It is perfect," he mumbled, "perfect. The perfect fluid. Ah, what would the Ptolomies have given for it?"

He then folded his short arms across his bosom and surveyed with dignity the five bodies which lay stiff and beautiful upon the five tables.

"One more injection," he mumbled, "and it is complete. But first another bath—one more bath."

Opening a drawer beneath one of the cabinets, Mr. Blute extracted a large bottle containing a violet liquid.

With this in his hand he approached first the body of Margaret Swinburne, looking as she had looked when he had asked her her name in his office two weeks ago. With the violet liquid he proceeded to bathe her face.

An odd spicy smell crept into the room.

The inanimate face underwent simultaneously a remarkable change.

The skin appeared to revive, the flesh seemed to bloom, a glowing tint of life suffused the throat.

"Four baths," mumbled Mr. Blute, "I must remember. Only four. And I must not forget the hair."

Darting to the cabinet he returned with a bottle of dark liquid and this he applied expertly to the head. The blonde hair, which he loosened, shimmered under the application. Slowly its color changed, Mr. Blute drenching it delicately with the contents of the bottle. It become a smouldering auburn. This accomplished, Mr. Blute returned to his long needle instrument.

"Now," he addressed the figure upon which he had been working: "We shall see. This way."

With quick little movements he inserted the point of the needle into the tips of the slender fingers, each time loosing some of the liquid by means of the silver plunger which formed the upper part of the instrument. The eleventh injection Mr. Blute made into the heart.

As soon as they were finished he seized the body in a frenzy and staggering under its weight carried it to a bench which stood near the cabinets.

"Now," he cried, "the pose, the pose. This way. No. Turn the head. The foot out. You will sit. A morning costume. So. The right foot in. The arm out. The fingers. My. God, are you stupid! The fingers, so; open one. Close the other. The knee less bent. Ah! Excellent. Leaning forward a bit. Ah, what grace. As if you listened. So. As if you had something to say, ha, ha."

As he spoke or rather ejaculated, Mr. Blute's hands manipulated the body before him. It resembled, the operation did, some weird sculpturing. But the pose he finally achieved seemed to delight him. He hovered around it. Now and then he added a finishing touch, a final angle. But soon the limbs ceased to obey his sensitive movements. He strained the wrist in an effort to undo a curve. He might as well have sought to undo the curve of some marble wrist. A gleam of triumph came into his eyes.

"You harden quickly," he gasped. "Quicker than ever. An hour quicker! I have barely time to adjust! Eh! And this time you will last longer; yes. Two years, my beauty. And then perhaps—who knows— the fluid which is forever. I think now, that you will do."

The remainder of the night Mr. Blute spent in similar ministrations upon the other four bodies. Each he bathed in the peculiarly smelling liquid. Each revived under his touch, losing its still ghastly stiffness, growing mysteriously alive, acquiring a delicate blooming transparency of skin as of death made beautiful. The hair of each Mr. Blute dyed a different color!

At dawn Mr. Blute had finished. The five were posed. They lay now upon the tables in impossible posturings, ludicrously sinister, lovely and vicious, like a family of houris caught by some sudden enchantment which had perpetuated them in their casual graces. Each had suffered the careful and elaborate adjusting of Mr. Blute.

Tired and disheveled, he stood in the center of the room and panted. The air was full of an almost suffocating odor. But a prodigious strength seemed to be his.

With a great sigh he lifted the body of Miss Swinburne upon his shoulder and carried her into an adjacent room.

On the floor of this room were laid six oblong boxes. Their lids had been opened and each of the boxes contained a naked wax model to which was affixed a wire standard.

It was Mr. Blute's purpose to sever the wire standards from the wax models and attach them to the bodies of his five young women. This he did carefully, placing each of the bodies, when he had finished, into each box occupied by the wax dummies.

V

An hour later Mr. Blute sat and waited for the arrival of the wagon from the *Maison des Robes*. He had washed his face and hands, changed his clothes, powdered his nose and violently brushed his hair.

The wagon came and Mr. Blute supervised the loading of the oblong boxes, which had been recrated and carefully relabeled by their owner. Seated then on one of them, the erratic Mr. Blute was driven into the avenue and around to a point in the rear of the *Maison des Robes*.

He emerged into his establishment and ordered his clerks to bring out the five costumes which had been selected. Then standing with the fluffy silken mass in his arms, he announced: "I do not wish to be disturbed until I ring," and retired into his office where the five oblong boxes had been taken.

He uncrated them one at a time, attiring them in lingerie petticoats, shoes and the costumes.

To the first he pinned a bit of paper on the hem of the petticoat. On the paper were the initials M. C. which, in Mr. Blute's mind, were obviously the initials of Mary Collins.

He placed the carefully dressed body in a corner and proceeded with the second. His actions were tender, wistful and expert.

It was well along in the afternoon when Mr. Blute issued from his office and summoned his pretty clerks.

"We will not place the figures in the window. We will take the figures which are in there out and put them in the boxes. Handle everything carefully, ladies."

The clerks stepped at the door of Mr. Blute's private office and gasped.

Confronting them were five beautiful young women attired in the height of exquisite fashion. One of them was standing smiling with a simple and yet startling grace to her outlines. A second was seated and gazing nonchalantly at her dainty boot. She seemed to be meditating upon the filmiest of secrets. A third was standing with her head turned and her mouth slightly opened in a look of pleasant surprise. A fourth was seated, leaning forward as if in conversation. Words trembled on her lips and there was about her the air of a woman who is struggling to reveal something of piquant importance. The fifth stood straight and tall, her eyes lowered, her arms listless, as if she were dreaming for the instant of some memories far distant. They were all radiant and appeared to the astounded clerks to be alive.

"Beauties, eh?" clucked Mr. Blute, rubbing his palms together.

The clerks admired his handiwork without a word.

Then amid the delighted exclamations of his employes and three fashionable customers, the five models were carried one by one into the spacious and wonderfully draped window of the *Maison des Robes.*

From the sidewalk Mr. Blute surveyed the effect and pranced excitedly up and down. His face moved with queer grimaces and he appeared obsessed by a deep and silent joy. He raised his eyes to the sky and blinked in a solemn sort of thanksgiving or prayer.

Within the shop his clerks talked among themselves.

"Those are certainly the most beautiful figures Blute has had yet," said the first one. "They are remarkable. I never saw anything like them."

The second one came out of the window shaking her head solemnly.

"Yes," she agreed. "They are far superior to the last three figures we had, although I can't see why Mr. Blute is throwing those last three out. They were better than anything on the avenue and hadn't begun to melt. *These* must have cost a fortune."

Miss Jones, the white-haired and regal-stepping one, interrupted in a superior manner.

"A man like Mr. Blute," she said, "does not balk at expense in pursuing his art. I have been here for eight years and during that time he has had four shipments from France, each one
better than the other. This is the fifth."

The conversation ceased as Mr. Blute re-entered his establishment. After gracefully receiving the congratulations of the occupants he retired to his office.

He closed the door behind him.

Then after a pause he opened the steel door of a wall safe and extracted from its interior a large ledger. This he carried to his desk.

Opening it to a blank page he wrote in it as follows:

Fifth Importation

For bodies from the Merville, Holmes, Wilmot and City Hospitals. $10 each.. $50
For poison gun and limousine attachment............................. 25
For embalming, mummifying chemicals.............................. 200
For rash statement to the press... 100
For expressage of hospital bodies to mouth of the river.......... 30
For wax models from France, destroyed.............................. 400

"I guess that's all," murmured Mr. Blute, and with a sigh he totalled the column.

A light of mystic satisfaction shone from him. He powdered his nose with the puff and rubbing his hands together added to himself:

"Eight hundred and five dollars! Twice as much as last time, ha! Hobbies cost money. Ah, well, art for art's sake."

Mr. Blute then returned the ledger in the wall safe, locked the steel door and with a light brisk step re-entered his display room.

On the sidewalk a crowd of men and women had gathered. The men stared intensely into the window, their eyes smiling, their hearts beating fast. The women gazed enviously fascinated as always by this Paradise of windows, this fairyland of silks and laces and tulles, and graces. Exclamations of delight and wonder came from all sides, exclamations of astonishment and joy.

Mr. Blute stood in the plate glass door of his establishment, his large head thrown back, his hands clasped behind him and regarded the admiring throng with an expansive, though modest, smile.

Si Mutare Potest Aethiops Pellum Suam . . .

Two late books intrigue me, not only because they are of intrinsic virtue, but also and chiefly because they expose a problem that will haunt this great Calvinist republic, in the days to come, like a persistent glycosuria or night sweat. I allude, of course, to the race question, now beautifully expanding and mellowing, and in particular to that part of it which has to do with the niggero. What, ladies and gentlemen, in hell or out of it, are we to do with the Ethiop? Who shall answer the thunderous demands of the emerging coon? For emerging he is, both quantitatively and qualitatively, and there will come a morn, believe me or not, when those with ears to hear and hides to feel will discover that he is to be boohed and put off no longer—that he has at last got the power to exact a square answer, and that the days of his docile service as minstrel, torch and goat are done. When that morn dawns, I pray upon both knees, I shall be safe in the Alps, and not below the Potomac River, hurriedly disguised with burnt cork and trying to get out on the high gear. Soon or late, I agree with William Archer (see his "Through Afro-America," 1910) it will come to rough work—and perhaps sooner than most of us fancy. The Southerners, even the honest ones, have botched the business abominably, and unless Providence intervenes with a miracle I suspect that it will jolly well botch the South.

I speak, not as a villainous Yankee and Abolitionist, but as one of Southern birth, and of Southerners born. I was brought up (or, in the local dialect, raised) among darkeys; I played with darkey boys in my nonage; I know hundreds of darkeys today; I am on good terms with them; I have never had a serious quarrel with an individual among them. I thus qualify, I hope, as a Southern gentleman, or, at all events, as a Southerner. More, I am and always have been in favor of slavery, not only for blacks, but also for all save a small and shrinking minority of whites. Yet more, I regard Stonewall Jackson as a great general, and believe that Ben Butler has never reached heaven, and prefer batterbread to *petit pain,* and voted for Bryan, and am sound on infant damnation and the crime of '73, and have the hookworm and used to write editorials for the Baltimore *Sunpaper.* I bore you with these qualifications in self-defense. It would shock and grieve me to be called a Yan-

Smart Set 53, No. 1 (September 1917): 138–44.

kee, and, what is worse, it would libel me. I hate everyone born north of the Mason and Dixon line, whether men or woman. I regard the surrender of General Robert E. Lee as the most calamitous human event since the discovery of America. I would rather be chained by the leg in the common jail of Yazoo City, Miss., fed only upon hoecake and coca-cola, than smothered in violets by all the gals of Boston. . . .

Nevertheless, it seems to me that the South has failed to solve the problem of the *Homo noir,* and that the completeness of its failure is growing more visible day by day. Not only is the coon not come to equilibrium; he is jumping up and rocking the boat more and more. For thirty or forty years after the war it was simply a question of how much should be given to him—freely or haltingly, generously or grudgingly, as you choose. But now it is fast becoming a question of how much he will demand and take—if possible, peaceably; if not, by force. And why the change? Simply because the niggero has been making fast and secure progress, not in mere education, but in competence, in self-confidence, in wealth—because he has begun to find out that he can make his way, Southerners or no Southerners—because, in all that is essential and last-ing, he has shown better progress than the Southern whites. A harsh fact, but still a fact. The South likes to think that it has recovered from the Civil War—the whole region, in truth, swarms with wind-machines who keep on trying to demonstrate it—but a glance at the evidence is enough to fill any impartial judge with doubt. Those four years were more terrible than anyone knew. They wiped out the old civilization, and they left the soil so sterile that a new one has never sprung up.

Consider, for example, Virginia—in the old days undoubtedly the premier American state, the mother of Presidents and statesmen, the hatchery of national ideas and ideals, the home of the first American university worthy of the name, the *arbiter elegantiarum* of the western world. Well, observe Virginia today. It is years since a first-rate man has come out of it; it is years since an idea has come out of it. The *an-cien régime* went down the red gullet of war; the poor white trash are now in the saddle. Politics in Virginia are cheap, ignorant, parochial, idiotic; there is scarcely a man in office above the rank of a petty job-seeker; the political doctrine that prevails is made up of hand-me-downs from the bumpkinry of the Middle West—Bryanism, prohibi-tion, vice crusading, all that sort of claptrap; the administration of the law is turned over to professors of Puritanism and espionage; a Wash-ington or a Jefferson, dumped there by some act of God, would be de-nounced as a scoundrel and jailed overnight. Elegance, *esprit,* culture? Virginia has no art, no literature, no philosophy, no mind or aspiration of her own. Her education has sunk to the Baptist seminary level; not a single contribution to human knowledge has come out of her colleges in twenty-five years; she spends less than half upon her common schools, per capita, than any Northern state spends. In brief, an intellectual desert, a paradise of the fourth-rate. There remains, at the top, a ghost of the old urbanity, a bit wistful and infinitely charming. But there is no thought under it, no cultural pressure and vigor, no curiosity and enterprise. The mind of the state, as it is revealed to the nation, is pathetically naif and inconsequential; it no longer reacts with energy and elasticity to great problems; it seems fallen to the bombastic trivialities of the camp-meeting and the Chautauqua. A Lee or a Poe or a Jefferson would be almost as unthinkable in the Virginia of to-day as a Huxley or a Nietzsche in Nicaragua.

I choose the Old Dominion, not because I disdain it, but precisely because I esteem it. It is, by long odds, the most civilized of the Southern states, now as always. If one turns to such a commonwealth as Georgia the picture becomes far darker. Here the liberated lower orders of whites have borrowed the worst commercial bumptiousness of the Yankee and superimposed it upon a culture that, at bottom, is little removed from barbarism. Georgia is not only ignorant and stupid; it is vicious. A self-respecting and educated European, going there to live, would not only find intellectual stimulation utterly lacking; he would actually feel a certain insecurity. The Leo Frank affair was no isolated phenomenon, no accident; it fitted into its frame very snugly; it was a natural expression of Georgian ideas of the true, the good and the beautiful. There is a state with more than half the area of Italy and more population than either Denmark or Norway, and yet, in thirty years it has not produced a single first-class book or picture or poem or scientific discovery or political or philosophical idea, or other sound contribution to human advancement. If it had been destroyed by an earthquake in 1875, the world would be exactly where it is to-day. If the whole of its present population were to be transplanted to Mars tomorrow, the news would be of no more interest to civilization than the news that a distillery had burned down in Kentucky.

If you want to get some notion of the intellectual and social backwardness of Georgia, turn to the last edition of "Who's Who in America," and particularly to page 15, on which the assembled *aluminados* are sorted out according to their places of birth. Georgia, with a population of 2,609,121, contributes 243; Michigan, with a population of 2,810,173, contributes 551; Vermont, with a population of 355,956, contributes 363. But we forget that Georgia is half black—we must chalk off the Moors. Very well, let us match that half of Georgia which is white against that part of the northern populace which is at least half American. (Georgia herself has very few foreign whites.) The result is almost as striking. The 1,300,000 whites of Georgia contribute 242

Whoswhoistas; the 1,433,375 inhabitants of Massachusetts who have "one or both parents native" offer 2,002. In New Jersey (perhaps the least civilized Northern state) the 1,213,601 American and semi-American whites give "Who's Who" 501 names—more than twice as many as Georgia. Here, remember, I always regard birthplace, and not place of residence. Georgia is no new state; it had half a million population in 1825, and more than a million before the Civil War. Yet it is now left far behind, both relatively and actually, by such new states as Wisconsin, Iowa and Michigan, none of which got on its legs until after the war.

Apply any other test and you will unearth the same sluggishness. The Southern white is falling behind the procession; not only is the Northern white forging ahead of him, but also the Southern *procyon lotor*. I turn to page 68 of the third revised edition of Ely's "Outlines of Economics," just published, and find this:

> In the South during the last census decade the number of negro farmers increased more rapidly than the number of white farmers; the acreage of land operated by white farmers decreased while that operated by negro farmers increased 10 per cent; the value of farm land and buildings owned by whites increased 117 per cent, but the value of farm land and buildings owned by negroes increased 156 per cent; while the number of negro farm owners increased 17 per cent as contrasted with an increase of 12 per cent in the white owners of farms.

More, the niggero is making equal, if not actually greater strides, in commerce and industry. When he learns to read and write he no longer sets up shop as a shyster lawyer, a quack doctor or a grafting ecclesiastic; he applies himself to a trade, or opens a store, or begins swindling his fellow blacks with some banking or insurance scheme. The number of such enterprises increases enormously in all the Southern states; there are whole towns given over to darkey business, and soon there will be whole regions. And then? Well, and then the band will begin to play. The black has learned the capital lesson that property is necessary to self-respect, that he will never get anywhere so long as he is poor. Once he is secure in that department he will take up the business of getting back his plain constitutional rights. Will he produce leaders fit for so great and delicate a venture? The answer is held *in petto* by the gods—but it is not to be forgotten that he produced a leader fit for the work of preparation. The Southern whites have pondered and debated the negro question for fifty years; it has been their first and almost only permanent concern; they offer its difficulties as the explanation of all their lack of progress. But let us not forget here that it was a black man, Booker Washington, who worked out the only intelligible solution so far heard of, and that he forced the whites, for all the concentrated horse-power of their joint meditation, to accept it. Booker liberated the niggeroes by teaching them the value of skill and money. Some later prophet may go a step further. The day he arises I shall retire to Interlaken.

All these lofty thoughts are inspired by the two books before mentioned—"His Own Country," by Paul Kester (*Bobbs-Merrill*), and "The Autobiography of an Ex-Colored Man" (*Sherman-French*), the first a novel and the second a record of fact. Mr. Kester's narrative runs to nearly 700 pages, but in structure it is quite simple. A young quadroon, the natural son of a Virginia planter, goes to Canada in his youth, acquires an education, accumulates money, and marries a white wife. Then, through an agent, he buys the decayed plantation of his old master, and returns as a gentleman of leisure. The circumambient gentry are horrified—what, a coon at Comorn Hall! But the worst is yet to come. The prodigal demands social recognition, goes into the courts to obtain his rights, defies the local *noblesse,* attracts the attention of the Northern newspapers, takes to the Chautauquas, horns into national politics, lunches at the White House, founds a black party, collects a war fund of millions, and tries to organize into one compact whole the financial, voting and even military strength of his 10,000,000 fellows. Alas, too soon! A cog slips, and down he goes, just as success seems yielding to his prehension. His Black Crusaders blow up, the newspapers turn upon him, his following falls away, he himself is amiably butchered by his white neighbors, and his son and daughter with him. . . . "'My son,' he gasped. 'My daughter—I have given all.' . . . Above Comorn rolled the leaped the sombre smoke and crimson flame. Against even the brightening glory of the morning sky the Black Crusader had unfurled and flung the awful challenge of his sable flag." . . .

A mere shocker? A book to harrow fat women? Nay, you mistake it. It is a serious attempt, by a man of Northern birth, long resident in the South, to project an experimental beam into the sinister and much muddled future. It is careful, thoughtful, persuasive, provocative; it stands as far above the gaudy balderdash of a Thomas Dixon as a novel by Dreiser stands above the boudoir goods of Robert W. Chambers. There is in it no sentimental propaganda, no childish tickling of the blackamoor. One sees in Brent, the Black Crusader, not only the unsuspected potentialities of the emerging negro, but also his deficiencies—his lack of self-restraint, his savage passion, his almost Jewish impudence and obnoxiousness. And in the lesser blacks of the chronicle these deficiencies are made even plainer; examine them carefully, if you are not a Southerner, and you will get some notion of what it means to live among such evil and intolerable Anthropoidea. Nor are the whites overdone in stupidity and hunkerousness. They are not the barbaric white trash of Georgia, but Virginians of gentle birth and rearing—the only genuine gentleman, perhaps, now extant in this moral republic. And they approach their problem, despite its final descent to bloodshed, in decency and soberness of mind, and with as much charity as human beings in trouble ever show. In brief, the story is artfully planned; there is no special pleading in it; it is an honest and discreet attempt to put living drama into a work of the imagination, and it comes, in places, to a very high level of achievement.

"The Autobiography of an Ex-Colored Man" is less sophisticated and reflective; all the author seeks to do is to tell his own story, with certain generalizations by the way. He is, like most Afro-Americans of any intelligence, chiefly white and of good blood; more, he is so nearly pure white that, in the end, he marries a white wife and passes over from the one race into the other. The value of his tale lies in the accuracy of its details—its pictures of the social life of the negro, North and South. He distinguishes three classes, (*a*) the tough niggeroes, (*b*) the order of niggero servants, dependent on the whites, and (*c*) the new order of well-to-do, industrious, self-respecting and aspiring niggeroes. It is the misfortune of the South that the first class is still numerous, and that the second is shrinking. It is the double misfortune of the South that the white Southerners still exhibit a vain and passionate intolerance of the third class. The brunette Napoleon (or Rockefeller, or Roosevelt, or Carranza, or Garrison), when he comes, will come out of Class III. . . . The anonymous author handles the question of miscegenation somewhat gingerly, though it is, in a sense, the main matter of his book. Interbreeding is going out of fashion in the South; it is no longer customary down there for every gentleman to have his xanthous mistress. But that is not because the Southerners have re-enacted the seventh commandment, but because the more sightly yellow girls have improved in education and aspiration and self-respect, and are thus less willing to enter into concubinage. A compensatory movement, not to be mentioned in a family magazine, shows itself in the North. You will find some notice of it in the present work. . . .

II

"The Mysterious Stranger" having escaped the public hangman, Albert Bigelow Paine now ventures upon the open publication of Mark Twain's "What Is Man?" (*Harper*). Of this book I have often discoursed at length; Mark wrote it back in the '80's, but did not print it until 1906, and then only in an edition limited to 250 copies, and not for sale. It contains, in brief, two ideas, neither of them very startling, the first being that man, in Dr. Crile's phase, is an adaptive mechanism, and the second being that altruism, when analyzed, always turns out to be self-interest in a long-tailed coat. These ideas, as I say, are not startling—most men of any intelligence subscribe to them today—but when they first occurred to Mark they were less prevalent, and so they shook him up a bit, and he set them down with the air of a boy pulling the cat's tail, and was afraid to circulate them. Even now they meet with horrified opposition from such pillars of forgotten nonsense as the New York *Times Review of Books*. In the issue for June 3 there is a long editorial denouncing them as naughty, and stating that "one refuses to believe that the book voices the settled, mature convictions held by Mr. Clemens—at least one does not wish to believe it." Refuses? On what ground? No more than a glance at Paine's life of Mark is sufficient to prove that he not only held to them to the last, but that he was fond of extending them and reinforcing them. If he was anything at all in this world, he was an absolute skeptic and determinist; nothing offended and enraged him more than the sloppy idealism and optimism which the *Times* now seeks to ram down his œsophagus. That such bosh should be seriously printed as criticism is surely a sorry indication of the depths to which criticism is sunk in These States.

But let us not be impatient. The fact that Mark was an intelligent man is one that will penetrate the caputs of the national grandmas of letters only slowly. They began by greeting him as a childish buffoon; they proceeded to hail him a purveyor of refined entertainment; they are now in the stage of praising him as a chaser of the blues—in the *Times* phrase, one "who has done so much, through his joyous humor, to lighten the burdens of his generation." Such judgments are worse than errors; they are indecencies. It is as if Italian organ-grinders should essay to estimate Beethoven. The truth about Mark is that he was a colossus, that he stood head and shoulders above his country and his time, that even the combined pull of Puritanism without and Philistinism within could not bring him down to the national level. The result is that he remains mysterious—a baffling puzzle to the critics of the country. Read Howells' "My Mark Twain" if you would see how even the utmost personal intimacy can leave a second-rate man with only a vague and inaccurate picture of a first-rate man.

III

"Those Times and These," by Irvin S. Cobb (*Doran*), is a collection of sketches and short stories which may be likened by the judicious to a sandwich made of very stale and leathery *Kriegsbrot*, but with an excellent slice of Smithfield ham in the middle. That slice of sweet hip bears title of "Hark! From the Tombs," and is a chapter from the history of Jeff Poindexter, body servant to Judge William Pitman Priest. It is an extravagant piece of buffoonery, and its central situation is as old as farce, but its presentation of niggero character and ways of thought is penetrating and irresistible. No feeble minstrel show is here; the authentic swart baboon is offered up; as for me I have fairly bawled over it. The tales of white folks interest me less, partly because they are full of a mawkish sentimentality and partly because their people are un-real. Consider, for example, Sergeant Jimmy Bagby, the *raconteur,* in "Ex-Fightin' Billy." He recalls to me, not any human being I have ac-tually known, but the creaking fun-machines of the late O. Henry.

IV

Long ago, in the early days of my pastorate, I used to woo the publishers with pleas for more plays in book form; of late they well-nigh swamp me. Let me call the roll of the arrivals since our last rub-bing of noses: Vols. XIX and XX of the Drama League Series (*Double-day-Page*), the first devoted to a translation of "Malvaloga," by the Spaniards, Serafín and Joaquín Alvarez Quintero, and the second given over to four pieces of the Washington Square Players; "Plays of Gods and Men," by Lord Dunsany (*Luce*), including "The Tents of the Ar-abs," "The Laughter of the Gods," "The Queen's Enemies" and "A Night at an Inn"; a separate printing of "A Night at an Inn" in a new Neighborhood Playhouse Series (*Sunwise Turn*); "The Son of Man," by B. Russell Herts (*Shay*); "Human Wisps," by Anna Wolfrom (*Sherman-French*); "Three Welch Plays," by Jeannette Marks (*Little-Brown*), the same being "The Merry, Merry Cuckoo," "The Deacon's Hat" and "Welsh Honeymoon"; "The Bravest Thing in the World," by Lee Pape (*Penn*); "Faust," by E. L. Viets (*Jackson*); "The Last Straw," by Bosworth Crocker (*Shay*), being the first instalment of Plays of the Washington Square Players; "Comedies of Words," by Arthur Schnitz-ler, translated by Pierre Loving (*Stewart-Kidd*), and including "The Hour of Recognition," "The Big Scene," "The Festival of Bacchus," "Literature" and "His Helpmate"; "Portmanteau Plays," by Stuart Walker (*Stewart-Kidd*), including "The Trimplet," "Nevertheless," "The Medicine Show," and "The Six Who Pass While the Lentils Boil"; "Five Plays," by George Fitzmaurice (*Little-Brown*), including "The Country Dressmaker," "The Moonlighter," "The Pie-Dish," "The Magic Glasses" and "The Dandy Dolls"; "Mrs. Leffingwell's Boots," "The Witching Hour," "Oliver Goldsmith" and "In Mizzouri," by Au-gustus Thomas (*French*), and "Maggie Pepper" and "The Third Degree," by the late Charles Klein (*French*). A formidable list, God wot. Seventeen different volumes, forty-two different plays.

Moreover, nearly all of them worth reading—nearly every one with its touch of interest. The four Dunsany pieces and the five by Schnitzler belong to the best literature of our time, and those by Miss Marks, Mr. Fitzmaurice and the Quintero brothers, if they fall below that high mark, are at least sincere, intelligent and deserving of respect. Even the Broadway confections of Augustus Thomas and the boob-shockers of Charles Klein are not to be sniffed at; if their publication is not a service to literature, it at least enables us to study the method of these skilful showmen at leisure, and so get at its secrets. In many of these playbooks one also finds prefaces, and some of them are as entertaining as the plays. Thomas prefixes one to each of his pieces, explaining how he conceived it, brought it to term and gave it issue—very curious bursts of frankness, not lacking in unconscious humor. In front of the Quintero pay John Garrett Underhill (an authority on Spanish literature) prints an instructive discourse on the modern Spanish drama. In front of the Portmanteau dramas Edward Hale Bierstadt tells how Stuart Walker came to do them and why. And by way of introduction to the Schnitzler one-acters, Mr. Loving offers the best critical consideration of Schnitzler the dramatist that has yet got into English.

I do not assault you with reviews of all these comedies and tragedies, for on the one hand the business would take up too much space, and on the other hand a good many of them have been presented in New York and hence noticed by the learned Nathan. More to the purpose of this pulpit is "The Contemporary Drama of Ireland," by Ernest A. Boyd (*Little-Brown*), author of "Ireland's Literary Renaissance." Here, for the first time, we have a complete and well-informed account of the most interesting movement in dramatic writing for many years. The Irish have not only built up a respectable body of drama in less than a generation; they have built up a body of drama that, at its highest points, overtops all others. Mr. Boyd, as editor and critic, has had a direct hand in the process, and he has put together a book about it that tells the whole story simply and adequately. In particular his volume is valuable for its illumination of the more shadowy areas of the field. We have had an avalanche of essays upon John Millington Synge and Lady Gregory and Yeats, and all the college professors are now pouring out their ideas about Dunsany, but Boyd is the first to include the Ulster dramatists with the Dublin dramatists and the first to deal understandingly with such men as Seumas O'Kelly, Lennox Robinson, Padraic Colum and George Fitzmaurice. A fine sense of proportion is in him; he is not so dazzled by the tarpons that he cannot see the herring. If you are interested in the new Irish movement, his book is one that you cannot afford to miss. . . .

Finally comes "The Dramatic Books and Plays in English Published During 1916," by Henry Eastman Lower and George Heron Milne (*Boston Book Co.*), a thin pamphlet, but one of daily use to the student of current dramatic literature. The thing is well done, and its appearance is the best of all proofs that the reading of plays is a vice that makes progress.

V

Of the books that remain, the most interesting by far are the reprints in The Modern Library (*Boni-Liveright*), an excellent series in clear type and at a low price. The volumes issued include Nietzsche's "Thus Spake Zarathustra," Robert Louis Stevenson's "Treasure Island," Anatole France's "The Red Lily," Kipling's "Soldiers Three," Oscar Wilde's "The Picture of Dorian Gray," Maeterlinck's "The Miracle of St. Anthony" and Strindberg's "Married"—in brief, a selection with sound taste behind it, and much less mush in it than usual. Some likely additions suggest themselves: Max Stirner's "Der Einzige und sein Eigentum," old Carlo Goldoni's autobiography (it is astonishing how little it is known), a volume of Ludwig Thoma's short stories, a complete "Robinson Crusoe," Zola's "Germinal," Huxley's debate with Gladstone, Dreiser's "Studies in Contemporary Celebrities," the Goncourts' "Madame Gervais," *u.s.w.* But why engaud such capital books with the limp leather of Garden City and East Aurora? Why not bind them simply in cloth, or boards, or linoleum, and so fit them for civilized libraries? . . .

Rosemary

BEING FURTHER SELECTIONS FROM A ROMANTIC CORRESPONDENCE

By Owen Hatteras

I

Dear Bill:

Being, as you are, adolescent, it was scarcely to be expected that you would ever have pored over the old *Standard* and *Vanity Fair,* but it does seem that Keppler's cartoons in *Puck* and the big-headed, tiny-bodied folk of F. M. Howarth would have been indelibly stamped upon your memory. And you recall with pride the Yellow Kid, but neglect the button craze that flourished as a more or less direct result of those cartoons.

But, bless me! You have a memory to be ashamed of, not to boast of; why, you've forgotten half the best things entirely! What about the drug store, just as popular as Holzapfel's smoke shop ever dared to be, with the big Diamond Dyes card hanging on the partition behind which they made up the prescriptions? Remember the red and blue bottles in the window, and the tiny gas-jets that lighted them at night? And the soda fountain painted all white to look like marble and in the centre a spray of carbonated water spouting up continuously under a glass dome?

You recall those things now, eh? Well, I'll try you again: Did you ever scan a Book of Views of the World's Columbian Exposition and point out the Administration Building and say, "Oh, I remember that"? Did you ever wear a short tan topcoat that struck you just below the hips? Or trousers so tight you couldn't hitch them up when you sat down? Or a black suit with a white vest? And do you remember when every sport wore patent-leather shoes every day and Sunday, too? And either a Windsor tie or an Ascot, unless he affected one of those new stocks?

He parted his hair in the middle, too, and plastered it down with military brushes and covered it with a straw hat as big around as a bi-

Smart Set 53, No. 2 (October 1917): 59–60.

cycle wheel. But with all this the chances were that he wore gold-buckled suspenders over his Jaeger's underwear and, if you will, his stiff- bosomed shirt.

But all those are easy ones. Why did you forget Regina music-boxes? And mackintoshes? And human-hair watch-chains? And eleven-bladed pocketknives? Why, oh, why, didn't you think of Mazie Follette? Or Sol Smith Russell? Or Helena Mora? Or the Harrison Sisters? Or Drina De Wolf? Or Ed. Delahanty? Or Jake Kilrain? Or the Wilbur Opera Company? Or "I Guess I'll Have to Telephone My Baby"? Or "Every Race Has a Flag But The Coon"? Or *The White Elephant Magazine?* Or the thin gold chains attached to nose glasses? Or Tourgee's "Fool's Errand"? Or Gilmore's Band? Or the Planchette? Or Charlie Mitchell?

Why, you don't even remember the night the gallery at the Opera House sank six inches with the crowd that gathered to see Jas. J. Corbett as "Gentleman Jim"! A mere infant you must be, else you would surely have mentioned Maude S., or the Gloire. de Dijon Rose, or Crokinole, or lightning-rods.

I don't believe, either, that you ever danced a quadrille or lancers. You don't remember your first Moxie, which you bought with a free ticket and the taste of which you didn't like. You evidently never saw a painted tambourine. And as for "Good-bye, Dolly Gray," or "Whistling Rufus," or "All Coons Look Alike to Me," you never heard any of them.

And what about Yale's "Twelve Temptations"? Better than the "Devil's Auction," if you had ever seen it. And I know you've never been in a First Chance and Last Chance saloon, or in the Buckingham in Louisville or the Standard in St. Louis. You never read "Beulah" and "St. Elmo," much less Frank Merriwell.

Did you hear your first phonograph by dropping a nickel in a slot and putting rubber tubes to your ears? And was your first moving picture shown in the same manner, minus the tubes? I doubt it. And how about the first Panama hat you ever heard of? Did or did you not believe it cost $500 and could pass unharmed through a finger ring?

Why continue? Your juvenility has been proven beyond the shadow of a doubt, but just to clinch it, answer me yea to these questions if you dare: Have you ever played Authors? Or worn a ring on your cravat?

Awaiting yr., etc.,

GUS.

II

Dear Gus:

. . . But what of Vesta Tilley? And Villa Knox ? And Mme. Steinheil? And Aunt Jemina's Pancakes? And Coal-Oil Johnny? And Sockless Jerry Simpson? . . . I am getting to be an old man, my boy. I remember the time when Coxey's Army came down the Chesapeake & Ohio Towpath. . . .

The other day I dropped into a little two-cent toy and candy store near a schoolhouse and asked for some peewees. Think of it: the woman said they were no longer made! How the devil can the boys of today play marbles without peewees? I asked her, and she told me that they now used boogies. I ordered up some of these boogies, and they almost made me weep: brown, dirty- looking spheroids, no two of them quite the same size. No wonder there is so little marble-playing in late years! . . . But the candy woman still had a drawer full of agates—aggies, we used to call them. I bought half a dozen for old-time's sake, and am still carrying them in my pocket.

Do you remember when every self-respecting boy had a whip-top in spring and spun it by lashing it with a home-made whip? I used to make the lash of my whip by stealing a towel from the cook and cutting it into long strips. These I nailed to half a length of broom-handle. A fine top whip—and very handy for defending the top. Any boy who happened along was free to grab it unless it had a "license" burned into it. This "license" was made with a piece of red-hot wire, and the wire was got red-hot by thrusting it between the front grates of the kitchen stove. That was long before gas stoves came in. The cook always burned coal. As I remember it, a top that was spun with a cord didn't need any "license." Or am I forgetting?

And did you ever make a baseball glove out of one of your father's old kid gloves, with an old sock stuck inside for padding? Did you ever chew Colgan's Taffy Tulu gum? And, tell me, my boy, do you remember the shavings of licorice root that used to be put up in little cheesecloth sacks in imitation of chewing-tobacco bags and sold in the candy store for a penny? Did you ever chew the stuff, pretending it was Fine Cut, and expectorate promiscuously in manly imitation of your Uncle Al?

Yours,

BILL.

Woman, Lovely Woman!

§1

In the midst of the war, the eternal woman question, that worse and damnder curse, continues to roost upon the subconsciousness of the race like the Sumerian basilisk upon the chest of U-sar-néph-ritus, the jitney Merodach. Scarcely a week goes by that I do not receive a book or two dealing with it—books chiefly wrote by suffragettes haunted by the vain wish that they were men, and thus able to vote for the barrel-house candidate, and to smoke five-cent cigars, and to duck through the swinging doors on hot days, and to read the *Police Gazette* in the barbershop, and to sit in the club-car, and to belong to the Elks and Freemasons, and to make a mock of the simple trust of poor working girls. Particularly this last. Once before I called dismayed attention to the fleshly favor of suffragette literature, and I now do so again, more in horror than in dudgeon. The inflammatory compositions of Christabel Pankhurst, LL.B., and other such specialists in the not-to-be-mentioned-by-ladies have convinced a number of the girls, it would seem, that the average male adult of Christendom leads a life of gaudy carnality, rolling magnificently from one liaison to another, and with an almost endless queue of ruined stenographers, telephone operators, manicurists, milliners, chorus girls, charwomen, parlor maids and wait-resses behind him, all dying of poison and despair. The life of man, as these alarmed (and envious) ones see it, is the life of a leading actor in a boulevard *revue*. He is polygamous, multigamous, myriadigamous, an insatiable and inconscionable debauchee, a monster of promiscuity; pro-digiously unfaithful to his wife, and even to his friends' wives; fathom-lessly sinful and superbly happy.

Needless to say, this picture belongs to fable. If the suffragette scaremongers (I speak without any embarrassing naming of names) were attractive enough to men to get near enough to enough men to know enough about them for their purpose, they would paralyze the women's clubs and boarding schools with no such flattering libels The simple truth is that the average man of our time and nation is vastly more virtuous, in the narrow American sense, than the authors of these alarming books and pamphlets ever dream. I do not say, of course, that

Smart Set 53, No. 2 (October 1917): 138–44.

he is pure in heart, for the chances are that he isn't; what I do say is that, in the overwhelming majority of cases, he is pure in act, even in the face of temptation. And why? For several main reasons, not to go into minor ones. One of them is that it takes a certain enterprise and courage to engage and betray the innocent affection of a sharp-eyed and highly-instructed working girl—and this is the sort of enterprise and courage that he hasn't got. Another is that he lacks the money: it takes more funds than he can withdraw from his wife's notice to en-snare even the most willing of bearable victims. Finally, and above all, he has a conscience, and that conscience stands immovably between his confidential aspirations and their lamentable fulfilment.

What! A conscience? Yes, dear friends, a conscience. It may be a poor one, a snide one, an artificial one. It may be indistinguishable, at times, from the mere fear that someone may be looking. It may be shot through with hypocrisy, stupidity, play-acting. But nevertheless, as consciences go in Christendom, it is genuinely entitled to the name—and it is always in action. A man, remember, is not a being *in vacuo;* he is the fruit and slave of the environment that bathes him; as Haeckel puts it, the cell does not act, it *re*acts. One cannot go to Con-gress or to the penitentiary without becoming, in some measure, a ras-cal. One cannot fall overboard without shipping water. One cannot pass through Harvard without carrying away scars. And by the same token one cannot live and have one's being in a great moral republic, year in and year out, without falling, to some extent at least, under that moral obsession which is the national hall-mark. An American, his nose buried in Nietzsche, the *New Republic,* "Man and Superman" and other such advanced literature, may caress himself with the notion that he is an immoralist—that he has emancipated himself from the Inter-national Sunday-school Lessons. But all the while there is a part of him that remains a sound Puritan, a moralist, a Presbyterian, just as there are parts of him that remain a baseball fan, a lodge-joiner, a democrat. And that part, in times of stress, asserts itself. It may not worry him on ordinary occasions. It may not stop him when he swears, or takes a nip of corn, or goes fishing on Sunday; it may even let him alone when he goes to a leg-show. But the moment a concrete Temptress rises before him, her nose snow-white, her lips rouged, her eyelashes dropping provokingly—the moment such a creature has at him, and his lack of ready funds begins to conspire with his lack of courage to assault and wobble him—at that precise moment his conscience flares into func-tion, and so finishes his business. First he sees difficulty, then he sees danger, then he sees wrong. The result? The result is that he takes to the woods, and another vampire is baffled of her prey.

In all this, of course, there is nothing new. Dr. Hatteras lately set forth the facts in this very journal. But the delusion persists, and I find it rampant in the literature of the suffragettes. Its propagation, I have no doubt, is fostered by three factors, the which I rehearse briefly:

(*a*) The idiotic vanity of men, leading to their eternal boasting, either by open lying or by dark hints.

(*b*) The notions of vice crusaders, Sunday-school superintendents and other such libidinous poltroons as to what they would do themselves if they had the courage.

(*c*) The ditto of certain suffragettes as to ditto ditto.

Here you have the genesis of the so-bogus generalization. Some pornographic Methodist, in the discharge of his enchanting duties as director of an anti-vice society, puts in an evening plowing through such books as "Night Life in Chicago," "The Confessions of a White Slave," "My Little Sister," the Cena Trimalchionis of Gaius Petronius and II Samuel. From this perusal he arises with the conviction that life amid the red lights must be one stupendous whirl of deviltry, that the shoe clerks he sees in Broadway at night are out for revels that would have caused a sensation in Sodom and Nineveh, that the average man who chooses hell and takes his chances leads an existence comparable to that of a Mormon bishop, that the world outside the Sunday school is packed like a sardine-can with betrayed salesladies, that every man who doesn't believe that Jonah swallowed the whale spends his whole leisure leaping through Hoop No VII. "If I were a sinner," whispers the vice director into his own ear, "this is what I, the Rev. Jasper Barebones, would be doing. The late King David did it; he was human, and hence weak. The late King Edward VII was not beyond suspicion: the very numeral in his name has its suggestions. Millions of others go the same sinister route . . . *Ergo,* Up guards, and at 'em! Bring me the pad of blank warrants! Order out the search-lights and scaling-ladders! Let us chase these hell-hounds out of Christendom, and make the world safe for virtue, the home, and infant damnation!"

Thus the anointed of God, arguing fallaciously from his own secret ambition. Where he makes his mistake is in assuming that the unconsecrated, while sharing his longing to be naughty, are free from his other weaknesses, *i. e.,* his timidity, his lack of resourcefulness, his conscience. As I have said, they are not. The vast majority of those who appear in the haunts of vice are there, not to engage in overt acts of ribaldry, but merely to tremble agreeably upon the edge of the abyss. They are the same timorous experimentalists, precisely, who throng the Midway at a world's fair, and go to burlesque shows, and take in hectic magazines, and read the sort of books that our Methodist friend reads. They like to conjure up the charm of devilishness, and to help out their somewhat sluggish imaginations by actual views of it, but when it comes to taking a header into the brimstone they usually fail to muster up the courage. For one shoe clerk who succumbs to the horrendous houris of the Broadway pave, there are 500 who succumb to lack of means, the warnings of Dr. Sylvanus Stall, and their own depressing conscience. For one "Fifth Avenue clubman"—*i. e.,* whiskey drummer or suburban deacon—who invades the department stores, engages the affections of some innocent miss, lures her into infamy and then sells her to the Italians, there are 1,000 who never get any further than asking the price of cologne water and emitting an oafish wink. And for one American husband who maintains a blonde stenographer in oriental luxury around the corner, there are 10,000 who are as true to their wives, year in and year out, as so many convicts in the death-house, and would be no more capable of any such loathsome malpractise than of cutting off the ears of their young.

I am sorry to blow up so much romance, but the facts are the facts, and curst be that dastard who would dodge them or pull their teeth. In particular, I am sorry for the suffragettes, for when they get into pantaloons at last, and have the vote and the new freedom, they will discover to their sorrow that they have been pursuing a chimera—that there is really no such animal as the male anarchist they have been denouncing and envying—that the so-called double standard, in a country so hagridden by moral qualms and hesitations as this one, has little more actual existence than honest advertising or free speech. They have followed the Sunday-school superintendents and pornomaniacs in embracing a piece of buncombe, and when the day of deliverance comes it will turn to ashes in their arms. Their error, as I say, lies in overestimating masculine independence, enterprise, sinfulness and courage. Men, in point of truth, are even more cowardly than women are—nay, many times. If the consequences, to a man, of the slightest descent from chemical purity, were one-tenth as swift and barbarous and overwhelming as the consequences to a young girl in like case, it would take a *capias ad computandum,* and perhaps even a *capias utlagatum,* to dredge up a single male flouter of that *lex talionis* in the whole of this grand and gaudy city of New York. As things stand today, even with the odds so vastly in his favor, the male hesitates and is thus not lost. Turn to the statistics of the vice crusaders if you doubt it. They show that the weekly and monthly receipts of female recruits upon the wharves of sin are always greater than the demand; that more young women enter upon the vermillion career than can make a living at it; that the pressure of the temptation they hold out constitutes a grave danger to our sophomores. What was the first act of the Army when it began penning its young clerks and college boys and plow hands in conscript camps? Its first act was to mark off a "moral zone" around each camp, and secure it with trenches and machine-guns, that the assembled *jeunesse* might be protected in their rectitude from the immoral besiegements of the propinquitous fair.

Quod erat demonstrandum.

§2

On a somewhat higher plane than the tracts of the suffragette viragos, but still full of sentimental fallacies, are such current works as "Woman," by Vance Thompson (*Dutton*), and "The Sexes in Science and History," by Eliza Burt Gamble (*Putnam*). A large part of Dr. Gamble's argument, for example, is based upon the following premiss:

> The beautiful coloring of male birds and fishes, and the various appendages acquired by males throughout the various orders below man, and which, so far as they themselves are concerned, serve no other useful purpose than to aid them in securing the favors of the females, have by the latter been turned to account in the processes of reproduction. The female made the male beautiful *that she might endure his caresses.*

The italics are mine. From this the learned doctor proceeds to argue that the male is little more then a chronic seducer, that his whole life is devoted to overcoming the reluctance of the coquettish and æsthetic female. In her own words: "Regarding males, outside of the instinct for self-preservation, which, by the way, is often overshadowed by their great sexual eagerness, no discriminating characters have been acquired and transmitted, *other than those which have been the result of passion,* namely, pugnacity and perseverence." Again the italics are mine. Well, what have we here? Merely the old, old delusion of masculine enterprise in amour, translated into quasi-scientific language—the Don Juan complex in a fresh bib and tucker. Dr. Gamble, of course, is speaking of the lower animals in the time of Noah. Now apply her theory to man today. Which sex actually does the primping and parading? Which runs to "beautiful coloring," sartorial, hirsute, facial? Which encases itself in gauds which "serve no other useful purpose than to aid in securing the favors" of the other sex? I leave the verdict to the jury. The more convincingly the ingenious doctor proves that the primeval mud-hens and she-mackerel had to be anesthetized with spectacular decorations in order to "endure the caresses" of their beaux, the more she supports the Shavian thesis that, in the human society of today, the principal business of women is to snare and conquer men.

In other words, her argument turns upon and devours itself. Carried literally to its last implication, it holds that women are all Donna Juanitas, and that, if they put off their millinery and cosmetics, men could not "endure their caresses."

To be sure, Dr. Gamble by no means draws this conclusion herself. On the contrary, she holds that the women of today are still victims of masculine rascality in amour, and that the coming millennium will set them free. But she can only reach this notion by admitting a contradiction into her chain of reasoning. On the one hand, she argues that splendor of attire is a bait to overcome the reluctance of the opposite sex, and on the other hand, at least by fair inference, she holds that it is not. My own inclination is toward her first position. It is supported, in the field of animal behavior, by the almost unanimous evidence of zoologists. It is supported, in the field of human behavior, by a large body of observation and experience. Shaw, as usual, did no more than state a platitude in scandalous terms—a trick that I have often exposed, and that I constantly employ myself (*e.g.*, in the present essay). If the thing had to wait for overtures from the male side, the business of marriage would blow up. Not one man in twenty makes any net gain by marriage; he may gain something, true enough, but he loses more. All the real profit is on the dexter side—and that is why all women, absolutely without exception, are eager to be married as soon as possible, and assiduous in attracting masculine attention, and pertinacious in trying to convert it into surrender. A normal man gives very little thought to marriage. He may roll an eye toward a likely cutie now and then, but in the main he devotes himself to other and more agreeable concerns. But a woman, unless she be downright insane, thinks about it incessantly. She never so much as buys a pair of shoes or has a tooth plugged without considering, in the back of her mind, the probable effect upon some unsuspecting and God-forsaken candidate for her "reluctant" affections. It is from the entirely theoretical pursuit of this enormously shy and unwilling victim that she now bawls for deliverance. This is the truth in the "sex-freedom" babble.

§3

Both Dr. Gamble and Dr. Thompson appear to be convinced that marriage, at least in its present form, bears harshly upon women. The former says flatly that "the institution of marriage, as it now exists, will disappear"; the latter indulges himself in vague rumble-bumble about "an equitable partnership-contract with man, which will enable woman to fulfill her duty to the race without yielding up her equally cogent duty to herself." What both have in mind is this: that the marriage of tomorrow will offer even greater advantages to women than the marriage of today. With the highest respect, this seems to me to be folderol. The truth, as I apprehend it after 27 years of unremitting study, is that tomorrow will see a determined masculine revolt against the intolerable conditions of today—conditions which steadily impose an increased burden of duties upon the husband and as steadily take away his rights. A century ago the husband, by American law, was the head of the family firm. He had authority over the purse-strings, over the children, and even over the wife. He could enforce his mandates by appropriate punishments, including the corporal. His autonomy and self-respect were carefully guarded by legislation. Consider his changed position today. Today by the laws of most American states, laws passed, in most cases, by sentimental orgy—all of his old rights have been converted into duties. He no longer has any control over his wife's property; she may devote its income to the family or she may squander that income upon her own follies, and he can do nothing. She has equal authority in regulating and disposing of the children, and, in the case of infants, more than he. There is no law compelling her to do her share of the family labor: she may spend her whole time in moving picture parlors an she will. She cannot be forced to perpetuate the family name if she does not want to. She cannot be attacked with masculine weapons—*e. g.*, fists and firearms—when she makes an assault with feminine weapons—*e. g.*, snuffling, invective and sabotage. Finally, no lawful penalty can be visited upon her if she fails absolutely, either deliberately or through laziness, to keep the family habitat clean, the children in order and the victuals eatable.

Consider, now, the case of the husband. The instant he marries, his wife obtains a large and inalienable share of his property—in most states, one-third. He cannot dispose of it without her consent; he cannot even deprive her of it by will. She may bring up his children carelessly and idiotically, cursing them with abominable manners and poisoning their minds against him, and he has no redress. She may neglect her home, gad about all day, put uneatable food on his table, steal his small change, pry into his private papers, and lie about him to the neighbors—and he can do nothing. She may compromise his honor by indecent dressing, write letters to moving picture actors, and expose him to ridicule by joining the suffragettes—and he is helpless. But let him, for one single week, withdraw from her the means to finance these follies, let him make a single attempt to bring her to terms by cutting off her supplies—and she can hale him into court and have him sent to jail. In brief, *she* is under no legal obligation whatsoever to carry out her part of the compact made at the altar of God, whereas *he* faces instant disgrace and punishment for the slightest failure to do so.

Such is human marriage in our fair republic. Such is the position of the husband under our *lex scripta*. The sentimentality of his own sex, reinforced by the demands of the suffragettes (whose actual though secret object, as I have hitherto shown, is the chimera of a so-called single standard of morality), has reduced him to a state of vassalage unmatched in any other country of Christendom. The moment he passes his head through the hymeneal knot, he is saddled with such a body of duties forthwith. And by exactly the same process his wife acquires a body of rights and prerogatives such as no despot now on earth could venture to claim without facing assassination instanter. Is it any wonder that sane men, in the presence of these facts, refrain from marriage as eagerly as they refrain from a mule's hind leg? Is it any wonder that women find it harder and harder to get husbands, so that many of them, despairing of succeeding by seemly means, turn to costumes which expose their persons in utter indecency, or to public activities which bring them into contact with men under false pretenses, or even to downright blackmail? Let us hear from Dr. Thompson on these points. Let us have from him a clear statement of the reasons, if any, which in logic and evidence urge any free man to embrace such hazards and take on such burdens.

§4

I have spoken of the husband's inability, given a lazy or incompetent wife, to force her to perform her domestic duties with diligence and skill. This inability is by no means merely theoretical; it lies heavily upon the gizzard of four American husbands out of five. The cause thereof is to be found in the fact that the rapid accession of wifely privileges hitherto rehearsed has filled the whole sex with a sense of freedom and irresponsibility, and fixed upon it the notion that a careful discharge of its duties is, in some vague way, discreditable and degrading. Thus the neglect of them takes on the character of a definite cult, and the stray woman who attends to them faithfully is laughed at as a drudge and a numskull, just as she is denounced as a "brood sow" (I quote literally, craving absolution for the phrase) if she favors her lord with progeny. The result is, on the one hand, the infernally bad cooking of These States—cooking so unspeakably distasteful to a cultured uvula that a French hack-driver, if it were set before him, would brain his wife with his linoleum hat. The second result is the abominable upbringing of American children, making cads and snobs of them. And the third (assuming three hands) is the general chaos and prodigality of American house-keeping, whereby the luxuries of life are put above its comforts, and waste is so lavish that a foreign expert, Dr. Hoover, has had to be imported to put it down.

All this, of course, is proof of the emancipation of the American woman. She has cast off the bonds which bind her sister of Europe, Asia, Africa and Oceania. Free from any obligation to squander her talents upon the ease and alimentation of her husband, and protected by the new laws in her liberty, she can devote her time to more stimulating business, *e. g.*, to shopping, politics and the uplift. Or, in time of war, to those bogus charities which cripple the army and get her picture into the papers. Meanwhile, her husband pursues his old round in the treadmill. If he cuts off her money, she can have him jailed for non-support. If he flees from her, she can jam him into the alimony club. If, exasperated, he attempts to correct her with the birch, he is good for a year in a reformatory. If, fearing to raise criminals, he takes his children to some place of safety, she can bring the catchpolls down upon him, have him slandered in the yellow press, and maybe get him put under bonds. And if, seeking a brief and healing respite from these horrors, he is lured into some imprudence by another woman, he can be given five years under the Mann act. . . .

For woes much lighter than these, the late Job von Uz, as we learn by Holy Writ, was advised to curse God and die.

§5

It is my sincere hope that nothing I have here exhibited will be mistaken by the nobility and gentry for moral indignation. No such feeling, in truth, is in my heart. Moral judgments, as old Friedrich used to say, are foreign to my nature. Setting aside the vast herd which shows no definable character at all, it seems to me that the minority distinguished by what is commonly regarded as an excess of sin is very much more admirable than the minority distinguished by an excess of virtue. My experience of the world has taught me that the average bartender is a far better fellow than the average prohibitionist, and that the average Elk is better than the average Swedenborgian, and that the average bordello piano-player is a decenter man than the average vice crusader. In the same way I am convinced that the average American woman, whatever her deficiencies, is greatly superior to the average American man. The very ease with which she bamboozles and victimizes him, in truth, is the clearest of proofs of her superiority. She has got him under her thumb because she is more enterprising than he is, and more courageous, and, above all, more intelligent. She is, at worst, an admirably cool-headed, sagacious and unsentimental creature; he is, at best, a mushhead and a stick.

The superior intelligence of women, and particularly of American women, must be obvious, indeed, to every impartial observer. They did not obtain their present high immunities as a free gift, but only after a long and bitter fight, and in that fight they exhibited forensic and tactical talents of a truly admirable order. Why they are so intelligent is a question that I discussed in the April number of this favorite family galaxy. For the present, suffice it to predict confidently that their possession of the quality will shortly get them the vote, and to say that I rejoice at the prospect, despite my sardonic view of the more ferocious species of suffragette. The majority of women are anything but suffragettes. The mere statement of the suffragette platform, and particularly of the hopes embodied in it, is enough to get them to laughing. A normal woman no more believes in democracy in the nation than she believes in democracy at the domestic hearth. She is far above all such man-made fallacies and sentimentalities. And once she has the franchise and becomes at ease in its use she will prove what I say. That is to say, her first great project of reform will be the recognition in law of the plain fact that democracy is unsound, unworkable and a nuisance. She will advocate, not the further extension of the ballot to children, criminals, the insane and horned cattle, but its gradual restriction to the small minority that is authentically human—say six women to one man. Thus, out of her sapience, she will make democracy safe for the world.

The curse of man is sentimentality. He is forever embracing delusions, and each new one is worse than all those that have gone before. But where is the delusion that women cherish? Who will draw up a list of things, believed by them, that are not true? (I allude here, of course, to genuine women, not to suffragettes and other such riff-raff, who are simply women with the defective intelligence of men.) As for me, I should not like to undertake such a list. I know of nothing, in fact, that properly belongs to it. Women, as a class, believe in none of the preposterous rights, duties and pious obligations that men are forever gabbling about. They distrust all haruspices and mes-

[*More of this anon*]

Wall-Paper

By Owen Hatteras

I

Mike Windle, like most married men, regarded the wife of his bosom as he did the wall-paper of his room—a thing to be favored with an occasional scrutiny and a vague speculation as to whether it would be worth while changing it. Like most married men his love for her was an inexplicable memory. At times, when in the throes of a rare philosophic mood, Mike was wont to look at her, to observe himself and to ponder how in the name of the multitude of protecting Gods he had ever been juvenile enough to mistake the fleeting, temporary, vague and ridiculous attraction the lady had exercised over him for a grand and eternal passion.

Mike was an author and associate editor of a popular magazine. He considered himself intelligent, cultured and sane, and what is more, he was. At such moments of cruel introspection as mentioned, he became poignantly aware of the fact that he had been tricked—cheated out of some vague heritage of ecstacy by an aberration of his intelligence, a lapse of his culture, an eclipse of his sanity, all of which had occurred when he was twenty-four, and had proposed to Clara Corky, only child of Bill Corky, a coffee salesman who played cribbage every Sunday evening with the elder Wimble. This was a matter of eight years ago.

In the light of developments the strange unfathomable mood which had inspired him to propose matrimony to Bill Corky's child, to protest to her on bended knee that she was the indispensable light of his suffering life, to seek out Bill Corky and argue, expostulate, threaten, cajole him into agreeing to yield up the treasure of his house and to bless them in their union—in the garish illumination of reason, culture and sanity which succeeded the marriage, the dreadful, the inexplicable, impulse seemed to Mike to have been the aboriginal workings of a mind and soul other than his. As time, that great healer, went its dumb way such cogitations grew less frequent with Mike. He lapsed into a

Smart Set 53, No. 3 (November 1917): 121–26.

state of amiable calm, performing his labors, composing his fables for the magazines, immersing himself in literatures of the past and of the moment.

Like most married men he was unable to sustain any sort of conversation with his wife for over five minutes, except during those ephemeral quarrels which agitate the serenity of the most smoothly routined lives. His ideas, his aspirations, his little daily dreamings he kept unconsciously to himself.

Thus for eight years he had lived in that state of uncommunicative and monotonous intimacy which is regarded as one of the cardinal glories of society.

Toward the end of the eighth year, however, the habit of meditation began to return to Mike Wimble, the old habit of lying awake nights, looking at the dark ceiling and wondering what there was to life, and why the devil he should be doomed because of a slip of the tongue and an eclipse of sanity eight years ago to spend the rest of his days harnessed to a creature in whom he had no interest, for whom he had no affection, with whom he had nothing whatsoever under the entire broad heavens in common.

Such thoughts naturally frightened Mike, and caused him to feel sad and remorseful, to bring home boxes of candy, to brighten up at the following breakfast table and expound the meaning of some item in the morning papers.

But once started the old habit grew. His faculty for pounding out fables seemed to be on the wane, his reputation as a fictioneer gradually came to a standstill and with it he became aware that his name had evolved into one of those syndicate nobodies fit only to capture the vacuous attention of people who ride on trains, who wait in doctors' offices, who tire of playing solitaire.

In the beginning of the ninth year, Mike Wimble's meditations no longer frightened him. His imagination, no longer employed in the evolution of tales, turned itself upon his own life with fascinating results. An illusion overcame him that without Mrs. Wimble life would unfold like some rare exotic. This was succeeded by a second notion that somewhere at large and mournful in the land there waited for him a creature intended by the considerate Gods for his happiness, a lady of astonishing loveliness, of infatuating brilliance, intelligent, cultured, rhapsodic—in short a mate for his soul.

Like most married men Mike began to dream of this suppositious person, to fashion her image in his mind, to indulge in piquant fancies. With her he sailed out upon the purple seas to far countries, toured strange places, walked with her over ground made sacred by the past. The idea grew, and, growing, grew less vague, became more real.

Together they passed through ennobling adventures. Sometimes Mike would have her commit suicide because of love for him, sometimes it would be a suicide pact consummated in a lyric and heroic manner. Often they traveled the mystical deserts the names of which Mike remembered from early geography readings. Often they sat beneath some luxurious tree singing each others' praises, understanding each other, in accord with each others' very pulse beats. Because of his somewhat more than average imagination Mike's dream world, which he shared with the woman he had missed, assumed more intricate proportions than that of the average married man.

Needless to say, Mrs. Wimble found life full of charm and happiness. She loved her husband, doted on his presence, fancied their existence together to be the Utopian blessedness which comes only to the most fortunate and gifted of law-abiding moral citizens. It is doubtful whether a single fear had ever intruded itself in her heart, a single qualm, quiver, foreboding.

Serene in her domestic ambitions, Mrs. Wimble regarded herself as an intelligent, cultured and sane woman who had earned the right to happiness by an unselfish devotion to her husband's weal, a shrewd knowledge of cookery and a cunning way with the tradesmen of the neighborhood.

She considered Mike, her husband, a surpassingly clever person, kept his books in good order, dusted his bookcases faithfully, read his printed fables with a delicious sense of pride (although she sometimes contented herself with merely glancing at the opening paragraphs) and looked forward to a docile, unruffled continuance of all that had been.

Mike was coming home from his office one afternoon in May in the ninth year of his married life, thirty-three years from the day of his birth, when his roving, aimless eye alighted upon a woman who wore a yellow hat, a green striped skirt, a white shirtwaist, a pair of brown oxfords with brown silk stockings to match. The woman's face revealed her to be passed her twenties, amiable, intelligent, cultured, sane. Further, there was a trim shapeliness about her. It was a windy day and just as Mike was passing her (he was at the moment wrapped in visioning himself and his phantom soulmate gliding down some jungle river) her hat blew off and rolled to Mike's feet. Whereupon Mike picked it up and handed it to her. These are the facts, uncolored, simple.

"Thank you, so much," the lady said, reaching forth for the hat.

"'sall right," Mike made answer, and in handing over the thing it blew away again.

There was nothing for him to do but give chase.

After a short pursuit he overtook the fleeing bonnet, returned with it again to the amused and somewhat chagrined owner and said,

"Seems to be a rather temperamental hat."

"Thank you, so much," the lady made answer.

An idea struck her, an uncalculating, more or less spontaneous idea—such as it was.

"I ought to have a regular hat chaser along when I go walking," she added.

It being spring, Mike's heart executed a great, an epoch-making leap. Of such remarks are destinies made and unmade.

Blushing, blinded, overcome with confusion, Mike yet managed to stammer out,

"Won't I do? I'm a—an accomplished hat chaser."

II

Thus it began, a delicate curbstone idyll on a spring afternoon, a thing to flick the emotions and no more. It would have ended with the first walk toward the lady's home—she lived five blocks from Mike's domicile—if not for another accidental meeting in a street car returning from work two days later.

During this ride Mike blossomed forth, giving vent to eight years of pent-up epigrams, repeating to the lady of the yellow hat a goodly part of the fascinating conversations he was wont to conduct with the mate of his imaginings.

For her part, the lady confided that her name was Mrs. Higgins, opened her mouth and gurgled with delight to learn that Mike was none other than Michael Wimble, author of the "perfectly wonderful Simon stories," and permitted her new friend to escort her again to her home.

From this point the idyll progressed and expanded. It required hardly a week for Mike to appreciate that the all indulgent gods had finally answered his prayers, that they had sent to him the queen of his dreams, the fairy of his yearnings. Their meetings increased, included a rendezvous at a matinée, a debauch at a soda fountain, a stroll in a park.

During the first of it Mrs. Higgins exhibited a timorous reluctance. She spoke, almost defensively of Jim Higgins, her husband, of his qualities, his kindness. She had been married seven years, their home had always been her shrine.

But under the spell of Mike's eloquence, his drolleries, his ecstasies Mrs. Higgins underwent the fatal change. Her words, at first, calm, meaningless, began to fashion themselves into whimsical repartee. Her manner, at first polite, moral, began to unfold itself into appealing kittenish ardors. Together they toured the Art Institute, paused in front of picture stores, of Japanese shops in Michigan avenue. Mike loaned her books and after her reading of them they would foregather in the park already made familiar to them and discuss with careful, with spontaneous phrases the meanings of life, the vistas of existence.

Mrs. Higgins and the lady of Mike Wimble's dreams gradually became one. Those delicate delights he had known in gliding down imaginary jungle rivers, committing imaginary suicides, touring imaginary deserts were completely effaced. In their place were the more material enthusiasms which these rendezvous with Mrs. Higgins furnished him, the more tangible joys of conversing in the flesh with the phantom of his former yearnings. If there were not the jungle, the desert, the ruins of ancient Greece, there were, on the other hand, the smile which lighted the familiar park, the eyes which illumined the familiar sun, the voice which sweetened the familiar noises of his life.

The first month resulted in no climaxes. Mike's home life progressed as serenely as ever, more so, perhaps, owing to the heightened interest which his adventure inspired in him towards his general surroundings.

For the first time since he came into the grip of that strange unfathomable mood nine years ago which had betrayed him into proposing matrimony to Clara Corky, Mike felt that delicious activity of the heart at the thought or sight of a woman which goes by the name of love.

But here the comparison ended, in his mind. Here the mood of nine years ago and the exultant disturbance of his senses today parted company. That had been a lapse, an eclipse, a disorder common to unthinking, unselective youth. This was a rhapsodic excitement born of the brain, the soul, the heart as well as the body. In Mrs. Higgins, Mrs. Belle Higgins her full name was, Mike perceived that there were qualities to call forth the finest in a man, to unleash his very soul.

No longer did he lie staring at the darkened ceiling pondering the why and wherefore of a lugubrious existence. No longer the meditations upon the wasteful futility of his days. His dreams formed themselves about the yellow head of Mrs. Higgins, inspired themselves by the blue eyes of that lady.

Already the first delicate tangible joys of their communion were exhausted and Mike's imagination was beginning to leap into mystic futures, to vault into splendid fancies. His appetite began to fail him, his mind to grow disordered. He began to live in dreams. He began to see that Mrs. Higgins was the indispensable light in his suffering life, that without her all—all was darkness.

When these perceptions first overtook him Mike reacted with a mixture of emotions. Clara Corky Wimble loomed before him, a wall of habit, a fortress of insurmountable convention. But gradually Clara Corky vanished, became mist.

And it was at this point in the second month of his communion with Mrs. Higgins that Mike approached the subject in her presence. Mrs. Higgins experienced a spasm of fear at the sound of his passionate outline of events as they might be. She shuddered, swallowed. hard, trembled in every fibre of her being and clung to his hand in a thoroughly bewildered and desperate manner.

They were sitting in the park hidden from view by the freshly leafed trees and shrubbery.

"Belle," he began, "don't you see. I need you. You need me. We are one. With you, good God, I could write such things as I once dreamed of writing. It is wrong, I admit. A sin, from one point of view. But—but—is it right for us to remain as we are, to live a lie, to—to go on in this terrible humdrum way and cheat ourselves of this wonderful thing? Oh, Belle, I love you."

He seized her other hand and crushed it. He eyed her lips and finally kissed them.

Mrs. Higgins became red, red from her hair to her toes. Shame, wonder, confusion and a peculiarly intruding emotion fell upon her.

"Oh, Michael," she whispered. "I can't . . . I just . . ."

Here Mike interrupted. He started anew. He pointed out to her such fascinating arguments as that she had been in his dreams from the first. He made it clear that he had known her in his soul from the earliest days of his youth.

"My mate," he cried, "my mate! Destined for me! Given to me! I will not permit you to pass out of my life, to leave me again in—in Hell!"

III

They arranged for another meeting and further discussion on the following day.

Mike returned to his home treading a fine high strata of air. Through his brain the events of the day whirled in radiant confusion. His heart, expanded almost to a bursting point, could barely contain its divine secret. He eyed Clara Corky Wimble with something approaching tenderness, and by dint of careful concentration, prevented himself from giving some fatal hint of what was brewing.

Mrs. Higgins came to him now wreathed in new splendors. Each gesture, each grimace of hers, each word, each everything appeared to him in a transfiguring light, as the saying goes. High above all women she loomed, in a Parnassian isolation, in a pillar of fire, in a cloud of gold. And he, Mike Wimble, loomed beside her, mate of her soul, companion of her heart, master and slave, one and inseparable, united forever.

They foregathered as appointed on the following day. They spoke to each other in low, vibrant tones. They held hands. Mrs. Higgins, behaving altogether like some unbalanced creature, clung to her adorer, wept, sighed, inquired, pleaded, kissed, choked, burbled, laughed, and to make it more strange, spoke at abrupt intervals of Jim, her husband of seven years whom she was deserting. True, he had always neglected her. She perceived this now. True, he had seldom addressed more than ten words at dinner to her. She saw this, too. But, what would he say, feel, do?

Mike answered all her timorous inquiries. Then came the business of practical arrangings. Again Mike rose to the occasion, reeling off train schedules, transportation statistics.

"When?" suddenly asked Mrs. Higgins.

They became silent.

Finally Mike husked,

"Tomorrow."

They parted. On the way home Mrs. Higgins decided not to elope. On the way home Mrs. Higgins perceived that it wasn't in her to elope, that she had been under the spell of a glittering, fascinating personality. On the way home Mike Wimble began to shudder. On the way home Mike Wimble decided eloping was impossible. On the way home Mike Wimble perceived that he had been under the influence of a glittering, fascinating personality.

Inwardly, Mike Wimble wept. Being intelligent, cultured, sane, he perceived further that he was not fitted for his destiny, that because of an inherent cowardice, a miserable habitual fear of Mrs. Clara Corky and all she stood for, he would cheat himself out of a heritage that was his. His emotions left him weak and ill. He repaired to his room. Clara Corky attended him with beakers containing physic, with powders pronounced infallible as relievers of headaches. But for his soul she brought him naught, naught but the kindly, patient smile which had taken on for him the qualities of a nightmare of the commonplace during nine years.

Mike Wimble hied him to no train depot the following day. He lay in bed, tossing, tossing, in almost actual pain, clinging to the hand of Clara Corky. A fever came upon him and finally the indulgent and comprehending gods sent him sleep. He awoke recovered, peculiarly recovered. At the breakfast table he expounded earnestly on the meaning of an item in the papers. And as he left his home he vowed to himself he would make amends—he would return with a box of candy.

As for Mrs. Belle Higgins, what was Mike's fate was in a measure hers. Jim Higgins came home the evening of the big pact to find the wife of his bosom strangely disturbed. He eyed her casually. He wondered what in Hell ailed her—if anything could possibly ail such a tor-pid, humdrum creature as was Mrs. Higgins.

Jim Higgins, like most married men, regarded the wife of his bos-om as he did the wall paper of his room, things to be favored with an occasional scrutiny and a vague speculation as to whether it would be worth while changing them. Like most married men his love for her was an inexplicable memory.

At times when in the throes of a rare philosophic mood Jim was wont to look at her, to observe himself, and to ponder how in the name of the multitude of protecting gods he had ever been juvenile enough to mistake the fleeting, temporary, vague and ridiculous attrac-tions the lady had exercised over him for a grand and eternal passion.

Jim was a salesman for a postcard firm. He considered himself in-telligent, cultured and sane, and what is more, he was! At such mo-ments of cruel introspection as mentioned, he became poignantly aware of the fact that he had been tricked, cheated out of some vague heritage of beauty by an aberration of his intelligence, a lapse of his culture, an eclipse of his sanity, all of which had occurred when he was twenty-three and had proposed to Belle Jolson, only child of Sam Jol-son, a cabinet-maker who played pinochle every Sunday evening with the elder Higgins. . . .

Whoopers and Twitterers

I

Compared to prose, what is all poetry save a kind of nonsense?—*Karl Marx.*

Of the poetry chuted into my cellars since our last bout with the bards, that of James Oppenheim strikes me as the fairest and best, and that of Louis Untermeyer as the next best, and that of Edgar Lee Masters as the next best, and that of Ezra Pound as the next best, and that of Orrick Johns as the next best, and that of—

But let so much be considered the reading of the minutes. Oppenheim enters two books, "The Book of Self" (*Knopf*) and "War and Laughter" (*Century*), and both are full of a furious and insistent earnestness, a gaudy and prodigious gusto, the driving force of genuine passion. It is not the sort of poetry that, personally, I adore. My taste is for more delicate things—to be honest, for more artificial things. I like a frail but perfectly articulated stanza, a sonnet wrought like ivory, a song full of glowing nouns, verbs, adjectives, adverbs, pronouns, conjunctions, prepositions and participles, but without too much sense in it. Poetry, to me, has but two meanings. On the one hand it is a magical escape from the soddenness of metabolism and the class war, and on the other hand it is a subtle, very difficult, and hence very charming art, like writing fugues or mixing mayonnaise. I do not go to poets to be taught anything, or to be heated up, or to be made reflective or indignant, but to be soothed and caressed, to be lulled with sweet sounds, to be wooed into forgetfulness, to be tickled under the chin. My favorite poem is Lizette Woodworth Reese's "Tears," which, as a statement of fact, seems to me to be as idiotic as the Book of Revelation. The poetry I regard least is such stuff as that of Matthew Arnold, which argues and illuminates. I dislike poetry of intellectual content as much as I dislike women of intellectual content, and for the same reason.

But I am employed by this great family magazine, not as a voluptuary, but (once a year, at all events) as a reviewer of the poets, and this job requires me to put away mere pleasure-seeking for a wider experimentation. The result of that effort, as I say, is the conviction that

Smart Set 53, No. 3 (November 1917): 138–44.

Oppenheim, of the current boiling, is by far the most worthy of applause. He offends my pruderies by stripping off his draperies in his poems and searching himself horribly with flashlight, scalpel and X-ray, and still more by exposing, not only the corporeal man, but the fearsome and mysterious psyche within; but he does it all with so persuasive an eloquence, so fine a dignity, so delicate a feeling for the sough and burble of words, that he overcomes my objections before I can voice them, and his dithyrambs reach my midriff in spite of my guard. It is, in brief, the skill that was in old Walt Whitman—the skill to make something grand and stately out of embarrassing confidences, soapbox philosophizing, the bald recital of facts. I don't like old Walt, but somehow he always fetches me. I could bring in an indictment of Oppenheim, but somehow he leaves me with the impression that I have heard music, and seen a panorama full of color, and smelt the smell of life. . . . Superficially, he seems to fall among the makers of *vers libre,* but that seeming is only seeming. The *vers librists* seek merely to experiment in hues and rhythms; Oppenheim has more sober and more interesting business. He is one of the few Americans of today whose originality is more than a tawdry endeavor to be different. . . . Nevertheless, the only one of his *opera* that I shall paste in my Bible is not a poem at all, but this little "Portrait of an Investigator of Vice":

> His nails were perfect:
> They were well-trimmed, shining and regular:
> But under each was a spot of dark dirt.
> In those nails I saw the man.

Untermeyer is a dervish of vastly different kidney. Oppenheim carries the thing off by the sheer weight of his sincerity; he is a sort of Brahms of prosody. Untermeyer is the Richard Strauss, the enormously adept and nimble craftsman, the virtuoso *par excellence.* Of all the poets of our national stud, he is the most dexterous, the cleverest, the most daring. There is no poetical job that he will not tackle, and there is none that he can't get through in a creditable manner. Does the foreman of the composing-room roar down the tube for two sticks of *vers libre?* Then Untermeyer has at him with some *vers libre* that Richard Aldington might own without shame. Is there a call for a ballade, a sonnet, a translation from the Bavarian, a bacchanal, a song for music, a couple of lengths of blank verse, some quatrains in strict form, a madrigal, a limerick? Then Untermeyer answers the summons with something that fills the order exactly. A gigantic ease in verse seems to be in him; he sets himself impossible tasks for the sheer joy of conquering them. In "These Times" (*Holt*), for example, he does a sonnet on a jewelry drummer; another on a dead horse. In ". . . And Other Poets," he essayed parodies so complex, metres so difficult, rhyme schemes so torturing, that the execution thereof took on the character of some fantastic feat of acrobatics.

But if you take this prodigious suppleness and ingenuity, this unmatchable mastery of the mere art of versifying, for no more than a hollow trick, then you are very much in error, for Untermeyer is not only the arch rhymster of the nation but also one of its most respectable poets, and in his latest book, as in "First Love" and in "Challenge," you will find abundant proof of it—proof here dished up in the form of a simple and beautiful song, and there in the form of a sonorous sonnet, and there again as a series of dithyrambs almost in the manner of Oppenheim. I give you "To the Child of a Revolutionist," the song in "Magic," "A Man" and "Moses on Sinai"; each suave and facile, each a clever thing, but each a good deal more. Facility alone, in truth, would not suffice for the concoction of such pieces; the more aptly they were done, the emptier they would seem. What Untermeyer gets into them, and into all of his serious verse, is a passionate exultation in the presence of beauty—a sort of æsthetic drunkenness, odious to the right-thinking, but not specifically forbidden by the police. This is the explanation of all his bawling against orthodoxy, which he himself often mistakes for moral indignation. He is really no reformer, even in poetry; he is merely one privy to the taste of Greek and Sinaian grapes, and hence gagged by the national buttermilk and coca-cola. . . . But despite the spiritual vine-leaves, he remains a bit cerebral and self-conscious: it is his broken leg. A true poet must be moony and unintelligent; the imagists disproved imagism when they began to prove it. I should like to see a book *on* poetry by this Untermeyer. But let him put away politeness when he writes it, and avoid cant; let him remember that an honest critic can never be a gentleman. Was Poe?

Masters, like Oppenheim, insists upon filling his compositions with ideas; he is, one may say, a programme poet. His poems are not so much exultations as exhortations, not so much rhapsodies as pronunciamentos. He is full of advice, persuasion, remonstrance, indignation; he likes to revile things, particularly things that the average numskull Methodist and democrat believes in. It is, perhaps, the easiest way to attract attention in the United States, provided one keeps within the bounds of the national superstition. That is to say, one must go so far but no further; one may dispute what it is a mere article of respectability to believe, but one must never dispute what it is an article of patriotism and virtue to believe. The Samuel Butler complex. The emancipated clergyman complex. Heterodoxy as a form of naughtiness. One finds it in such a piece as "Come, Republic." Here the republic is denounced for various errors and rascalities, but always on the ground that it is thus recreant to a lofty mission, to wit, to serve as model to the more backward nations, to "be a ruler in the world." So far, so good. That sort of belaboring is plainly merely flattery, and none too delicate. To dispute any such mission, to flout this alleged function and duty—in brief, to admit that, after all, there may be finer civilizations than the Yiddo-Presbyterian—this would get the bard a walloping, and the New York *Times* would never be hymning him as "the only poet with true Americanism (*i. e.,* department-store Potash-and-Perlmutterism) in his bones."

But though Masters is thus a bogus prophet, and, to me, at least, a poet only by courtesy, he possesses one faculty that is worth a great deal more than the gift of prophecy, and even more than the talent for making songs, and that is the faculty of being interesting, the faculty of holding the eye. There are bad poems in "The Great Valley" (*Macmillan*) and there are poems that are not poems at all, but there is nothing stupid, nothing tedious, nothing without its moments. That fact, it seems to me, explains Masters' great vogue. He is a thoughtful and in-genious man, a capital companion, a fellow who intrigues the atten-tion. In the midst of conventional poll-parrotting, he at least tries to do the thing in a new way—to deal with genuine people, to speak out his mind. Another poet who attempts that same thing is Conrad Aiken: his "The Jig of Forslin" (*Four Seas*) is something quite new: an effort to pump up poetry with the argon of the Freudian psychology. Un-luckily, this effort interests me only academically; I can't get into the swing of it. Politics in poetry is bad enough; when it comes to the sub-conscious and the Oedipus complex I retire to the woods. Oppenheim dallies with that dynamite too, but he does not embrace it as affection-ately as Aiken. The latter piles up complexes until there arises a sort of complex complex. This lifts the thing beyond my jurisdiction and comprehension. I have found "The Jig of Forslin" very muggy reading.

Pound and Eunice Tietjens, the former in "Lustra" (*Mathews*) and the latter in "Profiles from China" (*Seymour*), offer poetical evidence of that belated discovery of the Chinese spirit which has already had its influence in decoration. The Japs came first in Europe. They not only worked a revolution in actual painting; they also sent ripples through all the other arts, including poetry. That enchantment had its naif touches; the simian Nipponese were gravely accepted as the prophets of a new æsthetic. More sober inquiry has revealed the fact that they are really no more than facile imitators of the elder, lordier and far more honest art of China. The Japs, in fact, originate nothing; they are simply clever makers of deceptive shoddy. Their whole literature is Chinese; their art is Chinese in decay; their science is third-rate German; their politics is Italian; their philosophy is Oriental determinism tempered by English cant. If you would sense the nobler soul of the Chinaman read Herbert A. Giles' "History of Chinese Literature," one of the most charming books ever written by a college professor. Or go through the notes of the late Ernest Fenolossa, lately put together by Pound. Pound himself gets something of the true Chinese simplicity, the Chinese skill at image-making, the Chinese dignity and delicacy, into his transcriptions. And Mrs. Tietjens, though she never drops the Caucasian robe, nor even that of the frank tourist, yet gives us a glimpse of the unfathomable romance and mystery of old China in her disorderly pieces. Both poets war upon the commonplace, the obvious, the stale. Both achieve something that was worth attempting.

As for Johns, his "Asphalt and Other Poems" (*Knopf*) contains some of the worst verse of the year, and some of the best. It would be difficult, within the limits of seemly invective, to do justice to the cheapness, the vacuity, the downright imbecility of his poems in dialect. They are, in fact, truly atrocious—Chimmie Fadden in terms of a sick Kipling. But turn over! Specifically, turn to "The Melody"—a charming melody indeed. Or to "The Last Poet." Or to "The Answer." "Be clear! Be clear!" said Ivan Turgeniev. "But not too clear!" There is in these poems a shimmering and mystical vagueness, a hint of something beyond. They are not propositions in this or that; they are simply beautiful things.

II

If I had my way, I would give every poet a punch in the kishgish.—*Ulysses S. Grant.*

Come various tomes by cried-up poets whose sweetest burblings leave me cold. For example, Irene Rutherford McLeod, author of "Swords for a Life" (*Huebsch*). I find, in a sort of appendix to the book, lavish encomiums by O. W. Firkins, William S. Braithwaite, the New York *Times,* the *Athenæum* and other such authorities, but all that I can find in the book itself is some hollow stuff in the finishing-school manner—in brief, the sort of stuff every literate flapper writes when she falls in love with her first moving-picture actor. Turn to a pretentious piece called "Beethoven." What could be more machine-made, more obvious? This Mlle. McLeod, I suspect, is one of the bogus geniuses that English publishers are forever foisting upon American blockheads. Another is Sarojini Naidu, a Hindu lady, author of "The Broken Wing" (*Lane*). Her hard, strained stanzas take one back to the days of *Godey's Lady's Book.* Yet another is William H. Davies, a hobo Baudelaire discovered by the practical joker, Bernard Shaw. He says that his best poems are in "Collected Poems" (*Knopf*). Davies, to be sure, is a far more skillful versifier than the Naidu or the McLeod, but to call him "divinely gifted" and to compare him to Herrick—all that is plain poppycock. We have at least twenty poets in the United States who are vastly better than any of these imported prodigies.

Nor am I lifted up more than a millimetre or two by the 1917 volume of ""Some Imagist Poets" (*Houghton*) . As usual, the best work in the book is by Richard Aldington, by long odds the most talented of the imagists. John Gould Fletcher says the inevitable things about Lincoln, and assembles all the rubber-stamps of mad poetry—*e. g.,* flying clouds, wind-blown branches, swirling leaves, brown stubble, strangling cry—in a dull piece called "Armies." Amy Lowell, a year or two behind the procession, dallies with the Japanese. F. S. Flint and D. H. Lawrence begin their lines with small letters—and let that dazzling heresy serve in place of inspiration. Lawrence, beside contributing to "Some Imagist Poets," prints a volume of his own, to wit, "Amores" (*Huebsch*). I select one lush and lovely line:

> And the snore of the night in my ear.

Various other poets merely repeat themselves tiresomely. In "Harvest Moon" (*Houghton*) Josephine Preston Peabody offers one very excellent poem, "Seed-Time." For the rest, she does little more than offer evidences of the final collapse of a talent that was never very sturdy. "Livelihood," by Wilfrid Wilson Gibson (*Macmillan*), is simply a rechewing of cuds. Gibson, like many other current poets, writes far too much. Having achieved success with a new trick in poetry, he seems to be convinced that it can be done over and over again. The result is a very dull book. As for "Spectra," by Emanuel Morgan and Anne Knish (*Kennerley*), I find it nothing save a reboiling of the bones of Gertrude Stein, with music by the Greenwich Village *Stadtkapelle* of cigar-box ukaleles. With paper so expensive, it is astonishing that such drivel gets into print.

Far better stuff is offered by Scudder Middleton in "Streets and Faces" (*Little-Brown*); Morris Gilbert in "A Book of Verse" (*Privately printed*); Clement Wood in "Glad of Earth" (*Gomme*); Samuel Hoffenstein in "Life Sings a Song" (*Wilmarth*), Mary MacMillan in "The Little Golden Fountain" (*Stewart*); Pitts Sanborn in "Vie de Bordeaux" (*Brown*), and Ruth Comfort Mitchell in "The Night Court" (*Century*)—all of them, I believe, first books. Most of these poets have contributed to this favorite periodical. Miss MacMillan's "The Little Golden Fountain," a very lovely piece of free verse, first appeared herein. She opens her book with it, and adds another excellent poem, "Concerning Love," but she then spoils the feast by throwing in a lot of commonplace stuff, devoid of ideas and showing such banal rhymes as *jewels rare—colors fair*. Mrs. Mitchell also mixes the good and the bad. "The Night Court" is not a poem at all, and neither is "A Mountain Mummer." But pretty things go with them. Hoffenstein, I suspect, has a genuine poet in him, though he is yet somewhat awkward. In the case of Middleton there can be little doubt: he is already firmly on his legs. Wood, too, shows much promise, and so does Sanborn. Gilbert, a young fellow, prints some jejune stuff, but with it four or five poems of excellent quality. He has, moreover, a touch of humor: a rare quality in poets under sixty.

I see little else to interest you. William Rose Benét misses his mark in "The Great White Wall" (*Yale*). The thing needed sonority, and sonority is precisely what it hasn't got. Berton Braley in "Things as They Are" (*Doran*) and H. Stanley Haskins in "Cat's Cradle" (*Sherman*) stop at newspaper verse. Donald Evans in "Nine Poems from a Valetudinarian" (*Brown*) reins in his once-wild steed, and so drops out of the procession. In "Dust of Stars," by Danford Barney (*Lane*); "Californians," by Robinson Jeffers (*Macmillan*); "The Dance of Youth," by Julia Cooley (*Sherman*); "A Hidden Well," by Louis How (*Sherman*); "Rider of the Stars," by H. H. Knibbs (*Houghton*); "The Road of Everywhere," by Glenn Ward Dresbach (*Badger*), and "Out Where the West Begins," by Arthur Chapman (*Houghton*), I can find nothing save sound prosody. There is little that is positively bad in these books, but neither is there anything that is noticeably good. They fill the comfortable middle ground of current verse.

III

The true poet is of the devil's party.—*William Blake.*

It is sufficient to put Louis Untermeyer's "Poems of Heinrich Heine" (*Holt*) beside any other translation of the great Jewish lyrist, new or old, partial or complete, to see at once the extraordinary merit of the work. As I have said above, this Untermeyer is a clever rhymster—and never is his cleverness so plain as when he tackles the well-nigh impossible task of translating lyrics. Blank verse? It's easy enough: various Germans have done Shakespeare superbly. The epic? Recall only Chapman. But the lyric? Ah, there something rubs! The thing is so delicate, so fragile, so much a matter of overtones, that its transfer from one language to another is a business of truly staggering difficulty. Of all our lyric poets, only Poe has been done into French beautifully, and it took a Baudelaire to achieve the miracle. . . . But though his task was thus one for the collaboration of Hercules and the Graces, Untermeyer has, time after time, done a lyric of Heine into English with the utmost deftness and felicity. Now and then, true enough, he fails ingloriously. "The Two Grenadiers" is (and was inevitably) a mess. "The Lorelei" is a boiled violet. But these routs are curiously few. More often one is arrested by the address and ingenuity with which an obstacle is waved aside. Compare the worst of these translations with the work of Marguerite Münsterberg, a very competent translator, in "A Harvest of German Verse" (*Appleton*). Compare Untermeyer's version of "Die Nordsee" with that of Howard Mumford Jones in "Heine's Poem, The North Sea" (*Open Court*). . . . And, above all, don't forget the translator's capital introduction to his 325 translations. . . .

Two English versions of the lesser poetry of the late Emile Verhaeren are offered. Charles R. Murphy turns "Les Heures d'Après Midi" into suave verse in "Afternoon" (*Lane*); F. S. Flint does a prose translation of the whole cycle in "The Love Poems of Emile Verhaeren" (*Houghton*). These pieces exhibit the defunct poet in a somewhat unfamiliar mood: the dithyrambist of force and noise here sings the joys of love—more, of middle-age love. The version of Mr. Murphy is by far the more satisfying.

IV

Il doit y avoir toujours énigme en poèsie.—*Jules Huret*.

One of the worst curses of war is the cheap and imbecile versifying that it produces. It seems impossible, in the midst of the turmoil, for the poets to keep their heads. Consider, for example, Kipling. Fifteen or twenty years ago he wrote very excellent soldier songs; perhaps the best in English. But today all he can manage is an endless series of hysterical hymns of hate—bosh so highfalutin and so discreditable to a grown man that his admirers can only pray God that the next Zeppelin fetches him. During the Spanish-American War I collected American war poetry, and at the end of hostilities had a bale of 896 specimens. In the whole lot there was but one decent poem—a brisk little ballad by Arthur Guiterman. This, it would seem, was an accident; Guiterman has written nothing of any merit since, and has lately taken to lecturing on poetry, the last resort of cashiered poets. The Civil War produced one good poem and no more. The Franco-Prussian War produced none at all, either in French or in German. The Boer War squeezed "The Dirge of Dead Sisters" out of Kipling, but that was after he had ceased making faces at the Boers. "Recessional," unless I err, came later. Moreover, it is anything but a first-rate poem.

Glance through the current offerings. In "Rhymes of a Red-Cross Man," by Robert W. Service (*Barse-Hopkins*), there is some very fair verse, but it is to actual poetry as "Poor Butterfly" is to a song by

Brahms. Such stuff does well when recited by flappers with pigtails down their backs, and no doubt it heats up the blood of the brave devils who now rush up to enlist in the commissary department, but I doubt that the bogs in the trenches set much store by it. I have personally witnessed some of these boys at their recreations in camp and field. They were not reading poetry; they were playing *Schafskopf,* shooting dice, snoring beside their little stoves, or reading such periodicals as *Le Rire* and the *Police Gazette.* Their chief desire, after the longing for peace, was for a good burlesque show, with plenty of legs and a couple of rough gas-house comedians. I heard no demands for poetry. No doubt a small crowd would have turned out to see Sir Rabindranath Tagore, perhaps mistaking him for a sleight-of-hand performer. But a hundred times as many would have turned out to see Jess Willard, or Charlie Chaplin, or the Dolly Sisters.

Service's strophes, at worst, are at least self-respecting; they are written in a manly, though highly sentimental, frame of mind. The "All's Well" of John Oxenham (*Doran*) is simply squashy—a wet sponge—a volume of slobbering. It is astonishing to hear that some of this drivel, separately printed, has had enormous circulation in England. Let us suspect the best; that is, let us assume that it was circulated gratis by the Y. M. C. A. . . . . "The Shadow," by some anonymous minnesinger (*Houghton-Mifflin*), is even worse: 47 pages of witless folderol. As for "Great War Ballads," by Brookes More (*Thrash-Lick Pub. Co.*), it is a truly horrible collection of bad ballads. "Patriotic Toasts," by Fred. Emerson Brooks (*Forbes*), strikes bottom. It is the sort of cheap and obnoxious "patriotic" cant that makes a decent man ashamed of his country.

Perhaps "Women Are People," by Alice Duer Miller (*Doran*), also belongs to the war poetry. It is made up of bellicose stanzas in favor of woman suffrage, and shows a high degree of dexterity and no little humor. I am strongly in favor of the suffragettes and their cause; its success will quickly reduce democracy to an absurdity, and so give civilization a chance. I am more in favor of it after reading the waspish dithyrambs of this nimble-witted suffragette.

V

Of all mountebanks, a poet is the most bumptious.—*A. J. Balfour.*

What remains is doggerel so labored and so stupid that it is difficult to describe it without swearing. "Saber and Song," by William Thornton Whitsett (*Published by the author*), is made up of the heavy, empty versifying of a country pedagogue; there is no more poetry in it than in Billy Sunday's hymn-book. "The Newark Anniversary Poems," with introductory platitudes by Henry Wellington Wack (*Gomme*), are all bad and some of them are almost idiotic. No more gloriously unsuccessful combat of bards has been held in centuries; the prize-winning poem, by Clement Wood, is an unconscious burlesque of the style of Vachel Lindsay, one of the busted geniuses of year before last. "Ballads of the Wine-Mad Town," by Florence Wobber (*Published by the author*), are apparently the confections of an advanced-thinking high-school girl—all about dope fiends, vampires, succubi, California red wine and other such horrors of the moving pictures. In "Elan Vital," by Helen Williston Brown (*Badger*), I can find nothing whatever—in brief, a vacuum. In "The Singer," by J. T. (*Badger*); "When Leaves Grow Old," by Egbert T. Bush (*Sherman-French*); "Mystery, or, The Lady of the Casino," by David F. Taylor (*Badger*); "The Call of Life," by Charles V. H. Roberts (*Published by the author*), and "My Soldier Boy," by Mrs. John Archibald Morison (*Badger*), there is only a harmless balderdash. "Silence and True Love," by J. Brookes More (*Thrash-Lick Pub. Co.*), is a dull metrical version of Maeterlinck's essay on silence, itself very hard going. In "The Songs of Phryne," by Mitchell S. Buck (*Brown*), we have a series of prose poems in which the mistress of Praxiteles becomes a sort of Greenwich Village radical. A truly hideous cover design in blue, yellow and green completes the offending. "Across the Threshold," by Baron Vane (*McNair*), is a collection of the posthumous compositions of a talented Pennsylvania farmhand. A florid introduction by one Charles Sydney Barrett, M.A., Ph.D., "associate professor of English literature, research professor of Chaldean literature, holder of the Golden chair of belles lettres," indicates that criticism, like poetry, is an art foreign to the Pennsylvanians. How has this three-barreled professor doctor escaped an invitation to contribute to the *Nation?* Finally, there are "She Planted a Garden," by Albert L. Berry (*McClurg*), and "Songs of the Hills and Home," by Wallace Irving Coburn (*Sherman-French*)—sweet fluff, but no more poetry than I am an archbishop. . . .

This is all I can sweat through. Verse begins to sicken me. I shall bore you with no more of it for at least a year.

Addenda to Wilstach

By W. L. D. Bell

As appetizing as a boiled cocktail.

As flabbergasting as the amorous glance of a lady embalmer.

As naughty as a sister-in-law's kiss behind the door.

As depraved as the boy who made dominoes of his grandfather's femur.

As lardish as the smile of a fashionable rector.

As suffocatingly obese as Violetta dying of tuberculosis pulmonalis.

As musical as the air whistling through a maiden's teeth at the end of a long, adhesive kiss.

As heinous as the crime of J. Flavius Apprippus, who pulled his wife's incisors to make a necklace for the parlor-maid.

As fatuous as the Swedish slavey who tried to make charcoal white by scrubbing it with tooth-paste.

As well-fitting as a saddle on a cow.

Smart Set 53, No. 4 (December 1917): 108.

Critics Wild and Tame

I

The curse of criticism in America, and of literature with it, is the infernal babbling of the third-rate college professor, which is to say, of the overgrown sophomore. I am not one, of course, to deny the usefulness of the learned Ph. D. in the palace of beautiful letters, or, at all events, in the ante-chambers thereof. He, too, is one of God's creatures, and he has his high utilities. It is his business, *imprimis*, to ground unwilling school-boys in the rudiments of knowledge and taste, that they may comprehend the superiority of Ralph Waldo Emerson to Old Cap Collier, and know wherein the poems of Crabbe transcend "'Only a Boy." It is his business, *secondamente*, to do the shovel and broom work of literary exploration—to count up the weak and strong endings in "Paradise Lost," to guess at the meaning of the typographical errors in Shakespeare, to bowdlerize Hannah More for sucklings, to establish the date of "Tamburlaine," to prove that Edgar Allan Poe was a teetotaler and a Presbyterian, to list all the differences between F_1 and F_2, to edit high-school editions of "Tales of a Traveler," "Die Jungfrau von Orleans" and "La Mort de Pompée." But it is *not* his business to sit in judgment upon the literature that is in being, for that job requires, above all things, an eager intellectual curiosity, a quick hospitality to ideas, a delight in novelty and heresy—and these are the very qualities which, if he had them, would get a professor cashiered in ten days. He is hired by the God-fearing and excessively solvent old gentlemen who sit on college boards, not to go scouting for what is new in the world, but to concentrate his mind upon the defense of what is old and safe. It is not his job to inflame his pupils to the pursuit and testing of ideas, but to make them accept docilely the ideas that have been approved as harmless, and his security and eminence in the academic grove run in direct proportion to his fidelity to that programme. If you want to know what happens to a professor who departs from it in the field of social theory, examine the life, crimes, trial, condemnation and execution of the late Scott Nearing, B.S., B.O., Ph.D. And if you want to measure the extent of the pressure in the field of the arts, think of what

Smart Set 53, No. 4 (December 1917): 138–44.

would have happened to a Princeton instructor who pronounced Walt Whitman a great artist in 1867.

It is the curse of American criticism, as I have hinted, that our rev. professors do not stick to their last—that they are forever poaching upon the preserve of criticism proper, and that a large body of public opinion follows them in their gyrations there. Fool that I am, I once welcomed that extension of function, and even mistook it idiotically for a proof that the professors were growing intelligent. I now know better, and recant without reservation. This roving of the birchmen has been, almost invariably, a damage and a nuisance. It has set up and fortified the formulae of the college pump in the precise field where all formulae are most dubious and most dangerous. It has created a caste of class-room big-wigs whose ponderous stupidity and mania for senseless labelling have corrupted the taste of two-thirds of our people. And it has worked steadily, maliciously and lamentably against the recognition of every new writer who has had anything sound and original to contribute to the national letters, from Poe to Whitman, from Whitman to Mark Twain, and from Mark Twain to Dreiser, George Ade and Montague Glass, and in favor of every platitudinizing old woman who has offered tripe in the market-place, from John Greenleaf Whittier to George E. Woodberry, the New England spinsters and Henry Van Dyke.

If this reign of mush-heads went unchallenged it would bring complete disaster; we would have no literature at all, but only a manufacture of books. Fortunately, it is not. Challengers arise on all sides, or at least on a side or two, emitting red fireworks from their nostrils. Watchmen cry *"Halt! Wer da?"* Better still, seductive barkers invite to livelier and better shows. And none more eloquently, none with greater caress and plausibility, than James Huneker. Who shall ever estimate the value of this Huneker to the arts in America? Who shall figure out what the pedagogues might have done for us had he never broken into their solemn vespers? He has been, for nearly thirty years, the chief of all our aesthetic explorers. He has been our introducer of intellectual ambassadors. He has ranged, at home and abroad, the free field of ideas, and brought back all he could find that was valid, and stimulating, and significant. And always, to the lugubrious branding and ticketing of one school of professors and the puerile moralizing of the other, he has opposed the fluent and resilient criteria of a genuine culture, and the spacious tolerance of a civilized man.

Such a critic, it seems to me, is a definite national possession, a mammal to be valued. He is worth, not only a whole herd of Harvard poets and essayists, but the whole of Harvard. It is not that he has played fugleman to this or that exotic revolutionist, or held out a hand to this or that neophyte of the soil; it is that he has taken away from aesthetic experience its smack of schoolmastering and "improvement" and turned it into a kindling and even gay adventure. Time and again I go to his books to get rid of my cobwebs—particularly after arising from such a terrible piece of punditry as the "Standards" of W. C. Brownell. There, indeed, is eternal recuperation for the reader and reviewer—a Pierian spring that not only flows, but bubbles. There the thing is made joyous, and hence once more engrossing and important. It is just this faculty which sets off Huneker from all the rest: he can, without apparent effort, achieve that magic re-creation for which the learned Dr Spingarn, echoing Goethe, Carlyle and Benedetto Croce, so pathetically bawls. He is himself an artist, and so he is at home among artists, and is able to understand what they are trying to do, and to sympathize with them in their pains and hesitations, and to make them interesting to the rest of us.

The last volume of the Hunekeran canon, by name, "Unicorns" (*Scribner*), lacks the sound articulation of most of its forerunners. It is, in fact, largely a product of the scissors, and some of its contents go back ten or twelve years. But though there is thus no steady stream of elucidation in it, and it shows nothing of novelty and discovery, it is, nevertheless, a book drenched with Huneker, and hence a book that slips past the eye very agreeably. Frankly a round-up, its contents are vastly discreet—a rhapsody on Brahms, foot-notes on George Sand, Henry James and Cézanne, an old valuation of Edward MacDowell, tentative reflections on James Joyce and Artzibashef, discourses on the great American novel and on English prose style, estimates of fiddlers and piano-players, experiments in fiction, philosophical memoranda— in brief, a stew, indeed, but always savory, always with its touches. Any critic in long practice could throw together such a book in a week, or, for that matter, half a dozen of them—but they would not be Huneker books; they would lack the salt that is in this one. Moreover, its patchiness and casualness suggest a diligent engagement upon some more elaborate business. What it may be I don't know, but if I had a vote I should cast it for another volume of "Old Fogy." Schoenberg, Richard Strauss, Strawinsky, Debussy, Massenet, Puccini—surely they invite the assault of the fabulous Hungarian! "Old Fogy," indeed, is Huneker sublimated, the astral body set free from the dogged arthritis of reality, the Hunekeran juices twice distilled. *Tempus fugit!* On some not distant tomorrow I shall be in hell. I pray this boon before the blast catches me. . . .

II

Of the true school of Huneker, though differing from him at every pore, are Alexander Harvey and my virtuous *Corpsbruder,* George Jean Nathan. The formula of Nathan, as I have explained in this place in the past, is artless to the point of austerity: he simply tells the truth. That truth, on the one hand, finds the gizzard of the commercial manager who turns the theatre into a mere bull-ring and bawdy house, and, on the other hand, it shakes up the ego of the clownish Drama Leaguer. The result is a double prosperity for the legend of Nathan's iconoclasm, ribaldry and barbarism, for both factions find their only refuge from his devastating demonstrations in furious abuse. Here, alas, they get into fresh trouble, for when it comes to abuse, Nathan is a professor of the art. Is he called names? Then he calls names himself—but with the addition of a poisonous wit that no mere Barnum or Ibsenite can ever hope to bring to the business. Thus Broadway has its show, and the glory of God is humbly served.

The latest Nathan issue, "Mr. George Jean Nathan Presents" (*Knopf*), exposes his method very admirably. It is, superficially, a book of rocking mirth, a compendium of flouting and derision. It is, fundamentally, a book of sharp and accurate judgments, presenting a sound theory of the theater. And what is that theory? It is, in brief, that works of art are not to be estimated by classifying them and labeling them, but by examining each of them for itself—by looking into its essential form and organization, considering the intent behind it, and valuing it according to its interest and validity to a civilized spectator. This bars out, at one stroke, the play of empty sentimentality. It bars out the tin-pot melodrama. It bars out the moony mush of the jitney Ibsens and Maeterlincks. It bars out the mere circus, sensation and peep-show. But it lets in every play, however conceived or designed, that contains an intelligible idea and is competently worked out. It lets in every play by a dramatist who is a serious artist, and self-respecting, and able to think and to write.

Bear this theory in mind, and you have a clear explanation of Nathan's actual performances—first, his merciless lampooning of the trade-goods of Broadway and the solemn pifflings of the Drama League geniuses, and secondly, his ardent championing of such widely diverse men as Avery Hopwood, Florenz Ziegfeld, Ludwig Thoma, Lord Dunsany, George Bernard Shaw, Ferenz Molnar, Roberto Bracco and Gerhart Hauptmann, all of whom have one thing in common: they are intelligent and ingenious, and know their trade. In Europe there are many more such men than in America, and some of the least of them are almost as good as our best. That is why Nathan is forever announcing them and advocating the presentation of their works—not because he favors foreignness for its own sake, but because it is so often accompanied by sound achievement and by stimulating example to our own artists. And that is why, when he tackles the maudlin flubdub of the ex-bartenders and jejune college boys who pass as geniuses on Broadway, he does it with the slapstick and seltzer siphon of comedy. What would you? Is an educated man to waste serious argument upon a piece of balderdash by George Broadhurst, a nonsensical cream-puff by Belasco, a smutty leg-show disguised as a Biblical drama? Nay. The remedy for such offenses against decent taste is a blow with a bladder, and that is exactly the remedy that Nathan applies.

Necessarily, he has to lay on with frequency. For one honest play, honestly produced and honestly played, that gets to Broadway there are two dozen displays of bosh. So his criticism consists largely of ridicule, of comic exposure, of the *reductio ad absurdum*. But when the stray exception appears, when something sound and respectable appears, whatever its form or investiture, then he is prompter than any of them to blow the horn. I look back over a dozen theatrical seasons, and catch him in very few errors, either of commission or of omission. He has not missed many worthy things, patent or obscure. His eye has rolled ceaselessly, and it has made discoveries. There is no intelligent dramatist or honest manager or competent actor in America who has not got help from him, freely and constantly. And there is no noisy mountebank in the theatre, however successful in tweaking the noses of the boobs, who can't show the marks of his snickersnee.

Harvey is a critic in less active practice: it is a pity that he writes so little. His "William Dean Howells" (*Huebsch*) is the most readable and original piece of literary criticism that America has seen since John Macy's "The Spirit of American Literature." In it there is the exact antithesis of the professorial manner. It is frank, courageous, provocative, exhilarating. It tells some plain truths in an admirably forthright way; it presents ideas that, whether true or false, at least intrigue the mind. The chief of then seems to me to be grossly false, to-wit, that Howells is a great novelist, and the peer of Balzac. Balzac was a trickster and showman; he wrote "Père Goriot," the worst novel in the world. But at his best he at least tried to get beneath the surfcce; he saw human life as more than a childish parlor game; he had his moments of awe and wonder. In Howells I can see nothing of the sort. He is dexterous and amusing; his facility is positively astonishing; but his novels, in the end, remain as empty as ancient skulls. He is the Moszkowski, the Chaminade, the Saint-Saëns of fiction. To compare him with the Beethovens and Bachs and Brahmses is sheer nonsense.

Harvey himself seems to be aware of this. He starts off with his impossible thesis—and then disproves it magnificently. In the first half of his book he is the patriot defending Howells against the competition of third-rate Englishmen and tenth-rate Continentals. In the second half, having scared off the foe, he proceeds to bring Howells himself to autopsy. The result, for all the preliminary fustian, is a penetrating and brilliant piece of criticism. The Howells limitations are mercilessly exposed; the feeble Howells matter is dredged up out of the deceptive Howells manner. . . . But Howells, after all, is not the real subject of the volume. It deals with literature in general, loosely and largely. It is full of the reflections and conclusions of a man who not only knows books, but also loves him—in brief, of a man of sense and taste, and not of a snuffling pedagogue. It is unhackneyed, personal and delightful. I am sure you will like it.

III

The other critical works of the month interest me a good deal less. Louis V. Ledoux's "George Edward Woodberry" (*Poetry Review*) is a solemn discourse upon a campus poet whose chief peculiarity seems to be that he has never written any poetry. "The Journal of Leo Tolstoi, 1895–1899" (*Knopf*) I can't read: the secret maunderings of the old jackass do not arrest me. As for "A Son of the Middle Border," by Hamlin Garland (*Macmillan*), it is the autobiography of a man who spoiled a possibly useful life by going in for literature. Garland should have stuck to the Chautauqua, his first love. In the world of beauty he is as forlorn a stranger as a Methodist deacon at a *Kommers*.

Henry H. Finck's "Richard Strauss" (*Little-Brown*) exhibits another misfit, which is to say, Finck himself. The man cannot think clearly, he cannot write decently, and he seems to have a very defective knowledge ol music. His book, setting aside the innumerable newspaper clippings that he has borrowed from scrap-books and newspaper morgues, is an impertinent, often ignorant and always ridiculous slanging of a man who stands indisputably at the head of all living musicians, and has done work that deserves the profound respect of everyone with ears. Every preposterous piece of malicious Strauss gossip is dished up; everything that can be said against every Strauss composition is duly said; the impression that the uninformed reader must inevitably get, plowing through this morass of *Town Topics* and *Kaffeeklatsch* criticism, is that the composer of "Der Rosenkavalier" and "Tod und Verklärung" is a cheap charlatan. And not only Strauss is manhandled, but also Brahms and others, and with them music itself. I direct your attention, for example, to the astounding twaddle about the sonata form on pages 92 to 95, with its staggering doctrine that the four movements are "totally unrelated in subject" and that the whole has no intrinsic design or psychological basis. And to the various sneers at Brahms, particularly the one on page 148. "If the genius of a composer is to be rated by his slow movements . . . then Brahms also falls short." Think of the Fourth Symphony!

The one rational and judicious thing in the whole volume is a preface by Percy Grainger, himself a competent musician. What he says is in striking contrast to the chatter of Finck, for he not only knows Strauss thoroughly and can comprehend his aims; he is also able to put his conclusions into coherent English. His little essay, in fact, is a model of modest and yet well-maintained criticism; he has reasons for his doctrines and he states them engagingly. To me, at least, it seems that he under-estimates Strauss's skill at instrumentation—surely there are long passages in "Josefs Legende," "Der Rosenkavalier," "Elektra," and, above all, "Feuersnot," that are far more than "momentary inspirations"—but that is a matter in which Grainger's opinion is surely of much greater worth than a layman's.

IV

In the midst of the customary tosh and blather, various novels of laudable quality are to be found currently in the department stores— among them, "The Three Black Pennys," by Joseph Hergesheimer (*Knopf*); "The Cream of the Jest," by James Branch Cabell (*McBride*); "Marching Men," by Sherwood Anderson (*Lane*), and "A Chaste Man," by Louis Wilkinson (*Knopf*). Moreover, there is a new and better edition of "Sister Carrie," by Theodore Dreiser (*Boni-Liveright*)—in fact, the only good one so far, for that of Doubleday, Page & Co. was little more than a set of rough sheets glued together, that of Dodge was made hideous by a preposterous frontispiece, and that of the Harpers was bound in a figured cloth apparently designed for Mother Hubbards.

Hergesheimer, in his new book, attempts to show the painful and laborious reaction of character to environment, not in a single individual or a group of diverse individuals, but in three successive members of the same family. The constant element in the process is a peculiar romantic daring, a sort of Byronic talent for the baroque and the naughty, which flares up at intervals in the house of Penny. The shift of environment is from the mellowing barbarism of colonial Pennsylvania to the decadent artificiality of the Philadelphia of today, that most hoggish and hypocritical of all American towns. The first Penny, in the early eighteenth century, achieves an exogamous marriage via

Route No. 7. The second, in the early nineteenth, saddles himself with an intolerable affair of the morganatic order. The third, in our own time, wobbles between amorous futilities and æsthetic sentimentalities until death finally extinguishes him, and the Penny line with him. The last showing of the flame is in a woman, a Penny by the left hand. The exhibition begins with violent thrusts of fire; it ends in sputterings and dancing shadows.

The book suggests Galsworthy's "The Dark Flower," both in its plan and in its manner, but unlike that fine piece it is by no means a mere demonstration in sex. We hear far more about the three Pennys than their adventures in the Bunsen burner of passion. They are revolved as the thing goes on; we see them from different sides and in different lights; each character sketch is elaborately and capitally done. And the three are deftly hung together: the Pennyism of these Pennys, so to speak, has reality, despite its gradual petering out. As for the writing, it shows a degree of finish very rare in the American novel—a finish never forgotten for an instant and sometimes rising to hardness, but always appropriate to the business, and the mirror of fine skill, and charming for its own sake. This Hergesheimer, in truth, is pre-eminently a fine workman, a man who respects his materials and his craft, a novelist of sound culture. He doesn't write emotionally, evangelistically, gaudily; he writes like a gentleman. And here he has done a piece of work that ends his apprenticeship, and puts him in a secure and honorable position.

The Cabell book is another quite unusual composition, half novel and half essay in psychology, and with excellent writing in it from cover to cover. In ground plan it is an attempt to lay bare the secret soul of Felix Kennaston, a successful novelist—not the Bovaryan pseudo-soul visible to his wife and his neighbors, but that esoteric spirit which transcends time and space, and has its adventures in the super-world of the imagination. Outwardly, Kennaston is a discreet and reputable man—a convinced monogamist, a dutiful householder, a docile Presbyterian. But within him there dwells an adventurer who ranges the whole of the visible universe, and a lover who has found his heart's desire. So much for the framework of the story. Upon it Mr. Cabell hangs the loot of much intellectual marauding—brilliant bits of irony, penetrating reflections upon faiths and ideas, a whole agnostic philosophy. It would be difficult to match the book in American fiction; it has, from first to last, a French smack; one constantly hears overtones that suggest Anatole France and J. K. Huysmans. A thing obviously written *con amore*, joyously, without regard to markets. The reader it will attract is precisely the reader most worth attracting. It is not a popular novel, not a story, not a mere time-killer; it is a piece of literature.

Anderson's "Marching Men" starts off brilliantly, but toward the end he begins to load it with dubious sociological ideas, as he loaded "Windy McPherson's Son," and so it loses some of its early vitality. In brief, it is the history of Norman McGregor, a youth from the Pennsylvania mining region who goes to Chicago, studies law, sets up shop as a prophet, and organizes the floating workers out there into regiments of industrial soldiers. The idea is that of Kipling's McAndrews: "Law, Order, Duty an' Restraint, Obedience, Discipline!" Above all, discipline. The regular tramp, tramp, tramp of rank after rank, the subtle strength of the drilled man, the mob made one and irresistible. Thus the plan. But the end, the aim? Here, alas, McGregor is less explicit, and with him his creator. I put down the book with the wish that Mr. Anderson had not brought the prophet out of Coal Creek. There he is brilliantly projected against a background as real as the landscape you see out of your window. There, and not in the last chapters, is the proof that Mr. Anderson is a novelist with something to say. . . . The Wilkinson book belongs to a far different genus. It is, like "The Buffoon," an experiment in irony, and capitally done. Not a word of moralizing is in it, and yet how delightfully the immoral moral is rubbed in! I commend it to your search when your mood is for an antidote to the stodgy thickness and solemnity of current fiction. It is a *scherzo* with some fine, sonorous chords underneath.

The rest of the novels interest me very little. There are three well-devised short stories in "The Friends," by Stacy Aumonier (*Century*), but they suffer from repetition of ideas. In such confections as "Turn About Eleanor," by Ethel M. Kelley (*Bobbs-Merrill*); "The Indian Drum," by William MacHarg and Edwin Balmer (*Little-Brown*); "Temperamental Henry," by Samuel Merwin (*Bobbs-Merrill*); "Amarilly in Love," by Belle K. Maniates (*Little-Brown*); "Wings of the Cardinal," by Bertha Crowell (*Doran*); "Scandal," by Cosmo Hamilton (*Little-Brown*); "White Monarch and the Gas-House Pup," by R. G. Kirk (*Little-Brown*); "Bucking the Tiger," by Achmed Abdullah (*Shores*), and "Long Live the King," by Mary Roberts Rinehart (*Houghton*), I can find only the commonplace stuff of department-store fiction. If you crave detailed reviews of that sort of thing subscribe to the New York *Times*.

"Bromley Neighborhood," by Alice Brown (*Macmillan*), is rather hard going, and "The Dwelling Place of Light," by Winston Churchill (*Macmillan*), I can't read at all, but here a personal prejudice against certain varieties of fiction may be showing itself, and so I advise you to read them as in duty bound. "The Wanderers," by Mary Johnston (*Houghton*), exhausts me long before I finish it: it is a series of sketches, inordinately drawn out, showing the shifting position of woman through the ages. "The Unholy Three," by Tod Robbins (*Lane*) starts off brilliantly, but soon slides into conventionality and puerility. Nevertheless, it is a first novel of much more promise than usual—the work of a newcomer who shows plain signs of doing something notable, once he finds his legs. "Jap Herron," a novel written from the "Ouija board" (*Kennerley*), is simply an irritating imbecility. A long introduction by Emily Grant Hutchings asks us to believe that it was dictated to a medium by the ghost of Mark Twain. It is an intolerably childish piece of nonsense, and resembles the actual writing of Mark about as much as the average moving-picture actor resembles Socrates. I turn for relief to books frankly intended for children, especially to the excellent "Sandman's Tales" and "The Sandman's Hour," by Abbie Phillips Walker (*Harper*), and to "New Adventures of Alice," a continuation of "Alice in Wonderland," by John Rae (*Volland*). Christmas is on us. The young ones, I am sure, will delight in Mrs. Walker's ingenious stories.

Two volumes by eminent hands remain: "The Soul of a Bishop," by H. G. Wells (*Macmillan*), and "King Coal," by Upton Sinclair (*Macmillan*). The Wells tome offers an inept and ludicrous amalgam of his early pseudo-science and his latter-day pseudo-religion. It is one of the dullest, stupidest, most unconvincing compositions that these eyes have rolled through for many a day; to find its match one must go to the same author's "God the Invisible King." But even in "God the Invisible King" there is nothing to equal the idiotic dialect of Lady Sunderbund. Surely Wells is putting heavy strains upon his admirers. . . . "King Coal" is a picture of life in the Colorado mining region, and is full of meticulous and apparently very accurate detail. Its defect lies in the fact that its central character, a young millionaire who goes into the mines to help uplift the miners, is always a bit stagey and incredible. To me, at least, the facts which give the book consideration would have been far more appetizing as simple facts, without any varnish of fiction on them. But even so, the story goes down painlessly and is not without its moments. . . .

Made in the USA
Middletown, DE
01 February 2019